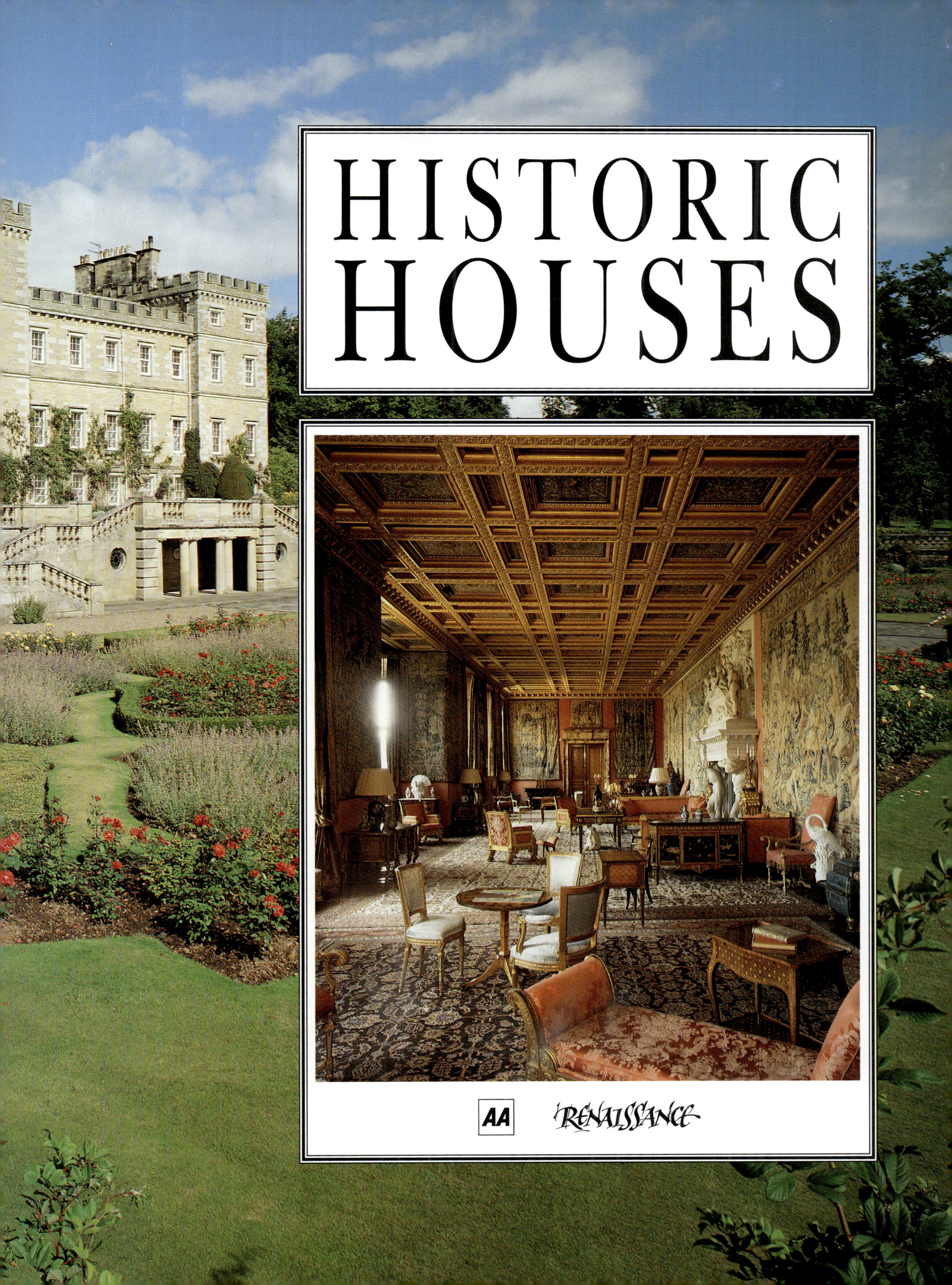

HISTORIC HOUSES

AA RENAISSANCE

Edited by Penny Hicks

Editorial contributors:
Tony Aldous, Juliette Barker, Sean Callery, Richard Cavendish, Elizabeth Cruwys, Cliff Hanley, Gail Harada, John Morrison, Paul Murphy, Ann Stonehouse, Hamish Scott, Daivd Winpenny, Michael Wright

Designed by Ian Muggeridge and Christopher Matthews

First published 1994. Reprinted 1999 and 2002

Published jointly by AA Publishing (a trading name of Automobile Association Developments Limited, whose registered office is Millstream, Maidenhead Road, Windsor, SL4 5GD. Registered Number 1878835) and Spero Communications Ltd. 'Renaissance' is an imprint of InFo Publishing Ltd, a member of the Spero Communications group of companies.

ISBN 0 7495 2102 3
ISBN 0 7495 2090 6

A CIP record of this book is available from the British Library.

Colour separation by Fotographics Ltd.
Printed and bound by Oriental Press, Dubai

HISTORIC HOUSES

CONTENTS

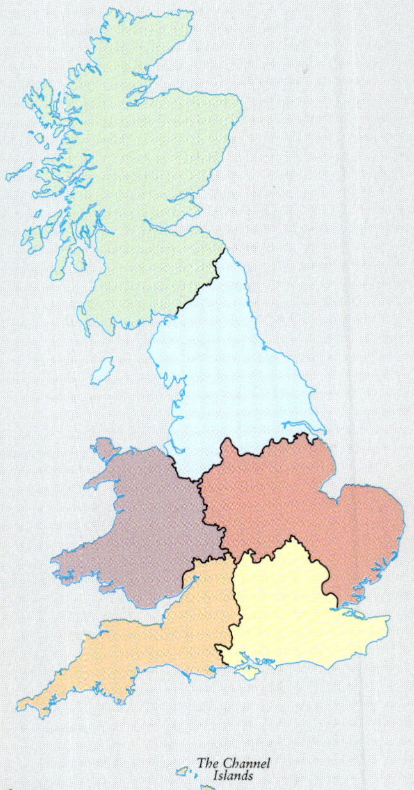

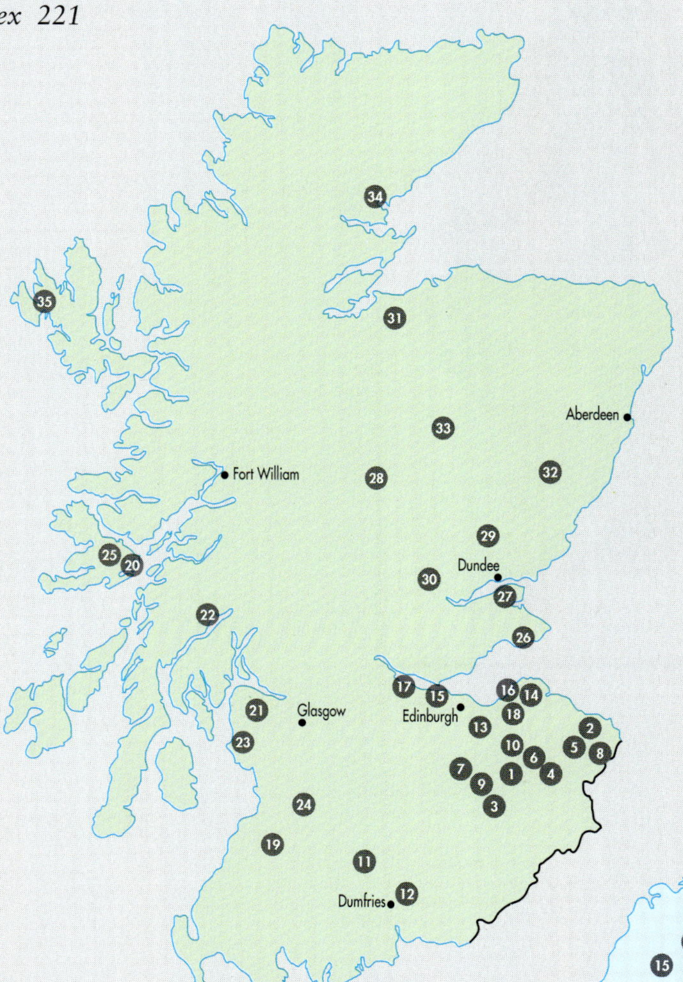

The North of England 126

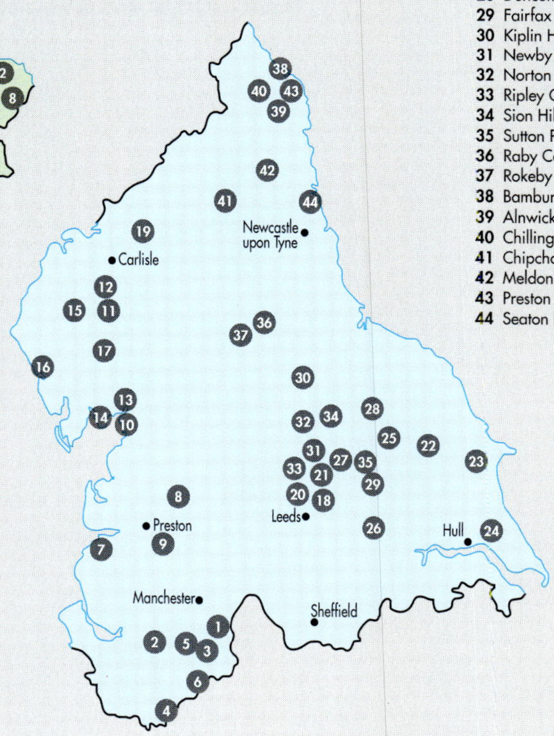

Scotland 186

Wales and The Marches 168

Central England and East Anglia 88

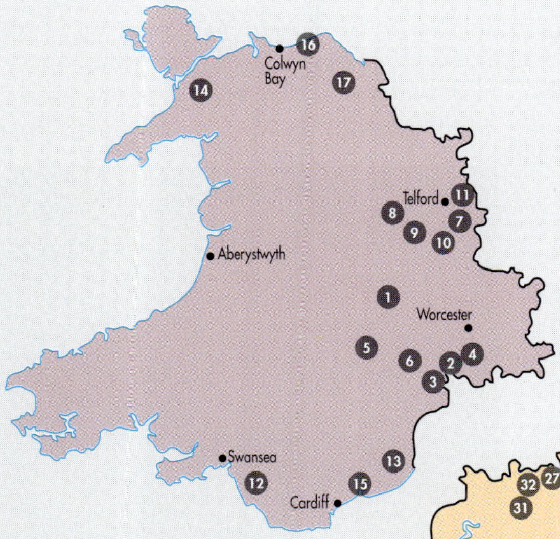

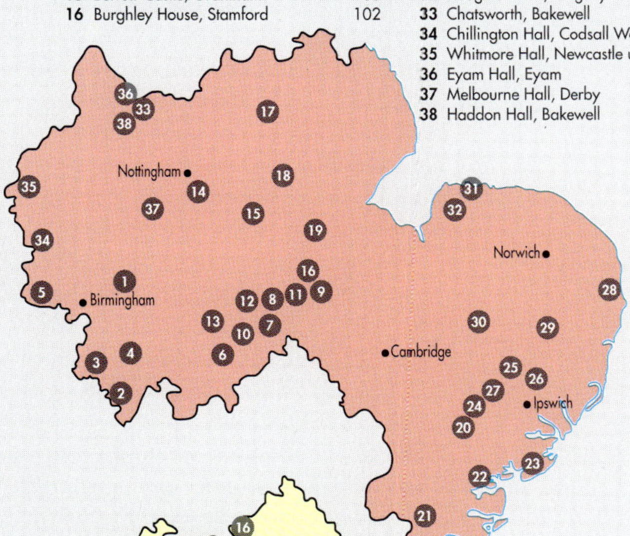

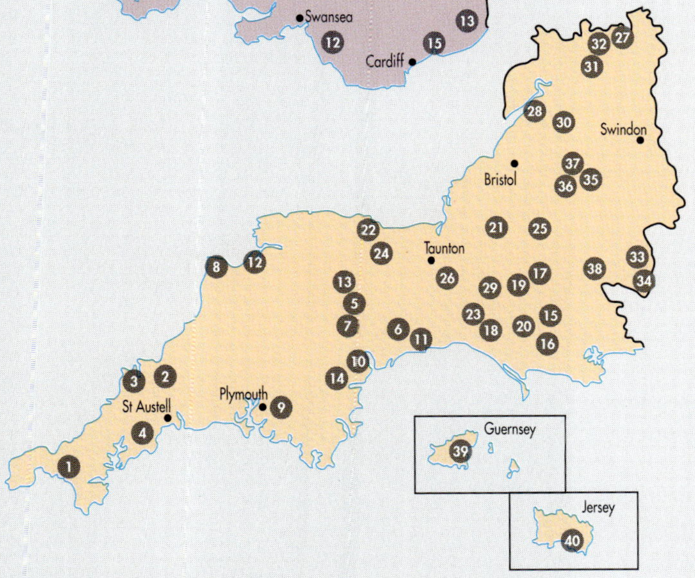

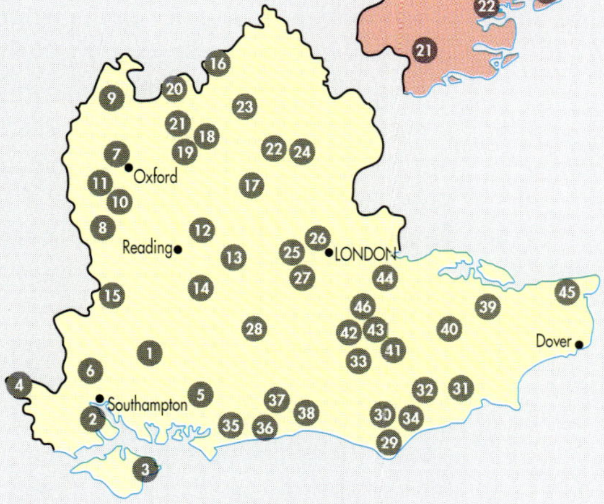

South-west England 10

South and South-east England 46

Introduction by His Grace the Duke of Norfolk

BRITAIN is known the world over for its enormous wealth of historic buildings, and visitors come from its four corners to see the ancient castles, abbeys and magnificent stately homes which can be found in every single county in the land. Many, many books have been published to announce the delights of these buildings, but this volume contains a selection of the most fascinating of all – those which are still the homes of the families who own them. Frequently, the houses have been cherished by the same family for many generations and their contents are not simply a display of fine antiques and works of art, but a documentation of the progress of that family through the ages.

Illustrious and romantic characters emerge from the pages of this book, for many of the houses have strong links with dashing figures from history – The Black Prince, The Duke of Monmouth, Bonnie Prince Charlie and 'Bonnie Dundee'; naval and military heroes include Sir Walter Raleigh, Sir Francis Drake and The Dukes of Wellington and Marlborough; statesmen such as Gladstone and Churchill are represented; there are literary connections with the likes of Shakespeare, the Brontës, Thomas Hardy, and Sir Walter Scott – and, of course, royalty. Kings and Queens really did 'sleep here'; there are tales of royal courtships, marriages and indiscretions, and of intrigue and murder! There are stories of elopement and unrequited love, of families divided by the Civil War, of strong principles, hopeless weaknesses and spectacular disagreements.

The contents of a house will often mirror the character and interests of the people who have lived there, whether it be a priceless collection of art and antiquities, or a curious hotch-potch of items which were the belongings of a particularly idiosyncratic collector. None will fail to delight the visitor. The buildings themselves are no less fascinating than their contents. Some appear as if frozen in a centuries-old time capsule; others have evolved with the architectural vagaries of each age, with, perhaps, traces of thick medieval stone walls, Tudor timbers and Jacobean panelling beneath the splendid classical features of an 18th-century remodelling. Many have been greatly enlarged as the fortunes and status of their owners increased, while others have passed their zenith and have settled down to a more modest and quiet life. Everything about these houses has its own story to tell.

Many families go back to the Norman Conquest, as do the homes in which they live, and some can trace their ancestry back even further. There is 'new money' too, for some of these houses have been taken on quite recently, often after years of dereliction or institutional use, and these owners are among the most enthusiastic when it comes to the restoration of the buildings to their former glory.

At Arundel I am privileged to be the custodian of many centuries of family heritage. Since Richard III created the title of Duke of Norfolk for my ancester, a title which carries with it the honour of being Earl Marshal, successive generations of my family have also been at the forefront of the heritage of Britain, and I have an abiding interest in the preservation of that heritage.

Over the past few decades, many of our historic houses, whether grand palaces or lovely old manor houses, have been under threat from a seemingly constant barage of soaring repair and restoration costs and punishing taxation. In many cases, the initial decision

to open a property to the public was prompted by the need to bring in additional revenue to assist with these financial burdens. It is a clear indication of how perceptions have changed towards our heritage that such measures can be so successfully embraced. The fact that visitors from home and abroad are captivated by these buildings has never been more apparent, but the modern owner's approach is vastly different from the attitude of many of their ancesters, who were more likely by far to have sold off the silver, demolished the building altogether or, of course, made an advantageous marriage. Today's owners have discovered the joy of sharing their heritage and treasured homes with an appreciative public, so that what started out as a means of raising much-needed funds has become a real pleasure and a new way of life, particularly for those who so enthusiastically conduct their own guided tours.

Most of all, this book celebrates the current owners of our selection of historic houses. Those who are prepared to tackle anything from dry rot to taxation in order to maintain their much-loved homes and their heritage, and who are prepared to share them with us.

Norfolk

SOUTH-WEST ENGLAND

IF ANY HOUSE in Britain rests cocooned in idyllic tranquillity it is Athelhampton, among its Dorset gardens. Sheldon Manor is another veteran of the centuries, sweetly scented with wood-smoke and packed with family treasures. Don't miss its platypus-skin quilt, while Powderham Castle has its venerable tortoise. Elsewhere there is grandeur. Longleat is palatial with its lions, the single and double cube rooms at Wilton are two of the most beautiful rooms in the country, and Bowood stands in one of England's most entrancing man-made landscapes. At Berkeley Castle the Berkeley family has spent 800 years turning the brutal Norman fortress where Edward II was horribly murdered into a civilised residence. Sudeley Castle contrives to be both a home and a romantic ruin, while Sezincote appears to have been brought from Mogul India on a magic carpet. But then, any conveyance which takes you round the delectable houses of the south-west will have magic qualities.

Godolphin House

HELSTON

A GREY, GRANITE MANOR HOUSE AMID CORNISH WOODS WITH AN IMPRESSIVE COLONNADED FRONT: ABOUT FIVE MILES NORTH-WEST OF HELSTON OFF THE A394 PENZANCE ROAD.

■ I can best describe the hold Godolphin has over me by quoting from A C Benson's letter after his first glimpse of the place, which he describes as '...one of the treasures of memory. I can only say the whole place seems to me, among all the houses I have seen, the most incredibly strange and romantic.' ■
Mary Schofield

Godolphin, solemn and grey among Cornish woodland, is a house unlike any other. Its dominant central section is early 17th century: a long, low, battlemented, granite building with great mullioned windows and a colonnade of monolithic Tuscan pillars. Behind it, two wings, dating from the 15th and 16th centuries, form the second and third sides of an inner courtyard. Ahead is a battlemented wall which used to front the Great Hall – demolished only a century ago.

The Godolphin family, pre-Conquest Cornish, settled on this upland site in Norman times. They rose to fame and power in Tudor times by fighting for the king in France, developing tin-mining technology, marrying heiresses, fighting pirates and Spaniards, and governing and fortifying the Scilly Isles.

In the Civil War the Godolphins were staunchly royalist, for which they paid in both lives and heavy fines. Francis Godolphin sheltered the future Charles II during his escape via the Scillies to France and after the Restoration, his son Sydney rose to high office. He was known as 'King Charles's honest treasurer', served three monarchs and was created Earl Godolphin. His son, another Francis, visiting Godolphin as a 12-year-old, described the house with its 'front upon pillars' as having 'about forty chimneys in it, and near a hundred rooms of all sorts belonging to it'. That Francis eventually became 2nd Earl Godolphin. Like his father, he bred racehorses and owned the famous stallion, The Godolphin Arab. His daughter Mary married the Duke of Leeds, that family becoming Godolphin's absentee landlords until the property was sold to their tenant farmers in 1921. Sidney and Mary Schofield bought the property in 1937 and it is still Mrs Schofield's home.

The dining room is the most complete room to survive from the 15th-century house; the Elizabethan bedroom has a 17th-century plaster frieze and a bed dating from about 1590. The 15th-century King's Room is thought to be where the future Charles II stayed while escaping to the Scilly Isles. Its carved doorway, with the Godolphin double-headed eagle on one side and the Sidneys' barbed arrow head on the other, celebrates the union of those two families in 1604. In the entrance hall is a remnant of the earlier fortified house: a 'squint', which allows a view – and, if necessary, an arrowshot – of the main gate.

The King's Room at Godolphin is named after the occasion when the 16-year-old future Charles II took refuge here in 1646.

THE KING OF THE WIND

There is a story that the remarkable Godolphin Arab was rescued from pulling a water cart in Paris, then brought to London and presented to the Earl of Godolphin – but that is hardly likely. Another version has it that the horse was given by the Emperor of Morocco to the King of France, but was found to be too high spirited. Whatever the true story, his acquisition by Sir Francis was fortunate indeed, for he became the sire of a whole string of winning racehorses and is one of only three stallions to which every horse now on the turf can trace its ancestry. He was also the subject of a best-selling children's book, *King of the Wind*.

Pencarrow House

BODMIN

AN ELEGANT, FINELY FURNISHED GEORGIAN HOUSE IN A BEAUTIFUL GARDEN AND WOODLAND SETTING: FOUR MILES NORTH-WEST OF BODMIN OFF THE A389.

Pencarrow House, at the end of a mile-long woodland drive, has been the home of the Molesworth-St Aubyn family since the Elizabethan age. Its original owners, the de Pencarrow family, lost it after an abortive Cornish rising against an unjust levy on tin in 1497. The first Molesworth here was John, Queen Elizabeth's commissioner for the Duchy of Cornwall; his grandson Colonel Hender Molesworth governed Jamaica under Charles II and William III, and was created a baronet.

It was, however, two 18th-century Molesworths who employed architect Robert Allanson to create the present house, with its Palladian-style entrance front. The long south front, with its roof of grey Delabole slate, has a Cornish feel to it, while the north-facing back of the house opens into a courtyard and was probably the main front of the earlier house.

A second stage in the development of Pencarrow occurred in 1841, when the 8th Baronet, Sir William, engaged a Plymouth architect, George Wightwick, to improve the interiors, one result being the particularly fine drawing room. Its beautiful rose-coloured damask curtains were a gift of a relative, Captain George Ourry, who took them as part of his booty from a Spanish ship, the *Santissima Trinidada*, which he captured off the Philippines in 1762

As well as its fine furniture and ceramics – notably the Pencarrow *famille rose* bowl – the house contains many family portraits, including that of the 18th-century Cornish MP Sir John Aubyn, identified by Prime Minister Walpole as the only Member he could not bribe. Another portrait is of the 8th Baronet, who was Palmerston's reforming Colonial Secretary, largely responsible for ending penal transportation to Australia.

The present owner's grandmother arrived at Pencarrow in 1918, to discover that previous generations had not always valued their heritage. Finely-crafted mahogany doors were hidden beneath ugly brown paint; beautiful 19th-century linen wall coverings were buried under layers of wallpaper; the water-gilt of the music room's fine Adam furniture had once been overpainted in black to provide a suitably funereal setting for the body of a family member awaiting burial. They even painted black mourning bands onto Reynolds portraits in the dining room! The present owners, Colonel Sir Arscott and Lady Iona Molesworth-St Aubyn, do take enormous pride in caring for the house, and have also cleared and restored the neglected 19th-century woodlands.

■ When we took over 20 years ago, everything was run down, unloved and sulking. Now it is quite different and is often remarked on. The house is smiling again – big houses were built to have lots of people in them. ■
Lady Molesworth-St Aubin

The walls of Pencarrow's Inner Hall are hung with outstanding paintings, including works by Scott, Brooking, Raeburn and Bower.

Prideaux Place

PADSTOW

AN ELIZABETHAN HOUSE, OCCUPIED BY THE PRIDEAUX FAMILY FOR FOUR CENTURIES, WITH CHARMING GEORGIAN AND REGENCY GOTHIC ADDITIONS: IN THE CENTRE OF PADSTOW.

Prideaux Place reflects its passage through the ages. Its E-shape plan is Elizabethan, as is its massive oak front door and its crowning glory, the Great Chamber with its superb plaster ceiling. Then in the 18th-century Edmund Prideaux returned from his Grand Tour and removed the pointed gables on the entrance front, and installed sash windows and coal-burning grates. He also bought a whole room from Lord Bath's doomed Restoration manor house at Stow – panelling, pictures, wine cooler and all. But Edmund's restrained Georgian style did not satisfy the taste of his grandson, The Reverend Charles Prideaux, and in about 1810 he started applying the Regency Gothic style. His particular influence is reflected in the drawing room, hall and library.

Among the many fine paintings in the house are a group in the morning room by John Opie, who had grown up on the Prideaux estate before becoming a famous Regency court painter. The group includes a rare self-portrait, left as a 'tip' for the housekeeper. Perhaps the most romantic painting is that of Humphrey Prideaux, painted by the Italian artist, Rosalba Carriera. She fell in love with him and hid a letter saying so in the frame of this picture. The letter was not discovered until 1914, so Humphrey never knew.

Prideaux Place has 81 rooms, 44 of them bedrooms, but of those bedrooms only six are habitable. The present owners, Peter and Elizabeth Prideaux-Brune, are restoring house and garden, and delight in showing it to visitors.

The Grenville Room houses Prideaux' important collection of Royalist Caroline paintings and 18th-century porcelain.

Trewithen

PROBUS

A GEORGIAN HOUSE AT ONE WITH ITS SETTING OF FINELY LANDSCAPED GROUNDS AND GARDENS: ABOUT SIX MILES NORTH-EAST OF TRURO ON THE A390.

The name Trewithen, home of the Hawkins family for 280 years, is Cornish for 'house of the trees', and the approach along the main drive displays a house that is very much at one with its landscape. The historian and Cornishman A L Rowse said of Trewithen 'As an ensemble (it) is one of the most perfect places in Cornwall, an integrated whole: house and gardens, the relation of one to the other and of both to the woods and landscape, the correlation of the exterior of the house to the interior.'

The house itself is in some respects a surprise. Its noblest elevation – looking south over lawns between mature woodlands – has a presence which belies the essentially domestic scale of the rooms behind it. This south front, dating from the late 18th century, is of an unusual pink-tinged stone from a family-owned quarry at Pentewan, and is a restrained and symmetrical Georgian composition with a projecting five-bay, two-storey centre, flanked by two-bay wings.

Yet behind this façade most of Trewithen's ground floor rooms, gracefully 18th century in their décor, are nonetheless relatively modest in size. Again and again visitors, shown the late 18th-century dining room, the earlier, panelled Oak Room, the comfortable-looking Smoking Room, remark, 'It feels so lived in.' These are not state rooms – not even the more spacious dining room, intended at one time to be the main entrance hall. They are comfortably human-scale rooms for daily living.

Part of the explanation is that successive remodellings of the house have, to a considerable extent, worked with and used the original plan and interior spaces of the house which Philip Hawkins acquired in 1715. Thomas Edwards, the Palladian architect he brought from London, proposed something grander, but Philip settled for a more limited rebuilding. His nephew Thomas, soldier, MP and sylviculturalist, developed woodlands, park and gardens, but also completed the open courtyard on the north front, using one pretty, well-proportioned flanking out-building (to sit in as local magistrate) and adding a matching wing for the stables and coach-house.

Thomas, seeking to persuade local people to undergo inoculation against smallpox, did so himself and died of it. It was his son, Christopher, employing another leading Palladian architect, Sir Robert Taylor, who gave the house its present form. He also went into tin mining, espoused the latest technology, and developed his own port at Pentewan – from where the stone came for Taylor's rebuilding of Trewithen's south front. George Johnstone, a Hawkins descendent who inherited the estate in 1904, spent 50 years developing the grounds. He worked with existing layouts but thinned and underplanted the tree canopy and, bringing in many new species from abroad, created one of the most significant and renowned plantsman's gardens of this century. His family, still at Trewithen, manage the estate and continue to build on his work.

Trewithen, 'house of the trees', is indeed within lovely wooded grounds.

Bickleigh Castle

TIVERTON

A ROMANTIC MOATED RANGE OF MEDIEVAL AND STUART BUILDINGS: OFF THE A396 FOUR MILES SOUTH OF TIVERTON.

In appearance both a farmhouse and a castle, Bickleigh has a complicated history. The manor, mentioned in the Domesday Book, was given to the Courtenays, Earls of Devon, in 1410. With vast estates elsewhere in the county, they regarded Bickleigh as the portion of their younger sons and built a modest castle that was in keeping with the troubled times. The Carews, who were given Bickleigh later in the century, lived there for 200 years, though they proved an ill-starred family. Sir George, an admiral under Henry VIII, was in command of the *Mary Rose* when she sailed past Spithead on her maiden voyage. Caught by a gust of wind, the greatest warship of the age turned turtle, sinking with all hands. In the Civil War, Sir Henry Carew, as a Royalist, was horrified to find the army of General Fairfax camped almost on his door-step. The house was slighted, leaving the ancient chapel standing amidst ruins. Sir Henry was permitted to continue living at his home, but only on condition that the house should never more pose any military threat. Fulfilling this condition he built a thatched cob farmhouse in part of what had been the castle courtyard. Fate was cruel to Sir Henry, for both his son and nephew died in early youth – and both on the same day – leaving him without an heir. Bickleigh was subsequently neglected and for more than 200 years was no more than a run-down farmyard, its crumbling buildings used as barns. Only the dedication of owners in the present century has saved it from oblivion and after years of restoration, Bickleigh is now once more a home.

The setting of the house is beautiful, between the River Exe and wooded hills. Its moat is now a water garden with irises and lilies growing beneath old stone walls. The gatehouse, dating from the 15th century, has a massive hall on the first floor with two great fireplaces and a minstrels' gallery. Smaller rooms below include an armoury, with weaponry and armour displayed on its bare stone walls, and a guard room filled with Tudor furniture and paintings. One portrait, of a lady in the habit of an abbess, still bears the scars of musket-balls, from the time when Cromwell's soldiers used her for target practice. Another is of Bampfylde Carew, who ran away from school to become king of the local gypsies!

The farmhouse is a separate building, with an old beamed dining room that was formerly the kitchen. In the Garden Room is a carved stone fireplace which was taken from the ruined castle to the safety of the local vicarage, where it remained until the present century. It bears the arms of Carew and the carvings may well represent incidents from local history or, more likely, of the Prayer Book Rebellion of 1545, which was suppressed by Sir Thomas Carew.

The Norman chapel is the oldest of the buildings and the only one to have survived unscathed from the Civil War. It is simple, small and utterly delightful, with a barrel-vaulted roof, medieval glass and an Early English font. For centuries it was a cattle-byre and fragments of a Carew tomb were discovered during renovation. There is also a museum with toys, maritime exhibits and equipment used by spies in World War II.

Bickleigh's armoury, in the oldest part of the castle, contains an impressive array of weapons and armour dating back to the 17th century.

ELOPEMENT AND RECONCILIATION

Elizabeth Courtenay was an orphan. Her grandfather, Sir Philip, asked William Carew to look after her at Bickleigh, where she led a lonely childhood until her guardian's young brother, Thomas, fell in love with her. One night the couple eloped – a disgraceful act in days when marriages were carefully arranged. Threatened by the fury of the mighty Courtenays, Thomas fled to fight in the war with Scotland where, at Flodden Field, he saved the life of his commander. Lord Howard happily repaid his debt by interceding with Sir Philip, who gave Bickleigh to the couple as a marriage gift.

■ **My wife and I were often asked why we bought Bickleigh Castle. The fact is that we were both very interested in history, and Bickleigh has plenty of that. It is also in a most delightful setting, with gardens and grounds bordering the River Exe.** ■
Noel Boxall

Cadhay

OTTERY ST MARY

AN ANCIENT HOUSE REFLECTING MANY CHANGES IN FASHION AND IN FORTUNE: SOUTH OF THE A30 BETWEEN HONITON AND EXETER.

The entrance to Cadhay is Georgian, giving little indication of the classic Tudor manor that lies within, and this is just one of the alterations carried out over many centuries to conform with the vagaries of fashion. When its first owner, John Haydon, died he left the property to his great nephew, Robert, who had ascended the social ladder somewhat by marrying Joan Poulett, the daughter of the Privy Councillor to Queen Elizabeth I. The new squire's wife, accustomed to the finest houses in the land, probably found life in Ottery something of a culture shock. She and Robert set about refurbishing Cadhay, adding on a Long Gallery in which they and their guests could perambulate in style.

Having scaled the social heights, the Haydon family fell into decline, supporting the wrong side in the Civil War and then amassing debts that by 1693 exceeded £17,000. By 1737 Cadhay was owned by William Peere Williams of Grays Inn, and the house was again remodelled in the latest style. He added an elegant façade, a second floor within the hall, new plasterwork and other fashionable additions. Cadhay then passed through marriage to a somewhat doubtful naval hero, Admiral Graves, who contributed to England's loss of North America through failing to relieve Lord Cornwallis. In spite of this, he was subsequently elevated to the peerage for his role in the Battle of the Glorious First.

A CLASSIC FIGURE OF THE TUDOR AGE

John Haydon was truly a man of his time – dedicated, ruthless and ambitious. Society was changing fast as old ideas were overthrown, new money flowed from trade and the foundations of the church itself were shaken. As a lawyer practising in Exeter, Haydon made his fortune from dealing in monastic lands. In 1539 the king's commissioners suppressed the College of Priests in Ottery, where Haydon was legal advisor to the manor. Buying up the buildings, Haydon used the stone to build a home in keeping with his status.

After the death of the admiral, Cadhay began an ignominious decline. Throughout the 19th century it was let out and divided up, with farm hands crowded in its bedrooms and pigsties built against the walls. It was not until 1909 that Cadhay acquired a saviour in Mr Dampier Whetham, a Cambridge academic and agricultural advisor to the government who rescued the house from ruin and carefully restored it.

The architecture of Cadhay reflects both the passing of time and its changing fortunes, but it remains essentially a Tudor house. The east front, with its mullions and projecting stair tower is still exactly as John Haydon knew it and Robert Haydon's Long Gallery still runs the full width of the upper floor. Use as a farmhouse kitchen for more than a century, together with the addition of an upper floor, has robbed the hall of something of its grandeur, but the enormous carved Tudor fireplace remains.

A visit to the roof chamber is a must. Though the hammer beams have gone, the arching chestnut timbers with chestnut boarding are a splendid sight and can be viewed at close quarters. Perhaps the finest feature of the house, though, is the internal courtyard that was created when the Long Gallery was built. The walls are faced with stone and flint in a random chequer-board design, whilst between the upper windows are immensely ornate niches containing statues of the last four Tudor sovereigns. Judging from the naïve style, they were probably the work of an itinerant mason who was possessed with more enthusiasm than sophisticated skill.

Despite the aspirations of its early owners, Cadhay remains at heart a charmingly provincial manor house, and it is a satisfying conclusion to the story that the present owners of Cadhay, the William-Powlett family, are descended from the family of Joan Poulett (Mrs Robert Haydon), who lived at Cadhay 400 years ago.

Fursdon

CADBURY

THE HOME OF ONE OF DEVON'S OLDEST FAMILIES, FILLED WITH HEIRLOOMS AND MEMENTOES: OFF THE A3072 NINE MILES NORTH OF EXETER.

The Fursdon family have remained loyal to the home that bears their name, living on the manor since the 13th century and seldom leaving. They were not a family to shirk their duties, though – in 1418 Robert was in France with the army of Henry V, and in 1643 George was killed fighting for Charles I. His shrewd and formidable widow, Grace, took over the management of the estate, continuing to run Fursdon even after her son came of age, and became a money lender, dying in her eighties worth £20,000. Another Fursdon bought himself a troop of Light Dragoons and saw

Right: Fursdon House, sheltered on all sides except the south, really does nestle in the soft contours of its unspoilt Devon surroundings.

service with the Duke of York in the Napoleonic wars, on one occasion giving up his horse when the royal steed was killed.

The 19th century saw a decline in the family fortune. George Fursdon was a gambler and though his son secured himself an heiress, her father's bank went bankrupt. The family invested in a local copper mine that suffered the same fate and the last few servants left to fight in the Great War. The Fursdons still stayed on, despite taxation and the problem of dry rot, and have in recent years reversed the tide by revitalising the estate and by converting some wings of the house to holiday accommodation.

The present house is 400 years old, though it was altered in the 18th century, and its rooms are elegant but unpretentious. It is furnished largely in Georgian style, though the table in the dining room has been in the house since Tudor times. Because the Fursdon family have neither moved house nor lacked for storage space, they have accumulated a fascinating array of treasures over the years, including portraits, historic costumes, mementoes, archives and bric-à-brac – forming a collection that celebrates the history of this English country family.

■ For me it is the tranquil setting, with a magnificent view, that makes Fursdon such a wonderful place to live. Walter de Fursdon took his name from the surrounding countryside, which was known as Furzey Down, and settled here 700 years ago. What a good decision! ■
Catriona Fursdon

This rare mantua, part of the Fursdon family costume collection, was worn by Elizabeth Fursdon in 1753, probably for her wedding.

Hartland Abbey

BIDEFORD

A GOTHIC MANSION WITH EXUBERANT VICTORIAN DECOR, ON THE SITE OF AN ANCIENT MONASTERY: 15 MILES WEST OF BIDEFORD, OFF THE A39 TOWARDS HARTLAND QUAY.

When the Augustinian monastery of Hartland was dissolved in 1539, Henry VIII gave it to the sergeant of his wine cellar, perhaps in jocular acknowledgement of his name – John Abbott. The Abbotts had family connections with Sir Richard Greville, the explorer and adventurer, whose great grandson John became a hero of the Civil War when he was only 12 years old. The property subsequently passed by inheritance and marriage through the Luttrells and Orchards to the Stucley family who are the present owners, but the monastic buildings were demolished in the 18th century and replaced with the gothic-style mansion we see today.

The fascination of Hartland Abbey lies in its portrayal of Victorian high life, with photographs of Stucleys fighting for the empire, shooting snipe and making social calls. The interior is High Victorian, with touches of Queen Anne. Murals in the dining room and inner hall, based upon designs found in the House of Lords, portray the historic exploits of the family. There are decorated ceilings and an extraordinary corridor commissioned by Sir George Stucley after visiting the Alhambra. And if all this inspires visions of heroics, romance and history, so much the better.

The contents of the house are varied and include a set of Meissen that belonged to Marie Antoinette and old documents from the medieval abbey which were discovered in an ancient box. In one of them a farmer swears by the sacred relics of St Nestan to desist from kidnapping and harming the king's messengers!

Below: Victorian splendour is the face Hartland Abbey presents today, but its history and its collections go back to the 12th century.

Hemerdon House

PLYMPTON

A GEORGIAN FAMILY HOUSE FULL OF INTERESTING MEMENTOES, FURNITURE AND PAINTINGS: TWO MILES FROM PLYMPTON, OFF THE A38 BETWEEN PLYMOUTH AND IVYBRIDGE.

■ My favourite room is the library, which contains a continuous record of the family's reading since long before the house was built. The earliest book was published in 1546, the latest in 1994. Repairs and rebinding are well advanced. ■
James Woollcombe

Hemerdon has belonged to Woollcombes since it was built 200 years ago. George Woollcombe was the son of Thomas Woollcombe, a Plymouth surgeon, and in 1782 married his cousin, Maria, daughter of another Thomas Woollcombe, also a Plymouth surgeon, who had bought the estate for her two years earlier. They began to build the house in 1793, though more than seven years passed before the house was finished, and from its somewhat curious arrangement it appears that Hemerdon was originally intended to be larger than it is. George had two sons: William, a soldier who fought at Waterloo and George, a sailor who rose to be Vice Admiral – his sword and naval uniform are in the house, together with a letter that he wrote after being wounded in the Battle of New Orleans. The house has survived largely unchanged, despite financial ups and downs, and in recent years Mr James Woollcombe, a former Shell executive, has undertaken a major restoration programme to preserve the house and contents intact for future generations.

The house, though unpretentious, is an attractive building of its period, and the documents and mementoes that the family have accumulated in two centuries of occupation are an added fascination. There are some fine pictures to be seen, including two portraits by Reynolds and others by Opie and Gandy – together with some local landscapes.

A portrait of the 3rd Viscount, the only boy in a family of 14, hangs over the fireplace in Powderham Castle's Music Room. He and some of his sisters painted the medallions around the walls.

Powderham Castle

KENTON

FINE GEORGIAN INTERIORS IN AN ANCIENT CASTLE OVERLOOKING THE RIVER EXE NEAR KENTON: EIGHT MILES SOUTH OF EXETER ON THE A379.

The soaring towers of Powderham recall the age of chivalry in a manner totally appropriate to this most romantic house. Late in the 14th century the castle was constructed by Sir Philip Courtenay, a younger son of the Earl of Devon. The castle was besieged and damaged in the Civil War, rebuilt in the 18th century and further changed by Wyatt in the 1790s. For centuries the Courtenays, though descended from a great historic family, prospered in a cautiously provincial manner, their only claim to notoriety being a youthful friendship of the 3rd Viscount with the wicked William Beckford. An exile in New York and Paris, it was the 3rd Viscount, William Courtenay, who discovered from his son's researches into ancient documents in 1831 that he was entitled to revive the Earldom of Devon, a title the family still hold today.

Powderham bears witness to the changing fortunes of the Courtenays. Its exterior is part medieval castle, part Gothic fantasy. The dining hall, though ancient in appearance, is in fact Victorian, with a splendidly romantic fireplace and coats of arms that proudly trace the Courtenay line back to the 11th century. Amongst the many other rooms, two are quite exceptional: Wyatt's music room, with a spectacular domed ceiling, and the staircase hall. The stairs themselves are grand and beautifully constructed, but the most amazing feature is the plasterwork. Birds and flowers, a cornucopia of fruit, even garden implements tumble in profusion against a bright blue background. The chapel too is interesting, converted from the grange of the medieval castle, with some fine old timbers in the roof. A sprawling house of many different styles and periods, Powderham is full of unexpected strange delights.

COURTENAYS CLOSE TO POWER

The Courtenays were a powerful but unlucky family. Their ancestors were related to the kings of France and had ruled as emperors of Constantinople in the 13th century. In England they produced a notable Archbishop of Canterbury in the 14th century, but in politics showed little judgement. One Courtenay took advantage of the Wars of the Roses to pursue his private feuds and was beheaded by the Yorkists; another was executed as a traitor by Henry VIII, having briefly been named Royal Heir. The earldom was extinguished when the 8th Earl, urged to marry Mary Tudor, died in exile, possibly by poison.

Sand

SIDMOUTH

THE SAME FAMILY HAS ALWAYS OWNED THIS HANDSOME TUDOR MANOR: ONE MILE NORTH OF SIDBURY OFF THE A375 BETWEEN HONITON AND SIDMOUTH.

On his retirement in 1560, James Huyshe, a successful London grocer, purchased Sand, and his descendants live there to this day. The present house was completed before 1600 by Rowland Huyshe and his wife Anne, whose initials are carved into a gable. In the Civil War the Huyshes, though Protestant in their beliefs, were staunch supporters of the Stuart cause, enduring fines and confiscations as a consequence. Both of their daughters, clearly girls of independent mind, married generals in Cromwell's army, one of whom, William Allen, was subsequently arrested for sedition whilst staying at the house.

In the 18th century the fortunes of the Huyshes declined and Sand was let out as a farmhouse, though when a neighbour's gamekeeper dared to trespass on the property, the Reverend Francis Huyshe wrote furiously that it was 'the miserable remains of an old family estate, which will be defended with family pride.' Sand was restored by Francis Huyshe early in the present century and though the house was subsequently let once more, the present owner, Colonel Huyshe, took up residence in 1967. Despite the many changes it has undergone, Sand still has Tudor fireplaces and old heraldic glass, whilst a staircase has survived from an even older house. A home that has adapted to the needs of modern life, Sand remains a fascinating relic of the squirearchy that seems, according to one visitor, 'to have grown out of the ground.'

Tapeley Park

INSTOW

THE MAGNIFICENTLY SITED HOME OF BRITAIN'S LEADING OPERATIC FAMILY: ONE AND A HALF MILES SOUTH OF INSTOW OFF THE A39 BETWEEN BARNSTAPLE AND BIDEFORD.

Set into a terraced hillside above the Torridge estuary, Tapeley Park enjoys splendid views of the lovely north Devon coastline and Lundy Island.There has been a house on the site ever since the time of the Domesday Book, and in 1702 it came to the attention of a naval officer, Commodore William Clevland, who had seen the house from his vessel as it sailed into the nearby estuary. Purchasing the property, he rebuilt the old cob manor as a fashionable brick mansion that after nearly 300 years still remains the home of his descendants.

The Clevland name died out in tragic circumstances, for the last male heir, Archibald, survived charging with the Light Brigade at Balaclava only to be killed at Inkerman, aged 21, leaving Tapeley to his sister, Agnes, and her husband, William Christie. Early in the present century the house was radically altered by Lady Rosamond Christie, who employed the architect John Belcher to redesign the main façades and lay out the Italian gardens that became her overriding passion. Her son, John Christie, married the opera singer, Audrey Mildmay, and they founded the Glyndebourne Festival – a fine display of operatic costumes are on show at Tapeley.

Despite its many changes, the house still retains much of its original decoration, including two fine ceilings – the work of a group of travelling Italian musicians in the 18th century who, when bookings for performances were slack, turned their hands to plasterwork! Amongst the furniture are many pieces made for Lady Rosamond by William Morris and there is also some interesting porcelain, but Tapeley's most delightful feature is undoubtedly the garden, an elaborate design of terraces, lawns and statuary, with palms, mimosa and hibiscus thriving in the shelter of the terrace walls alongside other rare and tender shrubs. Further from the house there is an experimental permaculture garden, where fruit, herbs, vegetables and nuts are grown in unison to produce a yield that varies with the seasons and is ecologically sustainable. Perhaps the far horizons which can be surveyed from Tapeley Park have inspired the idealism and enthusiasm inherent in so many of its owners.

Tapeley Park has lovely grounds and a superb situation, looking down over the north Devon coast, the Bristol Channel and the island of Lundy.

Tiverton Castle

Tiverton

A romantic home that has grown out of the ruins of a Norman castle: in Tiverton, six miles west of junction 27 of the M5.

Richard de Redvers, created Earl of Devon by Henry I, built Tiverton Castle to defend a vital crossing on the River Exe, completing it in 1106. When the de Redvers line died out, their lands and titles passed to Hugh de Courtenay, who strengthened Tiverton's defences in the 14th century, making it the stronghold of his volatile and war-like family in the feuds, rebellions and dynastic wars of late medieval England. It was an Earl of Devon whose notorious behaviour in the Wars of the Roses led to the triumph of the house of York and the forfeiture of Courtenay titles and estates.

When the family returned to favour after Bosworth, William Courtenay married Katherine Plantagenet, 'the daughter, sister and aunt of kings', who lived at Tiverton for 30 years. Their son, at one point Henry VIII's appointed heir, was later executed as a traitor; their grandson, having declined to marry Mary Tudor, died in exile, probably by poison. With the Courtenays' final and inevitable fall, Tiverton was rebuilt by Roger Giffard, who pursued a safer route to fortune through marriage to rich widows and transformed the castle into a comfortable Elizabethan house.

Following the Civil War, in which the castle's old defences were damaged, a new wing was built within the courtyard and Tiverton has since been home to important Devon families such as the Wests and the Carews. In 1960 it was bought by Ivar Campbell, a chieftain of the Campbells of Duntroon, who on his death in 1985 left it to his nephew Mr Angus Gordon.

The main part of the castle to have survived intact is the large gatehouse, dating from the 14th century, with walls more than five feet thick and vaults of pale Beer stone. Two other towers remain, one incorporating a medieval lavatory. Together with the Tudor and Elizabethan wings, they enclose a pretty courtyard.

Although much altered and redecorated, Tiverton remains a fascinating and romantic home, no longer under threat from Roundheads, but steadfastly defying the encroachment of the busy town on its ancient walls. Collections to be seen there include weaponry and armour from the Civil War, a fascinating display of clocks, continental furniture and pictures.

Ancient walls stand in ruins as a romantic backdrop to the part of Tiverton Castle which is now a comfortable and interesting home.

TIVERTON CASTLE BESIEGED

Both sides in the Civil War regarded the control of Tiverton and its river crossing as being vitally important. Garrisoned by Royalists, the castle was besieged by Sir Thomas Fairfax, overall commander of the Parliamentary army, who subjected its defences to a prolonged, intense bombardment. A spy, lowered from the walls to send for help from Exeter, was immediately apprehended and soon afterwards a lucky shot blew away the chains that held the drawbridge. The garrison was overwhelmed, with more than 200 taken prisoner, though it is said that some Royalists escaped from the castle through tunnels to the Red Lion inn.

Ugbrooke Park

Chudleigh

This Adam house is the home of one of England's oldest families: nine miles south-west of Exeter, off the A38 at Chudleigh.

An ancient and romantic family, the Cliffords claim descent from Viking kings and Dukes of Normandy. Arriving in this country with the Conquest, they played their part as warriors and barons in every conflict of the age. Roger fought for both sides in the Barons' War, Robert died at Bannockburn, his son was hanged at York after Lancaster's rebellion, and John, the 9th Baron, earned the nickname 'the butcher' for his ferocity in the Wars of the Roses. Victim of a chance encounter with an arrow, he was posthumously disgraced and his heir, 'the shepherd lord' was brought up in obscurity until he saved the Clifford name at Flodden in 1523.

A medieval house at Ugbrook belonging to the Precentor of the diocese of Exeter was seized by Protector Somerset and was later owned by Courtenays. Rebuilt as a Tudor manor, it passed through marriage to the Cliffords late in the 16th century. Though at first the poor relations of the family, the Chudleigh Cliffords rose to fame in the reign of Charles II, when Thomas, the first Lord Clifford, a hero of the war with Holland,

Left: Richly decorated and magnificent in its proportions, the chapel at Ugbrooke Park is a fine example of the work of Robert Adam.

became treasurer of the royal household and the king's most trusted confidant. Well-meaning but incompetent, his downfall came in opposing Parliament as a member of the King's 'cabal', when his opponents passed the Test Act to exclude all Roman Catholics from office.

Ugbrook was remodelled in the 18th century by Robert Adam, who paid tribute to the Cliffords' warlike heritage in the 'castle' style that he adopted, with battlemented towers at each corner of the mansion. The park was transformed by 'Capability' Brown, with a long and narrow lake the central feature of a gently rolling landscape. After the last war Ugbrook was neglected, with many of its finest rooms used for storing grain, but the house has now been beautifully restored. The library is a splendid Adam room, its plasterwork and colour-scheme exactly as they were 200 years ago. The house contains some fine old silver, tapestries and paintings, with a spectacular and unexpected bonus in the chapel. Designed by Adam in a most dramatic style, with a vaulted apse and open balconies, its marble columns, painted panels and elaborately worked decoration have an almost Byzantine richness.

Athelhampton

DORCHESTER

A ROMANTIC MANOR HOUSE WITH A MAGNIFICENT MEDIEVAL HALL: FIVE MILES NORTH-EAST OF DORCHESTER ON THE A35, NEAR PUDDLETOWN.

Athelhampton's roots are in Saxon times, dating from the time when Athelhelm was Earl of Wessex, but the present building was begun in 1485 when Sir William Martyn, a wealthy merchant and Lord Mayor of London, was granted a licence to enclose a deer park and build a battlemented house. Having backed both sides in the Wars of the Roses, he felt sufficient confidence in peace to build a home that, despite symbolic battlements, was designed for comfort rather than defence. The Martyns prospered for a century, but when Sir Nicholas died in 1595, though he left no less than ten daughters, he was without a male heir.

One later owner was the Earl of Mornington ('Mad Morny') – a nephew of the Duke of Wellington. The earl married an heiress with a huge fortune of £1million a year but gambled away her fortune and finally even lost Athelhampton in a game of cards.

Thomas Hardy made 'Athelhall' the setting for two rather gloomy poems and inscribed his signature into the lead of the dovecote roof. In 1891 Alfred Cart de Lafontaine built four courts walled with Ham Hill stone, as well as two garden pavillions. Yew trees were planted in the Great Court which have since evolved into topiary pyramids 25 feet high. The gardens as they stand today also owe much to the enthusiasm of Sir Robert Cooke, the politician, and his family, who continue his work today. This work has included the restoration of the house following a fire in 1992 which gutted much of the East Wing.

The glory of Athelhampton is its Great Hall, with a medieval roof of curved, braced timbers and an oriel with fine heraldic glass. For 500 years this has been the heart of the old house: Sir William warmed himself before the massive fire; Sir Nicholas gazed sadly at the Martyn crest (a chained-up monkey with a mirror) that is etched into the oriel; 'Mad Morny' listened to musicians on the minstrels' gallery as he wrote another begging letter to the Iron Duke ... Athelhampton, it is said, has more than its fair share of ghosts!

There is much more to be seen along the winding passages and unexpected stairs that link the different levels of this meandering house. The wine cellar has ancient liquor stains etched in the flagstone floor, other rooms have panelling and tapestries, pictures, furniture and china accumulated over the centuries and outside are complex and intriguing gardens with topiary and shady walks that, like the house itself, continue to grow with the years.

Beautiful Athelhampton, over 500 years old, has been completely restored after a terrible fire in 1992.

■ The architecture, the scale of the rooms and the quality of light all combine to make it a privilege to live in an historic house. The character of the building is stronger than one's own. ■
Penelope Duff

Ilsington House

DORCHESTER

A WILLIAM AND MARY MANSION WITH ROYAL AND SCANDALOUS CONNECTIONS: FOUR MILES EAST OF DORCHESTER NEAR TINCLETON, OFF THE A35.

The 7th Earl of Huntingdon built Ilsington in 1690 and it later passed through marriage to the Earl of Orford, son of Britain's first Prime Minister, Robert Walpole. The house was rarely lived in, though, until General Garth, a favoured courtier of George III, acquired the lease. The king visited Weymouth each summer for his health, and members of the royal entourage were accommodated by the general, who often rode to Weymouth twice a day – a total distance of some 50 miles.

In 1862 the Orfords sold the house to the Brymer family, who undertook 'improvements' to the village that outraged their neighbours, provoked a correspondence in *The Times* and upset even Thomas Hardy. Fortunately they did not tamper with Ilsington itself. In World War II, when the First US Infantry Division were based in Dorset prior to D-Day, the house was commandeered by the army and the wild parties held there were famed throughout the county. In the seventies, the Emir of Qatar was briefly the owner, but lost interest when he realised how far it was from Dorchester to Ascot!

The house now belongs to Peter and Penelope Duff, who have a fascinating and eclectic art collection, including modern works by Frink, Mahoney and Cecil Beaton. The interior has changed little in its architecture since the house was built, though many of the rooms have ornate plaster fireplaces that were installed by General Garth to please his royal visitors. The hall is copied from the Queen's Entrance to Kensington Palace, with a very pretty staircase and panelling of painted oak. In the gardens, the Duffs are gradually restoring the William and Mary design, with clipped yew hedges, sculptures, paths and lawns.

This 'Shy Goat' by Laurence Simon is on display in The Gallery at Ilsington House.

The entrance to Ilsington House is a copy of the Queen's Entrance at Kensington Palace.

A ROYAL INDISCRETION

Princess Sophie, the pretty, cosseted daughter of King George III, often stayed at Ilsington on her way to Weymouth. In 1800 she was found to be pregnant, though her father was convinced that she had dropsy. Born in secret, her son was adopted by Doctor Garth who, though 'an ugly old devil' more than 30 years her senior, was generally believed to be the child's father. Young Tom grew up handsome but disreputable and attempted to blackmail the royal family. Poor Sophie, despite all her princely brothers' unofficial offspring, was forced into reclusive spinsterhood for the remainder of her life.

The Manor House

PURSE CAUNDLE

A 15TH-CENTURY MANOR HOUSE IN THE VILLAGE OF PURSE CAUNDLE: SOUTH OF THE A30 FIVE MILES EAST OF SHERBORNE.

When the Blackmore Vale was a royal hunting forest in the 13th century, sick and injured hunting dogs were taken to Purse Caundle, where a steward nursed them back to health. A village legend claims that hounds can still be heard baying on Midsummer night and New Year's Eve. In 1429 Richard Long acquired the manor for 100 silver marks and his family began the present house, which was completed by their relatives, the Hanhams, before the onset of the Civil War.

The Hanhams, like most West Country squires, were Royalists and their property was confiscated. The hero of the household was their steward's son, Peter Mews, who fought at Naseby, fled to Holland, became a bishop with the Restoration, opposed King James and fought again at Sedgemoor. He died at the age of 91, still battling for his principles.

John Hoskins bought Purse Caundle from the Commonwealth Commissioners and the property then passed through inheritance and marriage to the family of Hudlestone, who were there throughout the 19th century. In those days there was an old stone staircase behind the fireplace in the hall, and ladies staying in the house frequently told stories of an over-friendly spirit that would rise out of the ancient well and follow them upstairs. So persistent were the tales that eventually the well was sealed and the staircase removed.

The splendid hall, still at its original height, was shared by the whole household until a separate bay was built to give the squire and his wife some privacy. Upstairs is the Great Chamber, with a barrel-vaulted ceiling and a pretty little oriel window that looks out on the village street – a vantage point from which the squire could keep an eye on local life. Many of the doorways are original and one bedroom window dates from the 13th century and probably came from the medieval lodge. From the gardens, the south front of the house forms the letter E, a popular conceit in Elizabethan times as a loyal gesture to the sovereign. Since 1984 Purse Caundle Manor has been owned and lived in by Mr Michael Pelet and his family.

Parnham House

BEAMINSTER

TUDOR ARCHITECTURE, A ROMANTIC HISTORY AND THE FINEST OF CONTEMPORARY DESIGN: A MILE SOUTH OF BEAMINSTER ON THE A3066.

In 1976 Parnham House stood derelict and crumbling, hidden by a wilderness of weeds that had once been croquet lawns and terraces. In three years on the market it had attracted no one brave enough to undertake its restoration and after a life-span of five centuries came very close to facing terminal decline.

Built when Henry VIII was king, Parnham was for its first 300 years the home of the Strodes – a powerful family with vast estates throughout the West Country. They were also firm in their convictions, risking their lives to shelter Charles II during his desperate flight in 1651 and beheading a cousin of the family, a Parliamentarian who disputed the estate's inheritance, for murdering Lady Strode.

In the 18th century Parnham passed by marriage to the Oglanders and in 1810 it was modernised by John Nash, who added pinnacles, battlements and other Gothic details. In 1896 the house was sold to Vincent Robinson, an eccentric antiquarian who was so passionate an atheist that he banned his sister from his home for having called a curate when she thought that he was dying. Eventually he forgave her and erected in her memory the Beaminster market cross. His body now lies buried in unconsecrated ground at Netherbury, between his sister and his favourite horse.

In 1910 Parnham was bought by Dr Hans Sauer, who swept away 'contemptible' Victorian additions and restored the house to Tudor purity, in the process finding a hidden room that had been sealed off for 100 years. For a period in the 1920s the house was a fashionable country club, visited by the then Prince of Wales and Sir Arthur Conan Doyle, who complained of 'restless ghosts'. During World War II the 16th US Infantry Division was billeted in the house, with officers indoors and other ranks in tents in the park. The assault on Omaha Beach in Normandy was planned here in conditions of high secrecy. In 1956 the Bullivants, owners since the failure of the country club, sold up and Parnham became a home for 'mentally frail old ladies' until stringent fire regulations forced its closure in 1973.

Its saviour three years later was John Makepeace, the internationally famous designer and maker of fine furniture. Parnham is now home to his own workshop and to the students of Parnham College.

Parnham's interior is exhilarating, proving that no ancient house need be frozen in a time capsule of 'heritage'. The Great Hall, restored to Tudor splendour and lit with true imagination, displays the innovative furniture that is the Makepeace hallmark. The drawing room's limed oak panelling and mullioned windows are a perfect backdrop to exhibitions of contemporary paintings and sculpture. On the first floor, each room reveals some new, imaginative quirk that never goes against the spirit of the house, while the *trompe-l'oeil* of the main staircase is a dramatic *tour de force*. The gardens, too, are fascinating – both formal and wild, and full of exciting surprises.

Top: The Great Hall at Parnham House reflects its Tudor origins.

Above: The Strode Bedroom has a four-poster bed made from a single English yew tree.

Sherborne Castle

SHERBORNE

THE 16TH-CENTURY HOME OF SIR WALTER RALEIGH, BUILT BESIDE THE RUINS OF THE OLD NORMAN CASTLE: ON THE EASTERN EDGE OF SHERBORNE, OFF THE A30.

When Sir Walter Raleigh first saw Sherborne whilst riding to his fleet at Plymouth, he was so enchanted by the view that he tumbled from his horse. Encouraged by a gift of jewellery from Raleigh, the queen herself put pressure on the rightful owner, the Bishop of Salisbury, to relinquish the estate. Raleigh first attempted modernising the old Norman castle, but later switched attention to a site across the River Yeo. Newly married and already with a son, he planned a home for his family and a refuge from his dangerous, fast life. In the grounds he laid out water gardens and a bowling green, planting trees from the New World with a bench of stone beneath their shade. This was perhaps where he was doused by an early anti-smoker whilst in quiet contemplation with his pipe – his servant thought he was on fire!

LIFE AT RALEIGH'S SHERBORNE

Raleigh's friends were brilliant and eccentric: the playwrite/secret agent Marlowe; the poetic Earl of Oxford; the astrologer John Dee. Life here was unorthodox and there were rumours of black masses in the tower study. Cleared on a charge of atheism, but bored with country life, Raleigh led an expedition up the Orinoco, returning sadder and no richer to the home he loved 'above all his possessions, of all places on earth.'

He was again parted from his beloved home, when James I considered him to be a threat to the new peace with Spain. After 13 years in the Tower, Raleigh was released to undertake one final expedition to the Orinoco coast. Failing to find gold, clashing with the Spanish and losing his own son, he returned to face disgrace and execution.

Present-day visitors to Sherborne Castle can see Raleigh's famous bench in the shade of trees he planted and admire the house he loved so much.

THE DIGBYS

Since 1617 the Digbys have owned Sherborne, many of them matching Raleigh in bravery and individualism. John, later 1st Earl of Bristol, was given the estate by King James I for his attempts to negotiate a Spanish marriage for Prince Charles. George became a Civil War hero when he led a charge at Lichfield into the heart of Cromwell's cavalry. His wife Anne was at Sherborne when the old castle was attacked. Learning that her brother was the Parliamentary commander, she stormed across the valley and ordered him to leave her home unharmed. Later losing patience with Charles II, George abused his monarch as dissolute and idle and was banished from Court. In 1688 William of Orange stayed at Sherborne for three days, proclaiming his 'bloodless revolution' from the house. Sir Kenelm Digby was a naval hero and practitioner of sympathetic magic who wrote recipe books and invented the ear trumpet. The 5th Lord would often visit the Fleet prison wearing beggars' rags, securing the release of the astonished prisoners by paying off their debts.

Sherborne Castle is now much larger than it was in Raleigh's time, but his square Elizabethan house remains the central block of the mansion. Most of the interior was refurbished by the Digbys in the 18th and the 19th centuries. The light and airy Gothic library is particularly pretty; other rooms are much grander, designed for entertaining royalty. Many of the massive fireplaces and elaborately plastered ceilings bear the Digby crest of a strange heraldic ostrich. There is an excellent collection of Japanese porcelain and many portraits of the Digby family, including works by Gainsborough and Lely.

'Capability' Brown's grounds take full advantage of the setting and the ruined castle; Raleigh's cedars are still growing and his favourite bench is still a vantage point, with views along the secret valley that he called his 'fortune's fold.'

RALEIGH'S FALL FROM GRACE

Elizabeth I was furious when told that Raleigh had seduced her maid of honour, Bess Throckmorton. Though already turning her attentions to the Earl of Essex, the Virgin Queen was nevertheless a jealous woman and the couple, now secretly married, were imprisoned in the Tower before banishment to Sherborne. Bess proved a loyal partner through all the hardships Raleigh faced and was with him at the end, when he addressed a last passionate poem to her before walking to the scaffold in Whitehall.

Wolfeton

DORCHESTER

LEGENDS AND ROMANTIC STORIES HAUNT THIS OLD ELIZABETHAN MANOR: ONE AND A HALF MILES NORTH OF DORCHESTER OFF THE A37 YEOVIL ROAD.

Luck has played an important part in the development of Wolfeton. In 1506 the young squire, Thomas Trenchard, heard that a great ship was sheltering in Weymouth from a storm. Riding to investigate, he met its occupants, the Archduke of Austria and his Spanish wife who were on the way to claim the Castile throne. For sheltering them in his home, he was subsequently invited to Windsor where his charm and talent earned him an important place at Court and eventually an earldom. He built the present house, which was extended further as his family continued to prosper.

Wolfeton is home of many legends: of the sceptre that fell from a statue of King Charles I before the Civil War; of the ghost of suicidal Lady Trenchard with a gash across her throat; of the footsteps of Sir George and even of a spectral coach that charges up the stairs to fulfil a bet made in the 18th century. Thomas Hardy used Wolfeton as a setting in *A Group of Noble Dames*, describing it as 'an ivied manor house flanked by battlemented towers.'

Wolfeton remains a most romantic and impressive manor, with enormous mullioned windows, turrets and a gatehouse which once housed 400 doves in its towers. There is a magnificent stone staircase, and much of the plasterwork is very fine, as are the great carved fireplaces. One, portraying Orientals and Red Indians, may have been inspired by tales told by Sir Walter Raleigh, who often visited the house when he lived at Sherborne Castle.

The Bishop's Palace

WELLS

A RARE OPPORTUNITY TO EXPLORE A PALACE OF PRELATES IN AN HISTORIC ENGLISH CATHEDRAL CITY: IN THE CENTRE OF WELLS, OFF THE MARKET PLACE.

Bishops' palaces are not often open to the public, and this one at Wells, frowning in machicolated defence behind its stout 14th-century walls and protective moat, seems certainly to have been built to keep unwanted callers at bay. A softer impression is given by the bell above the moat near the drawbridge, which the swans come and ring with their beaks when they want their tea. Or they do if visitors haven't overfed them.

Inside its warlike battlements the Palace has the peaceful air of centuries of clerical benevolence, its buildings set sweetly round a spacious lawn. There's a 13th-century chapel, which is still in daily use, and a beautiful ruined hall of the same period, which was deliberately made more picturesque in the 19th century. Both were built in the time of Bishop Burnell. What is regarded here as the 'modern' north wing was built in the 15th century by the formidable Bishop Beckynton, who was also responsible for the 'Bishop's Eye' gate which leads to the market place.

The State Rooms in the Palace were transformed in 'Italian Gothic' in Victorian times, and were subsequently abandoned by the bishops, who retreated to the north wing in the 1950s. A fine collection of portraits of past incumbents of the see includes the three most famous - Wolsey, Laud and Ken. The Long Gallery houses the cope which the bishops of Bath and Wells wear at coronations, sharing with the bishops of Durham the centuries-old privilege of supporting the sovereign.

The delightful gardens were landscaped by Bishop Law early in the 19th century, and contain the wells which give the city its name, the springs bubbling up at a rate of 40 gallons a second, day in and day out. And if you are particularly blessed, you will hear the choir singing seraphically in the ravishingly beautiful cathedral nearby.

Above: The Glastonbury Chair in the drawing room of the Palace.

Below: The medieval entrance hall.

Bottom: The Great Hall overlooking the south lawn.

Combe Sydenham Hall

MONKSILVER

MEMORIES OF SIR FRANCIS DRAKE IN A MAGIC, SECLUDED VALLEY IN EXMOOR: FIVE MILES SOUTH OF WATCHET ON THE B3188.

Hidden away in a delectable valley of the Brendon Hills in the Exmoor National Park, this Elizabethan house in its red-coloured sandstone is known for the beauty of its setting and its romantic connections with Sir Francis Drake and his second wife, Elizabeth Sydenham. The house was built in 1580 by Sir George Sydenham, the younger son of a well-to-do Somerset family. He married an heiress, Elizabeth Hales, and built his grand mansion at Combe Sydenham, with an inscription in Latin above the door. Translated, it means, 'This door shall always be open to you and yours, noble George, but closed to unwelcome souls.'

These sentiments were soon tested. Sir Francis Drake's first wife, an obscure Cornish girl named Mary Newman, died in 1583 and he came courting the Sydenhams' only child and heiress, the beautiful Elizabeth. According to the family tradition, for all his wealth and fame the Sydenhams looked down on Drake as an upstart, but that bold and piratical adventurer was not a man easily defeated. He may have been an 'unwelcome soul' to Sir George, but he and Elizabeth were duly wed in 1585. The new Lady Drake was his hostess at Buckland Abbey and survived her formidable spouse's death at sea in 1596. She then married one of the Courtenays of Powderham, but herself died soon afterwards in 1598.

The house has been through many vicissitudes and alterations, culminating in a long period of neglect, from which it has been rescued by the Theed family, who have made long strides in restoring it. The great hall, the Elizabethan courtroom and other rooms can be admired. Successful forestry and trout-farming have brought the estate back to earning its living and the beautiful grounds are now a delightful 500-acre country park, with Sir George's pond, a number of trails, including Drake's Leat walk, Lady Elizabeth's walk among the attractions. Others include a deserted hamlet, fallow deer in the deer park, woodland walks, a working corn mill and trout fishing, and gorgeous views northwards to the sea.

A SHOT ACROSS HER BOWS

According to a treasured Combe Sydenham legend, when Francis Drake wooed Elizabeth Sydenham she promised to wait for him while he was away at sea. In his absence, however, her family pressed her to choose elsewhere and she weakened and accepted a proposal from another suitor. The day of the wedding came and the bridal party was just about to enter the church when there was a blinding flash and a huge cannonball burst from the sky and smashed to the ground between the bride and the groom. Plans for the wedding were hastily abandoned, Elizabeth sent her intended packing and on the very next tide Drake sailed into Plymouth Sound and came to claim her for his own. The cannonball can still be seen in the house today, though some experts have identified it as a meteorite. Whichever it is, touching it is said to bring good luck.

Combe Sydenham Hall dates back to Elizabethan times and is now at the heart of a thriving rural estate and country park.

Forde Abbey

CHARD

MELLOW ABBEY BUILDINGS IN AN EXQUISITE GARDEN: FOUR MILES EAST OF CHARD OFF THE B3762.

From the bridge over the River Axe, close to the town of Chard, the buildings of Forde Abbey still appear as a monastery unaltered since the Middle Ages. Set in deep countryside, and framed by a magnificent garden, the golden tones of the Ham Hill stone have a tranquillity and a harmony about them that is rare in a building which has been a house for more than four centuries.

From the reign of Stephen until the Dissolution in 1539, Forde Abbey was a Cistercian monastery. In 1141, Adelicia de Brioniis offered the Manor of Thorncombe and a site beside the Axe for a new monastery, and within seven years the buildings were ready for occupation. The Abbey soon acquired a reputation for learning, and its third abbot was Baldwin, who became Archbishop of Canterbury and crowned Richard I.

Left: The monastic origins of Forde Abbey are still apparent, though today it is unmistakably a family home.

Thomas Chard, the last abbot, ruled from 1521 until 1539, and during his time the buildings were restored with great splendour and magnificence. The great Perpendicular tower over the entrance porch was his, and he proudly recorded the date, 1528, and his own name on the tall oriel windows when the building was finished. After the Dissolution, the Abbey went through a period of decay until 1649, when Edmund Prideaux, Oliver Cromwell's Attorney General, bought Forde Abbey and a new period of glory began. He changed the Abbot's lodging into private quarters for his family, shortening the Great Hall in the process, created a Grand Saloon out of the monks' gallery and added a series of State Apartments over the cloister.

The Great Hall, with its magnificent oak panelled roof, is a dignified Tudor room giving access to the Great Stair. Here, Prideaux's embellishments are strongly in evidence, with the wonderful pierced foliage panels instead of baluster rails beneath a plaster ceiling. The saloon, famous for its plasterwork, is hung with Mortlake tapestries, commissioned by Prideaux and based on Raphael cartoons of the Acts of the Apostles. With their magnificent borders by Cleyn, these are the most important works of art in Forde Abbey, but their delivery was delayed when Prideaux's son was implicated in the Monmouth Rebellion and imprisoned. The Upper Refectory, or monks' frater, still possesses its open 15th-century timber roof, while across the landing are the State Rooms, with wonderfully intricate plaster ceilings.

Gaulden Manor

Lydeard St Lawrence

A fine manor house noted for its Jacobean plasterwork: one and a half miles south of Lydeard St Lawrence off the B3224.

Gaulden Manor lies in the lovely rolling countryside between the Brendon and the Quantock Hills in Somerset. The house and its beautiful plasterwork speak today of the 17th century, and yet parts of the structure are 700 years old. Originally known as Gaveldon, Gaulden-in-Tolland was presented by Andrew de Bovedon to the Priory of Taunton in about 1250, and there was a monastic grange at Gaulden together with a large fishpool, which can still be seen.

At the Dissolution of the Monasteries the estate became privately owned and has remained so ever since. A number of families owned the property before it was bought in 1615 by John Turberville, grand-nephew of the Bishop, for his son, also named John. The plasterwork is most likely to date from 1639, the year when the younger John Turberville married Bridget Willoughby. The coats of arms of the two families are incorporated in the designs, appearing one in the hall and one in the upstairs Hall Chamber.

An oak door gives access to the entrance hall, which has a Tudor open fireplace, while the Great Hall is typical of those of the 17th century. Originally open to the rafters, the Great Hall has magnificent plasterwork including the overmantel, two ceiling roundels and a pendant, and a deep frieze. A carved oak screen divides the Great Hall from the chapel, in which the plaster frieze continues, while, above, the Turberville Bedroom, originally the solar, has a plaster overmantel dating from 1640.

The house is furnished with a fine collection of antique furniture, and also on display are embroideries worked by the present owner's wife.

The sitting room at Gauldon Manor is dominated by its magnificent plasterwork.

Longleat

WARMINSTER

The flamboyant 7th Marquess of Bath, the current owner of Longleat, with one of his own murals.

THE SEAT OF THE THYNNES FOR MORE THAN FOUR CENTURIES, THIS MAGNIFICENT ELIZABETHAN MANSION SURROUNDED BY 'CAPABILITY' BROWN'S PARK RETAINS A FINE GREAT HALL, TOGETHER WITH STATE ROOMS THAT EXPRESS THE OPULENCE AND GRANDEUR OF VICTORIAN NOBILITY: FIVE MILES WEST OF WARMINSTER, SIGNPOSTED OFF THE A36 BETWEEN SALISBURY AND BATH.

From Heaven's Gate, the view of Longleat is unforgettable. The trees that line the drive are suddenly drawn back to reveal a panorama stretching to the distant Mendip Hills, and a swathe of open parkland drops down into the valley, with a haze of darker woods beyond. Central to this composition is the house itself. Longleat at this distance is like some palace from a fairy tale. Honey-coloured stone and glass reflect the sun; the turrets, cupolas and chimneys are mirrored in the waters of a lake. The fantastic setting is entirely appropriate, for the history of this house is one of heroes, wicked villains, adventure and romance. As in many fairy tales, the story opens in a kitchen.

FROM HUMBLE BEGINNINGS

In the reign of Henry VIII, John Thynn was a youthful clerk working in the royal kitchens. Single-minded and ambitious, he came to the attention of Edward Seymour, Earl of Hertford, who appointed him his steward. In 1540 he became a man of property, paying £53 for a dilapidated priory at 'Longlete', which he started to repair and convert into a country home. Knighted at the age of 32, he took the crest his family still bear – a Scottish lion with a knotted tail. He also changed the spelling of his name to imply more noble origins and found a suitable young wife, a daughter of Sir Richard Gresham. His house meanwhile grew steadily until gutted by a fire in 1567. Within a year Sir John had bought a quarry of Bath stone, hired a hundred workmen and started to rebuild.

Longleat had no architect but Thynne himself, though he was assisted by his mason, Robert Smythson, his sculptor Allen Maynard and his joiner Adrian Gaunt, all three of whom have left at Longleat lasting evidence of their great talent. The result of this collaboration was a palace built to celebrate prosperity and peace, a modern home to suit a modern man. The site was chosen purely for its beauty, the house itself designed with no thought for defence, its great bayed walls of stone and mullioned glass setting a new trend in Elizabethan architecture. Thynne was a perfectionist, driving his masons to distraction as he changed his mind, rebuilt façades and added new details. He wanted the Gothic splendour of a Tudor mansion, yet he loved the classical perfection of Italian architecture. He gave each floor pilasters in ascending order of Doric, Ionic and Corinthian; he made the house symmetrical with matching wings, yet on the roof he threw away all classic elegance for Tudor quirkiness by the addition the 'banketting houses', where groups of friends might gather for an after-dinner drink. Five years after a disastrous fire, Thynne moved back into his home, together with his now extensive family and household. Soon afterwards, a most important guest arrived. Visits by Elizabeth I were often dreaded by her subjects, for, with a huge court in attendance, the expense could be colossal. Ever careful with his money, Thynne was a reluctant host, but he must have felt some quiet satisfaction with his life whilst dining with his sovereign in his own Great Hall. Just 40 years before, he had been working in her father's kitchen.

John Thynne died in 1580, leaving a substantial fortune and a building that though well advanced, was still far from complete. An accountant to the last, his books recorded that expenditure to date amounted to £8,016.13s.8d. His steward added that the nails for his coffin cost 11d.

Detail of A View of Longleat *by Jan Siberechts, the largest painting in the Bedroom Corridor, showing the house as it was in the 17th century.*

The Saloon, formerly the Long Gallery, is, at 90 feet long, the largest room in Longleat, and is hung with 17th-century Flemish tapestries.

MARRIAGES OF MIXED FORTUNE

The heir to Longleat shared his father's name, but not his character. Indolent, dishonest and foul-tempered, John Thynne tried to stab a Salisbury merchant who out-bid him at the market and was fined for mismanagement and fraud in performance of his public duties. Married to a wife who, like his mother, had been brought up as the daughter of a wealthy London merchant, he spent as little time as possible at Longleat and passed the last months of his life in hiding, convinced that a plot was afoot to kidnap him for ransom.

Jacobean marriages were seldom much concerned with love. Wives were chosen on the basis of their fathers' wealth or influence, though, as the Thynnes discovered, this did not always mean that women were content to be no more than good investments. Thomas Thynne's first wife Maria was spirited and independent-minded. When accused of failing to show her husband due respect, she promised he would find upon his bed tokens even from his dogs in gratitude for being fed! Following Maria's death in child-birth, Thomas married a daughter of the Duke of Norfolk, Catherine Howard, who, when her husband lay upon his deathbed, persuaded him to change his will. James, Maria's son, evicted her from Longleat, but Catherine stirred up endless trouble through her contests over the inheritance. Then James, far from being cautious, made the most disastrous match of all. Lady Isabella Holland was beautiful, well-connected and wildly eccentric. She attended church dressed as an angel, danced in public wearing a bare minimum of clothes and achieved the considerable feat of being banned from the court of Charles II for her disreputable behaviour.

A SELF-MADE MAN

John Thynn's meteoric rise was dependent on his patron's fortunes. With Henry VIII's death, Seymour was made Duke of Somerset and Lord Protector, a king in everything but name. He took his steward to the war in Scotland and knighted him at Pinkie. Sir John Thynne's future seemed assured until disaster struck when Somerset was overthrown. Twice imprisoned in the Tower, Thynne's persuasive powers saved him from his patron's fate upon the scaffold, but the experience made him a wiser and more cautious man, and he retreated to his Wiltshire home to concentrate on building his home and adding to his fortune.

THE END OF THE GENETIC LINE

In the Civil War James Thynne, though a Royalist and former soldier, avoided playing any noble part. He lent the King substantial sums of money whilst petitioning the Parliament for an Order of Protection, though this did not prevent the house from being looted. Following the Restoration and Isabella's death from alcohol, Charles II stayed at Longleat, grateful for Thynne's financial, if not military, support. At about this time, Christopher Wren was commissioned to work on the still uncompleted house and designed a splendid staircase, but tragically his work has not survived later renovations.

James Thynne died without a son, as did his nephew Tom, killed by hired assassins as he drove along the

The Great Hall is one of the few remaining Elizabethan rooms in Longleat.

Mall. 'Tom o' Ten Thousand', as he was dubbed after his income, died for a wife he did not love, for the killers had been hired by an admirer who wished to see her widowed. This break in the genetic line was probably quite fortunate, for when born to fortunes that seemed limitless, few heirs to Longleat could be trusted with either alcohol or money, let alone with women – though a grandson of the scheming Catherine Howard, the 1st Viscount Weymouth, proved a very different character. In 30 years at Longleat he expanded the estate to 50,000 acres, drank little, never gambled and remained devoted to his wife. His one extravagance was gardening; £30,000 was spent on formal beds and gravel paths, terraces and fountains, with a romantic little 'wilderness' enclosed behind neat railings. His masterpiece did not survive for long, for his successor to the title lived for years as a recluse showing little care for either house or gardens. By the middle of the 18th century the 'wilderness' had burst from its enclosure and threatened to invade the house itself. By then the age of formal gardens was in any case long over.

ROMANCE AND INTRIGUE

The 2nd Viscount Weymouth was a haunted man. Wild and wilful in his youth, he married a young wife whom he adored. To show his love he bought her a live leopard and a bear, he brought actors down from London to perform in the Long Gallery. But when Louisa died at the age of 22 there were rumours of a secret lover, a murder and her ghost seen in an upper corridor. The Viscount closed up Longleat and lived as recluse until his death. In 1915 workmen found a booted skeleton in a shaft below the corridor where Louisa's ghost is still occasionally seen.

A NEW LANDSCAPE

Few ages have seen such drastic changes to the English countryside as happened in the 18th century. Each year Enclosure Acts were passed, breaking up the common fields that had existed since Saxon times with hedges that denoted individual ownership. In great gardens on the other hand, complexities were swept away, largely at the instigation of one fashionable designer. 'Capability' Brown let nothing come between him and his vision of the ideal landscape. At Longleat, as elsewhere, he dug out lakes where none had been before and replanted trees as casually as daffodils. As Cowper wrote:

'He speaks; the lawn in front becomes a lake;
Woods vanish, hills subside and valleys rise.'

Though Brown's destruction of old formal gardens may seem sad, few would have survived into our present century, when having 50 gardeners is considered an extravagance. Instead, we can enjoy the prospects he envisaged two centuries ago, softened with maturity and at the peak of their perfection. Though Humphrey Repton later added some touches of finesse it is essentially Brown's view we see today from Heaven's Gate.

GEORGIAN PROGRESS

Thomas, the 3rd Viscount, pursued a career in politics that, despite his reputation as a drunkard, brought him friendship with the King. Elevated to the rank of Marquess, it was as the 1st Lord Bath that he received George III at Longleat in 1789, providing an enormous banquet for 125 guests. By early the next morning, 30,000 people had gathered in the park to cheer their sovereign and their landlord standing at an upper window. The Marquess died with massive debts, but his son was fortunately shrewd in business matters, ignoring all political ambitions to concentrate upon consolidating the estate and adding to its revenues. Bitterly aware that as a man of moderate habits he was a rare exception in his family, he attempted to disinherit his own son, who had eloped to Paris with the daughter of a local toll-keeper. Unable to reform his family, it was no doubt his distaste for chaos and disorder that drove him to improve the ancient and by now decrepit palace that he lived in.

Longleat, as John Thynne had envisaged its design more than two centuries before, still remained unfinished, for in place of a north wing there was only a dilapidated range of outbuildings. Moreover, the internal lay-out of the house was still Elizabethan, with the major rooms arranged in series without any form of private access.

James Wyatt was brought in to remedy these defects; he built a new north front that harmonised quite well with the Elizabethan wings, he added an enormous stable court and he managed to insert a maze of corridors that allowed the servants to perform their duties without disturbing family or guests. He also ripped out Wren's fine staircase and, as in so many houses that he worked on, replaced it with a bland and dreary substitute. After work that lasted for ten years and cost £100,000, Longleat was more comfortable and easier to live in, but a change in its Elizabethan character had started to take place – a change that would continue through the century.

THE VICTORIAN AGE

The Golden Age of Longleat was in the reign of Queen Victoria and even to this day the interior of the house remains a monument to this extraordinary period. Despite Reform Acts and a rising middle class, the English aristocracy had never been so confident; their estates were hugely profitable, their investments were secure, society was god-fearing and stable. They were the rulers of the wealthiest and largest empire that the world had ever known.

In 1837, the year of Queen Victoria's accession, the eloping Viscount Weymouth died, followed within months by both his father and his brother. Inheriting his title at the age of six, Alexander the 4th Marquess grew up to be a devoutly serious young man who at the age of 21 became master of a vast, well-run estate that stretched from Salisbury Plain into the depths of Somerset. There were 50 indoor servants, 30 gardeners, a man to iron his bootlaces and another to select and cut the flower for his button-hole. From gilded youth into respectable maturity, Alexander lived a charmed existence as a fine example of his class and age.

Alexander married an Italian wife, well-born and vivacious, to whom he was devoted all his life. Reticent and English in his character, he had loved all things Italian since the time of his Grand Tour, when he had seen Medici palaces whose splendours put to shame the drab interiors of Longleat. In 1876 he set to work upon the State Rooms, employing the designer J D Croce to express his baroque taste. With expense no object and the idea of conservation quite unheard of, Italian craftsmen were imported to transform Elizabethan rooms into apartments worthy of a Doge's palace, with ornately decorated ceilings, massive marble chimney-pieces and no corner left ungilded. The Marquess and his wife scoured Europe for Flemish tapestries, Cordoba leather and Italian paintings. In 1881 they entertained the Prince of Wales at a ball attended by 600 guests. They were at the pinnacle of High Victorian society, their home a fairy-tale palace.

A NEW BEGINNING

The fairy tale was ended by wars, recession and taxation. Servants were dismissed, vast tracts of the estate were sold. When Henry Thynne became 6th Marquess in 1947 he owed £700,000 in death duties and faced an annual bill of £30,000 to run the house. Under his direction, Longleat became the first of England's stately homes to be opened to the public, thus ensuring that the house could still remain within the family. It is now home to the 7th Marquess, who continues in the Thynne tradition both in living a defiantly unorthodox existence and by adding to the house the stamp of his own personality.

The Great Hall is the only room at Longleat that John Thynne would still recognise. High overhead, carved pendants hang from Tudor hammer-beams and Queen Elizabeth I, on her arrival at Longleat, must have warmed herself before the huge carved chimney piece. The State Rooms are, by contrast, pure Victorian and though extraordinary to modern eyes, should be seen as the exuberant expression of an age with very different tastes. The workmanship throughout is quite superb, particularly in the ceilings. Coffered, gilded, intricately decorated, they are designed to utterly intimidate anyone below the rank of Marquess.

The Red Library shows an unexpected aspect of Longleat's creator – a love of books that drove him to collect more than 6,000 volumes. There is also a fine modern table by John Makepeace, made from wood from the estate to commemorate Longleat's 400th year. The apartments of Lord Bath are another revelation. He has painted many of the walls with his own murals. Vast, exuberant and often of a most explicit nature, their lack of all restraint seems perfectly in keeping with the house.

Below: One of the State Dining Room's salt-cellars, representing the Cries of London, which were made for the Great Exhibition of 1851.

Bottom: Floodlights and a firework display pick out a night-time scene from across the lake.

Hatch Court

TAUNTON

AN ELEGANT PALLADIAN MANSION WITH A FINE STAIRCASE: SEVEN MILES SOUTH-EAST OF TAUNTON OFF THE A358.

Set in attractive parkland close to Taunton, Hatch Court is the very epitome of Georgian elegance. It was built in 1755 in the Palladian style for John Collins by a gifted amateur architect, Thomas Prowse. The Bath stone square towers have pyramidal roofs, reminiscent of Hagley Hall, in Hereford and Worcestershire, and the south front has an arcaded piazza of five graceful arches, while the curving wings were added between 1785 and 1829.

Although the Manor of Hatch Beauchamp traces its history back beyond the Conquest, and was held by the Seymour family during the middle part of the 16th century, it was only in the present century that a really remarkable personality owned Hatch Court. Andrew Hamilton Gault was born in England, but fought in the Boer War in the Canadian Mounted Rifles. In 1914, he conceived the idea of raising a regiment, the Princess Patricia's Canadian Light Infantry, and these volunteers fought in Europe from 1915 until the Armistice.

Inside the house, the most prominent feature is the splendid cantilevered staircase which runs through the centre of the house, divided from the entrance hall by a screen of columns. In the hall hang several paintings of horses by Sir Alfred Munnings, as well as a fine portrait of Brigadier Gault by Glyn Philpott. The dining room has simple Georgian decoration, with fine paintings by Sir Peter Lely's pupil, Mary Beale, but the drawing room ceiling is decorated with bold rococo plasterwork. Hatch Court is, indeed, a house where the elegance of the design is matched by the personalities of those who created and lived in it.

Right: Stanway House's beautiful mellow stone Gatehouse, between the church and the main house, is considered to be a gem of Cotswold architecture.

Stanway House

CHELTENHAM

A MELLOW JACOBEAN MANOR HOUSE WITH A FINE GREAT HALL: TEN MILES WEST OF STOW-ON-THE-WOLD ON THE B4077.

> **■ I think the unique charm of Stanway springs from its stone, its situation relative to the landscape and village and its trees. Together these give the impression of a community in which time has stood still. ■**
> Lord Neidpath

Nestling deep in the countryside at the edge of the Cotswolds is Stanway House, one of Britain's most romantic Jacobean manor houses. It was built between 1580 and 1640 in mellow golden limestone by the Tracys, a family which had owned land in the county since the Conquest. Later Stanway passed by marriage into the hands of the Charteris family, and is now occupied by Lord Niedpath, son of the Earl of Wemyss and March. In 715, the manor was given by two Mercian magnates to the Abbey of Tewkesbury as its first endowment, and it was on the Dissolution of the Monasteries that Stanway changed hands for the only time in 1,270 years when Richard Tracy obtained a lease of the property with the assistance of Thomas Cromwell.

Approaching the house from the beautiful village of Stanway, you pass the magnificent 14th-century tithe barn built by the Abbey, and also the charming gatehouse which dates from around 1630. The façade is dominated by the splendid gables and by the magnificent tall windows that give light to the Great Hall. Beyond the screens passage the hall still possesses an unmistakable Elizabethan atmosphere, with a raised dais at one end and at the other a minstrels' gallery, now made into a bedroom above the screen. The Audit Room has a rent table of 1780, where the estate still receives payment in person from tenants, while steps from the Great Hall lead up to the Great Parlour. Furnished today with two 'Chinese Chippendale' daybeds and Broadwood pianos and hung with family portraits by Romney and Raeburn, it was to this room that past generations of Tracys would have retreated from the mêlée of the Great Hall.

Berkeley Castle

BERKELEY

A ROMANTIC MEDIEVAL CASTLE WITH SPECTACULAR INTERIORS: OFF THE A38, SOUTH-WEST OF M5 JUNCTION 13 (NINE MILES) AND NORTH-WEST OF M5 JUNCTION 14 (FIVE MILES).

Few families can trace their ancestry back to the Anglo-Saxons, but the Berkeleys of Berkeley Castle are in direct descent from a Master of the Horse to Edward the Confessor. For 850 years the gaunt profile of

THE MURDER OF EDWARD II

In 1327 King Edward II was imprisoned and brutally murdered in Berkeley Castle by Sir John Maltravers and Sir Thomas Gurney. In the corner of the King's Gallery, we can still see a deep well – the pestilential vapours from the rotting corpses of dead animals rising into the room were expected to asphyxiate the King. Edward survived this barbarous treatment, only to be murdered in his bed by his jailers. Even today, there is doubt about the role Thomas Lord Berkeley played in this shocking crime, but it is probable that he was innocent of complicity in his sovereign's death.

Berkeley Castle has kept watch over the Severn and the Welsh Borders, seeming to grow powerfully out of the outcrop of rock on which it stands. Inside its thick walls, events of great importance have taken place: the West Country barons met in the Great Hall of the castle before placing their demands before King John at Runnymede in 1215; in 1327 the unfortunate Edward II was first imprisoned and then murdered in a room in the keep; during the Civil War Berkeley Castle was besieged for three days by Parliamentary forces, and though the castle was not seriously damaged, a large breach in the wall of the keep remains to this day.

Berkeley Castle was founded after the grant of a Charter by Henry II to Robert Fitzharding in 1153, and the entry to the Shell Keep is still through a Norman doorway in the inner courtyard. Most of the building that we see today dates from the 14th century, but the Drake Room and Tower Room contain a later but nonetheless remarkable collection of ebony furniture from the Portuguese East Indies which, by tradition, once belonged to Sir Francis Drake. In the picture gallery there are seascapes by Van der Veldes, portraits by Lely, a groom and horses by Stubbs and a hunting painting, *The Old Berkeley Hounds*, by Ben Marshall. Hunting is an ever-present subject at Berkeley, and the dining room is hung with portraits of three Masters of the Berkeley Hounds, by Raoul Millais, Orpen, and Teesdale. Beyond the medieval kitchen is the Housekeeper's Room, where the Godwin Cup is displayed – believed to have belonged King Harold's father.

The Great Hall still retains a medieval atmosphere, with its 13ft-thick walls hung with Oudenarde tapestries illustrating the story of Queen Esther, an unusual painted screen dating from the 16th-century, and a magnificent timber roof. Over the fireplace hangs a fine portrait of Admiral Sir Cranfield Berkeley by Gainsborough, and a well-preserved Berkeley Arch gives access to the Grand Staircase. This lovely wooden stair of 1637 leads to the Morning Room, which was once the chapel. The ribs of its ceiling are painted with verses from the Bible, translated into Norman French in 1387 by John Trevisa, a friend of Wycliffe, and are an early example of rendering the Bible in the vernacular. The walls are hung with magnificent early Brussels tapestries depicting the stories of Isaac and Rebecca and Sodom and Gomorrah, woven by Pannemakers from cartoons by Raphael, while the particularly fine refectory table reputedly came from Fountains Hall in Yorkshire. Now occupying the end of the Long Drawing Room is the King's Pew which used to stand in the chapel, while the Small Drawing Room is a charming evening room, hung with Brussels tapestries depicting episodes from Ovid's *Metamorphoses*.

From the castle the views over the gardens to the river are superb. The terraces have grass walks with borders of low plants, backed by shrubs and climbers, while the bowling alley is flanked by a high wall and ancient clipped yews. Beyond, cattle graze in the water meadows, creating as beautiful and peaceful a scene as anywhere in the country.

Top: The famous Godwin Cup, said to have belonged to King Harold's father, Earl Godwin.

Above: This Brussels tapestry by Jan Cobus is one of a delightful series in the Small Drawing Room.

Left: Smooth lawns contrast with the ancient stone walls of Berkeley Castle's south front.

The Manor House

WEST COKER

A BEAUTIFUL ELIZABETHAN MANOR HOUSE WITH A FINE GREAT HALL: FOUR MILES SOUTH-WEST OF YEOVIL ON THE A30.

In a part of Somerset rich in fine houses, stands this exquisite Manor House, built, like the other mansions and villages of the area in wonderful honey-coloured Ham Hill stone. The property suffered a great fire in 1457, and much of what we see today was the result of rebuilding by the Courtenay family during the following 50 years.

As was usual for the time, the Great Hall of the medieval house is situated in the centre and is entered by a porch dated 1600. Inside this wonderful room, the atmosphere is distinctly 16th century, with tall, elegant windows, each with two lights, giving a stunningly clear light into the hall. The bay window, which would originally have illuminated the dais end of the hall, now contains the staircase, and this also has two lights. The hall also has a splendid open timber roof and a most striking decorated frieze made up of quatrefoils, but it is possible that this handsome feature was added in the middle of the 19th century. The authentic layout of the Great Hall is completed by a vast fireplace.

On the upper floor, at one end of the Great Hall, is the Withdrawing Chamber, into which the owner of this great house and his guests would move away from the heat and confusion below. Here is a grand early 17th-century overmantel, decorated with fine plasterwork. In another upstairs room, a fireplace dates from the early part of the 16th century, and, on this upper level, many of the original open roofs can be seen.

The Manor House is one of those delightful houses, thankfully still numerous in this country, where historical changes are still quite apparent in the building we see today, but where harmony of stone, craftsmanship and setting are still successfully maintained.

■ I love the sense of continuity here, living and farming in a place where the boundaries haven't changed since Norman times and where only two families have lived since 1550. ■

James More-Molyneaux

Chavenage

TETBURY

AN ELIZABETHAN MANOR HOUSE OF MELLOW COTSWOLD STONE: ABOUT THREE MILES NORTH-WEST OF TETBURY OFF THE A46.

Only a short distance from Tetbury, in wonderful rolling Gloucestershire countryside, stands the mellow stone house of Chavenage. With a central porch and two projecting bays, it is a typical E-shaped house of the Elizabethan period, but when Edward Stephens began his reconstruction in 1576, Chavenage already had a long and distinguished history.

It had been part of the manor of Horsley since Anglo-Saxon times, owned by the sister of Edward the Confessor, and the place where Earl Godwin had gathered his forces with the intention of confronting King Edward at Gloucester.

A CHEQUERED HISTORY

After the Norman Conquest, a community of Augustinian monks from Tours settled at Horsley, and the estate was administered by the Church until Henry VIII's Dissolution of the Monasteries. Chavenage was part of the estate granted by Henry VIII to the Seymour family, but when they fell from favour, it was acquired first by Sir Walter Denys, of Dyrham Park, in 1553, and then, in 1564, by Edward Stephens of Eastington. With the exception of the ballroom, added in 1904, and the little chapel, the appearance of the house has not changed greatly since that time.

Approaching the porch, it is clear that, in converting the medieval hall, Edward Stephens re-used much of the original fabric, including the large stone in front of the door which might have been an altar from Horsley Priory. The main door also has a sanctuary ring and a spy hole, which again probably came from the priory. With its tall windows containing late-medieval glass, and a fine 16th-century screen with a minstrels' gallery above, the main hall still retains the authentic atmosphere of Elizabeth's reign. The stained glass shows a heraldic shield from the Stephens family, as well as other pieces, including an amusing picture of a naked lady. Originally the roof would have been completely open to the rafters, while the double doors of the hall are framed by Jacobean bedposts, perhaps from the bed upstairs, which is known to have been rebuilt at some stage in the past.

STEPHENS' FATEFUL DECISION

A kinsman of Oliver Cromwell, Colonel Nathaniel Stephens was eventually, after long meetings in the house, persuaded by Cromwell and Ireton to vote for the King's impeachment. Soon afterwards Stephens died, and the story is told of the Colonel's ghost being taken from the house in a carriage drawn by the headless king.

THE CIVIL WAR

During the Civil War, Chavenage played an important role on the national stage. Colonel Nathaniel Stephens was related to Oliver Cromwell, and he and his generals were known to have lodged here. Oliver Cromwell's room is clad in beautiful early 17th-century verdure tapestries made for the room, while those in Ireton's Room are unfortunately more fragmented, and of a later date. The contemporary bed is quite narrow, and is thought to be a sick bed, which could be hung from cords like a cot.

TREASURED POSSESSIONS

Queen Anne visited Tetbury and is thought to have lodged at Chavenage. The splendid bed which stands in her room is thought to have been converted for the use of her personal physician, and it has a Judgement of Solomon in bas relief on the headboard.

At the bottom of the stairs is a memorial chest dating from the beginning of the 17th century, while the ballroom has fine court cupboards and Cromwellian chairs upholstered in leather. The present chapel is from the early years of the last century, but contains not only a lovely Elizabethan monument to members of the Stephens family, but also has an important Saxon font.

Whittington Court's dining hall is furnished in true manorial style.

Whittington Court

CHELTENHAM

THIS ELIZABETHAN MANOR HOUSE STILL HAS PART OF ITS MOAT: FIVE MILES EAST OF CHELTENHAM OFF THE A40 OXFORD ROAD.

Whittington Court stands in the middle of its own agricultural estate on the western edge of the Cotswolds above Cheltenham, and even today the moat that surrounded the property still runs along two sides of the south garden. Many such houses in Britain had private chapels which have since become parish churches, and this is probably true of Whittington church, as it stands close to the Court and contains family memorials, including a brass to Richard Cotton (died 1556), for whom the house was originally built. The original plan was the usual E-shaped house, but during its history the porch was moved to the eastern end of the Great Hall, the present cross wing was rebuilt in the 17th century, probably to replace a solar where the library now stands, and the western wing was never built.

Although Whittington Court seems to be a house of the 16th and 17th centuries, its origins lie much deeper in history. Probably named Witetune in Anglo-Saxon times, the manor of Whittington belonged to the de Crupe family in the Middle Ages, and tombs to three members of the family are in the 12th-century church. Later it was owned by the Despencer family who were Earls of Gloucester, and after the death of the great Earl of Warwick, his widow, Anne, was persuaded to transfer Whittington to King Henry VII.

In 1545 the manor came into the hands of the Cotton family, and it was John Cotton who had the privilege of entertaining Queen Elizabeth at Whittington during a progress she made through Gloucestershire in 1592. Records state that she 'dyned at Mr Coton's at Whytinton'. The manor later passed to Ann Cotton, who was married to Sir John Denham, a courtier, poet and dilettante architect who, at the Restoration, was given the post of Surveyor-General of the King's Works. It is likely that his influence was brought to bear on some of the classical features added to the house in that era. The Grand Staircase has an original 17th-century dog gate on the first half-landing to prevent dogs from going to the bedrooms.

Whittington Court is the quintessential Cotswold manor house, with mellow golden stone, mullioned windows and delightful gardens.

Sudeley Castle

WINCHCOMBE

PART RUINED MEDIEVAL CASTLE AND PART VICTORIAN GENTLEMAN'S RESIDENCE IN LOVELY PARKLAND: TO THE SOUTH OF WINCHCOMBE OFF THE A46.

Set in deeply wooded countryside, Sudeley Castle incorporates the remains of a medieval castle. Some of 15th-century Sudeley is today in ruins, having been slighted by Parliamentary forces during the Civil War, but the mellow stone of the banqueting hall, the tithe barn and the dungeon tower reflect the extent and the beauty of the medieval castle. Both Edward IV and Richard III owned Sudeley, but the high point in its history came during the reign of Henry VIII. The King is believed to have visited the castle with Anne Boleyn in 1532, but after Henry's death, it became the home of his widow, Katherine Parr when she married Sir Thomas Seymour in 1547. Among the large retinue that the Queen Dowager brought to Sudeley was the ill-fated Lady Jane Grey.

After a long period of neglect, Sudeley was bought in 1830 by two brothers, William and John Dent, from a rich family of Worcester glovers. After their deaths, the castle was inherited by their cousin, John Coucher Dent, whose wife Emma devoted her life to the enrichment of Sudeley. With the help of the architect Sir George Gilbert Scott, who designed the beautiful tomb of Katherine Parr in the church, the house was restored.

Entry to the castle apartments is through the Rent Room, where the agent would have collected the tenants' payments, and the North Hall, which was once the guard room. This room displays a fine portrait of Charles I by Van Dyck. In the 15th-century drawing room there is a beautiful oil sketch by Rubens entitled *The Four Evangelists*, but in the Queen's Bedroom, named for the Aubusson tapestries that once belonged to Queen Marie Antoinette, is the remarkable allegorical painting by Lucas de Heere, *The Tudor Succession*. Blatantly political, it shows Queen Elizabeth I surrounded by the goddesses of peace and plenty, while, in marked contrast, her predecessor, Queen Mary, is depicted with her husband, Philip of Spain, and Mars, the god of war.

Among the relics of Queen Katherine Parr are her prayer book and a love letter to Seymour accepting his proposal of marriage. From the period of the Civil War, there is a display of armour discovered during excavations, as well as a fascinating letter from Charles I to the freeholders of Cornwall, painted on board and thanking them for their support during the war. The library displays the magnificent Sheldon Tapestry, depicting *The Expulsion from Paradise*, made in Worcestershire in the 16th century and a painting of the *Rape of Europa* by Claude Lorraine.

Sudeley Castle's gardens were laid out during the 19th-century restoration, with fine terraces and spectacular views over the ancient trees in the Home Park. The Queen's Garden, to the south of the church, however, has been designed as a Tudor parterre, between massive yew hedges in a form that would have been familiar to Queen Katherine Parr.

THE QUEEN DOWAGER AT SUDELEY

Queen Katherine Parr was Henry VIII's sixth and last wife. Very shortly after Henry died in 1547, Katherine's former lover, Sir Thomas Seymour, one of the most attractive men of his time, proposed marriage to the Queen Dowager, and they were married in the same year. Katherine Parr came to Sudeley with a large retinue, and new quarters were provided in the north quadrangle, of which the nursery, now 'Katherine Parr's Room', survives. In August of the next year, she gave birth to a daughter, Mary, but died a few days later.

Part of Sudeley Castle remains in ruins, making a romantic backdrop to the lovely parterre gardens.

Newhouse

SALISBURY

A JACOBEAN HOUSE, BUILT ACCORDING TO A MOST UNUSUAL PLAN: EIGHT MILES SOUTH OF SALISBURY, OFF THE B3080 AT REDLYNCH.

Newhouse was built in about 1619 as a hunting lodge for Sir Edward Gorges. Most unusual in design, it is built in the shape of a 'Y', perhaps to symbolise the Trinity – such 'devices' amused Jacobean architects, and Gorges' main house, Longford Castle, was constructed as a triangle. Sir Edward's fortune sank in the fens of Lincolnshire – or, at least, in a scheme to drain them – and Newhouse was subsequently sold to a family of prominent Cromwellians, the Eyres. It is their descendants who are the present owners.

In the early 18th century Sir Robert Eyre became Chancellor to the Prince of Wales and Lord Chief Justice of the Court of Common Pleas. Alexander Pope said of him that 'the end of the world would come before a smile from Lord Chief Justice Eyre'. His son, a trustee of the colony of Georgia, installed a second staircase and added to the north-west wing, whilst the south-east was extended later in the 18th century to provide a splendid drawing room.

One daughter of the house was married to a cousin of Lord Nelson, and his child by Emma Hamilton, Horatia, was brought up by the family at Newhouse. Her cot, made by a ship's carpenter, can still be seen, as can a portrait of Lord Nelson as captain of the frigate *Albermarle*. The most intriguing painting in the house is undoubtedly the 'Hare Picture', which portrays a triumphant band of hares hunting and mercilessly slaughtering humans.

When it was inherited by the present owners in the early 1970s, Newhouse was virtually derelict and it has taken many years of work to restore it. The impressive drawing room is Edwardian in décor, but Jacobean fireplaces and old panelling survive in other rooms.

Above: Detail from the remarkable tooled leather wall covering of one of the bedrooms at Hamptworth Lodge.

Left: A section of the painting The Hare's Turning on Man, *artist unknown, which hangs in the parlour at Newhouse.*

Hamptworth Lodge

LANDFORD

FASCINATING ARTS AND CRAFTS DECOR IN AN EDWARDIAN COUNTRY HOUSE: OFF THE A36 TEN MILES SOUTH OF SALISBURY NEAR LANDFORD.

At first glance Hamptworth appears to be a perfect Jacobean manor, half timbered and of old red brick behind the trimmed yew hedges of a formal garden. The house is in fact less than a hundred years old, but far from being a mock-Tudor fake, Hamptworth is an original, fascinating shrine to Edwardian ideals in architecture and design.

A genuinely Jacobean house at Hamptworth was pulled down in the middle of the 19th century and rebuilt, then largely altered again later in the century by George Morrison, whose family came from Islay. The typically Victorian house he built was inherited early in the present century by his nephew, Harold Moffatt, an extraordinary Edwardian whose energy and talents encompassed music, sport, design and woodwork. Detecting a faint smell of rot as he opened the front door, Moffatt instantly gave orders for the house to be demolished and set about designing a replacement with the assistance of Guy Dawber, the 'Lutyens of the west'. The house was built according to the strictest principals of the Arts and Crafts Movement, with all the timbers worked on site using traditional methods – even the lead-work was cast on the estate under Moffatt's personal direction. By 1914 Hamptworth had been reborn – a modern mansion that looked as if it had been there for three hundred years.

Passed on through inheritance and never altered or refurnished, Hamptworth has lost none of its character. The interior is panelled in exotic woods and much of the beautiful inlaid furniture was made by Moffatt himself, his workshop the vast Great Hall, with its organ gallery and elaborate 'medieval' roof. His pieces sit beside the Tudor furniture that provided his inspiration, including a remarkable four-poster bed, carved with naked figures, said to have belonged to Anthony Babington, the Elizabethan conspirator. Another bedroom is even more astonishing, with walls of ancient leather, tooled with flowers, birds and strange designs that have faded to a golden-silver sheen. Hamptworth Lodge is quite unique, seemingly halted in time just before the arrival of some Edwardian house-party.

■ To those of us who live in the house, and other members of the family, I think the most important point which we always have in mind is that the whole concept is a treasured tribute to my grandfather, Harold Moffatt. He was a most able man in many fields and we feel it is up to those of us now living to see that his concept is carried forward. ■
Nigel Anderson

Bowood House

CALNE

THE SURVIVING PORTION OF A MAGNIFICENT PALACE, FILLED WITH PRICELESS WORKS: SOUTH OF THE A4 BETWEEN CALNE AND CHIPPENHAM.

> **■ If we had to choose a favourite item in the house, it would have to be the collection of English watercolours. The pleasure grounds and rhododendron area are also a delight but the nicest thing about Bowood is that people all work together, like a little community. ■**
>
> Lord Shelburne

The splendid house at Bowood is only a small portion of the palace which once stood here, for in 1955 the Lansdownes sacrificed 200 rooms to create a habitable home and preserve the rest of their inheritance. As a rising family in the 18th century, immensely wealthy but without ancestral lands, they had bought a bankrupt's half-completed dream and Bowood grew in its magnificence with each successive generation.

ART AND INTELLECT

During the reign of George III, the 1st Marquess of Lansdowne was a statesman who negotiated peace in North America and was a friend of Franklin, Hume and Mirabeau. From his day onwards, Bowood was a centre of political and intellectual life, for the Lansdownes saw themselves as patrons of the mind as well as of the arts. Dr Johnson held court in the library, Joseph Priestley worked in the laboratory and Bentham stroked a leopard in the chambers set aside for wild animals. The 3rd Marquess became Chancellor of the Exchequer at the age of 25, the 5th served under Gladstone and, as Foreign Secretary, cemented the *Entente Cordiale*. Only one Lord Lansdowne, killed in World War II, has not held public office.

Some of Britain's greatest architects worked on the house. Adam, Dance, Cockerell and Barry designed ever more ambitious schemes to match the Lansdowne eminence. There were galleries in which the family could display their vast collections, conservatories to house exotic plants, a Great Room for their entertainments and a chapel for their prayers. 'Capability' Brown looked round the grounds, charged a 20 guinea fee and took five years to produce a plan, though he did later spend many years creating what is now regarded as one of his most distinctive landscapes.

Below: Robert Adam's library, which dates from 1769.

Bottom: Bowood's beautiful main terrace.

A BUILDING SACRIFICED

The loss of the great house is sad, but much remains, particularly of Adam's work, in the 'little house' that is now Lord Shelburne's still substantial home. The orangery, which served as a field hospital in World War I, now houses marbles that the first Lord Lansdowne brought back from his Grand Tour, whilst the walls are hung with Old Masters. The library remains, as does the laboratory in which Priestley discovered oxygen and Ingenhouse experimented with smallpox vaccine. Though now more like a study, in the 18th century it was equipped with a telescope, air pumps, a printing press and an early copying machine. Nearby, behind bronzed doors, the chapel is a reminder that even at the height of the Age of Enlightenment, the Church remained a social cornerstone. Upstairs are further exhibition galleries with a dazzling display of

THE PEACE-MAKING PRIME MINISTER

It was William, the first Marquess, who once remarked that any man could live, if careful, on an income of £50,000 – the equivalent of £1million today! Independent means allowed him to pursue an independent course in politics and his advanced ideas concerning free trade, income tax and education for the masses earned him many enemies, but he viewed the setbacks he endured at Westminster as opportunities to both proceed with work at Bowood and to entertain his friends at home. Despite his unconventional career, he became Prime Minister in 1782 and earned the Lansdowne title for negotiating peace in North America.

precious objects gathered by members of the family. Here are the glittering insignia and swords, the costume that Lord Byron wore for his portrait as a romanticised Albanian, the court suit made for the 1st Marquess, and Indian and Oriental art.

THE BOWOOD LANDSCAPE

The pleasure grounds were laid out by 'Capability' Brown at the peak of his career. Nature has been reproduced in an artistic form, conducive to high thoughts and contemplation. The Hermit's Cave may not have been pure decoration – many landowners employed professional hermits to sit within such dank interiors, dressed in ragged robes and reaching for a mouldy tome whenever house-guests sauntered by. The stunning Rhododendron Walks, over two miles long, reflect a later taste in gardening.

Corsham Court

CHIPPENHAM

A MAGNIFICENT ART COLLECTION IN AN ELIZABETHAN MANSION: SIX MILES WEST OF CHIPPENHAM ON THE A4.

Corsham Court was built in 1582 on the site of a medieval royal manor which had for centuries been part of the dower of the Queens of England. It was bought in 1745 by Paul Methuen, a wealthy clothier and ancestor of the present owner, who inherited his art collection from a relative – a distinguished diplomat who had acquired Old Masters in the course of a long and widely travelled life. 'Capability' Brown's designs were employed in the house as well as the grounds, and further changes were made by John Nash. However, the character of the house as we see it today dates principally from the middle of the 19th century.

In the 19th century Frederick Methuen, Lord in Waiting to Queen Victoria, married Anna Sanford, a young heiress who brought with her another collection of Old Masters, many of outstanding importance. Since then the Methuens, though often following a military tradition in the family, have shared a love of art and commitment to preserving their inheritance. The 4th Lord Methuen studied painting under Sickert and as a soldier in liberated France served as Montgomery's advisor on the preservation of monuments and art. In later years he let a large part of the house to the Bath Academy of Art, although the present Lord Methuen continues to make Corsham Court his home.

The State Rooms are splendid for their architecture and their furnishings as much as for the paintings they contain. The Picture Gallery, designed by Brown, is a triple cube, 72 feet in length, with an intricately plastered ceiling and walls of crimson silk that match the furniture by Chippendale. Van Dyck's superb *Betrayal of Christ* is here, together with Rubens' *Wolf Hunt* and works of the Italian School. In the elegant dining room are two Reynolds portraits of the children of Paul Methuen. Amongst other delights to be sought out there is an exquisite *Annunciation* from the studio of Filippo Lippi, a haunting portrait of the ageing Queen Elizabeth I and the sculpture of a sleeping cherub by Michaelangelo.

■ Among all the treasures in the collection at Corsham, my favourite is *The Sleeping Cupid* attributed to Michaelangelo. ■
Lord Methuen

Left: The harmonious arrangement of works of art in Corsham's Picture Gallery includes a magnificent Van Dyck Betrayal of Christ *and a superb equestrian portrait of Charles I.*

Sheldon Manor

CHIPPENHAM

KING EDWARD I PROVIDED THE TIMBER TO BUILD THIS LOVELY MANOR HOUSE: ONE AND A HALF MILES WEST OF CHIPPENHAM OFF THE A420.

Sheldon's fine stone porch dates from the 13th century, when Sir Geoffrey Gascelyn rebuilt a medieval house he had inherited from his father. As knights in royal service, Gascelyns fought at Bannockburn, Falkirk and Boroughbridge, and in 1327 Sir Esmund briefly freed Edward II from Berkeley Castle, though he failed to save him from his grisly fate.

In 1424 the Hungerfords acquired the manor, adding to their vast Wiltshire estates and allowing them, as it was said, to ride from Salisbury to Bath on their own land. Possibly damaged in the Civil War, Sheldon was almost totally rebuilt at the Restoration. For the next two centuries it was the home of squires and farmers and was almost derelict when the Gibbs, the present owners, moved back in after a long tenancy in 1952, embarking upon years of loving restoration.

Sheldon's setting is medieval, with traces of an ancient village in the grounds and yew trees that have stood for 700 years. The porch dates from 1282; above it is the Priest's Room, which has the original oak waggon roof. The beamed and panelled rooms contain some splendid Jacobean furniture, including an elaborately carved four-poster bed. Though neither large nor grand, Sheldon is a memorably atmospheric house that is all the more delightful for being still very much a family home.

■ I never chop an onion in the Sheldon kitchen without thinking of the generations of other women who have done so before me, or dandled their babies or grandchildren, or sat peacefully by the fire at the end of a long day, in this same place, as we have done. ■
Mrs Martin Gibbs

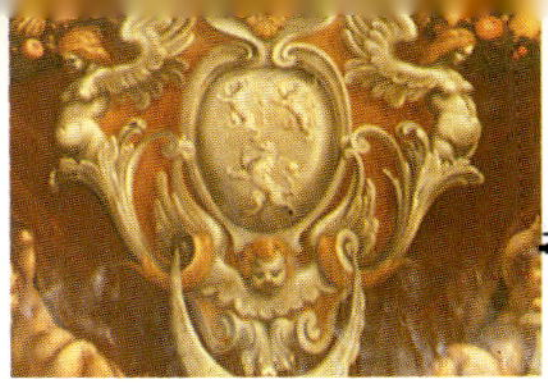

The current Earl and Countess of Pembroke.

Wilton House

SALISBURY

EARLS OF PEMBROKE HAVE INCLUDED PATRONS OF SHAKESPEARE, AN ARCHITECT, A STATESMAN AND EVEN A MURDERER. INIGO JONES DESIGNED THEIR HOUSE AROUND A STUNNING SET OF STATE ROOMS, HUNG WITH PAINTINGS BY VAN DYCK AND FILLED WITH RICHLY GILDED FURNITURE: THREE MILES WEST OF SALISBURY ON THE A30.

On a fine summer afternoon there are few corners of the English countryside so peaceful and idyllic as the grounds of Wilton House. The little River Nadder meanders lazily through splendid parkland, passing through the arches of a colonnaded bridge, as fine as any to be seen in Venice. The house, though large, is neither grandiose nor vulgar, but perfectly proportioned and delightful in design. Nothing, it would seem, could ever have disturbed this dreamy setting other than the click of croquet mallets or the chiming of church bells. Appearances can be deceptive. Since ancient times, before the birth of England, this has been a place where great events unfolded. The family who live here have never been content with quietly provincial lives, but have acted centre-stage in history, with Wilton as the back-drop. Their characters, exaggerated by enormous wealth and influence, have exemplified the nature of the times in which they lived and almost every generation has left some mark upon the house, altering its architecture, adding treasures to its contents or remodelling the landscape. Four centuries of drama have been played out by a quite extraordinary cast at Wilton House.

Like many of England's great country homes, Wilton is built upon monastic ruins. More than a thousand years ago the Wessex kings held court here and it was probably King Alfred who gave the palace to the Benedictine nuns. At one time the abbey was amongst the richest in all England, but had declined considerably by Lady Day in 1539, when the king's commissioners seized the estate, pensioning off the abbess with compensation of £100.

William Herbert, 1st Earl of Pembroke (1506-1570), the founder of the family.

THE TUDOR AGE

The Tudor period was a time of changing fortunes. As things that had been certainties were challenged and institutions tumbled, opportunists clawed their way to prominence in a Court where life itself could hinge upon the royal smile. William Herbert was a lowly courtier of doubtful ancestry and prospects, so insecure and violent tempered that he killed a tailor who insulted him whilst passing in the street, forcing him to spend some years in exile. He was, however, lucky in his choice of wife, Anne Parr, for her sister was soon married to the king himself. Katherine was the last of Henry's queens and amongst the many favours heaped upon her family was the gift of Wilton Abbey. William made full use of his opportunities. Appointed Earl of Pembroke, he became executor of Henry's will and was a guardian of young King Edward. Tearing down the abbey, he built a splendid mansion, part of which can still be seen in the great square tower with mullioned windows that formed the entrance to the house.

Marriage was equally significant to William's young son John, whose first alliance was with a sister of Lady Jane Grey, a contract that was hastily annulled when her family were disgraced as traitors. A second wife then died, but in early middle age the 2nd Earl married Mary, the fifteen-year-old sister of Sir Philip Sidney, a shining star in the Elizabethan firmament. The young countess was a girl of wit and education and in her day, according to John Aubrey, 'Wilton House was like a college, there were so many learned and ingeniouse persons. She was the greatest patronesse of wit and learning of any lady of her time.' As a writer of some talent she collaborated with her brother, who wrote *Arcadia* at Wilton House. The Queen herself was frequently a visitor, once arriving without warning when the Spanish envoy was a guest.

THE SHAKESPEARE CONNECTION

With the dawn of a new century, Wilton's reputation as a meeting-place for brilliant minds was enhanced still further by the Pembrokes' sons, William and Philip. Shakespeare was forever grateful to the family for their support and in 1603 his company performed *As You Like It* as an entertainment for James I at Wilton. William cut a dashing figure in his youth for his looks, intelligence and wild nature. A godson of the Queen, he was imprisoned briefly in the Tower for his seduction of a maid of honour, Mary Fitton, before his marriage to Lady Mary Talbot, a girl as notorious for her appearance as she was famous for her fortune. His brother Philip, who succeeded him in 1630, shared in his wildness but not his charm. When appointed Chancellor of Oxford University, it was said of him that he would prove perfect for the post 'were Oxford turned into a kennel'.

A favourite of both King James, who made him 1st Earl of Montgomery, and Charles I, who appointed him Lord Chamberlain, he accumulated profitable posts despite his unpredictable and often violent nature. Charles I loved Wilton 'above all other houses' and stayed there every summer, but this in no way inhibited Philip from switching his allegiance at the outbreak of the Civil War to go against the King.

HERBERTS AND THE BARD

Shakespeare's connection with Wilton and the Pembrokes spanned two generations and has been the subject of considerable speculation. He was certainly supported by the Countess and he dedicated the First Folio of his works to 'the incomparable pair of brethren', William and Philip, but could William Herbert also have been the mysterious Mr W H, the 'onlie begetter' of the sonnets? Was William's mistress, Mary Fitton, the 'dark lady'of the sonnets? Some have even gone so far as to suggest that all the works were written by a local member of the Herbert circle, swan not of the Stratford Avon, but of the Wiltshire river?

THE BUILDING OF A NEW PALACE

Wilton House was totally transformed by Philip. He began the work before the Civil War, laying out new gardens and employing a French architect, de Caus, to replace the Tudor mansion with a splendid modern palace. Then, in 1647, the half-completed house was gutted by a fire that was seen by many people as divine retribution for the Earl's disloyalty. Experts are divided over how much of de Caus' work survived this disaster, but before his death in 1650 Philip had already started to rebuild, employing in his service the greatest architect of the age, Inigo Jones. Jones had made his early reputation for theatrical designs, only later turning to a study of Renaissance buildings that resulted in such masterpieces as the the Whitehall Banqueting House and the Queen's House at Greenwich.

Now 75 years old, he had lost his livelihood as the King's surveyor, but his originality and genius were undiminished. Assisted by John Webb, his nephew, he designed a house that seems to have been built to welcome in the dawn of a new age. In place of massive bulk and Jacobean ostentation, he relied on classical proportion and restraint in a building that was to influence the style of English country houses for the best part of two centuries.

Wilton House presents a dignified, restrained appearance to the world, in keeping with an age of sober dress and outward gravity. What is found indoors is altogether something else. Jones once wrote that the interior, whether of a man or house, was where 'the imagination is set on fire and sometimes licentiously flies out.' This is certainly the case at Wilton, where he drew upon his love of theatre to create a set of State Rooms that are unparalleled in England. Their drama builds up gradually, through ante-rooms of mounting splendour to the glories of the Single Cube, followed by the still more dazzling Double Cube. This is a room that takes the breath away, both by its scale and through the richness of its decoration. Sixty feet in length, 30 feet in width and 30 feet to its coved and fabulously painted ceiling, its pale panelled walls are backdrops to a blaze of colour. Gilded swags and garlands, cornices and pediments create in their combined effect an impression of exuberant indulgence. The paintings are all by Van Dyck, dominated by his massive portrait of the Herbert family, the richly gilded furniture and mirrors were commissioned later for the room from William Kent and Thomas Chippendale. Many sovereigns, including the present Queen, have been entertained in this great chamber, which is all the more remarkable for having been designed and built at the height of Cromwell's Commonwealth, when displays of luxury were frowned upon. The 4th Earl may have been a man of fluid conscience, but he clearly had an iron nerve.

William Kent's statue of Shakespeare is the centre-piece of the Front Hall.

Wilton's solid and symmetrical exterior gives no hint of the extravagant interiors that lie within.

All the paintings in the magnificent Double Cube Room are by Van Dyck, or studio of Van Dyck, and his Herbert family group dominates the room.

THE NOTORIOUS 7TH EARL

Neither Philip's son nor grandson made any great impression on history or Wilton. Both died young and were succeeded by the 7th Earl, a Restoration rake who put contemporaries such as Lord Rochester into the shade so far as dissipation was concerned. That he was a gambler, drunkard and adulterer scarcely touched upon his notoriety, for it was said that he committed no less than 26 murders in his brief and violent life. He was proved a killer twice, once let off with a royal pardon and once convicted on a charge of manslaughter, an offence for which peers had the privilege of avoiding any punishment. Dying at the age of thirty, his only legacy to Wilton was a debt of £20,000 that necessitated the sale of many fine possessions from the house.

RESPECTABILITY REGAINED

His brother Thomas, who succeeded him in 1683, fortunately proved a total contrast and saved the family from ruin. With King William on the throne, respectability once more became the key-note of society and Thomas, with the Herbert genius for exemplifying the virtues or the vices of each each age, rose high in public office as a Lord Lieutenant, Lord Privy Seal and Lord High Admiral. He shared his ancestors' passion for collecting works of art, filling the gaps that his brother's wild extravagance had left in Wilton's rooms with many of the antique marbles, books and paintings that still grace the house today. 'Old Pem' was also popular, for by bringing in French weavers he helped make Wilton famous for its carpets.

In the early 18th century the study of antiquities was fashionable and the 9th Earl was in youth close friends with William Stukely, with whom he opened barrows in search of druid treasure and speculated on the mysteries of Stonehenge. Henry's next passion was for architecture, an interest that he shared with contemporaries such as Lord Burlington. In partnership with Roger Morris, 'the Architect Earl', he briefly turned professional, designing houses for his fashionable friends. His lasting monument is, however, to be seen at his own home, in the beautiful Palladian bridge that he built across the Nadder. Elegant and appropriately theatrical, this is still one of the delights of Wilton and arguably the prettiest of bridges ever built in England. Had its designer had less money to support him, he might well have found success and lasting fame in the profession that he loved.

A ROYAL VISIT

As the century advanced, society again grew coarser and more reckless. The 10th Earl matched the spirit of his times, with greater sporting instinct than any sign of common sense. A brilliant horseman, he wrote a text book about military equitation and was a major general by the age of 25. Married to a pretty heiress, he became a rising star at Court, where he was Lord of the Bedchamber to King George III. Then at the age of 28 he gambled all for love, eloping to the continent with Kitty Hunter. Though later reconciled with his wife, he proved throughout his life incapable of being faithful to her. The King also seems to have forgiven him, for in

1774 he and his Queen stayed at Wilton House. A grand reception followed by a banquet took place in the Double Cube Room and the royal couple passed the night in an exotic eastern bed borrowed from William Beckford at Fonthill and erected in the Colonnade Room. Lord Pembroke's chaplain was particularly proud that the Queen condescended to make use of an antique chamber-pot from his collection.

WILTON IN THE 19TH CENTURY

In 1801 James Wyatt was commissioned by the 11th Earl to modernise the house. He constructed the Gothic entrance hall and cloisters, which made the house more practical to live in by providing corridors to rooms, and also gave more space for the display of works of art. Sadly, Wyatt also swept away Inigo Jones's great Painted Staircase in favour of a very mean replacement and made clumsy changes to the north and west fronts. Ten years after work began, the job had still not been completed, leaving architect and client hurling insults at each other. Though the cloisters are very attractive, Wyatt's influence is perhaps the most unfortunate in Wilton's history.

Wilton in the days of Queen Victoria was home to Sidney Herbert, half brother to the 12th Earl, who spent his life abroad. As Secretary of State for War, though his mother was a Russian, he championed the cause of Florence Nightingale in the Crimea. Frail, overworked and subjected to unending pressure, poor Sidney Herbert was assisted to an early grave by 'the lady with the lamp.' His eldest son died unmarried, though briefly considering a princess in Tahiti as his bride, and the title passed on to a brother, the present Earl's great-grandfather.

WILTON TODAY

In World War II, when Wilton House was requisitioned as the headquarters of Southern Command, the Double Cube Room was the secret operations centre for the planning of the Normandy invasions. In recent years a huge amount of restoration work has been undertaken by the 17th Earl, who continues to make Wilton House his home four and a half centuries after William Herbert, his direct ancestor, was granted the old abbey. He also continues in the family tradition of following a fashionable career, for Henry Herbert is a film director.

Few houses can match Wilton in the richness of their history. An extraordinary family have played host here to their sovereigns and to the brightest figures of each reign. The house is fascinating for its architecture, incorporating Tudor elements, the masterpiece of Jones and Webb and the Gothicism of James Wyatt, with the finest bridge in England in its grounds. The State Rooms in themselves are worth a most determined detour. Those whose taste is for refined simplicity may find them ostentatious, but they successfully contrive to achieve a balance between baroque vulgarity and predictable good taste.

A MAGNIFICENT COLLECTION

If the rooms at Wilton are sumptuous, the contents of the house are well matched – collections built up through the centuries by individuals whose skill in recognising excellence has been matched by their ability to pay for it. As well as the Van Dycks, every room contains magnificent Old Masters by Rembrandt, Van Leyden and Jan Breughal, portraits by Reynolds and Lely, landscapes and sporting scenes. One of the most disturbing paintings is a portrait by an unknown artist of the homicidal 7th Earl, tense and restless as he turns, or possibly rips out, the pages of a book.

In the entrance hall William Shakespeare has greeted Wilton's visitors since the 9th Earl paid £100 to have him made, commemorating in a somewhat stilted form the bard's great debt of gratitude to Herbert generosity. Wonderfully unsubtle, it introduces all the grandeur of the palace in a way that makes such splendour understandable; the desire to be remembered by the future.

The forecourt gardens were laid out in 1971 by the 17th Earl of Pembroke as a memorial to his father. Beyond them is the Triumphal Arch, surmounted by an equestrian statue of Marcus Aurelius.

This delightful carving is on the stairway in the entrance hall.

Sausmarez Manor

Guernsey

A BEAUTIFUL 18TH-CENTURY MANSION ON A MANORIAL ESTATE OWNED BY THE SAME FAMILY SINCE THE 11TH CENTURY: ABOUT TWO MILES SOUTH OF ST PETER PORT.

A Queen Anne house with something different about it. Built in blue-and-gold-dappled Guernsey granite? To be sure. Rather more in the way of dormers sprouting from its roof than you might normally expect? Yes. Something else that's different? Yes, it was designed in America, in the 'colonial' variant of Queen Anne style then fashionable there, at the request of a Guernseyman Sir Edmund Andros, who was governor of New York, New Jersey, Virginia and large parts of New England. It was built, in 1714, after his death.

The illustrious Sir Edmund was a cousin of the de Sausmarez family who – with this one brief interruption when the fief passed in marriage to the Androses – have owned Sausmarez since before 1245. They have included wool merchants and wreckers; lawyers and privateers; navigators, cartographers and engineers; adventurers and sportsmen; generals and admirals; artists, designers and inventors; governors and diplomats; churchmen and spymasters.

And it was the exploits of one sailor forebear, Philip de Sausmarez, while serving under Anson in the War of Jenkins' Ear, which allowed the family to recover their patrimony. This was the result of Anson's daring foray, on behalf of George IV, to raid ports on the Pacific coast of South America. Ultimately his ill-equipped little fleet not only circumnavigated the world, but after a two-year chase captured a galleon, *Nuestra Señora da Cabodonga*, containing £500,000 of treasure, of which Philip was awarded a share.

'Sausmarez Manor is built on a smaller and possibly more comfortable scale than stately homes in Britain, compatible to the size of Guernsey' says Peter de Sausmarez, the present owner. 'The house and its contents reflect the changing fortunes of our family and of the Channel Islands during more than a millennium'. Its contents include rare examples of Guernsey Chippendale furniture, the wedding coat of James II, made in pure gold and silver thread, china from the Imperial Summer Palace in Peking and paintings of celebrated naval engagements. The former dining room is now the tapestry room, devoted to housing a fine collection of 17th-century tapestries depicting Ovid's *Metamorphoses*. The fascinating entrance hall is a remarkable hybrid, having been built in the 19th century with a mixture of Burmese carvings and woodwork bought from French churches during the post-Revolution wave of anti-clericalism.

Now, like so many stately home owners in the rest of the UK, de Sausmarez runs his 30-acre estate as a tourist business, and has installed additional facilities and attractions to provide an enjoyable day out for all the family. There is, for instance, a steam railway which takes visitors for rides through the Sausmarez

THE TREASURE GALLEON

The *Nuestra Señora da Cabodonga*, landed at Dover 250 years ago, was the richest treasure ship captured in history – it required 32 wagons to transport the booty to London. Philip de Sausmarez, in HMS *Centurion*, played a leading part, and was one of only 100 survivors out of an expedition of 2,000; but through some technicality he was foisted off with only a seaman's share. So great was the treasure, however, that even a seaman's share allowed him to buy back the family estate, with its fine new mansion, from the Androses. The vellum notebook in which Philip recorded the voyage has a proud place among the house's rich contents.

Below: Sausmarez Manor's fascinating entrance hall.

Below right: The Manor has one of the largest collections of dolls' houses in the United Kingdom.

woodlands; indoors, an immaculately-scaled '00' gauge model railway with up to eight trains running at a time, including request appearances by a model of Thomas the Tank Engine; a nine-hole pitch and putt course and the third largest collection of dolls' houses open to the public in the United Kingdom; and a 'clambering area' for children under 12. The Treasure Chest gift shop features a special section for doll's house collectors; the Old Grape House Café and lakeside tea garden are strong on Guernsey delicacies.

More peaceful is the lush woodland garden set around lakes and a stream and combining native and exotic plants, including hundreds of camellias, rhododendrons and azaleas, as well as bamboos and other species from many parts of the world, such as giant echiums. A variety of ducks, geese, jungle fowl, swans and guinea fowl – very tame and always anxious to be fed – complete the picture.

La Mare Vineyards

JERSEY

A BEAUTIFUL 18TH-CENTURY JERSEY FARMSTEAD, RESTORED AS THE CENTRE OF A WINE-MAKING BUSINESS; VISITORS SEE THE PROCESS AND TASTE THE PRODUCT: OFF THE B33 IN THE NORTH-WEST OF THE ISLAND, NEAR ST MARY VILLAGE.

La Mare is a rather different house from the others in this book. The house is a traditional Jersey farmhouse in St Mary, a tranquil rural parish near the island's north coast. Built of local granite, in which golden tints mix with greys, it has the simple solidity and harmonious quality of Jersey's Georgian vernacular: small-paned 18th-century sash windows set symmetrically in white surrounds, their grey lintels matching the generous stone-arched doorway; two wings stretching out behind to frame a workday courtyard.

A handsome building, certainly, and since its restoration by the present owners, Robert and Ann Blayney, designated a Grade I site of special historic interest – yet scarcely a stately home. Its treasure is of a different variety – wine.

The Blayneys, who moved to Jersey in 1968 from Northumberland, come from a family involved in the wine trade since 1831. They sold their wine interests in Newcastle-upon-Tyne to go into the wine business in Jersey's capital, St Helier. The house at La Mare was built in 1797 by a member of the old Jersey family of de Gruchy. When the Blayneys bought it, the property, known as Elms Farm, was so dilapidated that the obvious course was to rebuild. But they and their architects were reluctant to take so drastic a step with what was recognisably still a fine group of buildings. Instead, in 1969, they embarked upon restoration. They also decided to revert to the original name of the property, La Mare – which certainly sounds more convincing as a vineyard appellation!

Part of the original 17th-century farmhouse building of La Mare, now at the heart of a successful vineyard.

At the same time they were planning a vineyard for this typical 12-acre smallholding – a new crop to follow the others grown there in the past, which included apples, grazing for Jersey cows, potatoes and cauliflowers. After much research and experiment and some setbacks, they finally settled on making two wines: Clos de Mare, a fruity, medium Alsace-style white; and Domaine de la Mare, from the Seyval grape – a crisp dry white more akin to a Sauvignon and well-matched with Jersey seafood. The Queen, on visits to Jersey, has twice been regaled with Clos de Mare. A recent small planting of red grapes allows them the future possibility of producing a rosé, and perhaps some red.

Both they and the Jersey Tourist Board realised that wine-making, together with their beautifully restored buildings, were a considerable tourist attraction. A new winery has been skilfully fitted into the landscape so as to make minimum impact, and was designed to allow visitors to see and understand the process and sample its end results. Another building houses an audio visual show; and one wing of the farmhouse provides refreshment facilities alongside a tea garden.

But La Mare hasn't stopped with wine. Its latest venture is to revive Jersey Lightning, a Calvados-like apple brandy exported from Jersey in the 1920s via Canada to Prohibition USA. Today's version is, however, legal, and purer and much more polished than the potent brew of 70 years ago.

■ Wine is an art, and the feel for it often runs in wine families. We hoped that the inherited flair, combined with such a lovely property, would create fine wine – and it does! Now our son Andrew has joined us, the fifth generation: a growing tradition. ■
Robert Blayney

SOUTH AND SOUTH-EAST ENGLAND

THE AREA OF ENGLAND closest to London has always attracted the rich and powerful. Today it holds the palatial ducal mansions of the Dukes of Norfolk at Arundel, the Marlboroughs at Blenheim, the Bedfords at Woburn and the Richmonds at Goodwood, while the Dukes of Northumberland treasure the superb Robert Adam state rooms of Syon House. On a more modest scale is Stratfield Saye, the great Duke of Wellington's country house, and other historic homes are filled with memories – of Henry VIII and Anne Boleyn at Hever Castle, of a king's mistress and the first pineapple at Dorney Court, of cricket at Belmont. For the exotic, Japanese armour is alarmingly ensconced in Chiddingstone Castle, big game trophies at Quex Park and memories of Tutankhamun's tomb at Highclere Castle, while architectural pleasures run all the way from Tudor charm at Chenies Manor to the 18th-century splendour of Spencer House and High Victorian romanticism at Knebworth House.

Avington Park

WINCHESTER

A LATE 17TH-CENTURY RED-BRICK HOUSE WITH FINE PAINTED DECOR: FIVE MILES EAST OF WINCHESTER BETWEEN THE A31 AND THE B3047.

That redoubtable chronicler of 18th-century England, William Cobbett, once described Avington as 'one of the prettiest places in the country'. At that time its grounds stretched all the way to Winchester and it was the home of the Duke of Chandos, one of the richest men in England. The last Duke to own Avington left in 1848 and the grounds are now cut off from Winchester by new roads, turning it into a peaceful backwater.

Avington Park dates mostly from around 1670 and was remodelled by its owner, George Brydges, to serve as a place of lodgings and entertainment for his patron, Charles II. During the six-week racing season in Winchester, the king had formerly stayed at the Deanery, but when the Dean refused to let his mistress, Nell Gwynn, accompany him, he moved to Avington, where Nell was welcome. (Around a century and a half later, it is reputed that King George IV also used Avington as a regular tryst with Mrs Fitzherbert).

The portico is in the grand classical style, with tall columns and a triangular pediment, and displayed here are figures of Minerva, Juno and Ceres, made of lead and weighing an astonishing three tons. The painted entrance hall is a fine example of the late 18th-century work of the artist Clermont, who used eggs as a paint preservative, and the bright and glowing colours are as true as when they were first painted.

The ballroom has a splendid gold plasterwork ceiling, which dates from around 1760, its painted panels attributed to the Italian artist, Verrio. The gold decoration on the doors and doorcases were painted by the French artist, Valdrez, who mixed powdered gold and milk – a method which is claimed to be unique in England. The adjacent Red Drawing Room is another striking example of the talents of Clermont.

■ **Beaulieu offers a unique atmosphere of a lived in family home. I was brought up here, with flowers in the rooms and fires in the grates. Together with the Motor Museum it surely offers something for every member of the family.** ■
Lord Montagu

Palace House

BEAULIEU

AT THE HEART OF A WHOLE COMPLEX OF TOURIST ATTRACTIONS IS THIS VICTORIAN GOTHIC MANSION, BUILT ONTO A 13TH-CENTURY MONASTIC GATEHOUSE: ON THE B3056, ABOUT SEVEN MILES SOUTH-EAST OF LYNDHURST.

Beaulieu is far more than just an historic house. It is an unashamedly modern tourist attraction with a state-of-the-art museum, an overhead monorail and other Disney-style trappings. Yet the estate and home of Beaulieu dates back to 1204 when a Cistercian Abbey was founded here by King John. It was, until then, the site of a royal hunting lodge named *Bellus Locus Regis* – 'the beautiful place of the king'. The Cistercians, a French order, rechristened it *beau lieu* ('beautiful place'), pronouncing it 'bewley' just as it is today.

The Upper Drawing Room, one of the finest rooms in Palace House, was once a chapel.

The Abbey was dissolved in 1538 by Henry VIII and the estate sold to Sir Thomas Wriothsley. Most of the buildings were demolished, but Wriothsley turned the Great Gatehouse of the monastery into a modest manor house cum hunting lodge, which is the basis of the present house.

The Wriothsley name continued until 1667, when Elizabeth Wriothsley inherited Beaulieu and married into the Montagu family. After just one generation, however, the 2nd Duke of Montagu died without a male heir and the famous Scott family (the Dukes of Buccleuch) took over the Beaulieu estate. The Montagu name was revived in 1885 when Lord Henry Scott was created 1st Baron Montagu of Beaulieu.

During the 18th century the Great Gatehouse had been fortified and moated (against the threat of a French invasion) and gardens laid out. And by now it was known as Palace House. However when Lord Henry Scott moved into Beaulieu in 1867 it was essentially very little changed since monastic times and he commissioned Sir Arthur Blomfield to redesign the Great Gatehouse in Victorian-Gothic style. Lord Henry's son, the 2nd Baron Montagu was truly a Renaissance Man – pioneer motorist, world motor boat racing champion, journalist, politician, publisher and much more. But it was the present baron, Edward, who ensured the survival of the estate by opening the house up to the public in 1952.

The Picture Gallery contains a selection of interesting characters from the family tree. None were more handsome nor ill-fated than James, Duke of Monmouth who had married into the Buccleuch family. He organised a rebellion to claim the crown of England and was executed on Tower Hill. A picture of James's

father, Charles II, hangs nearby.

The Dining Hall and Lower Drawing Room, originally the Inner Halls of the monastic gatehouse, retain the ancient atmosphere of the house and still have their original fan-vaulting. The kitchen, by contrast is stolidly Victorian, with plenty of utensils from those days. The Upper Drawing Room and Ante Room are the finest rooms in the house – both were formerly chapels in the Great Gatehouse and still retain their splendid trefoil tracery stone windows. Look for the stone piscina (where the priest washed his altar vessels and hands) on the side wall in the Upper Drawing Room. There is another in the private dining room, off the Ante Room.

Apart from the Great Gatehouse, only two other buildings survived intact from the demolition of the monastery. The Domus, once the living quarters of the lay brothers of the order is now an atmospheric exhibition on the history of the Abbey; the monks' refectory is now the parish church of Beaulieu village.

The National Motor Museum, acclaimed as one of the finest autmobile collections in the world, has over 300 vehicles, from the oldest car in the collection – an 1896 Peugeot, to the latest, a 1993 Jaguar XJ220 – the world's most expensive production car at over £403,000.

THE TRUE PRETENDER?

Although James, Duke of Monmouth, was the son of King Charles II, he was prevented from taking the crown because it was always presumed he was illegitimate. James claimed to have his parents' marriage certificate and took up arms for what he believed was rightfully his. He was defeated at Sedgemoor and executed. However, according to family legend, the 5th Duke of Buccleuch discovered the actual marriage certificate. As a token of his loyalty to the crown, he gave the certificate to Queen Victoria, who watched him burn it!

Nunwell House

BRADING

CHARLES I SPENT HIS LAST NIGHT OF FREEDOM IN THIS PART JACOBEAN, PART GEORGIAN ISLE OF WIGHT HOUSE OVERLOOKING THE SOLENT: ABOUT THREE MILES SOUTH OF RYDE OFF THE A3055 SANDOWN ROAD.

This is a house full of history, with a fascinating and agreeable mixture in both its architecture and its contents. One family – the Oglanders – owned and lived in Nunwell from 1522 to 1982. They were staunchly royalist and the Jacobean part of the house includes the room where Charles I spent his last night of freedom, sheltered by a cavalier in a strongly roundhead island.

This western, Jacobean part of the house is in total contrast to the eastern, Georgian wing. They are linked by a 16th-century hall section, refaced in Queen Anne's time with mathematical tiles. Victorian and Edwardian extensions provide dining and music rooms in a style to match the lightness and grace of the Georgian and Jacobean interiors. The tearoom and old bakehouse are almost certainly the earlier farmhouse the Oglanders first occupied in 1522.

In 1982 Nunwell was bought by Colonel and Mrs J A Aylmer, originally from County Kildare in Ireland. Two rooms in the main house are devoted to the Aylmer family's military heritage. There is also a little Home Guard Museum, commemorating the fact that, between 1295 to 1945, whenever invasion threatened, Nunwell was the 'Home Guard' headquarters. Though the other rooms contain a wealth of fine furniture and paintings, including some lent by the Oglander family, it is evident that this is the Aylmer family home.

■ The Library, in which I work, with its 18th-century Florentine ceiling, English bookcases and tall windows, gives me a great feeling of peace and light. ■
Col J A Aylmer

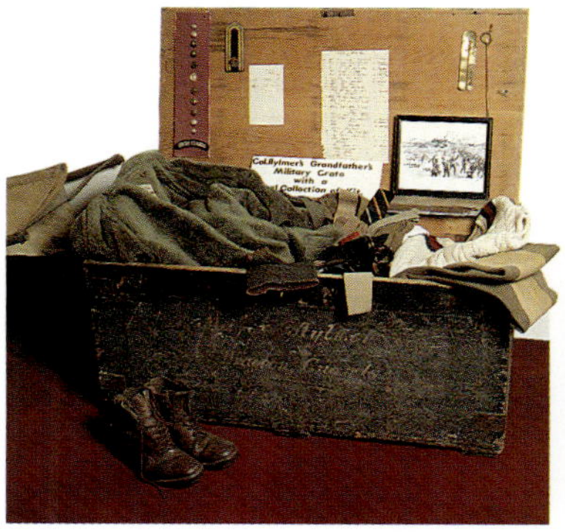

Top left: The name of Beaulieu is synonymous with Lord Montagu's National Motor Museum.
Above: This Campaign Chest of 1882 is from the Ayler family's military collection.
Below: The library at Nunwell House has an elaborate plaster ceiling and an interesting collection of books.

■ Breamore is very much a family home. The combination of deep ties with my ancestors and its beauty make it an enduring joy. ■
Sir Westrow Hulse

Breamore House

FORDINGBRIDGE

A LARGE, ATMOSPHERIC, ROSY-BRICK ELIZABETHAN MANOR HOUSE WITH MANY ART TREASURES: THREE MILES NORTH OF FORDINGBRIDGE ON THE A338 SALISBURY ROAD.

Breamore House lies in a picturesque secluded farmland setting, little changed in over 400 years. It has been owned by the Hulse family for nine generations, since its purchase in 1748 by Edward Hulse, Court Physician to Queen Anne, George I and George II.

The Tudor character of the house is immediately apparent in the dining room, with heavy oak furniture and a large stone fireplace. In the Great Hall is a Van Dyck painting of Charles I's children and a charming full-length portrait of Charles II as a boy, attributed to the studio of Van Dyck. Many visitors' favourite painting, however, is the village inn scene, *The Coming of the Storm*, by David Teniers. Teniers also designed the two superb Brussels tapestries (*c*.1630) here.

The Netherlands connection continues in the Blue Drawing Room with some immaculate Dutch marquetry furniture, the dowry of the beautiful Hannah Vanderplank, who married Edward Hulse III in 1741, and whose portrait is also here.

Colourful advertising signs at the Breamore Countryside Museum recall a bygone era.

The West Drawing Room contains probably the most memorable painting in the house. *The Boy with the Bat*, from the mid-18th century, is one of the very first paintings of cricket and has been exhibited internationally. More fine pictures line the Inner Hall. Lucas's sketch of the Duke of Wellington was the Duke's own favourite of all his many portraits, and a Canaletto hangs next to some acclaimed eye-witness battle paintings by Napoleon's war artist, Beaufort.

The staircase is dominated by a very rare and very beautiful 17th-century English carpet, reminiscent of a William Morris design. On the landing is an extraordinary series of 17th-century Mexican paintings, illustrating mixed marriages between Spaniards and indigenous South American peoples.

After the soft tones of the Georgian Blue Bedroom, the Tudor bedrooms restate the house's origins with dark heavy furnishings, a superbly carved Jacobean bed and fine tapestries. The kitchen has an excellent collection of copper pots, pans and moulds.

The Breamore Countryside Museum is a splendid evocation of village life of the past, where recreations include a farmworker's cottage, smithy, wheelwright's shop, dairy. There is also an important collection of tractors and steam engines, horse-drawn vehicles and fire-fighting equipment.

The Countryside Museum offers a fascinating insight into the days when the village was self-sufficient.

THE DODINGTON CURSE

The Dodingtons, who built Breamore in 1583, were an ill-fated family. William Dodington committed suicide in 1600 rather than await the outcome of a suit pending against him in the Star Chamber and 30 years later his grandson was hanged for the murder of his mother. The sad portrait of Mrs William Dodington in mourning clothes, dated 1604, hangs in the Great Hall. In 1748 when the house was sold to the Hulses it was on condition that the picture remained in situ. It is said that if you touch it, you will die the same day. The picture was the only one which remained in the house when the Americans occupied it during the war.

Stansted Park

ROWLANDS CASTLE

A RED BRICK NEO-CLASSICAL MANSION BOUGHT AS A HOME FOR THE BESSBOROUGH FAMILY AND THEIR FINE PAINTINGS AND FURNITURE: FOUR MILES NORTH-EAST OF HAVANT, SIGNPOSTED FROM THE A27.

The Lumley family built Stansted House on its present site in 1688, at about the same time as nearby Uppark and using the same architect, Talman. That house was altered in the 18th century by Wyatt, but burnt out in 1900, resulting in the present house being partly an Edwardian rebuilding by Sir Reginald Blomfield and partly Georgian with later additions. The original Stansted was a hunting lodge, shattered by Parliamentary cannon in the Civil War and now incorporated into the Regency Gothic chapel. This is probably the only church in Britain to display the Ten Commandments in Hebrew – Lewis Way, Stansted's owner in the early 19th century, aimed to persuade the local Jews to convert to Christianity.

Stansted's spacious interiors provide a worthy setting for the splendid furniture, paintings and other works of art belonging to the Bessborough family. Indeed, they bought it to house their historic and valuable collection of paintings after fire destroyed their house in Kilkenny in the Republic of Ireland. The Blue Drawing Room, still lined with its original blue silk, contains four large Arcadian landscapes by the Dutch artist, Dalens, and furniture brought by the 10th Earl of Bessborough's mother, who was French.

By contrast, the music room has mainly modern family paintings, but also William and Mary and Queen Anne chairs and an 18th-century square piano. The main dining room evokes wonder and admiration with its Chinese *famille-rose* dinner service, Georgian silver and Waterford crystal. The old kitchen contains such items as a teak sink and a butter cupboard, once wheeled nightly into cold storage. There is also a small but well-equipped theatre built in 1985.

Left: The Old Kitchen at Stansted Park was in regular use until 1956. Some of its copperware is very much older.

Broadlands

ROMSEY

A PALLADIAN MANSION BY THE RIVER TEST, WITH FINE INTERIORS AND MEMENTOES OF PALMERSTON AND EARL MOUNTBATTEN OF BURMA: ON THE SOUTHERN OUTSKIRTS OF ROMSEY, OFF THE BYPASS (A31).

It was Henry Temple, 1st Viscount Palmerston, who in 1736 bought the Tudor and Jacobean manor house and began to transform its riverside grounds into a landscape in the newly fashionable English manner. The 2nd Viscount engaged Lancelot ('Capability') Brown, who was an architect as well as master of informal landscape design. Brown completed the transformation of the grounds and, together with Henry Holland, his protegé and son-in-law, transformed the 'half-H' plan manor house into the elegant, four-square Palladian mansion we see today.

ILLUSTRIOUS OWNERS

In the 19th century Broadlands belonged to Henry John Temple, 3rd Viscount Palmerston, Prime Minister and Victorian political giant. Palmerston loved Broadlands, which he inherited at the age of 17 – before the railway, he would often travel the 80 miles from London on horseback to spend weekends there.

More recently, Broadlands was home to Lord Mountbatten, whose wife Edwina was descended from the Temple family. Great-grandson of Queen Victoria, Mountbatten joined the Navy as a young man and fought in both world wars. His World War II exploits became the basis of Noel Coward's film *In Which We Serve*. As Chief of Combined Operations and he played a key role in planning the invasions of North Africa, Italy and France; then as Supreme Allied Commander South-east Asia he retook Burma. As last Viceroy, he oversaw India's transition to independence. Assassinated by the IRA in 1979, he is remembered in a special exhibition in the 17th century stable-block.

BROADLANDS' INTERIORS

The most spectacular rooms include the Saloon, a dream of delicate plasterwork by Joseph Rose the Elder, the Wedgwood Room, with pale blue and white friezes and mouldings, and the domed hall and sculpture hall, the former with snowflake-like decorations in white plaster. When, during World War II, Broadlands served as a hospital, the walls of the Wedgwood Room were boarded up for protection, but patients in bed could still gaze at Joseph Rose's ceiling.

These rooms display the collections which Henry, 2nd Viscount Palmerston, brought back from his Grand Tour. They include an impressive collection of ancient Greek and Roman sculptures, and 18th-century pieces in similar style, and Henry returned to England determined to make Broadlands a fitting showcase for his acquisitions. The Oak Room, now Lord Romsey's private cinema, gives some impression of interiors before the house's 18th century transformation.

The aptly-named Wedgwood Room at Broadlands is where the family usually take tea.

Blenheim Palace

Woodstock

The Duke of Marlborough in Garter Robes, as portrayed by Sir Godfrey Kneller.

The story of Blenheim Palace has as many twists and turns as the most intricate of its decorations. It begins when a humble military man, John Churchill, married the future Queen Anne's lady-in-waiting and confidante, Sarah Jennings. As soon as she became queen in 1702, Anne gave him the title Duke of Marlborough. His career was a triumph, with a string of spectacular victories in the War of Spanish Succession. The first was over France and Bavaria in the Battle of Blenheim in 1704. In recognition of the nation's gratitude, Anne gave him the manor of Woodstock and the money to build a grand house. John Vanbrugh, the architect, designed a main block surmounted by four towers, with two projecting wings, which earned it the local nickname of Blenheim Castle. Some 1,500 men were needed to carry out the vast scheme. In 1711, the Marlboroughs fell out of royal favour, left the country and building work on Blenheim stopped.

Blenheim is England's answer to Versailles: a baroque palace filled with treasures, set in wonderfully landscaped grounds including a huge lake. Built in honour of the Duke of Marlborough, it is remarkable for the scale and theatricality of its design, by John Vanbrugh: in Woodstock, eight miles north of Oxford on the A44.

A Clash of Temperaments

After Queen Anne died in 1714, the Marlboroughs returned and began funding the project themselves. However, increasing tension between the cantankerous Duchess and Vanbrugh became unbearable as she tried to limit his extravagances, venting her fury at the changes he had made in her absence – and at the comfortable quarters he had allotted to himself – until he stormed off in 1716.

The Duchess banned him from returning and Vanbrugh died ten years later, having only seen his creation once, while Sarah was away. In the meantime, his erstwhile assistant, Hawksmoor, and many of the top craftsmen deserted Blenheim because of arguments over money. The 1st Duke died in 1722, and Sarah oversaw the project which was now her husband's memorial, persuading Hawksmoor to return and complete the job. The completion of the chapel in 1732 was the final element, and it is here that the 1st Duke and Duchess are buried. The nearby 134ft Column of Victory was her flamboyant memorial to him.

Blenheim forms a series of theatrical settings, and its façade is a magnificent sight. From the central block, curved walls lead to the east and west wings. As you enter through the east gateway, look out for the carvings of the English lion strangling the French cockerel. Inside, there is another reference to the Battle of Blenheim on the 67ft-high ceiling of the marbled Great Hall, in the oval painting by Sir James Thornhill. It depicts the Duke in the garb of a Roman general being presented with the laurel wreath of victory by Britannia. Ever resentful of paying bills, the 1st Duchess quibbled over Sir James's fee, costing him the chance to decorate the adjacent Saloon. In the dome-vaulted corridor leading west from the Great Hall, is Closterman's large painting of the 1st Duke and Duchess with five of their children.

The building of Blenheim Palace alone covers some four acres of ground.

Sir Winston Churchill

The passage leads to the small, plain bedroom where, in 1874, Jenny Churchill gave birth to a son, Winston. Churchill's father, Lord Randolph Spencer-Churchill, entered Parliament that year, later briefly becoming Chancellor of the Exchequer, but his son was to achieve far greater fame through his dogged leadership of Britain in World War II. A nearby exhibition about this imposing man includes a set of his young curls, and a maroon velvet boiler suit which he wore a great deal during the war, together with some of his oil paintings. Winston Churchill was born at Blenheim by chance (he was premature), but as the cousin of the 8th Duke, he was heir to the Dukedom until Consuelo Vanderbilt gave birth to the 10th Duke in 1897. A regular visitor, he maintained a great affection for the place, and is buried at nearby Bladon churchyard.

The ceilings of the three rooms east of the Saloon cleverly give an effect of great height through the coving and banding. The Green Drawing Room has portraits of the 1st Duchess (by Godfrey Kneller) and the 4th Duchess with a child on her knee (by Joshua Reynolds). The Red Drawing Room has a Reynolds too, this time of the 4th Duke in his Garter robes, with his wife and six of their children, two spaniels and a whippet. Opposite is Sargent's group of the 9th Duke with his first wife, Consuelo, and their family.

THE 9TH DUKE

Known as 'Sunny' (from his title of Earl of Sunderland) the 9th Duke is one of Blenheim's major characters. His disposition was anything but sunny, partly because he was badly affected by his parents' divorce, and suffered two rather unhappy marriages himself. The first was to Consuelo Vanderbilt, and was a balanced arrangement designed to increase the American Vanderbilt family's social standing, and the Spencer-Churchills' finances. Consuelo did her duty and produced an heir, but it was a miserable marriage which ended in divorce in 1921, after 15 years of separation.

Within a few weeks, the Duke married her old friend and fellow American, Gladys Deacon. She had made numerous visits to Blenheim – causing an international sensation on one occasion by flirting with the Crown Prince of Germany, one of many admirers. Gladys was an early casualty of cosmetic surgery, for the paraffin wax injected to change the shape of her nose slipped down under her chin. She remained a striking figure with intense, blue eyes, and her intelligence was matched only by her vanity.

Although she supported her husband in his restoration of Blenheim, she found the formal social life there dull, and the relationship deteriorated. The Duchess became increasingly eccentric, and eventually the Duke moved to London, finally forcing her out of Blenheim in 1933. He died the next year. Gladys survived, physically but not mentally, until 1977.

THE STATE APARTMENTS

The Saloon is a majestic room. Its *trompe-l'oeil* murals, and painted ceiling showing the 1st Duke driving a chariot through the sky, are by Louis Laguerre, who painted himself in next to the Duke's rather rotund chaplain, Dean Jones (who spent many hours indulging the Duke in his love of card games). The room was used as a family sitting room, but the large table now in its centre is a reminder that it often served as dining room, including for the visit of the German Kaiser in 1899.

The décor of the three drawing rooms that follow was rather over-embellished by the 9th Duke during restoration work in the 1890s. This fact (which he himself acknowledged) is a great shame as the rest of the work he had done was of such a high standard. Finally, on the west side of the palace, is the Long Library, at 183 feet the longest room in the house. The interior is by Hawksmoor, who treated the five sections of the room as separate compartments, beneath a luscious plasterwork ceiling by Isaac Mansfield. The result is said by some to be Hawksmoor's finest room.

This magnificent tapestry of 1708 depicts the Fall of Lille.

LILIAN'S MILLIONS

The 8th Duke, sometimes known as 'the wicked Duke', was a keen scientist who installed an early internal telephone system during the 1880s. Soon after, his adventurous nature allowed him to discover another source of funds. In 1888, he met and married a rich widow called Lilian Hammersley in New York. She changed her christian name to 'Lily' to avoid newspaper headlines rhyming Lilian with million, but they would have been accurate nonetheless. The marriage allowed for the re-leading of the roof, the installation of central heating and a number of other refinements. The upkeep of Blenheim Palace has been a terrible strain on the Marlborough finances over the centuries, and the 9th Duke was not alone in having to marry for money to keep up with the bills.

If you feel a slight chill during your tour of Blenheim, you are not alone. It may be the demented ghost of the 8th Duke, said to haunt the palace, or it could be a mere fact of life in this huge structure. At one time it took a ton of coal a day to keep the place warm, and that didn't always work. Noel Coward thought his bedroom here 'the coldest room I have ever encountered'. If at any time on your tour of Blenheim you feel a little lost, worry not, for again, you are not alone. Many servants in the past were quite unable to find their way around. A door keeper giving French writer André Maurois directions to a side door was asked exactly where it was. 'I don't know,' he admitted, 'I haven't been there'. When one house guest asked a maid for directions to the bathroom, she replied 'Oh miss, I wouldn't know that'.

A MIS-MATCHED PAIR

Gladys, wife of the 9th Duke ('Sunny'), was beautiful but increasingly eccentric, while her husband was rather dour and grim. In the 1930s, as their marriage fell apart, she took to keeping Blenheim spaniels, given the run of the house, and there were rumours that she had ordered dog flaps for the doors. Such licence had inevitable and damaging consequences for the furnishings. She exploited her husband's fury at this by placing fake messes in the Long Library just to annoy him. He would roam the house seeking stains in the carpets and curtains, which he would mournfully point out to his guests.

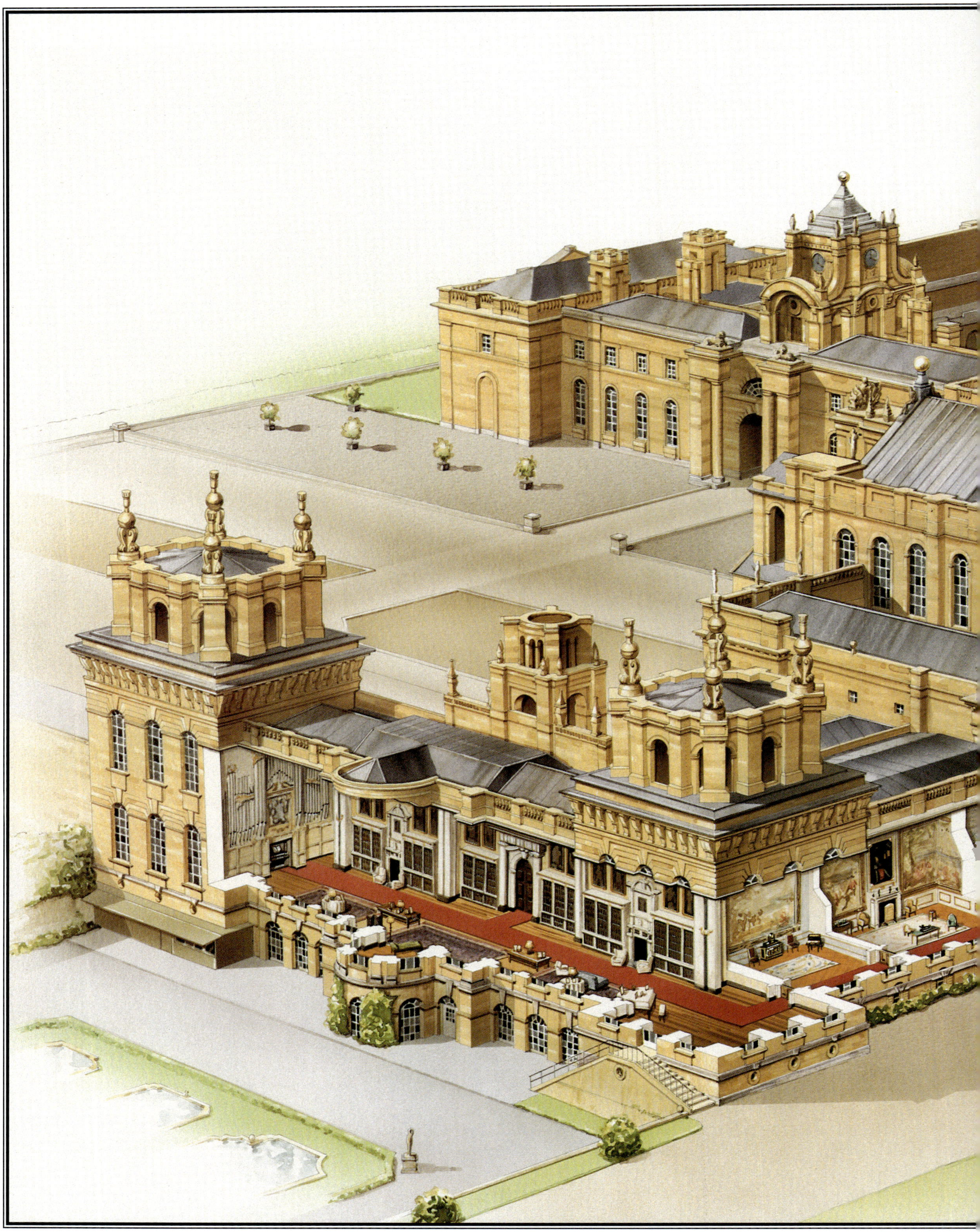

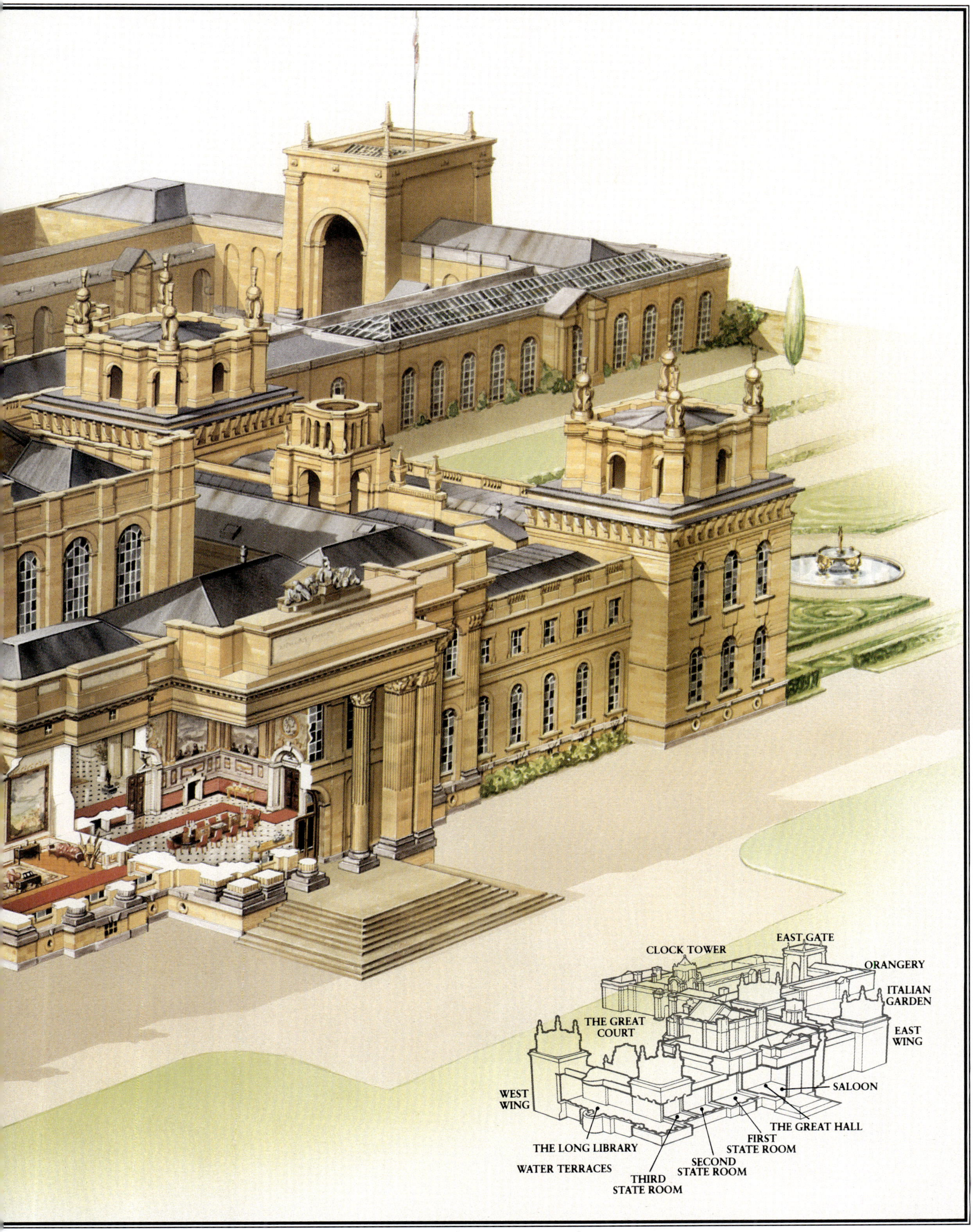
CLOCK TOWER
EAST GATE
ORANGERY
ITALIAN GARDEN
EAST WING
THE GREAT COURT
WEST WING
SALOON
THE GREAT HALL
FIRST STATE ROOM
SECOND STATE ROOM
THIRD STATE ROOM
THE LONG LIBRARY
WATER TERRACES

Ardington House

WANTAGE

THIS REMARKABLE BAROQUE HOUSE LED TO THE RUIN OF THE FAMILY WHICH BUILT IT: TWO AND A HALF MILES EAST OF WANTAGE, OFF THE A417.

Edward Clarke had excellent, if extravagent, taste, but poor financial judgment, and both facts were proved when he completed Ardington House in 1720 – he created a classical home set in formal gardens, but in doing so sealed the fate of his family. John Clarke had acquired the freehold to Ardington manor in the 16th century, and his grandson, another Edward Clarke, is buried with his wife (the daughter of Sir Thomas Temple of Stowe) in Ardington churchyard. No one accused the later Edward Clarke of wisdom, and the fact that his wife Mary's maiden name was Wiseman was of no help. They married in 1721, but they soon had to pull down both the Berkshire houses she inherited, Sparsholt Court and Steventon, to pay his debts. Even that wasn't enough to save the situation, and in 1728 he sold 450 acres – a large portion of the estate – to his neighbour Matthew Wymondsold of Lockinge.

The deal left Clarke without sufficent land to support the beautiful house he had built. After his death in 1733, the house was hardly changed until his grandson, William Wiseman Clarke, undertook some alteration towards the end of the century. He could not, however, improve the family's finances, and eventually, in 1831, William Nelson Clarke sold the estate.

Ardington was acquired by Mr and Mrs Desmond Baring in 1939, and they later added the kitchen pavilion on the east side of the house, carried out various restorations, and opened the house to the public. It is a Baroque house with remarkable brickwork: pale grey for the walls, and two kinds of red for the detailing. The major internal feature is the Imperial Staircase Hall occupying the middle of the ground floor. This continues the symmetrical theme of the design by having two flights on either side of the south door leading to a single flight to the upper landing – a spectacular feat of joinery. The painted ceiling in the panelled dining room is well worth seeing, and the house stands in grounds with fine cedar trees.

Broughton Castle

BANBURY

A MEDIEVAL HONEY-COLOURED STONE MANSION SPECTACULARLY REFLECTED IN ITS MOAT: THREE MILES SOUTH-WEST OF BANBURY ON THE B4035.

Broughton is a castle in name only, for it is really an early 14th-century mansion, later enhanced by Tudor architects. It was built by Sir John de Broughton, who enlarged an existing building within the moat to form a manor house. Since 1370, however, it has been in the Fiennes family (whose title is Lords of Saye and Sele). Indeed, it was Richard Fiennes who in 1554 altered it to meet the 'Court' style of Edward VI. He put in two floors above the Great Hall, two staircase projections to the south and added a pair of rooms to form the west wing, building on the foundations of a medieval kitchen. His son Richard embellished the interior, including the magnificent plaster ceiling in the Great Parlour, finishing the job in 1599.

Little has changed at Broughton since that time. It escaped a Regency 'restoration' because the 15th baron frittered away his time and the family fortune on a life of frivolity as a member of the set of the Prince Regent and Count d'Orsay. The family deserted Broughton,

Broughton Castle's moat was originally dug in the 13th century. The beautiful house that it encloses was enlarged between 1530 and 1600.

and in 1837 sold off most of its contents, including the swans on the moat.

The 'Gothick' ceiling pendants in the Great Hall are one of the few 19th-century additions. The groined passage beyond the dining room has some fascinating corbel heads at the base of its arches. A stone staircase leads to a rare 14th-century private chapel with its fixed altar slab. Queen Anne's Room is named after Anne of Denmark, wife of James I, who slept here in 1604. She is likely to have admired the exuberant plasterwork ceiling in the Great Parlour, completed five years previously. Broughton has two notable chimneypieces: one in Queen Anne's Room dates from at least 1551, possibly earlier; the other, of stone and stucco, in the Fontainebleau style, is in the King's Chamber, off the gallery. In addition to the family portraits including one of William Fiennes, the splendidly panelled Oak Room has a painting of Mrs Nathaniel Fiennes. Her daughter was Celia Fiennes, who became famous for the journals of her travels around England towards the end of the 17th century.

'OLD SUBTLETY'

The English Civil War, when Royalist cavaliers clashed with Oliver Cromwell's parliamentarian roundheads, was a time of great intrigue, and Broughton Castle was in the thick of it. William Fiennes, 8th Baron and 1st Viscount of Saye and Sele, was strongly puritanical and fiercely opposed to Charles I's attempts to rule without Parliament. From 1629 to 1640 Broughton became a gathering point for those who wished to bring down the King's government. William was an accomplished wheeler-dealer whose political skills earned him the nickname 'Old Subtlety'. When war broke out, he raised a regiment of blue-coats and four troops of horse which fought in the nearby Battle of Edgehill in 1642. The battle was inconclusive, but local Royalists captured and occupied the castle as a reprisal.

This leather bucket, dating from around 1740, shows the Fiennes family coat of arms.

Kingston Bagpuize House

KINGSTON BAGPUIZE

PARKLAND SURROUNDS THIS CHARMING, BEAUTIFULLY PROPORTIONED HOUSE: FIVE MILES WEST OF ABINGDON, ON THE A415.

Miss Marlie Raphael bought Kingston Bagpuize House from Lord Ebury in 1939, and when she died, in 1976, she was succeeded by her niece, Lady Grant, now Lady Tweedsmuir. Her father-in-law was the writer John Buchan, most famous for his action-packed adventure stories such as *The Thirty Nine Steps*.

Mystery surrounds the origins of Kingston Bagpuize House. Some experts date it to about 1710, because it looks like the work of Wren and Gibbs. However, the family has found deeds showing that the house existed in 1670, and other suggested architects are Sir Roger Pratt, who built nearby Coleshill in 1652, and William Townesend.

The high-ceilinged rooms have Queen Anne fireplaces and a wealth of architectural detail; the furniture is mainly a mixture of French and English pieces from the 18th century. One of the most striking features of the house is the staircase and gallery, magnificently cantilevered so that the wall supports all the weight, leaving the entrance hall free of pillars. You can best appreciate the symmetrical design of the house from the saloon, which was originally the entrance hall, and from where the main ground-floor rooms can be seen. There are some interesting pictures, including one of Miss Raphael as a child.

The dining room was panelled in oak in 1728, and contains a grandfather clock showing the phases of the moon. In the library is an intricately carved chimney piece in the style of Grinling Gibbons. The next room is a charming small morning room which may have been a bedroom at one time. Its panelling was removed earlier this century, but was found in the stables by the indomitable Miss Raphael, who had it restored to its rightful place.

Upstairs there are five bedrooms. One of these, the Rose Room, was originally the Great Chamber, when it was larger by one bay. Lady Tweedsmuir's Bedroom was the original drawing room of the house. Look out for the Victorian doll's house on your way down the stairs. The late Miss Raphael's influence goes well beyond the house, for she also laid out the English garden, extending it beyond the mellow brick walls, and creating a woodland garden and a large shrub border. There is also an early 18th-century gazebo built over an Elizabethan cockpit.

■ My family and I enjoy living in this lovely, peaceful old house, with its beautiful garden. ■
Lady Tweedsmuir

Kingston Bagpuize House, now owned by Lady Tweedsmuir, still reflects the considerable influence of her aunt, Miss Marlie Raphael, who lived here for nearly 40 years.

■ **One of the attractions to visitors seems to be that the same family that built the house still live here after 37 generations, including the youngest generation. Visitors see all the rooms in the house, which is still the family home, and if my husband happens to be in the kitchen making 'shooting soup', they walk past rather like 'Bisto Kids'. There are also nearly always traces of the grandchildren's visits, with toys and books exactly where they were discarded!** ■
Mrs Gascoigne

Right: The peacock is the Harcourt family crest.

The dining room at Stanton Harcourt.

Stanton Harcourt Manor

STANTON HARCOURT

UNUSUALLY WELL-PRESERVED MEDIEVAL BUILDINGS SET IN TRANQUIL GARDENS: FIVE MILES SOUTH-EAST OF WITNEY ON THE B4449.

The Harcourts were a Norman family who came to England at the time of the Conquest and acquired the Manor of Stanton in the mid 12th century upon the marriage of Isabel de Camville and Robert de Harcourt. Isabel was well connected – her mother was a cousin of Queen Adeliza, second wife of Henry I, and the Queen's wedding gift was the Lordship of Stanton. The family lived in the house until 1688, when Sir Philip Harcourt died, leaving it to his widowed second wife, Elizabeth. She promptly sold off its contents and furniture, and abandoned Stanton Harcourt to return to her own family home.

Her stepson Simon Harcourt had already built a house three miles away at Cokethorpe and the Harcourt family lived there until 1755. In that year, parts of the old house at Stanton Harcourt were pulled down to provide stone foundations for a Palladian villa at Nuneham Courtenay, and it was not until this house was sold in 1948 that the family returned once more to Stanton Harcourt.

The entrance to the house is through the gatehouse, partly dating from 1540, remodelled in 1868 and enlarged in 1953. Beyond it is Pope's Tower, named after the poet Alexander Pope who worked on his translation of *The Iliad* here in 1717-18. The ground floor is the original chapel, used only by family retainers; the family itself celebrated Mass from the Assembly Room above, following the service through an opening over the archway facing the altar.

Almost opposite the tower is the spectacular Great Kitchen, with foundations dating back to around 1380. In the absence of chimneys, smoke from the open fires collected in the cone of the octagonal roof and was released through wooden louvres.

The Harcourt family still lives in the Manor House, which houses their fine collection of pictures, furniture, silver and porcelain. The buildings are set in a beautiful formal garden, developed since 1948, and there is a delightful wild garden around the manorial fish ponds.

Stonor Park

HENLEY ON THAMES

FROM MEDIEVAL HOME TO GEORGIAN MANSION, STONOR HAS BEEN IN THE SAME FAMILY FOR MORE THAN 800 YEARS: FIVE MILES NORTH OF HENLEY-ON-THAMES ON THE B480.

Stonor evolved into its present state over many centuries, but at its core remains a group of medieval flint, chalk and clunch buildings. The oldest, dating from about 1190, is the Old Hall which retains the original arches. A buttery (now the study), a solar (an upper chamber which is now the library) and the chapel were added between 1280 and 1341 and over the next two centuries, timber and flint additions were built. When Sir Walter Stonor took over the estate in 1534, he linked the various buildings together to create a formal E-shaped Tudor house with a gabled brick façade.

These changes were financed by a fortune made from wool and sheep, and the acquisition of land by marriage. The Stonors also enjoyed the status of high office. However, interest in home improvement understandably lessened after the Reformation, when this staunchly Catholic family refused to change its faith, and was heavily fined and penalised throughout many years of Catholic repression. The family sheltered priests on the run, most notably Edmund Campion, who supervised the printing of his *Decem Rationes* (Ten Reasons for Being a Catholic) in 1581 from a room behind the chimney in the roof. Stonor became a national centre for Catholicism, and indeed its chapel is one of only three in England where Mass has been celebrated to this day without interruption.

In the 1750s, architect John Aitkins removed the Tudor forecourt, wall, gateway and lodges, in order to introduce fashionable Georgian features such as heavy cornice of the roof. A fascinating view of the important buildings of Paris in about 1816 can be seen in the dining room wallpaper by Defours. Paris was also the source of the shell-shaped bed and the shell chairs in Francis Stonor's bedroom, reflecting the flambuoyant, romantic character of this great-grandson of the 3rd Lord Camoys. Under the high, 16th-century barrel-vaulted ceiling of the library is a major collection of Catholic books, including many illegally printed or imported during the Recusancy. Surrounded by beechwoods, Stonor is on the site of a prehistoric stone circle which has been recreated in the grounds.

Left: The wallpaper in Stonor's dining room dates from 1816 and depicts important buildings along the River Seine in Paris.

A RETURN TO POWER

As Catholics, the Stonors were banned from holding public office for more than 150 years until the passing of the Catholic Emancipation Act in 1829. Thomas Stonor, then 32, was eager to make up for lost time, and was soon elected as a Whig Member of Parliament for Oxford. In 1838 Queen Victoria granted him the ancient Barony of Camoys which he had inherited through his great-grandmother Mary Biddulph. He served the indomitable Queen as Lord-in-Waiting for a record 32 years. Thomas Stonor was also a co-founder of Henley Royal Regatta, an early member of the MCC, and a local magistrate. 'Old Tom' had sufficient energy remaining to father 15 children.

Far left: The bronze of Neptune, holding a trident and sharing his plinth with a dolphin, is Italian and dates from the mid 17th century.

Left: The baroque saint is one of a pair of 18th century German woodcarvings in Stonor Park's library.

Dorney Court

WINDSOR

A PERFECTLY PRESERVED EXAMPLE OF A SMALL 15TH-CENTURY TUDOR MANOR HOUSE: AT DORNEY, THREE MILES NORTH-WEST OF WINDSOR ON THE B3026 ETON TO TAPLOW ROAD.

Dorney Court is the quintessential English Tudor house. It was built between 1440-1480 and is a picture-postcard property of blushing pink bricks, ancient timbered gables and soaring slender chimneys. The setting is an Anglo-Saxon idyll. Despite its proximity to bustling Windsor, the ancient meadowland of Dorney Common has a wild and timeless air, while the house is surrounded by clipped hedges.

Entering the house, there is again a feeling that little has changed over the centuries. Restoration has been sympathetic, and if there is a cobweb here or a crack there, then so much the better – this is still a family home. The Palmer family have lived at Dorney since 1620, with an unbroken lineage from father to son. There have been some notable ladies too, looking down now from the portraits in the parlour, including he pretty Barbara Palmer, Countess of Castlemaine, who was a favourite mistress of Charles II.

In the Great Chamber the barrel-vaulted ceiling is said to be held up only by ancient twig branches which creak and groan with the house and often bring down plaster. The panelled bedroom walls slope backwards at a drunken angle, and the last of the bedrooms, the Little Room, is haunted by a female form who enigmatically points to a panel in the room.

Adjacent to the William and Mary style dining room is the Great Hall, and the many portraits around the walls contain works by Kneller and Lely. There is also a rare and striking set of Turkish portraits, brought to Dorney by Sir Roger Palmer, then Ambassador to the East for Charles II. The most curious piece however is a large carved stone pineapple. It is said that Charles II gave Sir Roger the top of a Barbados pineapple. He planted this at Dorney and it became the first ever pineapple to be grown in England. The resulting fruit was presented to Charles II in 1661.

Stratfield Saye

STRATFIELD SAYE

A MODEST STUCCOED CAROLINE HOUSE, WITH A 17TH-CENTURY EXTERIOR AND 18TH-CENTURY INTERIORS: SIX MILES SOUTH OF READING OFF THE A33 BASINGSTOKE ROAD.

Following the Battle of Waterloo, its victor, the Duke of Wellington, was fêted as the saviour of England and to show its appreciation, 'a grateful nation' voted the great Duke £600,000 to buy a home fit for a hero. After some deliberation the Duke chose Stratfield Saye, a relatively small Caroline house, built *c*.1630, whose interiors were remodelled between 1730 and 1790. It is thought that he planned to build a grandiose 'Waterloo Palace', as a rival to Blenheim Palace, but the project was abandoned when its massive cost became apparent. Instead the Duke settled down to life at Stratfield Saye, improving his relatively modest house with such unheard-of comforts as double-glazing, water-closets and central heating. Stratfield Saye remains the main residence of the Wellesley family, and the lived-in atmosphere is demonstrated nowhere better than in the Lady Charles Room.

The Entrance Hall – very masculine, full of portraits and military memorabilia – sets the tone for the house. The elaborate French flags were originally intended for presentation by Napoleon to each French Département as souvenirs of his victory.

The library has hardly changed since the Duke's day and many of the books here are from Napoleon's own library. The adjacent music room is mostly devoted to the Duke's favourite charger – 'Copenhagen' carried the Duke all day at Waterloo and was buried at Stratfield Saye with full military honours.

The funeral of the Iron Duke was a sombre, but spectacular affair. His huge funeral carriage, resplendent in black and gold, is now on show in Stratfield Saye's old stable block.

In the print room and the gallery the prints are, unusually, stuck straight onto the walls. The Gallery is the oldest of the two rooms (*c*.1745), and its prints are edged with gilded wooden beads to indicate picture frames. Between each picture the wall is covered in gold leaf so that the Gallery positively glows. Gilded busts of emperors and kings and black and gold Boulle furniture complete the Midas effect.

The richest collection of paintings are displayed in the drawing room, including many pictures from the Spanish Royal Collection, looted by Napoleon's brother, Joseph, before being snatched back by Wellington's troops. The Duke offered them back to Spain, who declined to accept them as 'they came into your hands by just and honourable means'.

There is an excellent exhibition on the life of the Duke of Wellington in the old stable block, offering a first class introduction to the house, and its highlight is the Duke's enormous funeral carriage. This richly ornamented black and gold behemoth is 17 feet high, 21 feet long and weighs 18 tons. The state funeral was the greatest ever seen in England, its cortège watched by one million people.

Highclere Castle

NEWBURY

AN EXUBERANT HIGH VICTORIAN-GOTHIC MANSION WITH EXTRAVAGANT INTERIORS: FOUR AND A HALF MILES SOUTH OF NEWBURY OFF THE A34.

Driving through the 6,000-acre Highclere estate, past verdant rolling meadows and towering ancient cedars, there is a sense of high expectancy. And when the house dramatically heaves into view it doesn't disappoint. If it bears a strong resemblance to the Houses of Parliament, this is hardly surprising – Sir Charles Barry built Parliament and Highclere concurrently, the latter completed in 1842.

The entrance hall continues the exterior Gothic theme with polychrome marble and a fan-vaulted roof. The beautifully carved pair of wyverns (winged dragons with two legs and a serpent's tail) represent the family crest. Period contrasts are a hallmark of Highclere and the next room is a sumptuous Victorian library. This too is by Barry and has dark mahogany-painted columns, richly carved bookcases and glowing soft furnishings .

Between the drawing room and the smoking room are a curious set of pigeon-holes which were hidden for some 67 years, the doors locked and barred by heavy furniture. When rediscovered they were found to contain ancient artefacts from the 5th Earl's expeditions to Egypt. The 6th Earl had, while still grieving for his father, sold what he thought was his father's complete collection of finds to the Metropolitan Museum in New York. He had no idea that further pieces were hidden within the castle, and the horde was only uncovered (by

Left: The library at Highclere Castle represents Victorian style at its very best.

the family butler) after the 6th Earl's death. These are now on display in the basement. The other passion of the 5th Earl was horse-racing and he founded the now world-famous stud at Highclere. The present Earl is Racing Manager to the Queen and the castle has an exhibition on the Highclere Stud.

The architectural *tour de force* of the house is its Saloon. This is a pure 'Cathedral Gothic' grand hall, with a splendid first-floor arcaded gallery and a soaring vaulted roof. Other highlights include the Stuart Revival dining room with a classic equestrian Charles I by Van Dyck, and outstanding gardens.

THE MUMMY'S CURSE

The 5th Earl of Carnarvon first started excavating in 1907 and later that year teamed up with the expert archaeologist Howard Carter. In November 1922, the two men made one of the greatest discoveries in the history of archaeology – the tomb of Tutankhamun. But the earl's enjoyment was short lived. He was bitten by a mosquito, contracted blood poisoning and died in April 1923. At the moment of his death in Cairo, all the city lights went out and at Highclere his favourite dog died. Howard Carter however survived the 'curse of Tutankhamun' to complete the dig and died peacefully in England.

Chicheley Hall

Newport Pagnall

A Georgian house with a stylish touch of Roman baroque and superb craftsmanship: two miles east of Newport Pagnall on the A422 Bedford road.

Chicheley Hall is among the finest and least altered 18th-century houses in Britain. John Julius Norwich described it as 'a curious, but surprisingly successful marriage between early Georgian austerity and exuberant baroque'. The mellow, orange brick is of early Georgian date; the ornate stone window and door frames show strong traces of such architects of baroque Rome as Bernini and Borromini – but this is inventive adaptation, not slavish imitation.

Built between 1719 and 1723, Chicheley was the work of the Midlands architect and master-builder Francis Smith of Warwick. His client, Sir John Chester, did not follow the more severe Palladian style then in vogue, and not everyone approved. His friend Burrell Massingberd, who had advised him on its design, wrote to his wife in 1722 that he was 'so fretted to see such havoc made in the architecture ... that if Sir John had been at home when I first saw it, I should not have forborne the rudeness of exposing all the faults to the utmost.' The baroque features we admire today were for Massingberd unforgivable solecisms.

The entrance is as cool as the exterior brick is warm; it opens through green marble columns on to a wooden staircase of amazing intricacy and craftsmanship. Two of the best rooms – the dining room and Lord Beatty's study – take their character from superbly designed panelling; others, including the Jacobean room, are in lighter tones.

Sir John Chester's study appears at first sight to be a conventional panelled room with pilasters and unusual carved capitals; in fact almost every panel hides a cupboard, the pilasters are on hinges, and so is the frieze above the door. Altogether, Chicheley's brickwork, wood and stone carving, joinery and plasterwork are a poem in Georgian craftsmanship. Ironically the fact that Sir John Chester's later descendants rented it out, when an owner-occupier's fingers might have itched to 'improve', may have been crucial to its preservation. The house is still lived in by the family, and is full of flowers and people, giving the house its particular warmth and charm.

■ Living in Chicheley is a joy. All the rooms are panelled and have never been changed; none are too large and the sun pours in through the original glass, mostly with the old thick glazing bars. It is the happiest of houses. ■
Mrs John Nutting

Chicheley's superb classical hall is separated from the staircase by an arcade of marble columns.

Chenies Manor House

CHENIES

A TUDOR MANOR HOUSE WITH SECRET TUNNELS AND HIDDEN CHAMBERS, WHERE HENRY VIII AND ELIZABETH I STAYED: TWO MILES NORTH-WEST OF M25 JUNCTION 18, OFF THE A404 AMERSHAM ROAD.

Chenies Manor House, on the edge of its Chiltern village above the little River Chess, is a mellow brick Tudor house full of the idiosyncrasies of a house altered and matured over centuries. It has a secret chamber, possibly for hiding priests, tunnels running from the house to a nearby wood, a medieval well, rooms where Elizabeth I stayed and a ghost who may or may not be Henry VIII.

The manor house, built around two courtyards, is approached by a lime-tree-canopied forecourt alongside the parish church. Its oldest part, T-shaped and dating from around 1460, centres on a battlemented tower. The 'new' lodgings were added in the 1520s to provide better accommodation for guests and the same era saw the installation of the fireplaces and spectacular brick Tudor chimneys, of which 22 survive. It is said that Henry VIII so admired them that he had the same craftsmen work on Hampton Court which he was then in the process of enlarging.

The west-facing elevation of Chenies Manor House has a delightful outlook over the Sunken Garden.

The stone parlour, fitted out with mainly 17th century furniture, was the hall of the 15th century house and would originally have been open to the rafters, with smoke swirling up from an open central hearth. The 2nd Earl, a staunch protestant, was devoted to Elizabeth and frequently entertained her here along with the Earl of Leicester and her Secretary of State, Burleigh. Perhaps the house was noisy, for Burleigh asked to be accommodated in the nursery 'for my quieter lodging'.

Queen Elizabeth's room, where she probably held court, is an oak-floored parlour with 16th-century tapestries and furniture from the 17th century. The State Bedroom, where she is believed to have slept, is hung with family portraits, but now used as a billiards room. Another room full of history is the armoury – a primitive 140 feet long gallery on the top floor, where roundhead soldiers were quartered in the Civil War. The 4th Earl of Bedford, who owned but did not generally live at Chenies, was a friend of John Hampden, whose stand on Ship Money led to the Civil War. Hampden's son died in a skirmish near the house.

The manor house was subsequently let as a farmhouse and suffered neglect – it was described by Horace Walpole as being 'in piteous fragments'. Indeed, a surveyor reporting to the estate recommended wholesale demolition. Fortunately only the most decayed parts, including service buildings, were taken down; the Bedfords restored the finest Tudor section.

The house's present owners, Elizabeth and Alistair Macleod Matthews, have lived there since the 1950s – nearly all their married life – and take pleasure in welcoming visitors personally. Outside they have re-created a turf labyrinth as depicted in a 16th-century picture which is now at Woburn Abbey; and Mrs Macleod Matthews has established a physic garden of medicinal herbs.

THE HAUNTED CORRIDOR

When Henry VIII visited Chenies in 1541, his fifth wife, Catherine Howard, was having an adulterous affair with her cousin Thomas Culpeper, which later led to both of them being executed. During this visit, the ageing king was suffering from an ulcerated leg which made movement difficult. Legend has it that ghostly, halting footsteps have sometimes been heard on the stairs and gallery leading up to Catherine's bedroom. We may infer that a pain-racked and suspicious Henry sometimes returns, still, after four centuries, vainly aspiring to catch the lovers *in flagrante delicto*.

Lilies

AYLESBURY

AN ATMOSPHERIC COUNTRY HOUSE BY A PIONEERING VICTORIAN ARCHITECT, NOW A 20-ROOM BOOKSHOP: ABOUT FOUR MILES NORTH OF AYLESBURY OFF THE A413 BUCKINGHAM ROAD.

Lilies is built on the site of a medieval French monastery called 'Lelius' after the lily, emblem of France. A Tudor house replaced the monastery, and was remodelled in Georgian times, but the present house dates from around 1870 and is by the Victorian architect George Devey, who was largely neglected until recently, though he had pioneered the 'organic', vernacular approach to house design.

Victorian Lilies had its own gasworks to light house and drive, and even its 1920s and '30s owner, Miss Isabel Heap, maintained it in grand Edwardian style, with a large staff of indoor and outdoor servants. But when the present owners, Mr and Mrs Peter Eaton, acquired it 25 years ago, it was run down and empty after a period as a nurses' training centre. 'It had 30 WCs in working order and 20 baths in as many rooms,' they recall, 'and the roof had fallen into total disrepair'.

The Eatons have gradually restored both the fabric of this handsome and fascinating house and, they believe, something of its old atmosphere. But this is not your ordinary country house on show; instead it earns its keep as one of Europe's most unusual bookshops. Twenty of its rooms are given over to books on a wide range of subjects, including an antiquarian section which is open on request. Its atmospheric contents also include Pre-Raphaelite paintings and drawings by Ruskin, Rosetti, Lord Leighton, Watts and others, in addition to such diverse curiosities as part of the first gramophone record ever made, the first book and first newspaper with photographs, Rosetti's music stand and George VI's ration book.

Lilies speaks eloquently of a vanished society. Its first tenant was Ferdinand de Rothschild, who would daily ride seven miles to view progress on the building of his new mansion, Waddesdon. A later owner, Vernon Britain, used to ride the village street on his grey horse, tossing half-a-crown to each man who touched his forelock to him and two shillings to each woman who curtseyed.

Nether Winchendon House

AYLESBURY

A TUDOR MANOR HOUSE WITH 18TH-CENTURY GOTHIC ADDITIONS: NEAR LOWER WINCHENDON, SIX MILES SOUTH-WEST OF AYLESBURY, NORTH OF THE A418.

A medieval house? Parts of it are, with Tudor improvements, but the eye-catching battlemented screen wall of three arches which frames the front door is Regency gothic. It was designed and erected by an early 19th-century owner, Sir Scrope Bernard, who also clad older timber-framed buildings in stone. A far-reaching 19th-century transformation, but, with such earlier features as the tall, ornate Tudor chimneys, creating a delightful and harmonious ensemble.

Some of the most interesting and attractive parts of the house date from the early 16th century, when it was owned by the Abbey of Notley, but let to one of Henry VIII's top civil servants, Sir John Daunce. He added a parlour (now the drawing room), and his initials, portrait, rebus and coat of arms feature in the superbly carved Renaissance oak frieze.

The house was sold in 1559 to a London merchant, William Goodwin, and since then has changed hands only by inheritance. Goodwin's daughter married into an old Buckinghamshire family, the Tyringhams, and it subsequently went to their cousins, the Bernards, whose family still live there. The first Bernard at Nether Winchendon was Sir Francis, governor of New Jersey and Massachusetts, who is remembered in the names of four US towns: Bernard, Bernardston, Bernardsville and Winchendon. His third son, Thomas, was a lawyer and notable social reformer who promoted smallpox vaccination.

The dark-panelled great hall was the meeting place of the manorial court, presided over by the Abbot of Notley, and court rolls displayed there date back to 1530. On one wall hangs an early Flemish tapestry showing Henry VIII with Archbishop Cranmer and Lord Russell (later first Duke of Bedford). Leading out of the great hall is the walnut-panelled Justice Room, which incorporates the 'screen passage' which ran from the back to the front of the medieval house. Among items on view in the entrance hall is a summons to attend the Barebone's Parliament of 1653, signed by Oliver Cromwell. From the south front the garden runs down to the tranquil little River Thame.

This lovely Worcester and Spode Imari pattern pot pourri vase is among the treasured possessions at Nether Winchendon House (below).

Stowe School

BUCKINGHAM

A CELEBRATION TO A GREAT WHIG LANDOWNER'S POLITICAL POWER AND WEALTH, STOWE STANDS IN ONE OF BRITAIN'S FINEST 18TH-CENTURY GARDEN LANDSCAPES: ABOUT TWO MILES NORTH-WEST OF BUCKINGHAM ON UNCLASSIFIED ROADS.

This statue of Alexander the Great is one of many in Stowe's famous garden.

Stowe, both the house and park, are testimony to an era when men of wealth and political power celebrated by ostentatiously pursuing the latest architectural and artistic fashions. The Temple family supported Parliament in the Civil War and became steadfast (though sturdily independent) adherents of the Whig cause. They were against the Stuarts and absolutism, and in favour of the independence and power of the landowning aristocracy.

All this was expressed in lavish display by Sir Richard Temple (1675-1749). An outspoken soldier with political ambitions, he was, when he set about turning Stowe from a country house into a palace, probably the richest man in England. And the grand design for this celebration of power starts not at the north front door, but two miles away in Buckingham town, where the great vista of the approach avenue to Stowe begins. Visiting VIPs were driven along this for a mile, with impressive views of the porticoed south front with its curving colonnaded wings, then led away through trees to the carriage entrance on the north side.

Stowe's elliptical Marble Saloon, inspired by the Pantheon in Rome, is one of the most spectacular rooms in the country.

In the grandly furnished North Hall two features dominate: William Kent's fine ceiling, and a large painting showing Mars, god of war, handing a sword to Richard, ennobled as Viscount Cobham.

The Temple family went from strength to strength, becoming Earls, then Marquesses, and finally Dukes of Buckingham. They employed a whole string of celebrated architects, including Vanbrugh, Kent, Gibbs, Adam and Soane, to embellish and improve the house, and continued to develop its landscape setting.

They also applied their wealth and taste to furnishing and adorning its interiors, the State Rooms of the *piano nobile* or ceremonial first floor are particularly outstanding. The coolly classical State Music Room and its counterpart the Temple Room open into the central, oval-shaped Marble Saloon, which in turn gives on to a loggia overlooking the lake and that two-mile vista. The State Dining Room, library and Blue Room are three more components in a rich ensemble of interiors and contents nearly blown apart by demolition in the 1920s. It was saved by the establishment of Stowe School, the present owners, who contrive to reconcile the running of a 600-pupil boarding school with conservation of the house and its opening (in school holidays) to the public.

STOWE'S LANDSCAPE

Stowe's grounds constitute the most important 18th-century landscape in Britain, according to the National Trust which now owns and cares for them. Viscount Cobham and his successors pioneered the essentially English style of natural-seeming landscape associated with 'Capability' Brown, who spent a decade as Stowe's head gardener. It consists of a delightful combination of views and vistas, with an amazing 32 set-pieces in the form of temples, follies, bridges, towers, grottos and other features, often loaded with political symbolism: temples of Ancient Virtue, British Worthies and Conductor and Victory. These are now the subject of a phased £10million restoration programme.

Wotton House

WOTTON UNDERWOOD

AN EARLY 18TH-CENTURY HOUSE, ALMOST IDENTICAL IN DESIGN TO BUCKINGHAM HOUSE (LATER BUCKINGHAM PALACE): ABOUT EIGHT MILES WEST OF AYLESBURY OFF THE A41.

This early 18th century country house has a fascinating story. It was built between 1704 and 1717, and the inscription on the splendid portico above the west, garden front – attributed to Grinling Gibbons – reads 'Conceived in 1704'. A drawing of the house by Sir

John Thornhill exists, showing one of the pavilions. It is also one of several houses built to a similar plan to Buckingham House, the London home of the Duke of Buckingham, which was later remodelled and enlarged to become Buckingham Palace. Interestingly, Wotton was built by Richard Grenville, and one of his descendents became Duke of Buckingham and Chandos.

A fire in 1820 gutted the interior of the house, but the exterior remained intact. The Duke, a great friend of the architect Sir John Soane, sent post haste to London to invite him to restore the interior, which he did to superb effect. Contrary to claims by the then owners, there was no further fire in 1929. Apparently, this was their excuse to explain away the obliteration of the Soane interior! Fortunately, they simply superimposed their own taste upon the superb Soane features, and when the rooms were eventually restored, his splendid cornices came to light, along with the arches and the floating effect of the ceilings. Today, the house is once again as Soane meant it to be.

Among its treasures is a wrought-iron balustrade by Tijou which Soane re-used for his superb – and unique – cantilevered staircase. The gates and railings that enclose the courtyard are attributed to Robinson, a pupil of Tijou, and the landscaped grounds display the work of 'Capability' Brown at his best.

■ I am about to attack the grotto, having just finished the Palladian bridge. The 400 acres of landscaped gardens are nearly restored and are rich in wildlife – magic! It is hard work – but so rewarding. ■
Mrs Elaine Brunner

Luton Hoo

LUTON

A DIAMOND MILLIONAIRE'S ART COLLECTION AND RUSSIAN IMPERIAL RELICS ARE DISPLAYED IN LAVISH RITZ INTERIORS, SET IN A 'CAPABILITY' BROWN LANDSCAPE: 2 MILES SOUTH OF LUTON ON A6129.

Though only just over a mile from Luton's suburban edge, visitors to Luton Hoo, situated at the end of a drive which winds through parkland landscaped by 'Capability' Brown, enter a very different world. Here is a great house that has gone through many transitions. Robert Adam, Sir Robert Smirke of British Museum fame, and in the present century Mewes and Davis, architects of the Ritz Hotels in both London and Paris, have all contributed to its style and grandeur.

Amongst Luton Hoo's owners were George III's Prime Minister Lord Bute, who engaged 'Capability' Brown; a Liverpool lawyer called Leigh; a 19th-century Danish ambassador; and – crucially – the diamond millionaire, philanthropist and art collector, Sir Julius Wernher. Born in Germany, Wernher made a fortune in the South African diamond business, settling in England in 1881. Advised by a leading Berlin museum art expert, he set about using his fortune to build up a remarkable collection with a Renaissance and Continental rather than English emphasis. It is this art collection which is Luton Hoo's central attraction.

Julius Wernher, who became a British citizen and was later knighted, preferred to keep his collection at Bath House in London (since demolished); his wife was more enthusiastic about Luton Hoo, which he bought in 1903; they employed Mewes and Davis to remodel it in 18th-century French style, creating perhaps the richest and finest Edwardian/French interiors in Britain.

THE WERNHER COLLECTION

These stunning interiors are the setting for a sequence of art treasures which starts in the top-lit entrance hall with a magnificent Gobelin tapestry of around 1700, moves on to rooms devoted to Dutch and Italian masters, and continues with superb 15th and 16th century Italian ceramics and one of the largest private collections of the work of the Imperial Russian jeweller Fabergé.

This portrait of Alexandra Feodorovna, the wife of Tzar Nicholas I, is part of Luton Hoo's famous art collection.

The story behind this magnificent collection is a further colourful strand in the Luton Hoo story: the marriage of Sir Julius's second son, Major General Harold Wernher, to Zia, great-granddaughter both of Tzar Nicholas I and of the poet Pushkin. It was Sir Harold and Lady Zia who opened Luton Hoo to the public in 1950; and among the items on display are many mementoes of the Imperial family inherited from Lady Zia's parents and a collection of relics formed by Charles Gibbes, English tutor to the last Tzarevitch, the Tzar's eldest son, who with his parents was murdered in the 1918 Revolution.

Luton Hoo's Russian connections have been strengthened by the reordering of its chapel, created in the 1870s by the Victorian architect G E Street, as a Russian Orthodox chapel and gallery to house part of the Russian collection.

Woburn Abbey

WOBURN

A GEORGIAN NOBLEMAN'S PALACE SET IN A REPTON-DESIGNED PARK, AND FILLED WITH RICH FURNISHINGS AND WORKS OF FINE ART: EIGHT AND A HALF MILES NORTH-WEST OF DUNSTABLE, OFF THE M1 AT JUNCTION 12.

Woburn Abbey shows few outward signs of having once been a religious foundation. It is an 18th-century English nobleman's palace built on the foundations of a Cistercian abbey – a palace adorned with treasures assembled by a dozen generations of a family with both taste and money. Its grand State Apartments, including the State Saloon and State Dining Room, are palatial both in scale and the magnificence of their décor. These, and the more comfortably-scaled family rooms, house an astoundingly rich art collection – for instance, a room full of views of Venice by Canaletto, commissioned by the 4th Duke; another hung with family portraits by Sir Joshua Reynolds.

GRAND INTERIORS

Perhaps the most serenely beautiful room in this south (family) wing is the library. In effect, it comprises three rooms, divided by screen walls with fluted Corinthian columns, and is lined with recessed bookshelves of finely bound volumes (predominantly on the subject of natural history) which beautifully complement the decorative plasterwork above. Hanging over the bookcases are a series of remarkable portraits, including a Rembrandt self-portrait and his wonderful study, *The Old Rabbi*.

Another of Woburn's grandest interiors is the Long Gallery, designed in the mid 18th century by Henry Flitcroft. He remodelled an earlier gallery, giving it new scale and proportion by using Corinthian columns to divide it into what are, visually, three inter-connecting rooms. Their plaster ceilings are beautifully moulded, with chandeliers hanging from delicately worked central roses of twined foliage. Among the paintings is a portrait of a dashing 16th-century soldier, Henry Danvers, Earl of Danby, depicted in armour outside his tent and showing the scars of battle. Danvers had been page to the soldier poet Sir Philip Sidney.

Other interiors to please the eye include a Chinese Room lined with exquisite 18th-century Chinese wallpaper with delicately painted and marvellously coloured birds and foliage; a grand staircase which climbs its lofty stair-well, each step supported by the one below without other visible signs of support; and the Racing Room, which was redecorated as a drawing room in the 18th century and is now refurnished by Lady Tavistock, wife of the present heir to the dukedom, with paintings and photographs of horses owned by the family.

At ground level on the north side of the house is an early 17th-century grotto, its ceiling carved to resemble seaweed, seashells and stalactites, and originally designed as an open loggia for the family to sit and breathe in good, fresh Bedfordshire air. Below ground, the crypt is used to display porcelain and Woburn's gold and silver collections – installed securely here after recovery from a 1984 burglary.

THE STATE APARTMENTS

In the State Apartments, which were generally kept empty except when royalty came to Woburn, two rooms recall a visit by Queen Victoria and Prince Albert. The room now called Queen Victoria's Bedroom was remodelled in the late 18th century and contains two portraits by William Fowler of Victoria as a young princess and as queen, as well as etchings done by the royal couple and given to their hostess, the 7th Duchess. Long before its remodelling, this room accommodated other royal visitors, notably Charles I and Henrietta Maria in 1636 and Charles again in 1647. The adjoining Queen Victoria's Dressing Room now contains a fine collection of 17th-century Dutch and Flemish paintings; previously a small drawing room, it has good views of the park and basin pond.

THE RUSSELL FAMILY

The family of the Dukes of Bedford – the Russells – have owned Woburn for 450 years, and lived there for more than 300 years. The present house, with its columned portico and great west-facing classical front, is largely the work of two Georgian architects, Henry Flitcroft and Henry Holland; but also includes parts of an earlier Jacobean house built by the family and remains of the 12th-century abbey.

The Russells acquired Woburn shortly after the Dissolution of the Monasteries: Edward VI granted it in 1547 to Sir John Russell, who became successively Baron Russell and 1st Earl of Bedford. Russells did not

Woburn Abbey, the ancestral home of the Dukes of Bedford, is set in a 3,000-acre deer park.

live at Woburn until 1619, however, and it was the 4th Earl, Francis, the original developer of the Covent Garden piazza in London, who rebuilt Woburn Abbey as a mansion appropriate for a 17th-century nobleman.

The 5th Earl, William, lived through five reigns and became 1st Duke of Bedford. The 3rd Duke did his best to squander the family fortunes; the 4th Duke, John, rescued them and began making the Abbey the treasure house it is today. He employed Flitcroft to rebuild Woburn as a Georgian palace, and filled it with works of art and furniture. Flitcroft's improvements included a hot-water bath and a water closet.

The 4th Duke and his successors greatly extended the family's Bedfordshire landholding – by 1877 it comprised about a tenth of the county. The 6th Duke engaged Humphry Repton to transform the park with lakes, wooded drives, waterfalls and a Chinese Temple. Roaming it are nearly 600 Père David Chinese deer, saved from extinction by the 11th Duke and recently reintroduced into China.

The 5th Duke, Francis, employed Henry Holland to rebuild the south wing, providing the family with more comfortable rooms than the cold, north-facing Jacobean wing. Flitcroft's west wing was always reserved as the State Apartments – strictly for entertaining royalty and other VIPs. More recently, in 1949, it seemed that dry rot had taken such a hold that the only realistic solution was to demolish the east wing and adjoining sections of the north and south wings. The family engaged leading neo-classical architect Sir Albert Richardson to clothe the two stub ends in appropriate style, and created a formal terraced garden on the site.

THE 'STATELY HOME BUSINESS'

At that time the present (13th) Duke was, as heir to the dukedom, grappling with death duties and horrendous repair and running costs. But he was absolutely determined that the Russells would go on living at and caring for Woburn, and to achieve this set about exploiting it. He did not 'sell the family silver' in the sense of parting with it – not to part with it was the object of the exercise. Instead, he 'sold' Woburn as a tourist attraction. In this way he effectively pioneered the modern 'Stately Homes' business.

For centuries only the gentry had been able to view Woburn; now a broader public were given an opportunity to see how a Duke and his family lived. He also added greatly to its attractions and promoted them by very professional advertising to Woburn's new mass market; this was much frowned upon at the time by owners of other stately homes – but they later followed his example. And to boost desperately needed funds, the Duke made Woburn the venue for all kinds of events – they currently range from the East Midlands Doll Fair to rallies of historic vehicles and aircraft. One wing of the huge and impressive stable block houses an antiques centre with 50 shops and showcases set behind old shopfronts.

Woburn Abbey is now lived in and managed by the heir to the dukedom, the Marquis of Tavistock and his wife and family. They aim to provide a range of attractions that give all members of a visiting family a worthwhile day out.

Woburn has one of Britain's most important private art collections. Above: Mary I and Philip II, dated 1558 and attributed to Hans Ewerth (or Ewoutsz). Below: The Long Gallery is just one showcase for Woburn's works of art.

THE FLYING DUCHESS

Mary, wife of the 11th Duke, yearned in her youth to train as a doctor, but such a career was forbidden by her father. At Woburn she designed and built a cottage hospital, and during World War I helped to care for wounded soldiers there. She also loved flying, qualified as a pilot, and became known as 'the Flying Duchess'. One afternoon in 1937 she took off in her Gipsy Moth to view flooding in the Fens – and never returned. Wing struts recovered from the sea are displayed in the Flying Duchess's Room, and Woburn's public restaurant is named after her.

■ Knebworth is a part of the great heritage that belongs to all of us. At the same time it remains a family home. My children have grown up here, as I did. We love the atmosphere of the house and we hope that visitors will do so too. ■
David Cobbold

Above: Knebworth House is adorned with a fantasy of Gothic battlements and heraldic beasts such as this.

Knebworth House

KNEBWORTH

A ROMANTIC VICTORIAN PILE WITH SPARKLING MEMORIES OF 19TH-CENTURY LITERARY LIONS AND BRITISH INDIA: JUST OFF THE A1(M) AT JUNCTION 7.

Edward Bulwer, author of *The Last Days of Pompeii* and other best-selling novels and successful plays, inherited Knebworth House from his mother, who was a Lytton, in 1843. Armed with a romantic disposition and plenty of money, he added Lytton to his surname and transformed the old Tudor manor house, which his mother had already 'Gothicked', into the medieval fantasy of towers and turrets, battlements and machicolations, domelets and heraldic beasts that greets the astounded eye today.

Gothic horror films have been made here, and scenes for the remake of *The Big Sleep* with Robert Mitchum were shot at Knebworth, too. Inside, however, is no vampire's lair, but a charming old family home, with the warmth of five centuries of hospitality since Sir Robert Lytton built his house here in about 1500. There is a portrait of Sir Robert in the banqueting hall, as well as a painting of the room by Sir Winston Churchill, who was often a guest here. The door at one side allowed robust 18th-century drinkers to retire to the wine-cellar and finish a bin in peace.

KNEBWORTH'S TREASURES

A vast portrait of Bulwer-Lytton as a young man hangs above the noble main staircase, which was created by his designer, the brilliant John Crace, and on the landing is a famous, melodramatic painting of him by Daniel Maclise. There's yet another painting of him in his study, smoking one of his extraordinarily long cherrywood pipes, which looked like alpenhorns. The crystal ball he loved to gaze into is there, too. Crace designed the grand State Drawing Room with its Gothic furniture. There's one room in which, according to family tradition, Elizabeth I spent the night, and another which was occupied by the almost equally formidable Elizabeth Bulwer-Lytton, the novelist's mother, who ruled Knebworth from 1811 to her death in 1843.

Among the house's treasures are fine furniture and china, paintings and sketches by Lely, G F Watts and Rex Whistler, a crucifix which belonged to Mary, Queen of Scots, a ring owned by Charles I, a Dutch musical clock and children's toys including an engagingly horrible Japanese clockwork toad. The rare Chinese bronze, some 2,500 years old, was presented to the 2nd Earl of Lytton in the 1930s.

Knebworth's romantic, turretted exterior conceals the original simple, red brick Tudor manor house.

THE BULWER-LYTTONS

Bulwer-Lytton's son and grandson scored a remarkable family double as respectively Viceroy of India and acting Viceroy. The novelist's son, Robert, 1st Earl of Lytton, was a distinguished diplomat who was ambassador to Paris (and a poet under the pseudonym of Owen Meredith). As Viceroy, he formally proclaimed Queen Victoria Empress of India in 1877, in a ceremony of stupendous magnificence in Delhi. His son, Victor, the 2nd Earl, was acting Viceroy in the 1920s. A special exhibition at Knebworth, in the old squash court, glows with the colour and finery of the Raj in its great days.

In the library there's a display relating to Lady Constance Lytton, the suffragette, who called herself Jane Wharton to avoid being given special treatment because of her title when she was arrested. Sir Edwin Lutyens, who was married to her sister, Lady Emily, remodelled the Knebworth gardens. Following the death of the 2nd Earl in 1947 the estate passed to his daughter and her husband, Lord Cobbold, the distinguished banker, whose family have lived at Knebworth ever since.

FASHION AND THEATRICALS

Bulwer-Lytton was a notable dandy as a young man and one of his novels was said to have inspired the fashion of wearing a black coat for evening dress. He was an MP for many years and knew the most prominent and interesting figures of his day. Charles Dickens was a good friend and a frequent visitor to Knebworth, where he indulged his passion for amateur theatricals. In 1850, for example, the banqueting hall saw the great man and his amateur cast put on a play by Ben Jonson, *Every Man in his Humour*. The house has a collection of more than a hundred letters from Dickens.

Syon House

BRENTFORD

GLITTERING ROBERT ADAM STATE ROOMS BLAZE WITH SPLENDOUR IN THE DUKE OF NORTHUMBERLAND'S PALACE: OFF TWICKENHAM ROAD IN BRENTFORD, VIA PARK ROAD.

Adam's cool, classical Great Hall has fine decorative stucco work and statues by Joseph Rose.

The Dukes of Northumberland are the descendants of the formidable Percy dynasty, which for centuries held the north against the Scots. The family's northern seat is Alnwick Castle in Northumberland (see pages 160-163). Syon was their country refuge a few miles outside London, its grounds running down to a quiet stretch of the Thames – along which it could be reached more easily from the city than by road. The estate was named after Mount Zion in the Holy Land by the nuns who owned it at the end of the Middle Ages. In 1547 Lord Protector Somerset began to build the house that stands there today, though it has been greatly altered, and the two mulberry trees he planted in the grounds still survive and bear fruit.

Lady Jane Grey was fatally offered the crown at Syon, which came to the Northumberlands under Queen Elizabeth and James I. The 'wizard' Earl of Northumberland, nervously famed for his chemical experiments and his dabblings in the occult, spent time there when he was not incarcerated in the Tower of London. In the 18th century the 1st Duke of Northumberland found the place 'ruinous and inconvenient'. To remedy these defects he poured out money on the estate in quantities that astounded his contemporaries. 'Capability' Brown was called in to work his magic on the grounds and Robert Adam to design the State Rooms which are the glory of the house today.

During World War II 69 bombs fell on Syon, but the great mansion somehow survived virtually unscathed. Do not be misled by the heavy, battlemented exterior – the interiors are breathtaking. These are not apartments for anything as humdrum as living in. They are for entertaining, showing off, politicking, intriguing, flirting, gossiping and looking one's absolute best in, and they are superbly adapted to the purpose – a succession of brilliant rooms, each a satisfying creation in itself and also an integral part of a larger, skilfully planned whole.

The entrance hall at Syon has claims to be the finest in all England. Cool, quiet, soothing in grey, white and blue, it is staffed by statues of noble Romans in marble. Steps lead up to a second, contrasting hall which is ablaze with lifesize gilded statues on marble pillars in black and swirling shades of grey. Through Corinthian pillars you proceed into the delectable dining room, 66ft long and a splendour of cream and gold. The Three Graces pose sweetly in a roundel over the chimneypiece and above them, in a graceful compliment, is a portrait head of Northumberland's duchess.

There's another artful contrast as you go into the warmth and comfort of the richly red drawing room, which is hung with crimson silk. The carpet was designed by Adam to echo the ceiling with its medallions. Then comes the Long Gallery, a masterpiece of deception which is 136 feet long but only 14 feet wide and 14 feet high, but the eye is tricked into seeing it as far broader and higher than it really is.

In and amongst all this are family portraits, pictures by Rubens, Van Dyck, Lely, Reynolds and Gainsborough, Chippendale furniture, Sèvres porcelain, plasterwork by Joseph Rose, Vulliamy clocks, elegant busts and statues, ornate looking-glasses and chimney pieces. Outside, as well as the beautiful grounds, are an art centre, a butterfly house, a miniature steam railway, a soaring glasshouse which was a forerunner of Crystal Palace, and one of the best garden centres in the South.

Spencer House

LONDON

A SLEEPING BEAUTY OF A PALACE, AWAKENED AND MUNIFICENTLY RESTORED TO ITS 18TH-CENTURY GLAMOUR: OFF ST JAMES'S STREET; NEAREST UNDERGROUND – GREEN PARK.

London's last remaining aristocratic 18th-century palace belongs to the Earls Spencer, The Princess of Wales's family, though they have not occupied it for many years – it was used as a ladies' club in the 1920s and 1930s, as offices after the war and is now let to Lord Rothschild's investment company, which is estimated to have spent some £16-17million so far on restoring the magnificent principal apartments.

The house was built as a classical temple of love, bounteous hospitality and the arts for the young John Spencer, the 1st Earl Spencer, and his childhood sweetheart and bride, Georgiana Poyntz. They were secretly married in 1755 and, being young, in love and colossally rich, they built themselves a sumptuous neo-classical style town house. Lord Spencer's architect, John Vardy, designed the exterior and the ground floor rooms in the manner of Imperial Rome; James 'Athenian' Stuart decorated the upstairs rooms in the classical Greek taste and, as he liked 'an easy and convivial life', it took him eight years to finish them.

In a succession of superbly proportioned rooms of dazzling grandeur, the most extraordinary is the Palm Room, its gilded columns in imitation of palm trees – symbols of marital fertility. The Painted Room by 'Athenian' Stuart, one of the most famous 18th-century rooms in the country, is a celebration of 'the triumph of love'. The decorations of the dining room were described in 1772 as 'in the finest taste and the richest of their kind.' There is a most unusual and satirical statue showing William Pitt as the infant Hercules strangling Lord North and Charles James Fox in the form of the many-headed Hydra of radical Whig politics. Replica marble chimney pieces are being made by the Yorkshire master carver Dick Reid and his team, and the rooms are stocked with appropriate paintings, sculpture and furniture. Though Spencer House is mostly used for functions, the public now has a chance to feast its eye on a brilliant epitome of elevated 18th-century taste.

The Painted Room at Spencer House is one of the most famous 18th-century interiors in the country and is the earliest complete neo-classical ensemble in Europe.

Southside House

WIMBLEDON COMMON

A 17TH-CENTURY HOUSE, ORIGINALLY A PLACE OF RETREAT FROM THE PLAGUE: ON THE SOUTH SIDE OF WIMBLEDON COMMON, OPPOSITE THE CROOKED BILLET INN.

The owner of Southside House for many years was Mrs Hilda Munthe who, in 1907, married Axel Munthe, the Swedish doctor and philanthropist, best-known as the author of *The Story of San Michele*. Parts of the book were written in the garden at Southside, where the youthful Lord Byron had liked to sit years before. Mrs Munthe, a beauty who, as a girl of 16, had declined a proposal from King Alexander of Serbia, was originally Hilda Pennington Mellor, a descendant of Robert Pennington. He retreated here in the 17th century from a plague-ridden London after the loss of his small son, converting a farmhouse into this grand house.

The property passed through a succession of descendants, including John Pennington, something of a Scarlet Pimpernel during the French Revolution, helping aristocrats to escape, and a pearl necklace which fell from Marie Antoinette's dress when she was guillotined is still in the house. The house was restored after the war and there are family portraits and pictures by Van Dyck, Hogarth, Reynolds, Gainsborough and Burne-Jones. There are personal belongings of Anne Boleyn, distantly related by her sister's marriage, paintings by Viking Munthe, son of Axel and Hilda, and many other family treasures.

THE LAST RIDE

During World War II, after the house had been bombed, Hilda Munthe decided to retire to the country. She had neither car nor petrol, but a 100-year-old coach was discovered gathering dust in the coach-house. Upholstered in crimson satin, weighing two tons and with only the most rudimentary braking system, the ancient vehicle trundled gamely out on its last journey, driven by a local riding-master and carrying Mrs Munthe and her maid to Herefordshire.

Loseley House

GUILDFORD

A SPLENDID TUDOR MANSION AND HOME TO THE SAME FAMILY FOR FOUR CENTURIES: TWO AND A HALF MILES SOUTH-WEST OF GUILDFORD OFF THE B3000.

This beautiful Tudor mansion in its spreading park preserves both the mellowed stone of medieval Waverley Abbey and handsome panelling from Henry VIII's vanished Nonsuch Palace. Sir William More built his new manor house in the 1560s, since when it has descended to successive generations of the More and More-Molyneux families, and it has the atmosphere and the much-loved possessions of a cherished home.

The estate was bought originally by Sir Christopher More in Henry VII's time. The famous Sir Thomas More, executed by Henry VIII, was the stepson of Sir Christopher's sister and there is a portrait of him in the house. Sir Christopher's son, Sir William, was a devoted friend and servant of Elizabeth I. He was succeeded by Sir George, whose daughter Ann secretly married the poet John Donne when she was only 17; Sir George had his son-in-law put in prison for a year, but they were later reconciled. Elizabeth I and James I both visited Loseley on more than one occasion, and James I presented the portraits of himself and his queen which hang in the Great Hall.

The gilded ceiling in the drawing room is decorated with moorhens, mulberry trees and cockatrices – all family emblems – and the ornate chimneypiece, astonishingly, is carved from a single block of chalk. Queen Elizabeth I herself is believed to have worked the cushions on the two Tudor chairs.

The estate is well-known today for its Jersey herd and Loseley dairy products, and the house has often been used as a film location.

This screen depicting The Nativity, by Henri met de Blois is among the treasures to be seen at Loseley House.

Firle Place

WEST FIRLE

A TREASURE-HOUSE BENEATH THE SOUTH DOWNS, HOME TO THE GAGE FAMILY FOR FIVE CENTURIES: FIVE MILES SOUTH-EAST OF LEWES, OFF THE A27.

A line of great houses and stately parks lies beneath the northern slope of the South Downs in Sussex, and Firle is the easternmost. The Gage family have been notable collectors and the house is a living gallery of the lives and tastes of successive generations.

Today's Georgian mansion conceals an older Tudor house. This was later enlarged by Sir John Gage, a distinguished soldier and leading light of the court of Henry VIII. He commanded against the Scots in 1542, when King James V was killed at Solway Moss. He was also Constable of the Tower of London, which gave him the disagreeable duty of superintending the executions of Queen Catherine Howard and Lady Jane Grey; the future Queen Elizabeth I spent a period in the Tower under his stern eye. His son, Sir Edward, as Sheriff of Sussex, oversaw the burning of the Lewes Martyrs, but later, as staunch Roman Catholics, the family had to retire from public life, and their house was often searched for concealed priests and weapons. In the 18th century Sir William Gage conformed to the Church of England and he and his cousin and successor, Sir Thomas, rebuilt the house in the Palladian manner with rococo elaborations.

Items of special American interest in the house come through General Thomas Gage, younger brother of the 2nd Viscount. A career soldier, he served gallantly against the French in North America and married an American, Margaret Kemble of Morristown, New Jersey. He was in command in Boston in 1775 and his men's skirmish with the rebellious colonists at Lexington was the first encounter of the War of Independence.

A feature of the house is one of the finest Georgian staircases in the country and a splendid collection of Old Masters, which includes works by Van Dyck, Fra Bartolomeo, Reynolds, Lawrence, Gainsborough and Rubens, as well as Sèvres porcelain and French and English furniture.

Firle Place, home of the Gage family for 500 years, contains a diverse and remarkable collection of works of art as well as such historic items as this splendid suit of armour.

Glynde Place

Glynde

Memories of 'the Beauty of Holiness' in a venerable Elizabethan manor house: three miles south-east of Lewes off the A27.

In the gap where the Glynde Reach cuts through the South Downs is the village of Glynde, with its beautiful manor house (Glyndebourne with its new opera house is a mile or so away). The manor has been handed down by family descent, generation by generation, for no less than 800 years. The piers of its great gates are surmounted by ferocious heraldic wyverns, placed there when the house belonged to Richard Trevor, who was Bishop of Durham. There was a medieval house on the site long before this, though – the home of the Waleys, one of whom fought with Henry V against the French at Agincourt.

The estate passed to the Morley family when a Waley heiress married Nicholas Morley, and it was the Morleys who, in 1579, built the house we see today – a construction of Sussex flint, blocks of chalk and Caen stone, which had to be ferried over from Normandy by boat. Colonel Harbert Morley was a strong partisan of Parliament against Charles I in the 17th century. His wife was a Trevor, and it was through her that the house passed to the Trevor family, of Welsh origin, who had amassed their fortune in England under Elizabeth I and James I. In 1712 the Trevors gained their peerage when Queen Anne needed twelve extra peers in order to force the Treaty of Utrecht through the House of Lords.

The house later passed to Richard Trevor, who was Bishop of St Albans and Durham. The bishop left the exterior of the house as it was, but reconstructed the interior in the 18th-century classical spirit, creating the elegant Georgian hall, with its wooden columns painted to imitate marble. In the drawing room there is a picture of Durham Cathedral in Bishop Trevor's time and his portrait hangs with those of serried ranks of Trevors in the main room of the house, the gallery.

In 1824 the house passed by marriage to the Brands, who have lived there ever since. Henry Bouverie Brand had a distinguished political career and the colossal Victorian silver object presented to him in 1867 is one of the sights of Glynde. From 1872 to 1884 he was Speaker of the House of Commons, and he presided over the longest single session of the House ever recorded – it lasted for over 41 hours. On retirement he became Viscount Hampden, resurrecting an earlier Trevor title. His son, the 2nd Viscount, was Governor-General of New South Wales in the 1890s. The present owner is the 6th Viscount.

Paintings by Kneller, Lely, Greuze, Zoffany, George Richmond, Copley and Oswald Birley, with fine furniture and silver, Italian bronze frescos and Davenport china combine to make this a distinguished and lovable family home.

'THE BEAUTY OF HOLINESS'

Bishop Richard Trevor, who looked so wonderful in his episcopal robes that George II called him 'the Beauty of Holiness', inherited Glynde in the 1740s. The locals somewhat understandably thought him eccentric: he had the whole village inoculated against smallpox, which involved locking up each protesting villager in the stables for six weeks. On the other hand, he handed out a free tankard of his home-brewed beer to any of the locals who called at the house.

The home of one family for over 800 years, Glynde Place enjoys a beautiful South Downs setting.

Great Dixter

Northiam

Two medieval halls, charmingly blended by Lutyens, above the valley of the Rother: off the A28, on the outskirts of Northiam.

Great Dixter is best known for its garden, but the house is a treat as well, with its crazily tilted porch and spacious Great Hall. Like other houses in this area where there is little stone for building, it was constructed, in about 1460, of oak timbers filled in with lath and plaster. The household lived together in the Great Hall, a huge room open to the roof some 30ft above, through which the smoke from the central hearth filtered out. Its combination of tie beams and hammer beams, some of which are carved with coats of arms, is unique. The lord's comfortable solar or withdrawing room is still to be seen, too. In the following century the occupants of such houses began to develop a taste for more privacy,

preferring to have more rooms. Here at Great Dixter the open hall was split up with partitions and two upper floors were fitted between the floor and the roof.

Great Dixter was in a run-down state in 1910, when it was bought by Nathaniel Lloyd, a printer with a business in London. He called in Sir Edwin Lutyens to restore it and the hall was opened up to the roof again. It is exceptionally large – 40 feet by 25 feet and 31 feet high – and has a unique combination of tie-beam and hammer-beam roof construction. High up at one end is the squint window, looking into the hall from the solar, the 'withdrawing room' of the lord of the manor. This room retains its original stone fireplace and the fire-back bears the emblems of kings Henry VII and VIII. As restoration cut down the amount of living space, Mr Lloyd spent £70 on another old hall-house, nine miles away at Benenden, which was taken down, brought over to Dixter in numbered sections and reconstructed there, while Lutyens added a new building of his own in a suitable vernacular idiom to connect the two together. Lutyens also designed new gardens and the result is altogether a delight.

Nathaniel Lloyd died in 1933, since when Great Dixter has occupied much of the lives of his sons Christopher and Quentin, both born in the house. Christopher Lloyd, the well-known gardening writer, became a life member of the Royal Horticultural Society at the age of five and his many articles and books – which include *The Year at Great Dixter (1987)* – have made Dixter a household name among lovers of beautiful gardens. Laid out on the site of the farmyards, the gardens incorporate many of the original farm buildings, including an oasthouse which was last used for drying hops in 1939.

Haremere Hall

ETCHINGHAM

A JACOBEAN AND VICTORIAN HOUSE OF CHARACTER STANDING IN DELECTABLE SUSSEX COUNTRYSIDE: BETWEEN HURST GREEN, ON THE A21, AND ETCHINGHAM, ON THE A265.

Built of stone and brick in about 1616, Haremere Hall was substantially enlarged in the 1680s and once more in the 1860s. It is set in an ample park of 150 acres, looking out over the valley of the River Rother, not far from the Sussex/Kent border. The house was built originally for a family named Busbridge, who bought the manor of Haremere in 1612, and soon passed by marriage to the Temple family. In the 18th century it was sold to Sir John Lade, a diminutive Regency buck, gambler and gentleman-coachman, and friend of the Prince Regent, who visited him at Haremere.

From the Lades the house passed through a succession of other hands and is now owned by Jacqueline, Lady Killearn, whose husband, Lord Killearn, was British Ambassador in Cairo at the time when the substantial frame of the notorious King Farouk occupied the throne of Egypt. Farouk abdicated in 1952, leaving power theoretically to his nine-month-old son, but actually in the hands of a military junta, and died in exile in 1965.

Lord Killearn's knightly banner of the Order of St Michael and St George hangs above the main oak staircase, which dates from 1682, and there are handsome 17th-century fireplaces and panelling of the 17th and 18th centuries. The main part of the house is now available for conferences, weddings and other functions, and can be rented for holidays.

Left: Dating from the mid 15th century, Great Dixter was restored by Lutyens and is now most famous for its gardens.

Haremere Hall has seen many splendid social gatherings in the past, including a visit from the Prince Regent.

Hammerwood Park

East Grinstead

A TEMPLE TO APOLLO IN SUSSEX IS BEING RESTORED TO BOTH SPLENDOUR AND FAMILY LIFE: THREE MILES EAST OF EAST GRINSTEAD, VIA THE A264.

■ On a hot summer's day one cannot but agree with the discoverer of the dedication of the house to Apollo – that the main room of the house is not the hall, nor the dining room, drawing room or library where concerts are held, but the 'hunting room' – the delicious landscape park which surrounds the place and invites one outside. ■
David Pinnegar

Visitors to Hammerwood Park can enjoy their cream teas in the former kitchen below a replica of the Elgin Marbles. There could be no more appropriate way of ending a tour of this extraordinary Greek Revival mansion, which was derelict when David Pinnegar took it over in 1982. It previously belonged to the Led Zeppelin rock group and before that had been clumsily converted into flats. The dining room has been left untouched to give an idea of the scale of the desolation, while the Pinnegar family, who conduct the lively guided tours of their house, are tackling the restoration with heroic enthusiasm.

The house was built in 1792 as a grandiose hunting lodge. In spirit it is a temple to the Greek god Apollo, lord of hunting and the arts, and an inscription in Coade stone dates the house to the second year of the 642nd Olympiad. It was designed by Benjamin Latrobe, later famous for his work on the White House in Washington DC. There were subsequent modifications by S S Teulon, better known as an ecclesiastical architect. The house surveys in Olympian calm a beautiful view over rolling country to the south.

Inside the house antiques complement the elegantly proportioned main rooms and the noble hall has been beautified with a delicious mural by two French artists, who spent three months on scaffolding in Michelangelo style. At the same time, prams and Wellingtons scattered about the place are reminders that this is a family home as well as a showplace.

The murals which fill the walls of Hammerwood Park's Staircase Hall give an impression of ascending through a classical landscape of ancient Greece.

Michelham Priory

Hailsham

A REMARKABLE BLEND OF MEDIEVAL RELIGIOUS COMMUNITY AND COUNTRY HOME, IN THE LOCAL RED-TINGED IRONSTONE: TWO MILES WEST OF HAILSHAM OFF THE A22 UCKFIELD ROAD.

Michelham Priory is separated from the everyday world by one of the biggest moats in England, which was created in the 1380s by diverting an arm of the River Cuckmere. A substantial stone gatehouse was constructed to keep attackers at bay, but the moat was probably intended as much for seclusion as for defence. All this happened in the time of Prior John Leem, Michelham Priory's most distinguished figure and an agent of John of Gaunt.

The Priory of the Holy Trinity had been founded in 1229 by a prominent local family. It was staffed by canons of the Augustinian Order – not monks exactly, but priests living together here and serving the local parishes. After the Priory was closed down, in 1537, the house was turned into a country gentleman's residence, principally by Herbert Pelham, a Sussex ironmaster who bought the property some 50 years later. In 1601 it was sold to the wealthy Sackville family, of Knole in Sevenoaks, who became Earls and later Dukes of Dorset, though they never took up residence at Michelham.

The Sackville era ended in 1891, when Michelham was sold to James Gwynne, who commenced a programme of restoration. Work on the Priory continued from the 1920s by the Beresford-Wright family (whose money came from Wright's Coal Tar Soap). Canadian troops were billeted here in the 1940s and a plan for the ill-fated Dieppe Raid of 1942 can still be seen, outlined on one of the gatehouse walls.

Since 1959 Michelham has belonged to the Sussex Archaeological Society, and the tapestries, furniture, samplers and other items on show in the Priory come from its collections. They include a marvellous assemblage of musical instruments from the Alice Schulmann Frank Collection (Alice was the cousin of Ann Frank, of diary fame). These are on display in the Music Room, with its beautiful walnut panelling and modern stained glass windows.

There is a piquant contrast between the medieval religious sections of the house, such as the Prior's Chamber in the 13th-century Undercroft, and the later domestic conversions and additions. The outlines of the church and other priory buildings which were destroyed can be seen around the grounds, and there is also a watermill which is kept in working order. Other historic buildings to have survived include a magnificent Tudor barn and a 19th-century farmyard. On the south lawn is a recreation of a monastic physic garden, containing nearly 100 different types of medicinal plants.

Left: The name of Michelham is Anglo-Saxon for 'large piece of land in a river bend'. The river is the Cuckmere, which was diverted to feed the moat which encircles the Priory.

Goodwood House

CHICHESTER

THE DUCAL PALACE STANDS IN A HUGE PARK RUNNING UP TO THE CREST OF THE SOUTH DOWNS: THREE MILES NORTH-EAST OF CHICHESTER, BETWEEN THE A285 AND THE A286.

Famous for its downland racecourse, Goodwood is the Sussex home of the Dukes of Richmond and Gordon, romantically descended on the wrong side of the blanket from King Charles II. The 1st Duke of Richmond, Charles Lennox, was his illegitimate son by the fascinating Louise de Kéroualle, who was sent to England by Louis XIV as a spy. The family also accumulated the dukedoms of Lennox and Aubigny in France and the earldoms of March, Darnley and Kinrara. In the 19th century the 5th Duke inherited the title and vast Scottish estates of the Dukes of Gordon, and changed the family name to Gordon Lennox.

The unusual flint house was originally a hunting lodge, bought by the 1st Duke in 1697. It was rebuilt in an H-shape in the 1760s for the 3rd Duke by Sir William Chambers (the architect of Somerset House in London) and altered at the end of the century by James Wyatt, who added the towers at the corners as part of an immensely expensive plan to enlarge the building into a giant octagon, which was never completed. It was also the 3rd Duke (whose debts were titanic) who collected the superb Sèvres porcelain and pieces of French furniture while ambassador in Paris. He also built kennels of unrivalled comfort for his hounds and initiated the horseraces up on the Downs which developed into 'Glorious Goodwood'.

His nephew and successor, the 4th Duke, was a friend of the great Duke of Wellington, who attended the Duchess of Richmond's famous ball on the eve of the Battle of Waterloo (there is a painting of the occasion in the house). In the early years of this century King Edward VII used to enjoy the stately banquets given in Goodwood's ballroom for the race meeting, and the present royal family have frequently been entertained here.

Successive dukes have collected treasures which include magnificent Van Dycks of the royal Stuarts, Canalettos – the London ones painted from the family's town house – family portraits, horse pictures by Stubbs, Louis Quinze and Louis Seize furniture, 18th-century Gobelin tapestries, and Chelsea porcelain. In the Long Hall stands a monstrous silver centrepiece of colossal proportions, presented to the 5th Duke (a note comments restrainedly that, 'It has not been an easy object to house over the years'). A table in the yellow drawing room was made from twenty of the quarter of a million trees on the estate which were destroyed in the hurricane of 1987.

DEAREST FUBS

There's a portrait by Kneller at Goodwood of Louise de Kéroualle, the plump Breton charmer who, in her early 20s, was sent to the court of Charles II as a secret agent by Louis XIV. The part of her mission which involved gaining access to the royal bed was fairly swiftly accomplished, though her convincing show of resistance at first quite alarmed the French ambassador. Charles, who called her his 'dearest, dearest Fubs', remained attached to her among his many other mistresses all his life. After her son was born in 1672 and named Charles Lennox after his father, the King gave her English nationality, a substantial income and the title of Duchess of Portsmouth. She long survived her royal lover and all her rival mistresses. Voltaire, who met her when she was 70, thought her still attractive. She died intensely respectable in 1734 in Paris, at the age of 85.

■ Perhaps my favourite picture is Reynolds' portrait of the 3rd Duke, the predecessor I most admire for his vision. He filled Goodwood House with lovely things – many of them French and many gathered while he was British Ambassador to Louis XV in 1765. ■

The Duke of Richmond

Goodwood and horses have always gone together. This painting by Stubbs shows the 3rd Duke of Richmond and his family watching horses in training on the Sussex Downs.

Detail from Daniel Mytens' portrait of the Earl of Arundel in his Gallery.

Arundel Castle

ARUNDEL

THE IMPOSING 700-YEAR-OLD STRONG-HOLD OF ENGLAND'S PREMIER DUKES: IN ARUNDEL.

The gargantuan Barons' Hall of Arundel Castle, 133 feet long and 50 feet high, is a suitably grand tribute to the two great families which have owned the fortress for the last 700 years and more: the Fitzalans, Earls of Arundel, followed by the Howards, Dukes of Norfolk and Earls Marshal of England. The 4th Duke of Norfolk married the Fitzalan heiress in 1556 and generations of Howards have played leading and sometimes perilous roles in English life. One was killed at Bosworth in 1485, one defeated the Scots at Flodden in 1513, one was uncle to two of Henry VIII's queens – both of whom were beheaded – two more were executed and yet another, a Roman Catholic saint, died a prisoner in the Tower of London.

NORMAN ORIGINS

The castle was founded soon after the Battle of Hastings by the Norman warlord, Roger of Montgomery, to command the Arun gap through the South Downs. The 12th-century oval keep, perched up on its high mound, is where the medieval lords of the castle and their families lived, and the gateway through which visitors enter the castle is also medieval.

Almost everything else that meets the eye is of more recent date. The castle was badly knocked about in the Civil War in the 1640s. The 8th and 11th Dukes began rebuilding operations in the 18th century, but were far outdone by the 15th Duke, a formidable builder who succeeded to the title in 1860 as a boy of 13. A devout Roman Catholic and a leading figure in the Catholic Revival, he decided to rebuild his ancestral fortress in medieval Christian and heraldic grandeur. His architect was Charles Alban Buckler and the results he achieved are enormously enjoyable – enormous being the operative word. As visitors walk up the path on the approach to the barbican, Buckler's massive south and west fronts rear up, grey and churchly, studded with soaring, smooth towers.

The size of the castle, imposing enough from the ground, can be truly appreciated from above.

A REMARKABLE INTERIOR

Inside, the chapel, with carvings by Thomas Earp and stained-glass by John Hardman Powell, is a moving expression of Catholic spirituality. A deliberately understated stairway leads up to the surprise of the colossal Barons' Hall and its huge, hooded fireplaces, hammerbeam roof and paintings connected with the family history. The Long Gallery is crowded with more family portraits. Charles Alban Buckler was an enthusiast for heraldry (he was Surrey Herald Extraordinary) and the stone beasts which stand guard over the grand staircase hold shields with the family quarterings. The bed specially made for Queen Victoria in 1846 is still in her room.

The castle's riches include Tudor furniture, armour, tapestries and clocks, and paintings by Van Dyck, Lely, Reynolds, Gainsborough, Lawrence, Opie, Millais and de Laszlo. As hereditary Earls Marshal, the dukes are responsible for the organisation of coronations and other major occasions of state, and their baton of office can be seen. There are 10,000 volumes in the remarkable library, hushed and cool under its vaulted ceiling and solemn in dark mahogany.

A POWERFUL FAMILY

The Howards were originally a Norfolk family, with a long history in the county before they emerged on the national stage. John Howard was a strong supporter of Richard III and may have played a part in the murder of the little princes in the Tower. The king made him Duke of Norfolk and Earl Marshal in 1483 and he and his son both fought for Richard at Bosworth. The 3rd Duke, whose portrait at Arundel is a masterpiece, was a ruthless politician and courtier who could have given Machiavelli a lesson or two. He manoeuvered two of his nieces – Anne Boleyn and Catherine Howard – onto the throne as queens to Henry VIII and stirred not a finger to save either of them from the block. His son is famous as the poet Earl of Surrey, who was executed on a trumped-up charge of treason in 1547. The 4th Duke plotted to marry Mary, Queen of Scots and went to the block in his turn. His son, canonised in 1970 as St Philip Howard, was a zealous Catholic who was imprisoned for his faith and died in the Tower in 1595, possibly poisoned.

TWO FAITHS UNDER ONE ROOF

For 500 years the Fitzalans and Howards have been laid to rest in the Fitzalan Chapel, which is a rarity – a Roman Catholic chapel in an Anglican parish church, from which it is separated by glass walls. The church was built in the 14th century by one of the Fitzalan Earls of Arundel. The chapel was desecrated by the Parliamentary troops who besieged the castle during the Civil War, and was subsequently restored. Here can be seen the bronze effigy of the 15th Duke, who died in 1917. Besides his other creations at Arundel, he paid for the town's Roman Catholic cathedral. Designed by Joseph Hansom, the building contains the shrine of St Philip Howard, whose remains were removed to it from the Fitzalan Chapel after his canonisation.

'LORD THURLOW HAS LAID AN EGG'

Take care not to miss the stuffed owls at the foot of the stairs going down to the armoury. A special breed of giant size, they were imported from America to colonise the keep, but unfortunately died out. It was difficult to establish their sex and there is a story about one which was called Lord Thurlow – the butler appeared one day to announce, 'Please, Your Grace, Lord Thurlow has laid an egg.'

Parham Park

PULBOROUGH

A SUPERLATIVE COLLECTION OF NEEDLEWORK AND MANY OTHER TREASURES IN A BEAUTIFUL ELIZABETHAN HOUSE: OFF THE A283 WEST OF STORRINGTON.

On January 28 1577 'at about ten of the clock in the forenoon' the foundation stone of the new house at Parham was formally laid by a boy of two-and-a-half, Thomas Palmer. The Palmers, who had made money in London, came by Parham in 1540 after the Dissolution of the Monasteries. The estate had previously belonged to the monks of Westminster and the new house incorporated an older one on the site. An Elizabethan creation in greyish-brown stone, the house is today a treasure trove of rare needlework, paintings, furniture, tapestries, china and oriental carpets.

The principal Elizabethan room is the Great Hall, light and airy with its tall windows, a double cube with a moulded ceiling and carved oak screen, where the whole household ate together. There is an old tradition that Elizabeth I dined here in 1593. The hall also contains a portrait of James I's eldest son which, when cleaned in 1985, revealed a new and entirely unsuspected allegorical picture.

The Great Parlour, charmingly panelled, was the family's private sitting room in the 16th century, while the elegant Saloon was redecorated in cream and gold in about 1790. Upstairs, the Long Gallery is 160 feet in length and in the Great Chamber the four-poster bed has 16th-century needlework, traditionally attributed to Mary, Queen of Scots.

Thomas Palmer, the little boy who laid the foundation stone, served at sea under Sir Francis Drake and sold Parham in 1601 to Thomas Bysshop, who obtained a baronetcy from James I and whose descendants lived here for three centuries. In 1816 Sir Cecil Bysshop successfully claimed the title of Baron Zouche of Haryngworth, which had been in abeyance since 1625 and which, unusually, can descend in the female line. In 1922 Parham was sold to The Hon. Clive Pearson, son of the 1st Viscount Cowdray, and he and his wife devoted themselves to restoring and bringing life back to the house.

It was Mrs Pearson and her mother, Lady Brabourne, who assembled Parham's wonderful collection of embroidery and tapestry from the 17th-century and later, which is probably the best in the country. Their own work can also be seen in the house. There are also portraits and other memorials of Sir Joseph Banks, the great 18th-century naturalist who explored Australia and the Pacific with Captain Cook and had much to do with the establishment of Kew Gardens.

The Great Hall at Parham Park has always been, and remains the heart of the house. Its walls are hung with fine portraits and the room is furnished with Early English pieces.

Saint Mary's

Bramber

A BLACK-AND-WHITE VETERAN WHOSE HISTORY RUNS FROM MEDIEVAL INN TO MUCH-LOVED PRIVATE HOME: IN THE VILLAGE OF BRAMBER, ABOUT FOUR MILES NORTH-WEST OF SHOREHAM OFF THE A283.

This haunting and venerable building – the finest example of Sussex half-timbering of its time – began life in 1470 as a galleried inn, kept by monks for the sustenance of pilgrims on the southern road to Canterbury. Besides its huge black interior beams, it has a unique 'shutting window' from that time. After the Dissolution of the Monasteries, St Mary's was turned into a private house and in the 16th century it belonged to Lord Calthorpe, who was Queen Elizabeth I's cousin. She came to visit him and the beautiful Painted Room was specially prepared for her, with superb *trompe-l'oeil* pine panelling. A later visitor was the young Charles II, who waited anxiously in the house on his way to escape across the Channel to France after the Battle of Worcester in 1651.

In the 1890s the house was bought by The Hon Algernon Bourke, a son of the Earl of Mayo, owner of White's in London and a notable wit and *bon viveur*, who added the beautiful music room where concerts are again held today. Alfred Musgrave bought the house in 1903 and the Sherlock Holmes story of *The Musgrave Ritual* is set here, mentioning the two huge trees which stood in the garden until the 1980s.

In the 1940s St Mary's was only just saved from a developer who would have knocked it flat. In 1984 it was bought by Peter Thorogood, and the Thorogood and Linton families have been busy sensitively and stylishly restoring it. An unexpected bonus for today's visitor is Mr Thorogood's unrivalled collection of material related to Thomas Hood, the 19th-century humorous writer, while outside the charming garden has delightful examples of topiary and is said to be stalked by spectral monks.

Belmont

Faversham

AN UNRIVALLED COLLECTION OF CLOCKS ADORNS THE HOME OF A REDOUBTABLE FIGURE IN THE HISTORY OF CRICKET: FOUR MILES SOUTH-WEST OF FAVERSHAM, VIA THE A251.

Commanding beautiful views over the countryside and the Thames estuary from the eminence which gave it its name, Belmont was built in 1793 in dignified neo-classical style. The architect was Samuel Wyatt, who had worked under Robert Adam, and the principal fronts are covered in stone-coloured tiles, with attractive decorations in Coade stone. The house was built for a retired army officer, Colonel John Montresor, who had served in North America. Unfortunately, in 1799 he was falsely accused of embezzling army funds and packed off ignominiously to Maidstone prison, where he died protesting his innocence. His two sons, both generals, spent more than 20 years in a campaign which eventually cleared his name.

Meanwhile, the Belmont estate had been put up for sale by public auction in 1801. It was bought by General George Harris, who had made substantial prize money in a military career in India, culminating in the defeat of the Indian ruler of Mysore, Tipoo Sahib, at Seringapatam. In 1815 he was created Baron Harris, and Belmont has been the home of his descendants ever since. His son, the 2nd Lord Harris, had a distinguished

Belmont is pure 18th-century, though built in two stages. The original house, now the office wing, can be seen from the stable block at the back of the main house, which was completed in 1793.

KING IN FLANNELS

The 4th Lord Harris was born in Trinidad in 1851. A fine batsman, he was captain of cricket at Eton and Oxford, captained the Kent county side in the 1870s and 1880s, took a touring side to Australia in 1878-79 and captained England against the Australians at home. A member of MCC for more than 60 years, he dominated the administration of the English game through his mastery of the principal committees and he had a leading role in popularising cricket in India during his time there. He was Governor of Bombay in the 1890s and was said to have caused some surprise by wearing his cricket flannels to meet the Tsar of Russia on an official visit. He has been described as 'the uncrowned king of cricket' during the period from 1870 to his death in 1932.

Left: Belmont's drawing room is an interesting example of the Regency-style decoration of the period between the two world wars.

military career during the Napoleonic Wars and fought with conspicuous gallantry at Waterloo. The 3rd Lord was Governor of Trinidad and subsequently of Madras in India, playing an important role during the Indian Mutiny. He became a close friend of the Governor General, Lord Canning, and Lady Canning once described Lord Harris as 'so easy and comfortable in his manner, so amiable and agreeable, so full of appreciation of fun, a real friend.' The most famous member of the family, however, was the 4th Lord, a powerful figure in the history of Kent and English cricket. After captaining the Eton and Oxford teams, he went on to captain Kent and England, managing to combine his love of the game with an active public life.

A lion, which fell to the 4th Lord's gun in India and was subsequently stuffed, is one of many objects in the house related to the family's Indian connections. Tipoo Sahib's hat is among them, along with fine furniture and family portraits. They include a huge group of the 1st Lord and his numerous offspring by Arthur William Devis, with the future 2nd Lord in his Black Watch uniform. Other family portraits adorn the beautiful staircase hall – Wyatt's triumph – with its cantilevered stairs. The house is also full of marvellous clocks, from one of the finest private collections of the kind in the country. It was formed by the 5th Lord Harris, who died in 1984.

Boughton Monchelsea Place

Boughton Monchelsea

Time and tide have passed for four centuries since the young Robert Rudston built his house: off the A229, five miles south of Maidstone.

Built of the local grey Kentish ragstone in 1567 and commanding fine views over its landscaped, deer-grazed park and the Weald towards Romney Marsh, the Elizabethan house was given a Gothic and battlemented look during the Regency period. A succession of families have filled it with treasures. Boughton (pronounced Borton) is an Anglo-Saxon name meaning 'beechwood clearing', while the Monchelsea part of the name is a legacy from the powerful Norman family which planted itself here early in the Middle Ages.

In 1551 the manor was bought by Robert Rudston, son of a successful Yorkshireman who had made money in business. Described as 'a brave gentleman and of a very loving disposition', but also 'furiously choleric', he rashly involved himself in a Kentish rebellion against 'Bloody' Mary and was lucky to escape with a heavy fine. The expense apparently delayed the building of his new house. His descendants in the female line – Barnhams and Riders – followed him here in continuous succession until 1888. In the 1680s Thomas Rider installed the handsome main staircase that visitors admire today and around the turn of the 18th and 19th centuries Ingram Rider and his son Thomas gave the house its present appearance.

One of the odd things about the place is the length of time for which Boughton Monchelsea was undisturbed by the patter of tiny feet. In all the time between 1728 and 1903 there were children in the house for only 30 years, and for 98 years it belonged to two bachelors. For many years after 1945, again, there were no children here. Between 1888 and 1903 the house was let or left empty. It was then bought by Colonel G B Winch, who was chairman of a Maidstone brewing firm. Tragically, his only son was killed during World War I and his adopted son died in Word War II. Michael Winch, who succeeded his uncle in 1953, was another bachelor and the house now belongs to his adopted son, Charlie Gooch.

The local quarries which supplied the Kentish ragstone for Boughton Monchelsea Place also provided some of the stone for Westminster Abbey. The stone was equally prized for the making of cannon balls.

Chiddingstone Castle

EDENBRIDGE

THE IDIOSYNCRATIC ENTHUSIASMS OF A PASSIONATE COLLECTOR IN THE HOUSE OF A DYNASTY OF IRONMASTERS: TEN MILES SOUTH-WEST OF SEVENOAKS, OFF THE B2027.

There is a good view of the house – it is a castle only by courtesy – looking across the lake from the road out of the village towards Hever. The village itself is a showplace of wonderfully preserved Tudor houses, owned by the National Trust and frequently used for period scenes in films. In earlier days it belonged to the Streatfeild family, the rich local ironmasters who built Chiddingstone Castle.

Early in the 1500s the first of the dynasty lived in a Tudor house at the end of the village street, where the castle is today. In the 1670s the old house was pulled down and replaced by a new one, High Street House, which lasted until early in the 19th century. The Kentish iron industry had died out long before this, but Henry Streatfeild came into an inheritance and employed the architect William Atkinson to turn the house into a mock-medieval castle. Atkinson's plans were, in fact, a scaled down version of Scone Palace in Scotland which he was building for the Earl of Mansfield, but Henry Streatfeild had overstretched himself financially, and the building work was called to a halt with only the north and south wings completed. However, some cottages were demolished, simply because they spoiled the view, and a lake was installed, which is now popular with anglers. A famous bream of colossal proportions was caught there in 1945. Henry's son added the battlements to the roof and various other embellishments, but he, too, was unable to see the original plan through to completion.

The Streatfeilds eventually found the house too expensive to keep up and Colonel Sir Henry Streatfeild

Battlements and towers at Chiddingstone live up to the name of 'castle', but this is more a home than a fortress.

sold it in 1938. Troops were billeted there during the war, leaving it in a very sorry state, and it was later used as a school. By the time that the late Denys Eyre Bower bought the house in 1955 it was in a bad way. Mr Bower, originally from Derbyshire, had been an obsessive and eccentric collector since his teenage years – all the works of art displayed in the castle today were collected by him. He worked as a bank clerk, but spent so much of his time and energy collecting antiques that he was first moved to the most obscure country branch the bank could find and finally forced to leave. He then set up in London as an antique dealer. He made very little money, but the house today is a museum of his wide-ranging enthusiasms. Denys Bower died in 1977, leaving everything to the nation, and it was his hope that the castle and contents would be preserved, as they have been, intact. There's a portrait of him in the study, along with Chinese porcelain, Derbyshire landscapes, the bust of an Egyptian pharoah and the drawings chest of Telford, the great engineer. For a fleeting moment he thought of presenting it to the Institute of Civil Engineers, but the weakness soon passed. The mixture is entirely typical.

Mr Bower had a romantic enthusiasm for the House of Stuart and gathered a treasury of Stuart and Jacobite memorabilia. Charles I's linen handkerchief – thought to be the one he had with him at his execution – the spectacles of Cardinal York, the titular Henry IX, swords from Culloden and a steel knife captured from the Young Pretender's baggage after the battle. A particular rarity is the 'Bonnie Prince Charlie' bowl, rare because it was treason to make such items. All are displayed beneath the alluring gaze of Nell Gwyn, painted sexily in the nude by Lely.

When the tomb of Tutankhamun was discovered, Denys Bower was inspired to turn his attention to Egyptian artefacts, seeking the guidance of the great Egyptologist, Sir Flinders Petrie. He soon built up one of the finest private collections of antiquities, which includes a mummy lying silent and sinister in its wrappings, a crowd of little tomb figures (*ushabtis*) and a mummified cat some 2,000 years old ('Alas Poor Pussy!' Mr Bower characteristically captioned it). The striking Japanese collection includes exquisite laquer work – again regarded as probably the finest private collection in the world – as well as a typical Bower assortment of ferocious armour, swords, kettles and teapots, Noh theatre masks and articulated figures of insects, a lobster and a dragon made by armourers in iron and bronze to show off their skill. The collection of exquisite lacquerwork is probably the finest in private hands in the West.

Bower's interest in Japanese art led to an interest in Buddhism and he went on to amass a beautiful collection of Buddhist works of art, now displayed in the old east wing. There are some fine Stuart portraits in the Georgian drawing room – named the White Rose Drawing Room, after the Jacobite emblem. The Great Hall, in 19th-century Gothic, is a particularly impressive room and contains a working barrel organ – another of Mr Bower's little idiosyncrasies – which dates from *c.*1805 and provided music for both dancing and for family prayers. The kitchen has its old baking ovens and a handsome black 1860s range. Mr Bower has departed, but his engaging spirit lives on.

■ The trouble with white elephants is that you can buy them cheaply, but they have voracious appetites. ■
Denys Eyre Bower

WEALDEN IRON

In the days before the Industrial Revolution, the forested Weald of Kent and Sussex was a major source of iron. The area had ample supplies of both iron ore and trees for fuel, and the forests rang to the noisy din of hammering at the 'bloomeries' where the ore was smelted in kilns. Iron was used for nails and horseshoes, for pots and pans, for firebacks and fire-irons, for cannon and cannon balls, and in iron districts for tombstones, as can be seen in Chiddingstone church. The church has many monuments to the Streatfeilds, including a memorial to Sophia Streatfeild, who died in 1835. An intellectual friend of Dr Johnson, she was admired for her ability to weep on demand.

Haxted Mill

EDENBRIDGE

A FINE VETERAN WATERMILL ON THE RIVER EDEN: ABOUT TWO MILES WEST OF EDENBRIDGE ON THE MINOR ROAD TO HAXTED.

The double-fronted mill stands handsomely beside the road, spick-and-span in its smart white weatherboarding and red brick. A mark surprisingly high on the front wall indicates the height which the great flood of 1968 reached, not so very much lower than the old Victorian postbox which is let into the wall.

The mill is on the border between Surrey and Kent. The western half was built in about 1580, with the eastern part added in 1794. The older section stands on 14th-century foundations and this may have been one of the two watermills in Edenbridge mentioned in a document of 1347. The oldest certain reference to it comes in a will of 1361. The mill remained in use for grinding corn until 1919. After that, like most windmills and watermills, it eked out an existence producing animal feed for local farmers until it closed in 1945.

Inside, the mill is a maze of massive, ancient timbers. The 150-year-old overshot waterwheel and mill race have been restored, a much older wooden wheel has survived and there is a collection of machinery and exhibits from other mills, with a Cornish tin mine wheel, milling machines, grindstones and old postcards, photos and drawings. There's a steep climb up the three upper floors. The museum is open only for parties by appointment.

Hever Castle

Hever

Anne Boleyn, Henry VIII's second wife, spent her childhood at Hever Castle.

Royal romance, Tudor gallantry and Edwardian comfort blend sweetly beside the River Eden: three miles south-east of Edenbridge off the B2026.

Hever is not really a castle, but a double moated manor house in the north-western corner of Kent. There are four crucial periods in its building and family history – the 13th century, the mid 15th and 16th centuries and the early 1900s – and four famous figures dominate Hever's story. The first is the bewitching Anne Boleyn, second wife of King Henry VIII and the mother of Queen Elizabeth I. Hever Castle was her childhood home. She lived dangerously and died young when the executioner's sword cut through her pretty, slender neck in the Tower of London.

The second figure is King Henry himself, who came to Hever to court her. The third is his fourth wife, the distinctly unbewitching Anne of Cleves, to whom he gave the estate. The fourth, 350 years later, is the American multi-millionaire William Waldorf Astor, who rescued Hever from gentle decline and with admirable taste and judgement, and a mountain of money, created the romantically beautiful house and grounds of today.

The oldest part of Hever is the sternly massive gatehouse, which was built in about 1270 and today houses some torture and punishment instruments. There was a strong wall around the bailey, or yard, and the whole place was protected by a moat. Nothing else of much importance happened for two hundred years or so, until the appearance of the Bullens, or Boleyns.

The oldest part of the castle, still enclosed by a moat, dates from about 1270.

The Bullen family came originally from Norfolk. Geoffrey Bullen made money as a merchant, was Lord Mayor of London in the 1450s, was knighted and bought both Hever Castle and Blickling Hall in Norfolk. The Bullens rapidly ascended the social ladder. Sir Geoffrey's son, Sir William, married a rich heiress of the Butler dynasty, Earls of Ormond. His son, Sir Thomas Bullen, in turn, made a spectacularly advantageous match with Elizabeth Howard, of the Duke of Norfolk's family. Most of their children died as babies. The three who survived were George, born in 1503, Mary, born a year later, and Anne, who was born, possibly at Hever, in 1507 (but the dates are disputed).

The Bullens transformed Hever from a crude castle into a comfortable residence, built round a central courtyard. What is now the inner hall, with its rich Edwardian woodwork, was their Great Kitchen. There's a copy of the famous Holbein portrait of Henry VIII, with portraits of both Anne and Mary Boleyn, and the clock on the mantelpiece is a copy of the one which Henry gave Anne as a wedding present. The splendid dining hall was the Great Hall of the Tudor house and the linenfold panelling, minstrels' gallery and stone fireplace are careful Edwardian reconstructions of the Tudor originals: so carefully done that William Waldorf Astor would not allow any tools to be used that had not been known in the Tudor period. The locks on the doors are replicas of the royal lock which was carried everywhere that Henry VIII went and was fitted to the door of any room he occupied by his personal locksmith.

Upstairs, Sir Thomas Bullen built a Long Gallery, in the fashion of the day, 100 feet long and running the full width of the house. It was used for entertaining and for taking exercise on wet days. It is thought that Henry VIII may have held a formal court in this room. Today's court consists of fibreglass figures clothed in Tudor costumes, by Bermans and Nathans, the theatrical costumiers. They include Henry and Anne, Sir Thomas, Cardinal Wolsey, Sir Thomas More and others, posed in dramatic tableaux.

Anne and the King

Sir Thomas was a dedicated servant of the Tudor dynasty and his children were often with him at the royal court. Anne also spent time at the glittering court of France, and by the time she was a sophisticated teenager she found remote, provincial Hever painfully dull. From about 1525, however, life ceased to be dull – far from it. Henry VIII, who had already enjoyed Mary Bullen's favours, and would soon make Sir Thomas an earl, now turned his attention to Anne. He came repeatedly to Hever to visit her, usually without warning, bringing with him his numerous retinue and causing frightful disruption and enormous expense. Anne's mother complained bitterly, but Sir Thomas was rich and ambitious, and hoped to have a queen in the family.

Henry had a queen already, Catherine of Aragon, but she had failed to give him the son and heir he needed to secure the future of the dynasty. That he fell genuinely in love with Anne can be seen from transcripts of his letters to her, but she refused him. 'Your wife I cannot be,' she wrote to him, bravely, for he was not a man to cross, 'both in respect of my own unworthiness and also because you have a queen already. Your mistress I will not be.'

The Pope would not allow Henry a divorce. Wanting Anne and needing a son, he took a decision which changed the course of English history by breaking with the Pope and the Roman Catholic Church, declaring himself the head of the independent Church of England, divorcing Catherine and marrying Anne. They were wed early in 1533, when she was already pregnant. By this time, she had taken to spelling her surname more grandly as Boleyn and on 1 June 1533 she was crowned Queen of England in Westminster Abbey.

She had less than three years left to live. When her baby was born, it was a girl. No one could know that the little girl would grow up to be one of the greatest monarchs ever to grace the English throne, and Henry, desperate for a son, was profoundly disappointed. Poor Anne conceived again and miscarried, then bore a stillborn son, then miscarried again. In May of 1536 she was arrested and sent to the Tower of London on charges of high treason and adultery with five men, one of whom was her own brother George, now Lord Rochford. She wrote to Henry from the Tower, firmly denying the charges. 'But let not your grace ever imagine that your poor wife will ever be brought to acknowledge a fault, where not so much as a thought ever proceeded. And to speak a truth, never a prince had wife more loyal in all duty, and in all true affection, than you have ever found in Anne Boleyn...'

There is no reason to believe there was the slightest truth in the accusations against Anne, but Henry was ruthlessly determined to be rid of her. On May 19th she was beheaded on Tower Green with a sword by an executioner brought over from France. She had asked for a sword rather than the customary axe and had joked that her slender neck would give the executioner little trouble. She was buried in the grim little chapel in the Tower and there have been many reports of her ghost haunting the fortress – some say that she has been seen at Hever, too, a phantom in white, almost transparent. Her brother and her other alleged lovers were also executed. Ten days later, Henry had a new queen, Jane Seymour, one of Anne's ladies in waiting.

At Hever are touching mementos of Anne's short life, including embroidery which she worked. In the little bedroom that was hers as a girl are portraits of her and the prayer book which she carried with her to the block on Tower Green. In it she wrote, 'Remember me when you do pray, that hope doth lead from day to day, Anne Boleyn.'

Twice in the course of its history Hever Castle was found to be too small by the people who lived there. Unable to extend because of the moat, the Waldegraves simply moved out in the early 1700s. The Astors solved the problem in the 20th century by building the lovely 'Tudor' village outside the moat.

THE LAST GRANDEUR

Anne Boleyn's father, Sir Thomas, died a broken man, his ambitions for his family shattered. He was Elizabeth I's grandfather, but never had the satisfaction of knowing it. His tomb stands near the altar in the village church, surmounted by a magnificent brass of him dressed in his Garter robes with a falcon, the family crest, at his right shoulder. It was the last assertion of Bullen grandeur. Also in the church are many memorials of the Meade Waldos, later owners of Hever, including a stained glass window to Edmund Meade Waldo, who was a keen ornithologist, which is why there is an owl at St Francis's feet in the window. Close by is the window in memory of the 2nd Lord Astor of Hever, the last Astor to own the castle.

THE FLANDERS MARE

Anne's mother and father both died before the decade was out. The king took Hever for himself and presently bestowed it on one of Anne's successors, Anne of Cleves, known unkindly as 'the Flanders Mare'. After Jane Seymour's death in childbed – she at last produced the much needed son and heir, the future Edward VI – Henry was told that Anne of Cleves was a raving beauty, 'as well for the face as for the whole body'. Ambassadors were sent to Cleves, which was a small principality on the lower Rhine, to inspect Anne and her sister Amelia, and then Holbein was packed off there to paint them. On seeing the paintings, Henry much preferred the look of Anne. When she arrived, however, at the end of 1539 and Henry hurried to Rochester to see her, he was disagreeably disappointed. 'I like her not,' he announced.

They were married, but the union was apparently not consummated and the pair were divorced within seven months. Anne, perhaps thankful to have kept her head on her shoulders, was granted Hever as part of her divorce settlement and owned it for 17 years, until she died in 1557 and was buried in state as a Queen of England in Westminster Abbey. In her room at Hever are two portraits of her, one which is flattering and attributed to Holbein, and the other which is neither. Her room also contains the finest of the castle's many tapestries. It was woven at Tournai (then in France, now in Belgium) in the 1520s for the marriage of Princess Mary Tudor to King Louis XIII, and Anne Boleyn is said to appear in it as a lady-in-waiting.

THE ANNUAL OUTING

Among many Astor family items in the house are photographs of the huge gatherings in the 1st Lord Astor of Hever's time, when the entire staff of his newspaper, *The Times,* were brought down to Hever with their families by special train for their annual outing. It was always held on a July Saturday and the guests were feasted in giant marquees. The day's events included dancing to a band, competitive golf, tennis and shooting, swimming and rowing races and a baby show. Lord Astor was unusually democratic for his time, and the Hever staff were allowed to use the tennis court and the golf course, and swim in the lake, when the family were not on the scene.

The Staircase Gallery, built in 1506, is dominated by a portrait of Elizabeth I. There are also portraits of her half-sister Mary Tudor and of her mother, Anne Boleyn.

DECLINE AND RESCUE

After the death of Anne of Cleves, Hever was bought by the Waldegrave family, who owned it for 150 years. They were Roman Catholics and constructed the little secret chapel off one of the bedrooms, concealed behind panelling. In the 18th century the Humfreys family owned Hever for a time, to be succeeded by successive Waldos and Meade Waldos down to 1903. Hever mouldered gently away during these long, quiet years, as can be seen in a painting of it in 1850 by David Cox, in the house, where it looks like the ideal nesting spot for moping owls and moonbeams. During part of this period the local farmers were keeping animals in the ground floor rooms, where once Henry VIII and his gallant court had sparkled and shone.

In 1903, however, a whole new lease of life opened up, when Hever was bought by William Waldorf Astor. The Astors' rags-to-riches story had begun with a German butcher's boy, John Jacob Astor, who emigrated to the New World in 1783 and made a fortune in the fur trade. He bought New York real estate with his profits and when he died in 1848 he was reckoned the richest man in America. Under his children and grandchildren the family fortunes prospered and the Astor empire grew.

William Waldorf Astor was a great-grandson of the original John Jacob, and rich from his cradle. Highly educated and cultivated, he was Ambassador to Italy in the 1880s and when he left the United States for good in 1890 he was estimated to have taken no less than $100 million with him (worth at least ten times as much today). He bought Cliveden in Buckinghamshire in 1893 and Hever ten years later. He was not a man to spare trouble or expense. At Hever he had the River Eden and the main road moved further away from the house. This was in order to make room for a warren of extra rooms for guests and staff, artfully designed by the architect F L Pearson to look convincingly like a variegated Tudor village from the outside, but actually all one complex. The Astor family sometimes lived in the Tudor Village, sometimes in the old house.

Mr Astor – who was later created Viscount Astor – had 800 men working for two years to dig out a handsome lake in the grounds, which he beautified with walled gardens in the Italian style. In the old house he restored the exterior and many of the original Tudor rooms, but in the Tudor Village he created marvellously comfortable apartments in the style of his own time, with luxurious bathrooms, modern plumbing and carefully concealed central heating and electricity. Agents were sent out, amply provided with funds, to buy paintings, furniture, tapestries, carpets and *objets d'art* with which to furnish the apartments. The result was a harmonious arrangement which contrived triumphantly to both blend and contrast the Tudor and Edwardian elements.

As you proceed round the house, you have to keep mentally switching from the 16th century to the 20th and back. The drawing room, morning room and library are wonderfully luxurious Edwardian creations, but at the same time eminently liveable-in. You feel you could sink into one of the comfortable chairs and stay there happily for ever, nibbling the occasional crumpet from a silver dish or enjoying a gargantuan cigar. Astor employed the great craftsman W S Frith, whose work in the house includes the carvings in the library in an iron-hard South American wood called sabicu (it is so dense that it will not float). Other items to look out for include Astor family portraits, walnut chairs of Charles II's time, sumptuous Persian carpets, beautiful 17th-century marquetry, porcelain and Tunbridge ware.

Before William Waldorf Astor died in 1919 he had given Cliveden and Hever to his two sons. His elder son, Waldorf, who inherited *The Observer* newspaper, lived at Cliveden in Buckinghamshire with his wife, the famous and formidable Lady Astor, who reigned at the centre of the celebrated 'Cliveden set'.

Hever went to the younger son, John Jacob Astor V, who was an MP, took control of *The Times* newspaper and was created Baron Astor of Hever in 1956. He was succeeded at Hever by his son Gavin, 2nd Lord Astor of Hever, who opened Hever to the public for the first time, in 1963.

The 2nd Lord Astor died in 1984, a year after selling Hever to the present owners, Broadland Properties Ltd. Besides keeping the castle and grounds open, Broadland Properties has developed the Tudor Village as a centre for conferences, corporate entertainment and private functions. Outside in the grounds there is a maze and some fine topiary work, and the new Guthrie Miniature Model House Collection of three period houses. Made to one twelfth of real scale, they are like exceedingly grand dolls' houses, furnished in style to depict English country house life over the centuries. Special events which take place during the season include a lively summer theatre festival.

Above: The Inner Courtyard at Hever shows both 1[illegible]- and 15th-century building.

This portrait of Henry VIII by Holbein hangs in the Inner Hall of the castle.

Lullingstone Castle

EYNSFORD

MEMORIES OF HENRY VIII AND QUEEN ANNE CLING TO THIS HISTORIC MANSION IN THE DARENTH VALLEY: ABOUT ONE AND A HALF MILES SOUTH-WEST OF EYNSFORD, OFF THE A225 SEVENOAKS ROAD.

When Queen Anne went to visit Percival Hart at Lullingstone Castle, he provided a new staircase for her to reach the State Drawing Room. It was specially designed with shallow treads to help the queen heave her colossal weight upstairs. There's a portrait of her in her royal robes in the room, and also one of her favourite dolls, but the room itself dates from Queen Elizabeth's time and has a remarkable barrel ceiling with medallions of Roman worthies. Next door is Queen Anne's Bedroom and its fine four-poster bed of the period, and a tiny room opening off it was the royal powder closet.

The history of the house goes back well before Queen Anne's time. Hiding behind its Georgian exterior is a Tudor manor house, built in the time of Henry VII by Sir John Peche, who in the royal jousts in 1494 won the prize of a golden ring set with a ruby. His jousting helm is still at Lullingstone and the flat area west of the massive Tudor gatehouse was the jousting ground. He became a close friend of Henry VIII, who often visited him at Lullingstone.

Sir John was succeeded by his nephew, Sir Percyval Hart, who died in 1580 after being Chief Server to all the sovereigns from Henry VIII to Elizabeth I. His portrait in the house shows him with the silver knife, the symbol of his office, at his belt. The last of the Harts was the Percival who entertained Queen Anne, a stout Jacobite. When he died in 1738, Lullingstone went by marriage to the Dyke family and the Hart Dykes have owned the house ever since. One of them, Sir William Hart Dyke in the 19th century, helped to draw up the rules of lawn tennis. There is fine embroidery by his daughter in the house and a splendid array of family portraits, with much heraldry and armour. The church near the house contains magnificent monuments of the owners of the house from Sir John Peche onwards.

Quex Park

BIRCHINGTON

TRIUMPHS OF THE TAXIDERMIST'S ART PROWL, SNARL AND GRAZE AT THE POWELL-COTTON MANSION IN THANET: ABOUT THREE MILES SOUTH-WEST OF MARGATE OFF THE A28.

■ I was born at Quex over 70 years ago and although I served abroad for much of my working life, I always returned to the quiet and peace of Quex with a feeling of content and of welcome, which I believe today's visitors still sense in the smaller family rooms in the house such as the library and the boudoir. ■
Christopher Powell-Cotton

Major Percy Powell-Cotton, who inherited the family estate of Quex Park in 1894, was a formidable naturalist, hunter, explorer and collector who loved 'to wander in distant lands'. He wandered to some effect, making 28 expeditions to Africa and Asia, shooting hundreds of animals. Bringing his specimens back home, he had them stuffed by the London taxidermy firm of Rowland Hill, the masters of the craft, and displayed in dioramas of their natural habitats. In one of them is the lion which savaged him, almost fatally, in Africa in 1905. The jacket which the lion tore to bits can still be seen in the museum.

Powell-Cotton pioneered this type of display and the house at Birchington became home to more and more of his exotic exhibits, which started in the billiard room, colonised the house from there and spilled over into a specially built pavilion outside. The major opened his museum to the public in 1921. By the time he died in 1940, aged 74, there were 500 animal specimens as well as thousands more objects gathered on his travels, one of the finest African collections ever put together, an enormous assemblage of cannon and firearms, and a unique collection of Chinese imperial porcelain, from the 17th century on. The collections are now in a purpose-built museum next to the house, where the Powell-Cotton family still live.

Stuffed animals are out of favour today, but although Powell-Cotton was a keen and deadly shot, he was also a genuine scientist, concerned to preserve specimens for serious study. He financed his expeditions by developing the family's London estate in West Hampstead. The curious name Quex comes from the Quek family, which owned the estate during the 15th century. It later belonged to Charles James Fox for a time and subsequently to John Powell Powell, who had a new house designed for him by Thomas Hardwick in 1805. Having a passion for bellringing, he also constructed one of the strangest objects in Kent, a brick Gothic tower 124 feet tall with a soaring iron spire, to house a peal of 12 bells specially cast for him and still in working order.

From Powell, Quex passed to the Cottons, who changed their name to Powell-Cotton and in 1883 substantially enlarged the house. Today, as well as the dioramas and museum exhibits, many of the rooms in Quex House are still much as they were in Major Powell-Cotton's time, delightfully furnished in the Edwardian manner, and set in 250 acres of park and woodland.

These carved and painted heads from the former French Congo are among the ethnographical collections displayed in the galleries at Quex Park.

Squerryes Court

WESTERHAM

A CHARMING KENTISH HOUSE HAS BEEN CHERISHED BY THE SAME FAMILY FOR OVER 250 YEARS: ON THE WESTERN EDGE OF WESTERHAM OFF THE A25.

The manor house in mellow red brick is in the William-and-Mary style, though it actually dates from Charles II's reign. In the 18th century it was owned by the Villiers family, Earls of Jersey. Meanwhile, a Yorkshireman named Sir Patience Warde had made himself a fortune in London (his father, having had one daughter and six sons, insisted that if he had another son he would call him Patience). Sir Patience became Lord Mayor of London in 1680, just as Squerryes was about to be built. The two strands came together in 1731, when the 3rd Earl of Jersey sold Squerryes to his friend John Warde, who was Sir Patience's great-nephew. The Wardes have lived there ever since and the house is a delightful monument to the family.

There is also a strong connection with General Wolfe, the famous 18th-century soldier who grew up at Quebec House nearby. As a boy he was a friend of the young Wardes. A monument in the garden marks the spot where he was given his first commission and a room in the house is devoted to his memory. The portrait of him as a boy by Benjamin West was commissioned by George Warde and in a glass case is Wolfe's mother's alarming hand-written recipe for a medicine for consumption, involving ground snail-shells and earthworms freshly sliced with herbs, all simmered in milk and taken two spoonfuls at a time. The two 18th-century mahogany library or cock-fighting chairs in the room make an unusual matched pair. They are equipped with adjustable writing pads and compartments for writing materials.

The second John Warde, son of the one who bought the house, collected Dutch and Italian paintings. The successive generations of Wardes are commemorated by a fine array of family portraits and there are pictures in the house by Van Dyck, Ruysdael, Stubbs and Opie, and a giant portrait of Philip II of Spain in which the figure of Fame was painted by Rubens. Fine furniture and clocks, china, mirrors, Soho tapestries and lacquer work are added attractions and in the beautiful grounds can be seen a circular 18th-century dovecote. All the pigeons were exterminated during World War I because their depredations in the neighbourhood were felt to be a negative contribution to the war effort.

THE FATHER OF FOXHUNTING

Many of the Wardes were notable horsemen and lovers of hunting, especially the John Warde who has been nicknamed the Father of Foxhunting. A large and cheerful man, he is said to have been the first person to have kept hounds exclusively for foxhunting (stag hunting is much older) and he was a Master of Foxhounds for 57 years. In the house is a portrait of him, painted in 1829 on the horse which he bought from a gin merchant and christened 'Blue Ruin'.

■ We feel fortunate to live at Squerryes and hope to be able to share the treasures of this lovely house with others for many years to come. ■
John Warde

Squerryes Court is a fine example of late 17th-century domestic architecture, which remains largely as it was when it was first built.

Central England and East Anglia

The contrast between the Duke of Rutland's two great Midlands houses, Haddon Hall, immemorial in medieval stone, and Belvoir Castle magnificent in 19th-century mock-Gothic, conveys that this region of England has a lesson in architectural styles to teach. It starts with the mighty medieval fortifications of Warwick Castle. From Tudor times there is the moated mellowness of Kentwell Hall. The Cecils' grandeur at Burghley House is expressed in a riot of Jacobean domes and pinnacles. Two of the grandest Palladian palaces in the country vie for supremacy in Norfolk – Houghton Hall and Holkham Hall – while Somerleyton Hall embodies Victorian lavishness. At Deene Park you can see the head of the horse that led the charge of the Light Brigade, at Ingatestone Hall there are priests' holes, at Stanford Hall memories of early flying. The same families have treasured their homes for centuries past – the Ishams at Lamport Hall, the Fanes at Fulbeck Hall and many, many more here in England's heartland.

Arbury Hall

NUNEATON

THIS CHARMING GOTHIC MASTERPIECE, SET IN INFORMAL GARDENS, INSPIRED NOVELIST GEORGE ELIOT: TWO AND A HALF MILES SOUTH OF NUNEATON OFF THE A444.

On 22 November 1819 Mary Ann Evans was born at South Farm on the Arbury Estate, a daughter for the estate's agent, Robert Evans. Under her pen name of George Eliot, she became one of the great English novelists, and Arbury Hall and its surroundings were among her earliest inspirations. Arbury features as Cheverel Manor in her *Scenes of Clerical Life*, in which she describes how the house grew 'from ugliness into beauty' under the direction of Sir Christopher Cheverel. In real life, this was Sir Roger Newdigate, who is largely responsible for how Arbury looks today. He is also remembered through his 21-guinea Newdigate Prize for verse at University College, Oxford, first awarded in 1806.

Arbury Hall was originally an Elizabethan courtyard house, to which the handsome symmetrical classical stable block to the north-west was added in the 1670s. Its main decorative feature is the porch, designed by Sir Christopher Wren. From 1748 to his death in 1806 Sir Roger transformed Arbury Hall into an outstanding work of the Gothic Revival. The light, exuberant style of the rebuilding was a reaction against the strict classicism which had come to dominate English architecture.

Entry is through the vaulted corridor known as the Cloisters, off which is the chapel with its late 17th-century rich plaster ceiling. In addition to the high fan-vaulted ceiling and marble inset fireplace in the adjoining School Room, look out for the embroidered stools which were worked by Sir Roger's first wife, Sophia Conyers. The playing cards and fans in these designs are a fond reminder of her habit of leaving things untidily lying around.

Past the Little Sitting Room is the saloon, which has amazing plaster hanging loops and lace-like tracery in its ceiling. The room also has full-length portraits of Sir Roger and his second wife, Hester Mundy. There is another spectacular ceiling, this one barrel-vaulted, in the drawing room.

From here, cross to the dining room, which was originally the Elizabethan hall, hence the great height of its fine fan vault. In addition to the Gothic splendour of the décor, particularly the high chimney-piece, among the portraits in the canopied niches is the striking painting by John Bettes of Queen Elizabeth I. Outside, the informal gardens extend away from the house and are a real joy.

The splendidly battlemented Arbury Hall looks out over lovely informal gardens.

Honington Hall

SHIPSTON ON STOUR

THIS ELEGANT HOUSE WITH ELABORATE ROCOCO DECORATION HAS SUPERB PLASTERWORK: TEN MILES SOUTH-EAST OF STRATFORD-UPON-AVON, OFF THE A3400 SHIPSTON ON STOUR ROAD.

Honington Hall was built for a lawyer called Henry Parker in 1682. A member of the Merchant Taylors Company, he owned a coffee house near the Temple and had other interests in the City. He combined these with his enthusiasm as a collector, and, for three separate periods, with being an MP. The house is in the Caroline style, built in mellow brick with stone quoins and window dressings, and a heavy wooden cornice. Henry Parker's eldest son died in 1712, a year before his father, and they are buried together in a marble tomb in the nave of the local church.

The family eventually sold the house to Joseph Townsend, also an MP, and from the 1740s onwards he made a number of changes to Honington Hall. He lavishly redecorated the interior and brought in the ornamental plasterwork. More drastically, Townsend inserted an octagonal saloon to fill the indent on the west side of the house's original shape, a 'thickened H'. The son of a London brewer, Townsend married Judith

Gore, an heiress and daughter of yet another MP, in 1744. The family's social standing rose again when their son, Gore, married Lady Elizabeth Windsor, daughter of the fourth Earl of Plymouth. The ceiling in the dining room and the large, classical temple-fronted portico now to the north-west of the house are thought to have been introduced by Gore.

Sir Charles Wiggin purchased the house from Sir Grey Skipwith, great grandson of Harriet, Gore's third daughter, in 1924, and it is his grandson who now occupies Honington Hall.

The plasterwork in the hall is thought to be by Charles Stanley, an Anglo-Danish sculptor and plasterer who worked in England between 1727 and 1746. It features six bas-relief panels, and two larger classical ones balancing each other at each end.

The grand octagonal saloon dates from 1751 and is a marvellous example of mid 18th-century English craftsmanship. A large and grand main staircase was replaced with a more modest construction to allow for the new room. The rococo plasterwork in the eight angles of the room represents the four elements and the four seasons. Every one of the 96 rosettes in the coffers of the ceiling is different. The designer's estimate for the work on this room was £600, including £100 'for a little carving, gilding and embellishment for the ladies'.

Ragley Hall

ALCESTER

THIS IMPOSING HOME, SET IN DELIGHTFUL GARDENS, FEATURES BAROQUE DECOR AND MANY TREASURES: ON THE A435 TWO MILES SOUTH-WEST OF ALCESTER.

Ragley Hall was merely a shell when the Seymour family inherited it, and they did not get around to filling it in until 1750, when James Gibbs designed the baroque plaster decoration with Britannia as its centrepiece in the Great Hall. Thirty years later, James Wyatt redesigned the Red Saloon and the two Mauve Rooms in anticipation of a visit by George III. He also built the stately portico and the stable block.

Architecturally, little has changed since then, partly because many of the later Seymours (who held the title Marquess of Hertford from 1793) did not allow it to distract them from their colourful lives. The 2nd Marchioness caused a scandal through her close friendship with the Prince Regent. The 3rd Marchioness inherited two huge fortunes from men who thought they were her father. Her husband was an avid art collector, a trait shared with their son, who spent his life in great luxury in Paris, and these two men founded the Wallace Collection in Hertford House, London. The next pair of Marquesses worked hard on running the Ragley estate, although the 6th put more effort into hunting and shooting. Incidentally, in 1916, he personally captured the German machine gun displayed in the North Staircase Hall. He considered his son such a reprobate that he disinherited him, and the house was in a sorry state when it eventually came to Hugh, 8th Marquess, who spent many years refurbishing it. In 1991 he handed it over to his son the Earl of Yarmouth, who has continued with the restoration.

Apart from its superb interior décor, Ragley Hall is home to treasures old and new. The furniture is outstanding, and there are several Old Masters, including van Haarlem's *The Raising of Lazarus* in the Red Saloon. The dining room features several royal portraits and a collection of silver including a Paul Storr cruet set dated 1804. This room was used for concerts and recreation during World War II, when the house was a hospital. There is a spectacular mural called *The Temptation*, completed in 1983 by Graham Rust in the South Staircase Hall. It is one of a number of modern works which are displayed at Ragley Hall. The Hall is set in 400 acres of parkland with an Adventure Wood, and the Stables and Carriage Collection.

AN OWNER AT LAST

The Seymour family alone has occupied Ragley Hall, but it was not built for them. It was designed by the 1st Earl of Conway in 1679 for his own use, but was half finished when he died in 1683. It was inherited by his daughter and her cousin and fiancée, Popham Seymour, an extravagant fop and son of the politician, Sir Edward Seymour. However, she died, and Popham was killed in a duel. As a result, Ragley Hall's first owner was Popham's younger brother, Francis Seymour, later given the title Baron Conway.

The Great Hall at Ragley Hall is a confection of superb plasterwork, designed by James Gibbs in the mid-18th century.

Warwick Castle

WARWICK

WARWICK CASTLE IS A MAGNIFICENT 14TH-CENTURY FORTRESS PACKED WITH TREASURES: IN THE CENTRE OF WARWICK, TWO MILES NORTH OF M40 JUNCTION 15.

Warwick Castle is everyone's idea of what a castle should look like, from the forbidding exterior to the suits of armour and the baronial proportions of the rooms within.

You can easily see why the Normans built a castle on this site in 1068: the high escarpment offers a superb view of the surrounding countryside, and one side is formed by the cliff over the banks of the River Avon. The motte and bailey fortress was put under the control of Henry de Newburgh, who was to become the 1st Earl of Warwick. Traces of the motte (or mound) survive today, and it has been restored, but most of the structure today was built in the 14th century by Thomas de Beauchamp and his son of the same name. Funding was provided by Thomas's booty from the Hundred Years' War.

THE MEDIEVAL FORTRESS

They constructed the north curtain wall with its pair of towers, and the main gatehouse, through which visitors enter today. In the gatehouse there is an exhibition on the life and times of Richard III, who once owned Warwick and began some new fortifications before his death in 1485. The Beauchamps' masterpiece was Caesar's Tower, a 150-feet high wall tower with an unusual double parapet. This was once a prison, with three vaulted storeys of cells above a dungeon, where the unluckiest captives languished in damp murkiness below the level of the courtyard. The tower now houses a menacing collection of torture instruments. Some must have looked all too familiar to the younger Thomas Beauchamp, who was arrested by Richard II for conspiracy, and had a miserable stay in the Tower of London in what is now called 'Beauchamp Tower'. The family restored its good relationship with royalty, however, and his son Richard (a famously chivalrous warrior) was responsible for the education of the future Henry VI. Nearby is an exhibition devoted to the most famous of the Warwicks, 'Kingmaker' Richard Neville. The waxwork figures here are a clue to the identity of the castle's owners, for it was acquired by Madame Tussaud's in 1978.

THE CASTLE AS A FAMILY HOME

Warwick Castle was in awful condition in 1604 when James I granted it to Sir Fulke Greville, who spent a fortune on the house and grounds. The family lived here for 374 years, and earned the right to the lapsed title of Earl of Warwick. Some of the private apartments they occupied were damaged in a fire in 1871, but are now peopled with 30 waxworks including a tableau recreation of an actual weekend party of 1898; among the guests are the future Edward VII and Winston Churchill. This display is reached through the main entrance to the vast 14th-century Great Hall, the focus of medieval life at the castle. This, too, was damaged in the fire, and is home to a huge collection of weapons and armour, including that of the 2nd Baron Brooke, who held the castle for Parliament during the Civil War until his death in 1643. This is one of the six state rooms at the castle, which are sumptuously decorated in the styles of the 17th and 18th centuries. Look out for the intricate plaster ceiling and white and gold panelling from about 1760 in the State Dining Room, where there is a striking painting of two lions by Frans Snyder, a pupil of Rubens, over the fireplace. The finest room in the suite is the Cedar Room, named after its wonderful wood panelling, produced by local carpenters. The bed in the Queen Anne Bedroom was given to the 1st Earl (after the title was revived) by George III, and the room also contains tapestries dating from 1604 showing people and animals frolicking in formal garden settings. Right at the end, in the Blue Boudoir, is a formidable study of Henry VIII, whose cold eyes stare out from a solid, square face. In a small group of 17th-century lodgings around the Watergate Tower, the study is reputed to be frequented by a ghostly apparition of Sir Fulke Greville.

THE GROUNDS

Don't miss a walk on the ramparts between Clarence Tower and Guy's Tower, for here you get a strong feeling of what it was like to defend this fortress from attackers. The other benefit is that you get a good view of River Island and the tranquil gardens. These cover 60 acres and were landscaped by the great 'Capability' Brown. Peacocks roam contentedly through the grounds, which also feature a woodland garden, and a conservatory where a replica of the late-Roman 'Warwick Vase', acquired by the 2nd Earl, is displayed. Another attraction is the fully restored Victorian Rose Garden which, like the attractive parterre in front of the conservatory, was created by Robert Marnock in around 1868.

THE KINGMAKER

The most famous of the Earls of Warwick is Richard Neville, who earned the title of 'Kingmaker' because of his influence on who wore the crown in the 15th century. Having been largely responsible for placing the Yorkist Edward IV on the throne, he quarrelled with the new king. The ambitious Warwick led a series of uprisings, at one stage holding Edward prisoner at the castle for five days. He engineered the restoration of Henry VI to the throne in 1470, but the next April Edward proclaimed himself king again at Warwick Castle, and Richard died fighting him at the Battle of Barnet.

Hagley Hall

STOURBRIDGE

HAGLEY HALL HAS A BRILLIANT ROCOCO INTERIOR, AND IS SURROUNDED BY PICTURESQUE PARKLAND: ABOUT TWO MILES SOUTH OF STOURBRIDGE, ON THE A456 NEAR HAGLEY.

Hagley Hall has been in the Lyttelton family for nine generations, and the family has held this land since 1564. This last of the great Palladian houses is largely the creation of George, 1st Lord Lyttelton. Secretary to and chief favourite of Frederick, Prince of Wales, he was a poet, man of letters, politician and briefly (1755-56) Chancellor of the Exchequer. George acquired his Italianate taste on his Grand Tour of 1728-31, and this is reflected in the house, which he had built between 1756 and 1760. He celebrated its completion with a three-day house-warming party, and the house remains much as it was then. Although there has been a park here since the 14th century, the present landscape with its follies and Rotunda was created in the 11 years up to 1758. Amiable, absent-minded, but a model of integrity, George Lyttelton's character is a marked contrast to that of his son, Thomas. Commonly called 'the wicked Lord Lyttelton' ('Naughty Tom' to the family) he was remarkably badly behaved, and was a founder member of Sir Francis Dashwood's notorious Hell Fire Club. After marrying Apphia Peach, widow of a former governor of Calcutta, he published some pious verses in her honour, then ran off to Paris with a barmaid, though he did return to sit in the House of Lords. On the night of 24 November 1749 he dreamed that a bird changed into a woman and told him he had three days to live. He made light of it, but, true to the prediction, died the next Saturday. 'Naughty Tom' is said to haunt Hagley.

The Drawing Room at Hagley Hall is a splendid showcase for the Soho arabesque tapestries which are among the Hall's most treasured possessions.

Hagley Hall's splendid interiors include the intricate plasterwork of the White Hall, the spectacular rococo ceiling by Vassalli in the dining room, and best of all, the marvellously preserved Soho arabesque tapestries of the drawing room. In the 19th century the columned Gallery was found to be ideal for family cricket practice, with inevitably damaging results! Luckily, the pair of elaborate pier glasses, attributed to the famous carver, Thomas Johnson, survived the onslaught of bat and ball. A fire virtually destroyed the library in 1925, but it has been faithfully restored around its centrepiece, a portrait of Alexander Pope, who advised on the early stages of the landscaping of the grounds which surround the house.

■ One of the many reasons I love Hagley is its perfect symmetry. It is a joy to work on restoring a family home of perfect proportions and where such spectacular Italian plasterwork abounds. ■
The Viscountess Cobham

■ There can be few houses in Britain which have changed so much and so frequently as Althorp over the past 450 years: from country house to palace, to elegant stately home, and now to a successful blending of all three. It is a fascinating building, constantly giving up old secrets, while remaining a warm and much-loved family home. ■

The Earl Spencer

Althorp

Northampton

One of the finest private collections of art in England, housed in the Spencer family home: five miles north-west of Northampton off the A428 Rugby road.

In 1981, the 8th Earl Spencer, owner of the country house of Althorp, escorted his youngest daughter up the aisle of St Paul's Cathedral where she married Charles, the Prince of Wales. Princess Diana is not the first Spencer to become a figure of national importance – the family can be traced as far back as the 15th century, and many of them are recorded in the history books – the wealthy Robert, 1st Lord Spencer, was a diplomat for James I; his grandson fought for the Royalists in the Civil War and was created Earl just three months before he was fatally wounded. Later Spencers included a First Lord of the Admiralty and a Chancellor of the Exchequer.

Sir John Spencer bought Althorp in the early 16th century. The house dating from this time was built of red brick and was surrounded by a wide moat and formal gardens. It is likely that the house remained unaltered until the mid 17th century, when the widow of the 1st Earl of Sunderland roofed the courtyard over and added an imposing staircase to form what is known today as the Saloon.

The flamboyant 2nd Earl of Sunderland decided that the dignified red brick house did not properly reflect his position at court as a man of power, and set about altering it. He added Corinthian columns and a balustrade to the front of the house, drained the moat, and turned the Elizabethan Great Hall into a long gallery. Thirty years after the 2nd Earl's death the splendid Italianate stable block was built in warm yellow ironstone, and remains one of the best architectural features of Althorp.

In 1772, part of the roof fell in, and it became necessary to undertake some major repairs. George John, the 2nd Earl Spencer, planned to have his house made structurally sound with a few modest alterations. The

The Machiavellian 2nd Earl of Sunderland

Robert Spencer, 2nd Earl of Sunderland, has been described as brilliant, but scheming and unscrupulous. He lost his position of Secretary of State for trying to stop the Catholic James II from succeeding Charles II. When James was crowned, Robert promptly became a Catholic and made himself an indispensable adviser to the King. In 1688, Robert fled England after backing James against the Protestant William of Orange. Two years later he was back, renouncing Catholicism and offering William his services. Although greatly disliked, he had undeniable skills for turning situations to his advantage, and was a highly cultured man.

Below: The Saloon at Althorp was created when the inner courtyard of the Elizabethan house was roofed over in the mid-17th century. It now houses family and other portraits.

Below right: Van Dyck's double portrait of Lords Digby and Russell is popularly known as 'War and Peace'.

architect he employed, Henry Holland, had different ideas, and ran up a bill of more than £20,000, which included some new buildings, landscaping of the grounds, and a refacing of the whole house with grey-white tiles made to look like bricks. In the mid 19th century, the gardens were remodelled, and the 5th Earl added the State Dining Room so that food did not have to be cooked in one wing, and eaten in another.

Althorp has a staggering collection of works of art – far too extensive to be fully appreciated on one visit. There are paintings by Old Masters and 20th-century artists, Chinese and Japanese porcelain, and Chippendale, Sheraton and Saunier furniture. The famous Wootton Hall was designed especially for Wootton's equestrian paintings; the Marlborough Room contains works by Gainsborough and Reynolds; there is a room dedicated to the work of Rubens; the Picture Gallery has paintings by Van Dyck and Lely; and the 'China Corridor' has wonderful displays of Sèvres, Meissen, Nantgarw and Derby porcelain. The dining room has 54 matching mahogany chairs designed by George Seddon in 1800, together with sideboards and mirrors by Henry Holland.

Above: The State Chariot outside Althorp House.

Displays in the Armoury at Boughton House.

Boughton House

KETTERING

A SPLENDID FRENCH-STYLE PALACE, THE COUNTRY SEAT OF THE DUKES OF MONTAGU: THREE MILES NORTH-WEST OF KETTERING.

Although formerly a monastic building, it is difficult today to imagine a simple life being led in what is now known as 'The English Versailles'. The building was finalised by the cultivated Ralph, 1st Duke of Montagu, over the rambling Tudor house on the site. Ralph was a member of the Courts of his Stuart kings and of Louis XIV, where he had been sent as ambassador. His frequent visits to France and the palaces of Louis XIV gave him the model for his country home, as well as giving him a great love for all things French. He married a wealthy widow, the Duchess of Albemarle, whose finances doubtless speeded up the building works at Boughton in the 1690s.

Ralph spent a considerable time in France, not only carrying out his duties as ambassador, but also collecting treasures for his house. He returned with an elegant writing table from Versailles, but more importantly he brought back with him several Huguenot artists, who he commissioned to work at Boughton. They included Louis Chéron, who painted the friezes and decorative ceilings. By the time of Ralph's death in 1709, Boughton was virtually completed. Although Ralph had planned this glorious house, and his son had married the daughter of the great Duke of Marlborough, his dynasty did not last and by the end of the 18th century Boughton had passed by marriage to the Dukes of Buccleuch. Essentially a Scottish family, the Buccleuchs continued to live north of the border, leaving Boughton to survive in a comparatively unaltered state.

The whole building is amazingly well preserved. The colours of the many tapestries and carpets are unfaded and most of the furnishings still have their original upholstery. Throughout the house, the French influence can be seen. There are fine writing tables with Sèvres porcelain inlays, a pair of Meissen swans made for Madame de Pompadour, Boulle furniture and an outstanding collection of porcelain, including the personal dinner service of Louis XV. Among the English pieces are some delicate Caroline glass candlesticks, many tapestries from the Mortlake factory which was owned by Ralph, landscapes and portraits, including a set of over 40 grisaille oil sketches by Van Dyck. The collection at Boughton includes many pieces from Ralph's London Montagu Houses, one of which stood on the site which is now the British Museum.

■ **I, for one, am quite intoxicated by Boughton's atmosphere, which is further enriched by more positively identifiable factors. For instance, there is a unique blend of fragrances exuded by the panelling, the dust in the tapestries, the smoke from particular oak logs, together with seasonal variations from new mown grass and the great Philadelphus bushes peering through the south windows. To this can be added the mystery sounds, the creaking woodwork, a sudden fall of soot down a chimney, the whistling of wind through ancient window frames, the ticking of clocks and – hopefully no longer – the munching of death watch beetles.** ■

His Grace,
The Duke of Buccleuch
and Queensberry KT

Right: This print depicts the Charge of the Light Brigade which was led by the controversial, but heroic 7th Earl of Cardigan.

Deene Park

CORBY

THIS STATELY PART-TUDOR AND PART-GEORGIAN MANSION HAS BEEN IN THE BRUDENELL FAMILY SINCE 1514: FIVE MILES NORTH-EAST OF CORBY.

Standing in carefully tended gardens in rural Northamptonshire, Deene Park was acquired by Sir Robert Brudenell in 1514, and has been the family home ever since. An Elizabethan building was erected on the foundations of an earlier house, and a Jacobean range was added a few years later. The fine Georgian façade was added in the 18th century, but alongside all these major building works, Deene Park has been altered by each successive generation of Brudenells, resulting in a fascinating, if a little confusing, assemblage of architectural styles.

The house boasts many fine features. The Great Hall has original 16th-century panelling and an impressive hammer-beam roof. The 17th-century stained glass was badly damaged when an American war plane, complete with a full complement of bombs, crashed nearby and was only repaired in 1959.

The first Brudenell to own Deene Park was Sir Robert, a lawyer who invested his large fortune in land. His grandson Edmund married a rich heiress, but the marriage was an unhappy one. His wife died after a long illness, and Edmund's ghost is said to haunt the house, filled with remorse for his neglect and infidelity. Edmund's nephew Thomas was offered an earldom if he would send £1,000 to Charles I. Thomas quickly obliged, and the earldom was bestowed upon him after the Restoration.

The Bow Room now houses a magnificent collection of 16th- and 17th-century books. Many of them belonged to the 1st Earl of Cardigan, who lost them temporarily when Deene Park was sacked by Cromwell's troops during the Civil War. To his fury, the Earl was made to buy them back when the war was over. The White Hall contains a painting by James Sant of the 7th Earl describing the Charge of the Light Brigade to Prince Albert and his children. The story goes that Queen Victoria was originally included in the picture, but insisted on being removed after being scandalised by the Earl's flagrant affair with his mistress.

The 7th Earl's widow died in 1915 and towards the end of her life the house began to fall into disrepair, mainly due to the expense of its upkeep. It was used to billet soldiers during World War II, and by 1946 had degenerated into a sad condition. However, since then it has been painstakingly restored to its former glory.

This bust of Field Marshall the Earl of Cardigan can be seen in The White Hall at Deene Park.

MILITARY GLORY AND SOCIAL INDISCRETION

James, the 7th Earl of Cardigan, inherited Deene Park at the age of 40. He was famous for leading the Charge of the Light Brigade during the Crimean War, and infamous for taking a young woman 27 years his junior as his mistress. He eventually married her a few weeks after the death of his first wife, when he was 61, but they were ostracised by Victorian society. Deene Park contains many relics of the Battle of Balaklava, including the stuffed head of the horse Cardigan rode, and a painting by de Prades of Cardigan leading the Charge.

Elton Hall

PETERBOROUGH

THIS CHATEAU-LIKE PALACE IS AN INTRIGUING MIXTURE OF ELEGANT ARCHITECTURAL STYLES: SEVEN MILES SOUTH-WEST OF PETERBOROUGH.

An avenue of lime trees leads to the front of this splendid palace, which looks more like a French château than an English country house. The back of Elton Hall is even more glorious, and is a Gothic extravaganza of turrets, battlements, pinnacles, and pointed windows.

There has been a house where Elton Hall now stands since the Norman Conquest. The earliest parts of the present house are the 15th-century gatehouse and a chapel with fine fan vaulting. These were later incorporated in Sir Thomas Proby's Jacobean building completed in 1666. A hundred years later, more buildings were added using labour from French prisoners of war, but most of this work was undone by the architect Henry Ashton in the mid 1800s. Seventy years later, the 4th Earl of Carysfort added the large central tower and some more rooms, so that the remaining house is a complex mixture of styles and remodelling.

The guided tours lead visitors through room after room of treasures gathered over 300 years. Paintings by Gainsborough, Hobbema, Poussin, Henry O'Neill, and

Constable vie for attention with Louis XV cabinets and 18th-century ceilings. Also outstanding among the contents of the Hall is the library, which contains some early bibles and psalters, including a prayer book owned and inscribed by Henry VIII and two of his wives. In stark contrast to the cosy book-lined walls of the library is the flamboyant white and gold drawing room, designed by Ashton. Gilded chairs are covered by Beauvais tapestry, while the walls are hung with paintings by Reynolds, Allan Ramsay and Hoppner. The adjacent Octagon Room, in Strawberry Hill 'Gothick' style, contains cases of delicate Sèvres porcelain, some of which is from a service made for Catherine the Great of Russia.

The estate at Elton was granted to Sir Peter Proby, Lord Mayor of London and Comptroller of the Royal Household, by Elizabeth I, and has been the home of Probys ever since. Sir Peter's descendant, John Proby, was created 1st Earl of Carysfort in the 18th century. The Probys were very active in social and official life in the old county of Huntingdonshire – and before county boundaries were altered, the boundary with Cambridgeshire ran through the middle of the Victorian dining room, so that Lord and Lady Carysfort could claim to dine in different counties.

Elton Hall, a fascinating mixture of styles, reflects the changing tastes of many generations of the Proby family. In the foreground is the Victorian rose garden, planted with nearly 1,000 specimens.

Lamport Hall

NORTHAMPTON

THIS ITALIANATE PALACE HAS SOME UNUSUALLY FINE FURNISHINGS AND FAMILY PORTRAITS SPANNING 400 YEARS: EIGHT MILES NORTH OF NORTHAMPTON.

In 1212, historical records say that King John stayed at Lamport. Nothing remains of the medieval hall, and the earliest part of the building today is a stable and some foundations of a house which was enlarged in the early 1600s by the 1st Baronet. The 2nd Baronet, Sir Justinian Isham, commissioned John Webb, Inigo Jones' principal assistant, to double the size of the Hall. Webb was working at the time of the Commonwealth, when Oliver Cromwell's puritans frowned on displays of extravagance. The result was the plain, but handsome, 'Italian palace' which now forms the central part of the house.

In the 1730s, the Ishams engaged Francis and William Smith of Warwick to add to the original building. Further alteration and rebuilding work was undertaken in the 19th century by Henry Hakewill. When the 10th Baronet, the charismatic Charles Isham, succeeded to the title, he took such a dislike to the Hakewill design, that he commissioned William Burn to build a new façade to hide it. Charles was also responsible for the abundance of family mottos on the front of the house and in the High Room.

Lamport Hall is crammed with all manner of treasures, including 17th and 18th century Chinese porcelain, some beautiful early Victorian furniture, and family portraits than span an unbroken 400 years. The library is an elegant early 19th-century room which contains a bible belonging to Charles I.

The Isham family dates back to the Conquest, and they have lived at Lamport for 400 years. Royalists during the Civil War, they were penalised during the Commonwealth. The most colourful of Isham was the 10th Baronet, who created the 20 feet-high rockery in the garden. The garden gnomes that he imported to decorate it are reported to be the first in England. A Victorian eccentric, he was especially noted for being a nature-lover, a vegetarian, and a doggerel poet.

In 1976, Sir Gyles Isham, 12th Baronet, died, and Lamport Hall passed into a Trust he had founded with the aim that the Hall should be kept open to the public, and used 'to promote historic and aesthetic education'. Thanks to his foresight, the Hall and its estate are alive with activity, ranging from school visits and local exhibitions to live dramatic and musical performances.

Lamport Hall, a splendid classical building which dates back to the Commonwealth, is now devoted to promoting 'historic and aesthetic education'.

Southwick Hall

OUNDLE

THIS SMALL, ELEGANT MEDIEVAL MANOR HOUSE HAS BEEN A FAMILY HOME FOR MORE THAN 600 YEARS: ABOUT TWO AND A HALF MILES NORTH OF OUNDLE.

Although altered many times during the course of its history, Southwick Hall still retains much of its original medieval layout.

Southwick Hall in spring is ablaze with glorious yellow daffodils, although a visit to this handsome medieval hall and its interesting gardens is rewarding at any point during its opening season. Three families have owned Southwick since the first buildings were erected about 1300. The Knyvetts owned it until 1441, and the two towers, one in the courtyard and the other at the front of the house, are the remains of this early building. The circular stair turret, crypt, and 'Gothic Room' date from this period.

In 1441, the manor passed to John Lynn, who had married into the Knyvett family. He and his descendants lived at Southwick until 1840 and made a number of changes. The main part of the house and the west wing were built in the 16th century, and elegant Georgian improvements to the interior of the house were made 200 years later. The hall, Oak Room, and study date from the 16th century, while the parlour is a fine example of early Georgian architecture.

Being almost 700 years old, it is not surprising that Southwick Hall has played its part in English history. One of the Knyvetts was Lord Chancellor to Edward III, and another was taken prisoner by the French in the Hundred Years War. It was possibly the enormous ransom for his return that forced the Knyvetts to sell the house in 1441. Southwick was sold to George Capron, a distant relative of the Lynns, in 1841, and the Capron family has lived here ever since. They rebuilt the east wing and the stables, as well as adapting the house to provide more modern living conditions.

One of John Lynn's descendants, George, was a banner-bearer at the funeral of Mary, Queen of Scots, and there is a legend that her burial certificate is secreted in one of the walls at Southwick. The following year, George was required to pay £50 towards financing a fleet against the Spanish Armada, and it is possible that Sir Walter Raleigh himself may have visited the Hall. In the 18th century, another George, an amateur astronomer and meteorologist, set up a large telescope to watch the eclipses of Jupiter's satellites. The Caprons have served in public office as magistrates, High Sheriffs, and Deputy Lieutenants.

Rockingham Castle

MARKET HARBOROUGH

ONCE A ROYAL FORTRESS, NOW A FAMILY HOME, ROCKINGHAM CASTLE IS ALIVE WITH HISTORY: TWO MILES NORTH OF CORBY OFF THE A6003.

■ Rockingham has a magical quality about it, derived from its long and largely happy life, which captivates all our visitors as it captivated Charles Dickens. ■
Commander L M M Saunders Watson, D L

Rockingham Castle stands on a high hill overlooking Rockingham Forest, and was a stronghold in Saxon times. William the Conqueror ordered the building of a castle here in 1066, and it had close royal links for 543 years. Henry I planted a vineyard, King John hunted here at least 14 times, and Edward I made numerous improvements. In 1485, Henry VIII had a hunting lodge put up because the castle had fallen into disrepair, and it was the huge, imperious king who leased the castle to Edward Watson in 1544. He spent thirty years converting it into a Tudor home, dividing the Great Hall into separate rooms in the process. It was finally sold by James I for £350 to his grandson, Sir Lewis Watson, in 1619.

Sir Lewis maintained the Watson's good relationship with the crown, but his wife, Eleanor, was sister to the Earl of Rutland and her Parliamentarian associations divided the family during the Civil War. Poor Sir Lewis tried to play safe by sending his treasure to his brother-in-law's home, Belvoir Castle, but he was unlucky: Royalists took Belvoir, while Rockingham fell to the Parliamentarians. The badly vandalised castle was returned to Sir Lewis after the war, and its restoration took up the rest of his life, and most of his son's. However, by 1669 it was complete, and much as it is today, apart from some remodelling and the addition of a tower in 1838.

Visitors come in via the Servant's Hall where some of the Norman stonework remains, and then go along the charming cobbled 'street', once the centre of life for the self-sufficient community of the castle. Beyond the kitchen are the hall and panel room, once part of the Great Hall. In the hall (now used as a dining room), is a round-topped chest said to have been left here by King John. There is an excellent collection of post-impressionist and modern paintings in the panel room. Upstairs is the 17th-century Long Gallery, possibly the finest room in the house, with its Chippendale and other furniture, and more fine paintings. Here large parties were held in the 19th century and Charles Dickens produced and acted in several of his own plays.

Stanford Hall

LUTTERWORTH

A DIGNIFIED WILLIAM AND MARY HOUSE SET IN ATTRACTIVE PARKLAND BY THE RIVER AVON: FOUR AND A HALF MILES SOUTH-EAST OF LUTTERWORTH, NEAR SWINFORD, EAST OF M1 JUNCTION 19.

The Cave family has lived on this site since 1430, but Stanford Hall itself dates from the 1690s when Sir Roger Cave, MP for Coventry, commissioned well-known Midlands architect William Smith to build the house. Neither lived to see their plans come to fruition, and the building was completed by Smith's sons for Thomas Cave, 3rd baronet. Relations between Thomas and his father had been strained. He had angered his father by marrying Margaret Verney, a woman of unimpeachable ancestry but, according to Sir Roger, insufficient cash. The already tense atmosphere of the wedding was not improved by a delay in the ceremony because the clergyman was drunk!

The 5th Baronet, also Thomas, added the fine stable block and courtyard, and in 1745 put in the beautiful ballroom. Antique collector, barrister and musician, Thomas Cave was a lively and able man who also widened the nearby River Avon so that he could sail the sloops he built on it, and he is silhouetted playing the viol in a group portrait displayed in the library. The oldest of the 5,000 books and manuscripts in this room is a grant of land dating from 1150, and there is also an eye-witness account of the trial and execution of Charles I, and of the coronation of James I.

Thomas's collecting habits continued with his descendant Sarah Otway-Cave, who travelled widely, especially to Rome, and bought many of the items on display in the house today. In 1839, the abeyance of the Braye Barony was terminated in her favour and she became the 3rd Baroness Braye. It is thought that Sarah journeyed abroad as a respite from an unhappy marriage (from which there were nine children), but the details of her unhappiness were erased from her diaries by a puritanical member of the family. Among her purchases were Stuart portraits and relics of Henry, Cardinal Duke of York, last of the royal line of Stuarts.

When Sarah died, the estate was left equally to her four surviving daughters, which led to its neglect, but it was restored in 1880 by her grandson Alfred, the 5th Lord Braye. Further extensive work was completed in 1957. It is now occupied by Penelope, the 8th Baroness Braye. Most of the rooms at Stanford have their original panelling and fireplaces.

Above: Stanford Hall, together with its fine stable block, stand beside the lovely River Avon. Left: The ballroom is beautifully proportioned, with a painted ceiling, coving and shell corners.

■ The Green Drawing Room was my grandmother's favourite room before the last war. It is a beautiful room and we have recently started to use it again when we entertain friends on summer evenings. ■
Lady Braye

THE FERRET ELECTRICIAN

When Adrian Verney-Cave, later 6th Lord Braye, wanted to replace the old oil lamps and candles at Stanford with electric light in the 1890s, he had a problem. He didn't want to rip up the house's handsome floorboards to put in the wiring. His ingenious answer was to tie the flex to a ferret which was then encouraged to scamper under the floor between the two holes by the bait of a smelly hunk of rabbit!

This splendid boy's coat is among Stanford's treasures.

Holme Pierrepont Hall

NOTTINGHAM

AN EARLY TUDOR MANOR HOUSE, ONE OF THE EARLIEST BRICK-BUILT HOUSES IN THE COUNTRY: FOUR MILES EAST OF NOTTINGHAM, NEAR THE NATIONAL WATER SPORTS CENTRE, OFF THE A52.

Holme Pierrepont was probably built by Sir William Pierrepont at the end of the 15th century, when it was one of the first brick buildings in the county. Sir William married the daughter of Sir Richard Empson, Henry VII's financier. The family prospered in the 16th century, and the earldom of Kingston was bestowed by Charles I. The 1st Earl extended the house in 1628, but later in the 17th century the family moved to Thoresby, leaving the Hall as a dower house. Most of the Jacobean work was demolished in the 1730s, so the family allowed Holme Pierrepont to moulder until the 1st Earl Manvers carried out some repairs and stuccoed the walls in about 1810. In the 1870s the house was extended again, and a courtyard garden with an elaborate formal box parterre, rose beds and herbaceous beds was added. In 1969, after almost another century of neglect, the present owners, Mr and Mrs Robin Brackenbury, bought the house to keep it in the family and began extensive restoration. This has included removing the stucco exterior and restoring the garden, which is enclosed by the three ranges of the house, the fourth being the church.

Visitors enter through the old lodgings, with their wooden partitions and brick walls, where family portraits hang, and which still has its original garderobes (lavatories). Upstairs, at the east end of the entrance range, is a superb open medieval timber roof with cusped wind-braces. The Long Gallery features two Tudor fireplaces and some 18th-century walnut furniture. There are also two Victorian bedrooms with four-poster beds, one with original William Morris fabrics.

However, the main decorative interest at Holme Pierrepont is the grand wooden staircase with elaborately carved floral panels, dating from about 1660 to 1680 which leads down to the courtyard garden.

Belvoir Castle

GRANTHAM

DRAMATIC HILLTOP CASTLE REBUILT BY THE DUKES OF RUTLAND IN REGENCY GOTHIC: SIX MILES WEST OF GRANTHAM.

Belvoir (pronounced 'Beaver') comes from the French *bel voir*, 'beautiful view'; its site, on a hill overlooking the Vale of Belvoir, cried out for a castle. From Norman times, when Robert de Todeni, the Conqueror's standard bearer, first built there, it has always had one – though two civil wars and an early 19th-century fire meant that it was often in ruins or being rebuilt. The present castle – the home of the Dukes of Rutland, and arguably the grandest and most picturesque of them all – dates largely from the Regency period; it was designed not for defence, but for display.

The Guardroom at Belvoir Castle contains an impressive array of arms and equipment, including muskets and flags of the Leicestershire Militia, who used a tower of the castle as their armoury.

THE RESHAPING OF BELVOIR

By 1816, when fire devastated it, Belvoir Castle was already being refashioned to the designs of James Wyatt, master of the picturesque Gothic. What we see today may be regarded as the work of three people: Wyatt, the Rev Sir John Thoroton, the 5th Duke's chaplain, and Elizabeth, his duchess, who was a knowledgeable and gifted amateur architect. Wyatt's Gothic

THE 5TH DUCHESS OF RUTLAND

A sumptuous interior in cream, red and gold, the Elizabeth Saloon celebrates the role in rebuilding Belvoir of Elizabeth, 5th Duchess of Rutland. A Howard from Castle Howard, she was a knowledgeable and discriminating amateur architect. She entrusted the saloon's decoration to James Wyatt's son, Matthew Coates Wyatt, who also sculpted the statue of her which stands at one end, and painted the amazing ceiling: four huge expanses full of classical gods, goddesses and mythological incident. The face of Jupiter, immediately above the duchess and busily hurling thunderbolts, was an admirable likeness of the then Duke of York.

was reacting to dull Palladianism; Belvoir's castellated towers – pierced not by arrow-slits but tall Gothic windows – form a deliberately asymmetrical and highly dramatic grouping.

MILITARY MEMORABILIA

The grandeur of Belvoir's interiors is evident from the outset. The 'pre-guardroom' turns out to be a lofty, vaulted corridor, its roof full of elaborate tracery, its walls hung with arms for 200 men and a vast number of leather buckets, painted with the Rutlands' coronet and cypher and meant to quench any further conflagration. Here and in the guardroom proper are spectacular star-shaped displays of cavalry sabres. A little side room where the Duke traditionally interviewed tenants is still called the 'speak-a-word-room'.

The guardroom is, again, not what one might expect. The castle's entrance hall, it is a dramatic place of high gothic arches, opening into the equally impressive grand staircase. This part of the castle contains an array of historic weaponry, banners and other military items associated with army units with which the family has links: Leicestershire Yeomanry, Leicestershire Militia, and 17th/21st Lancers. The castle gives houseroom to the Lancers' regimental museum, which covers their exploits from 1759 onwards. The regiment derives from the 17th Light Dragoons, raised in 1759 by the 3rd Duke's eldest son, the celebrated Marquis of Granby, whose military exploits won him lasting popular fame via a host of inn signs.

ART AND DECOR

If the ballroom looks ecclesiastical in style, that is because Sir John Thoroton based his design on parts of Lincoln Cathedral. Set above the piers supporting its pointed arches are the arms of the Duke of Rutland as Knight of the Garter; paintings here include full-length portraits by Hoppner of the 5th Duke and by Reynolds of Captain Lord Robert Manners, who died while commanding HMS *Resolution* during Admiral Rodney's victory at Les Saintes.

The Chinese Rooms consist of a bedroom with walls hung in hand-painted 18th-century Chinese silk, its high-canopied bed covered with an embroidered Chinese silk bedspread, and its wardrobe doors gold-on-black lacquer, and a dressing room with hand-painted 18th-century Chinese wallpaper brought from the east by Elizabeth, the 5th Duchess. Her most splendid memorial is the Elizabeth Saloon.

The Grand Dining Room comfortably seats 30 at table under a many-panelled ceiling decorated in gold with various flowers in relief on a cream plaster background. This motif is continued in the walls, where windows and mirrors are crowned with arches similarly adorned. There are sculptured marble fireplaces and Regency mahogany sideboards by Gillow; above the fireplaces are full-length Reynolds portraits of the 4th Duke and his father, the famous Granby.

The picture gallery, with its domed gold-and-cream ceilings and semi-circular clerestory windows contains many fine 16th- and 17th-century paintings, but is dominated by the Great Bed, a lofty Queen Anne four-poster upholstered in velvet and silk, rescued from neglect in another of the family's houses, Haddon. Recalling the visit to Belvoir of the Prince Regent, later George IV, are the King's Rooms and the 131ft-long Regent's Gallery with its Gobelin tapestries illustrating *The Adventures of Don Quixote*. The chapel – still in use for worship – contains other important works of art and the tomb of Belvoir's founder, de Todeni, excavated from the site of the nearby priory he founded.

Kitchen and beer cellars tell of another age, in which the thirsty inmates of the castle justified having some 6,000 gallons of beer on hand; one immense barrel held 1,300 gallons. It was filled in 1816 when an heir to the dukedom was born, and tapped on his coming of age. The statue garden alongside the drive is a landscape full of incident, including six classical statues by Charles II's sculptor, Caius Cibber.

The painted ceiling of the Elizabeth Saloon is the crowning glory of what is probably the most beautiful room in the castle.

Burghley House

Stamford

An Elizabethan palace built by the queen's chief minister to reflect his success and ambition: a mile south-east of Stamford on the B1443.

This charming figure, 'The Wrestling Boys', is among Burghley's varied collections.

Burghley, greatest of England's Elizabethan houses, was built by fits and starts between 1563 and 1489, though mostly from 1574 onwards. Its builder was William Cecil, Elizabeth I's Lord Treasurer, her chief minster for 40 years and, from 1571, her Lord Burghley. He wanted a palace, full of splendour and visual drama, grand enough to entertain monarchs. It was and they were. He largely designed the building himself, aided by an Antwerp mason named Henryk, and its exterior was very much as we see it today. Though Cecil was certainly aware of the classical architecture of France and Italy, and indeed incorporated French decorative features, Burghley House does not follow that path. It is Renaissance without really being classical, and signalled a robustly English route for the architectural fashion of the age – an exuberant, uninhibited Gothic romanticism, full of riotous decoration and without the rigid symmetry found in its Continental counterparts.

The scale of the building is such that it can carry this diversity. In appearance it is not so much a house as a small city, set in the little principality of its walled park. Each of the four main elevations is different, ringing wide changes on a basic structural grid. Its projecting corner towers, crowned by turrets with cupolas, contrive to unify it. Its roofline is broken by a riot of ornate stair-towers, chimney stacks in the shape of tall paired Ionic columns, all manner of decorative finials and a pyramid-shaped obelisk which might at first sight be mistaken for the spire of a parish church. All this is indeed meant to impress, and impress from a distance – as it does when seen through Jean Tijou's superb wrought-iron, gilded west gates. These gates were, in fact, commissioned by a later Cecil, John, 5th Earl of Exeter, who in the last quarter of the 17th century combed Europe for pictures, tapestries and furniture to adorn his house. He also recruited the finest craftsmen from far and wide – the Frenchman, Tijou, the painter Louis Laguerre, that prince among wood-carvers, Grinling Gibbons with his pupils, and yet another painter, the Italian Antonio Verrio, fresh from the royal palaces of Windsor and Hampton Court.

THE STATE APARTMENTS

Verrio was responsible for the great sequence of state apartments, called the George Rooms, which brought the baroque to Burghley. These six rooms give the effect of being peopled even when empty, because of paintings and tapestries covering the walls, and above all Verrio's ceilings. The Heaven Room is the ultimate masterpiece – walls and ceiling filled with an immense population of mythological beings who, thanks to superlative *trompe-l'oeil* technique, seem to be spilling into the room and about to invade its central space and furniture. Are these columns and pediments structural or painted? Are those heroic smiths with hammers mere static two-dimensional creatures? We almost hear the clang of their hammers and feel the sparks from their anvil.

In the 18th century the 9th Earl enlisted 'Capability' Brown not only to redesign the grounds, but also to make changes to the buildings, though in a way which would be respectful of the 5th Earl's improvements. In the 19th century the George Rooms were visited by Queen Victoria and Prince Albert; their host, the 2nd Marquis, had decorated for them the magnificent scarlet and gold tester bed, one of four spectacular state beds in the house, all now restored to their former glory. Of Burghley's original Elizabethan interiors, three survive: the Great Hall, its double hammer-beam roof an essentially medieval structure, its chimneypiece following a 16th-century model; the old kitchen, whose vaulted ceiling to let the smoke of open hearths escape is reminiscent of the kitchens of some medieval monas-

The West Front, originally intended to be the main entrance, was completed in 1577.

BURGHLEY'S BUILDER

William Cecil, Lord Burghley, was a remarkable man. Son of Richard Cecil, who had served Henry VIII, he studied law and theology, began his career under Mary, but corresponded with Elizabeth. She on her accession appointed him Secretary of State, later making him baron and Lord Treasurer. Remarkably liberal and far-sighted for that age, he strove to abolish monopolies and throw trade open. He found time to design and build two great houses – Theobalds in Hertfordshire and Burghley – and to entertain and discourse with scholars, setting aside his gown and staff of office and saying, 'Lie thou there, Lord Treasurer!'

teries; and a stone-vaulted staircase with its French renaissance design and ornament. Notable buildings in the grounds include a Gothic revival Orangery, by Lancelot 'Capability' Brown, and the endearingly eccentric Bottle Lodges which guard the entrance from the old London road.

Doddington Hall

LINCOLN

AN UNSPOILT ELIZABETHAN HOUSE WITH GATEHOUSE, WALLED GARDENS AND GEORGIAN INTERIORS, REFLECTING FOUR CENTURIES OF FAMILY OCCUPATION: FOUR MILES WEST OF LINCOLN OFF THE B1190.

Doddington Hall is a particularly fine Elizabethan E-shaped house in local stone and pink brick dug and fired on site, with chimneys and domed gazebos rising above its roof parapet. It was built in 1600 for Thomas Taylor, the Bishop of Lincoln's registrar, by Robert Smythson, architect of Hardwick Hall, Wollaton and other great Midlands houses. Externally it remains much as it was built – thanks largely to the sensitive care of its Georgian owner, John Delaval.

Most of the rooms – notably the Great Hall, drawing room, Imperial Staircase and Long Gallery – are early Georgian in style, while the library and parlour retain Queen Anne panelling and decorations. These rooms are filled with beautiful furniture, pictures, porcelain and textiles, in marked contrast with the original sparse interiors revealed by an inventory taken when that first Thomas Taylor died in 1606. There were then only 85 pieces of furniture in 40 rooms!

The house passed from the Taylors by marriage, first to the Hussey family and then to the Delavels of Seaton Delaval (see page 167), who owned the house until 1830. At this time the Jarvis family inherited the estate as a result of a romantic attachment in Dover between George Ralph Payne Jarvis and Sarah, the widowed Delavel heiress. The house is approached through a Dutch-gabled Tudor gatehouse and across the East Garden Courtyard. The gardens nearest the house are walled, formal and traditional; beyond are more natural areas, with a very convincing Temple of the Winds – built with his own hands by the present Mr Jarvis in order to mark his father's 65th birthday.

Left: In Elizabethan times architects would frequently outline their monarch's initial in their plans. Doddington Hall remains a fine example of the E-shaped building.

Among many lovely pieces at Doddington Hall is this pretty Coalport clock which dates from 1830.

■ I think more than anything, the reward for the great responsibility of looking after this place is its unique and timeless beauty which never fades, no matter how many times one returns. ■

Antony Jarvis

Fulbeck Hall

GRANTHAM

GEORGIAN COUNTRY HOUSE RESCUED AFTER DISASTROUS 1940S FIRES AND NOW DELIGHTFULLY RESTORED: ABOUT EIGHT MILES NORTH OF GRANTHAM ON THE A607.

If Fulbeck Hall reminds you of 'Middlemarch', that is entirely understandable. Much of the TV serial was set in the delightful Georgian town of Stamford; and when in 1733 Francis Fane rebuilt his fire-gutted house, he employed a Stamford architect. Though there were later additions and parts of an earlier house remain, today's building is essentially a Stamford-style Georgian town house scaled up for a more spacious site.

Fulbeck has been the home of the Fane family since 1622, and that it survives at all is thanks to the stolid determination of the late Mrs Dorothy Fane, mother/mother-in law of its present owners Mary and Michael Fry. Requisitioned by the army in 1940, the Hall suffered three fires which, along with water pouring through the roof, destroyed much of the fabric and contents. She and her husband moved in and set about the task of restoration – continued by the Fry's and now substantially complete.

Its largely Georgian interiors are full of family treasures, often with romantic stories attached. One 19th-century Fane, Georgina, was so infatuated with the Duke of Wellington that she pursued him relentlessly for 30 years, as a letter on the subject, written when he was in his 80s, testifies.

Grimsthorpe Castle

BOURNE

A MEDIEVAL CASTLE, SPLENDIDLY REBUILT BY VANBRUGH FOR AN 18TH-CENTURY DUKE: ABOUT THREE MILES NORTH-WEST OF BOURNE ON THE A151.

Grimsthorpe, with its great avenue, the Chestnut Riding, lake and fishpond, deer park and woodlands, is one of eastern England's most imposing stately homes. Though called 'castle', it is in reality an 18th-century palace, designed for the Duke of Ancaster by that most dramatic of architects, Sir John Vanbrugh. It was the last great house he designed.

The name Grimsthorpe, Norse in origin, means 'Grim's hamlet', but the estate has its origins in a Norman castle and nearby Cistercian abbey, both built of stone quarried here. Little remains of the monastery; its stone was reused for the castle which was substantially rebuilt in the 14th, 17th and 18th centuries as desire for comfort and grandeur superseded the need for defence. Its oldest part is the 12th-century King John's Tower at its south-east corner which, though considerably restored, still has arrow slits and some walls 7 feet thick. Henry VIII gave Grimsthorpe to William the 10th Lord Willoughby de Eresby in 1516 when he married Catherine of Aragon's cousin, and members of the Willoughby de Eresby family live there to this day.

It was around 1533 that Charles Brandon, 49-year-old Duke of Suffolk, married his 14-year-old ward Katherine, Baroness Willoughby de Eresby in her own right. Brandon used stone from the abbey to convert the medieval castle into a commodious Tudor courtyard house. His 17th-century descendant, the 14th Lord, who fought for Charles II in the Civil War, partly rebuilt it in Restoration times, but the big rebuilding came after George I had created the 16th Lord first Duke of Ancaster.

The stately Grimsthorpe Castle bears little resemblance today to that which Fuller described during the 17th century as 'an extempore building set up of a sudden'.

The new duke commissioned Sir John Vanbrugh, architect of Blenheim and Castle Howard, to transform the castle into a palace, but did not live to see it completed. His son presided over the building of Vanbrugh's new north front before both funds and enthusiasm dried up. Yet what was achieved transformed Grimsthorpe. The palatial north front is typical of Vanbrugh, a dramatist as well as an architect. Its skyline is topped by balustraded towers, ornate chimneys and statues; the grand courtyard in front is enclosed by wing walls lined with niches and ending in corner pavilions which echo the main towers. Completing the ensemble is a splendid iron grille and gates.

Within are opulent state rooms filled with rich furnishings and family pictures. The Great Hall, 110 feet by 40 feet, is Vanbrugh's finest room here. Its arcaded galleries echo his north front exterior; English Kings painted *en grisaille* by Thornhill look down from above a coronet-topped chimneypiece. Openings in the east arcade lead to a superb double-flight staircase, and the oval pattern of the concave ceiling repeats in the floor's black and cream.

Hedingham Castle

CASTLE HEDINGHAM

THIS MAGNIFICENT NORMAN KEEP IS OWNED BY THE ANCIENT DE VERE FAMILY: FOUR MILES NORTH OF HALSTEAD OFF THE A604.

The vast tower of Hedingham Castle looms over the surrounding countryside as a great monument to the Norman Conquest. The original Saxon owner of the lordship of Hedingham was dispossessed by William, and the title was given to Aubrey de Vere. Aubrey's son, Aubrey II, built the huge tower around 1140, using the Archbishop of Canterbury as his architect. It is 73 feet tall, with a further 20 feet gained by the two corner turrets. There are four floors, although the enormous Great Hall is twice as high as the other storeys. The entire building is faced with Ashlar stone, which, since it was very expensive to transport, is an indication of the great wealth of the early de Veres.

A GREAT DEFENSIVE FORTRESS

Norman towers were designed for strength and defence, and Hedingham is no exception. The main entrance is on the first floor, not the ground floor, so that attackers would find it more difficult to enter. The walls of the keep are between 10 and 12 feet thick, to provide protection against battering rams, undermining and missiles. Small rooms and passages are built into the thickness of the walls, many with arrow slits through which invaders could be attacked.

The massive chamber on the second floor houses the largest Norman arch in Europe. This magnificent arch is 28 feet across and 20 feet high. The chamber's arched windows and doorways are richly carved, and there is

THE INFAMOUS 9TH EARL

Robert, 9th Earl of Oxford, was only nine when he inherited his title. He quickly made himself a favourite of Richard II, who rewarded him with honours and estates. This, and the King's inclination to listen to Robert rather than his councillors, made him unpopular with the other nobles. He was made Duke of Ireland in 1386, but his inexperienced attempts to deal with the uprising there resulted in a dismal failure. The nobles accused Robert of High Treason, and he was forced to escape to Flanders, where, at the age of 30, he was killed by a boar while hunting.

a gallery running around the entire room in the thickness of the walls. There is no evidence that there was either a chapel or a kitchen in the tower. The absence of the latter is understandable, for one of the biggest hazards to castle dwellers was fire, and it is likely that the cooking and baking buildings were outside the main tower for safety reasons.

BATTLING EARLS OF OXFORD

The de Veres distinguished themselves in many battles and campaigns against the French, Welsh and Scots, as well as being prominent in politics and courtly life. Aubrey III was created Earl of Oxford by Matilda in the mid 1100s as a reward for his support during her struggle for the throne against Stephen. When Stephen agreed that Matilda's son (Henry II) should succeed him, she came to Hedingham to die peacefully after a life of conflict.

Robert, 3rd Earl of Oxford, was one of the 26 barons who forced King John to sign the Magna Carta. In retaliation, John laid siege to Hedingham. Robert surrendered it after a long and fierce resistance, and it was not restored to him until after John's death. The 4th and 5th Earls fought for Edward I against the Welsh, and the 6th Earl fought for Edward I, Edward II and Edward III in France and Scotland. The 7th Earl was present at the victories at Crécy and Poitiers with the Black Prince, and was feted for his courage and tactical skills. He was killed at the Siege of Rheims in 1360. Richard, the 11th Earl, proved himself at Agincourt with Henry V.

Throughout the Wars of the Roses, the de Veres remained loyal to Henry VI. When the Yorkist Edward IV was crowned, the 12th Earl and his heir were beheaded on Tower Hill. The 12th Earl's second son, John, inherited the title, and was imprisoned in France for his part in several battles against Edward. He escaped in order to take part in the Battle of Bosworth Field, where the Yorkists were defeated and Henry VII became king. The 15th Earl fought with Henry VIII, and the 16th Earl distinguished himself at the Siege of

Above: The magnificent square Norman keep of Hedingham Castle is among the best preserved in Europe.

The chair of the Lord Great Chamberlain was presented to the 9th Earl in the 14th century. The de Vere family have held the hereditary Chamberlain's office for 550 years.

Boulogne in 1544. The 17th Earl has been credited as the true author of Shakespeare's plays, mainly because of a mysterious £1,000 per year that Elizabeth I paid him until his death.

The 18th Earl, the last to own Hedingham, died from wounds received during the Battle of the Hague. Hedingham was sold by the 17th Earl's widow in 1713. It was bought by Sir William Ashhurst, one-time Lord Mayor of London, who built himself a comfortable house near the old castle. The present owner, Thomas Lindsay, can trace his ancestry to the de Veres through both his father's and his mother's families.

■ Having been brought up at Ingatestone Hall, I naturally think of it more as a home than as an historic house, and my family and I try to transmit the same feeling to visitors. The records show that, in the 16th century 40 or more 'strangers' would be entertained in the Great Hall every day, and it is a pleasure to welcome visitors to the house and hence restore something of the bustle of yesteryear. ■
Lord Petre

Ingatestone Hall

CHELMSFORD

THIS ELEGANT TUDOR COURTYARD HOUSE CONTAINS THE FAMED PETRE FAMILY PORTRAITS: FIVE MILES SOUTH-WEST OF CHELMSFORD OFF THE A12 BRENTWOOD ROAD.

In 1535, Thomas Cromwell's assistant, a young lawyer called William Petre, prowled southern England persuading monasteries and abbeys to give up their riches to the King. When he reached Barking Abbey, he took a liking to its manor of Yenge-atte-Stone (Ingatestone). After the Dissolution of the Monasteries, Petre bought the manor for £849. 12s. 6d. Simultaneously he endowed an almshouse for the poor so that, in the eyes of the Pope, his purchase would not be construed as plundering church property.

Petre built himself a fine house befitting his rising position at court. His son, John, bought nearby Thorndon Hall, and the two houses remained in the Petre family for the next 300 years. William was appointed Secretary of State by Henry VIII, and he remained in this office until ill-health forced him to retire in the reign of Elizabeth I. He has been described as the 'first civil servant' and also re-founded Exeter College, Oxford. William's son, John, was made 1st Lord Petre by James I, and was one of the patrons of the composer William Byrd. His great-grandson, the 4th Lord, was implicated in the 'Popish Plot' of Titus Oates and died in the Tower of London. The Petre family retained their Catholic beliefs, even through the Commonwealth years. The 9th Lord was a prominent figure in the movement for Catholic emancipation in the 18th century, and his great-great-grandson, the 13th Lord, was ordained priest.

In the 18th century Ingatestone's old west wing was demolished, the whole house was 'modernised' with corridors and sash windows and the house was divided into self-contained apartments which were rented out. The 16th Lord Petre died in the Great War, and in 1919 his wife began the restoration of Ingatestone. The contents reflect one family's collection of personal treasures over 450 years – a charming jumble of lovingly tended heirlooms. In the Long Gallery is the famous collection of Petre family portraits, an almost complete set from William, Ingatestone's builder (1505–1571), to the present day.

The beautiful mellow brick walls of Ingatestone Hall are arranged around a delightful courtyard.

Layer Marney Tower

COLCHESTER

ONE OF THE FINEST FACADES IN TUDOR ENGLAND DOMINATES THIS MAGNIFICENT BUILDING: SEVEN MILES SOUTH-WEST OF COLCHESTER OFF THE B1022.

On 22 April 1884, an earthquake shook eastern England. Chimneys toppled from Layer Marney Tower, and its walls and roofs were damaged, making it unsafe and virtually uninhabitable. Fortunately for Layer Marney, and for the thousands of visitors that admire it every year, the house has had a succession of caring owners who have gone to considerable effort and expense to ensure that it has been restored to its full glory.

The Marney family was first recorded here in 1166 and they remained until 1525. Henry Marney, began building the tower in 1520, but died three years later, and his Renaissance courtyard mansion was never completed. The east and west wings adjoin the central tower, but the south side remains isolated from the rest of the house.

The tower is the tallest Tudor gatehouse in the country, and has two hexagonal turrets eight floors high with finely moulded brick topped with terracotta dolphins and shells. The use of terracotta, relatively recent in England, indicates Henry Marney's sophistication. Between the turrets are two spacious rooms with huge windows that may have been used as a royal suite.

Henry Marney served on the Privy Council during the reigns of Henry VII and VIII, where his sound advice and integrity earned him his knighthood in 1510, and his baronetcy in 1523. Sadly, he enjoyed his title for only six weeks before he died. His son John died two years later, and having no male heirs, the estate passed to the Tuke family. In 1580 it was sold to Sir Samuel Tyron, 1st Baronet of Layer Marney, after which a succession of owners included Nicholas

HENRY MARNEY'S FUNERAL

Just two days before his death, Henry Marney organised a splendid funeral for himself. His coffin was placed in a carriage draped in black velvet with a white satin cross and the Marney coat of arms. Six horses pulled it from London to Marney, a journey of well over a week, and at every parish representatives were given 3s. 4d. The enormous funeral entourage included knights, friars, relatives and paid mourners carrying torches. At Marney, the requiem masses and dirges of the burial ceremony lasted for two days, and were eventually concluded with a good lunch.

Corsellis, whose memorial in Layer Marney church claims (falsely) that he had printed books five years before Caxton. The current owners, Nicholas and Sheila Charrington, inherited the Tower in 1989.

■ The fact that it was never completed has been Layer Marney's saving grace; it has all the magnificence of a Tudor palace, but is still a friendly, manageable family home which our children love to run all over. ■

Sheila Charrington

The Gatehouse of Layer Marney Tower is eight storeys high and is one of East Anglia's most remarkable landmarks.

Saint Osyth's Priory

CLACTON

A SUPERB GATEHOUSE AND PAINTINGS BY STUBBS ARE AMONG THE ATTRACTIONS OF THIS MEDIEVAL HALL: THREE MILES WEST OF CLACTON OFF THE B1027.

In 653 a small group of marauding Danes landed at the little village of Chiche on the Essex coast. They tried to force the abbess of Chiche nunnery to worship their gods, and when she refused they cut off her head. Legend has it that the stricken abbess carried her head to her church, half a mile away, and died at its doors. Where she fell, a fountain sprang up and many miracles were subsequently attributed to it. The abbess was St Osyth, daughter of the king of the East Angles, and 450 years later a priory was established on the site and dedicated to her memory.

Around 1200 the priory was upgraded to the status of abbey, and became one of the most powerful Augustinian houses in Essex. Like others, it fell during Henry VIII's Dissolution of the Monasteries, and became the property of the Crown. Since then it has had a series of owners, and is currently owned by Somerset de Chair.

The site is dominated by the vast late 15th-century gatehouse, a magnificent building decorated with carvings of saints and dragons. Little remains of the other early monastic buildings. In the early 16th century the last abbot but one, John Vyntoner, built himself a range of stately apartments to the north-west of the cloister, with a lovely oriel window above the main door. Vyntoner's successor passed the abbey to the Crown in 1537 where it eventually came into the hands of Thomas Darcy, later Earl Rivers. He added the eye-catching 'Abbot's Tower' and the octagonal clock tower, and incorporated parts of the old monastic buildings into his elegant three-storeyed house.

In 1642, St Osyth's was owned by the Catholic Countess Rivers, and was sacked and badly damaged by Puritans. The Rivers family retreated to their home in Cheshire, and the priory remained empty until it passed into the hands of Frederick, the 3rd Earl Rochford who, with his heirs, was responsible for much restoration and rebuilding.

■ For me the most interesting work of art at the priory is the famous life-size painting by Stubbs of the horse *Whistlejacket*, on loan to the Kenwood Museum until inherited by my wife. We had to lower the floor nine inches and alter the sash window to a French window nine feet high in order to get the ten by eight feet painting into the room. The picture was commissioned from Stubbs by one of my wife's ancestors, the 18th-century Prime Minister, Lord Rockingham. ■

Somerset de Chair

The splendid oriel window above the main door is dated 1527 and incorporates some outstanding architectural detail.

Right: Thomas Hopper's Great Hall of c1820.
Below: Armour on display in the Great Hall

Kentwell Hall

Long Melford

An impressive moat protects this lovingly restored Tudor house, which also has a rare-breeds farm: four miles north of Sudbury, turning off the A1092 at Long Melford.

In the Domesday Book, the manor of Kentwell was valued at £4 and was owned by Frodo, brother to the first Abbot of Bury St Edmund's. Nine hundred years later, the estate at Kentwell still survives, its centrepiece being the delightful Tudor manor house. Built in soft red brick the Hall seems to change colour when viewed at different times of the day, and is reached by an elegant avenue of lime trees that stretches almost a mile from the front gates. The Hall is surrounded by a wide moat that is seven feet deep in places.

The manor of Kentwell has been sold several times during its long history. It remained in Frodo's family until it passed to a family that took the name of the manor itself – the de Kentwells. By 1250, it was in the hands of King Henry III, who granted it to his half-brother, Sir William de Valence. At this point, the manor comprised 440 acres of land. De Valence's son, Aymer, was made Guardian and Lieutenant of England in 1320, and was murdered in France three years later.

The Hall was owned briefly by the 14th-century poet John Gower, and eventually came to Sir William Clopton through his mother Katharine Mylde in 1403. William's son, John (1423–1497), seems to have been responsible for the earliest parts of the existing complex. John was perhaps the most eminent of the family. He was Sheriff of Norfolk and Suffolk, and was imprisoned in the Tower of London accused of being part of a Lancastrian plot with the wife of the deposed Henry VI. He was pardoned and released, and promptly backed the Yorkist forces against the Lancastrians. John built Melford church; it is supposed that he also established the first large house on the present site. William Clopton (1509–1562) is credited with erecting much of the surviving Hall.

Kentwell was in the hands of the Clopton family for more than 250 years, until it was sold to the wealthy lawyer, Sir Thomas Robinson in 1676. He planted the lime tree avenue. Sir Thomas died seven years later when he jumped out of a window to escape a fire in his London chambers. Being unusually fat, he sustained such serious injuries from his leap to safety, that he died within an hour from the bruises.

Kentwell was sold yet again in 1706 to John Moore, who paid £21,200 for the estate. Although John appears to have made little alteration to the Hall, his descendant, Richard, made more changes. The estate was then sold to Robert Hart Logan, who had amassed a fortune in the Canadian timber business. He began a programme of restoration, engaging Thomas Hopper as his architect. Hopper's grand reception rooms, including the main dining room, the billiards room, and the Great Hall, can be seen on the ground floor. Kentwell was sold again after Hart Logan's death, and its subsequent owners leased it to several people,

■ **Kentwell has the most inspiring and tranquil atmosphere of any house I know. It is my pleasure that what I first felt when I came here, and still savour today, is shared and enjoyed by so many visitors. They may not wish to do what I have undertaken, but I think they understand what moves me to do it.** ■
J Patrick Phillips

Below: Kentwell's main front.
Bottom right: The Tudor Rose Brick Maze.

including the founder of the law company Norton Rose, and the engineer who built the first Aswan Dam. The house was sold to Patrick Phillips, the present owner, in 1971.

RESTORATION IN PROGRESS

Since 1972, the Hall and its gardens have undergone extensive restoration. Visitors to the house can admire the work in progress to return this splendid old house to its original glory. Rooms on all three floors can be explored. The ground floor includes the Great Kitchen, the Panelled Room, Hopper's masterpieces, the 'Jacobethan' Main Dining Room and the Gothick Great Hall, the drawing room, the billiards room, the hall, and the library. The various passages and staircases are also worthy of attention. The top floor includes the 'Victorian Room' and the reformed State Bedroom, its boudoir converted into a Roman-style bathroom.

No visit to Kentwell would be complete without admiring the grounds. The Moat House is a charming timbered building dating from the 15th century, which is reached by a pretty three-arched bridge. The walled garden is in the process of being restored to its original 17th-century layout, and the rare-breeds farm, based on four fine timber-framed buildings, is worth a visit.

RICHARD MOORE AND HIS ILL-MANAGED FINANCES

Richard Moore was born in 1769, and was only 13 when he inherited the Kentwell estate from his father. Perhaps this early access to wealth contributed to Richard's spendthrift tendencies – it is said that he built a large farmhouse on his estate so that he might escape his creditors if necessary. In 1812, he divorced his wife of 16 years, Sidney Arabella Cotton, for her 'unlawful familiarity, criminal intercourse and adulterous conversation' with John Miller, his steward. Richard was bankrupt by 1823, and even the sale of Kentwell could not keep him from the Debtors' Prison, where he died in 1826.

Haughley Park

STOWMARKET

AN EXTENSIVE COLLECTION OF 18TH- AND 19TH-CENTURY DUTCH PAINTINGS DISTINGUISH THIS IMPOSING RED-BRICK MANSION: FOUR MILES NORTH-WEST OF STOWMARKET.

When the sickly Edward VI died in 1553, Mary Tudor, Edward's half-sister and heir to the throne of England, was forced to flee from the supporters of Lady Jane Grey. On her way to the safety of Framlingham Castle in Suffolk, she was helped by John Sulyard, whose family owned the manor of Haughley. It was John Sulyard's grandson, another John, who built the E-shaped red-brick Jacobean mansion that can be seen today. The building started in around 1620.

Haughley Park is surrounded by delightful gardens and grounds.

The Sulyard's owned Haughley until the late 18th century, when it passed by marriage to another ancient Suffolk family, the Jerninghams. A drawing by the last Sulyard to own Haughley shows the house in excellent condition, with an impressive battery of Jacobean chimneys, and some handsome mullioned windows facing out onto the gardens. After the Jerninghams, the house had a succession of owners, but seems to have been fairly well looked after. In the 1820s it was remodelled, and the mullioned windows were replaced with Georgian bay windows. The present owners, Mrs and Mrs Williams, have owned the house since 1957. Sadly, only four years after their purchase, Haughley was seriously damaged by a fire that swept through all but the south end of the house.

The damage to this beautiful Jacobean mansion was devastating. However, a sensitive programme of restoration was started to recreate the house as it was in its Jacobean heyday, and the result is impressive. The solid oak 'Jacobean' staircase, a replica of the original one from the 1620 house, and the plaster cornices are examples of the restoration work. A fine Regency fireplace was brought from a house in London to replace the one that was destroyed.

Haughley Park is noted for its fine collection of 16th- and 17th-century Dutch and Flemish paintings. This includes a series of period portraits by Honthorst, flowers by Verelst, and a rustic *Last Supper*. There are also some interesting scenes of Venice by Alfred Stannard, a local artist of some repute.

Otley Hall

OTLEY

A CHARMING 15TH-CENTURY MOATED TIMBER-FRAMED HALL WITH A FINE ARRAY OF GABLES AND CHIMNEYS: SEVEN MILES NORTH OF IPSWICH OFF THE B1077.

In 1602, Captain Bartholomew Gosnold, one of the Gosnolds of Otley, set sail for the New World in his ship *Concord*. Martha's Vineyard was named after his deceased daughter. When he returned, his enthusiastic reports led to the foundation of Jamestown, Virginia, the first permanent English settlement in America in 1607. Gosnold was the community's prime mover, but he died of swamp fever within four months. The Earl of Southampton was patron of Shakespeare and Gosnold, and it is possible that Shakespeare's stormy sea scenes in *Twelfth Night* and *The Tempest* were based on Gosnold's own descriptions.

Around 1450, Otley Hall came into the possession of the Gosnolds, who were descended from Edward III, and there it remained until the Civil War. The War proved the undoing of this respected family. They supported the King, and suffered badly for their loyalty when Cromwell won. Colonel Robert Gosnold, who had lived for nine months on little other than cereal, rats and dogs during the siege of Carlisle, had his estates confiscated by Cromwell, and was imprisoned in Kings Lynn. The Gosnolds 'sank with the Royal Cause'.

Otley Hall is not only outstandingly beautiful, its history is full of famous names and fascinating stories.

Otley was then bought by the Rebow family, and over the next two centuries the hall and its lands were rented to a series of farmers who did little to maintain the fine Tudor buildings. It was not until just before World War I that the hall received any serious restoration, when the owner, Dorothy Sherston, embarked on a programme of repair and modernisation The present owners, John and Anna Mosesson, are continuing the programme of restoration work with the help of their seven children.

The earliest part of the house dates from the beginning of the 15th century, and became the wing of an elaborate H-plan Tudor mansion protected by a moat. The later house was started by John Gosnold, and completed by his grandson Robert the Justice. Parts of the house were later demolished, and the remaining buildings are in the shape of a T.

Perhaps the most impressive room in the house is the Great Hall. This dates from about 1500, and has a fine screen passage at one end which used to lead to the servants' wing, no longer there. There are also large mullioned windows, a beautiful carved ceiling and some handsome panelled walls. The walls of the room next door are decorated with 'linenfold' panelling, where the wood has been carved to look like folds of fabric.

Otley Hall has ten acres of formal and informal gardens and grounds. Parts of the garden were designed by Francis Inigo Thomas. Otley also offers a pleasant rose garden, shady avenues of nut trees, a croquet lawn, a mount and peaceful walks along the canal.

The Priory

LAVENHAM

THIS BEAUTIFUL 13TH-CENTURY HOUSE WITH TUDOR ADDITIONS HAS SOME FINE DECORATIVE PARGETTING AND BOSSANYI STAINED GLASS: ABOUT TWO MILES EAST OF THE A134 BETWEEN BURY ST EDMUNDS AND SUDBURY.

Despite its name, there is little evidence that The Priory at Lavenham was ever used for religious purposes. The Domesday Book states that the manor of Lavenham was owned by the rich and powerful de Vere family, and when Alberic de Vere founded the Benedictine Priory at Earl's Colne, he granted land at Lavenham to the monks. It is possible that the first buildings on the site were used by the Benedictines, but the parts of the house that date from the 13th to the late 16th centuries would appear to have been more closely connected to the cloth trade. Some of the fine decorative plasterwork, known as pargetting, at the front of the house is in the shape of a fleur-de-lys, which was one of the Lavenham cloth marks.

At the Dissolution of the Monasteries in 1539, the

Benedictines lost their priory, and with it they lost their estates at Lavenham. Henry VIII sold the priory back to its original owners, the de Veres, and it eventually became the property of the unscrupulous Edward, 17th Earl of Oxford. Edward was involved in a great many plots and schemes, and when Sir Philip Sidney refused to vacate a tennis court that Edward wanted to use, it was rumoured that Edward began some serious plans for his murder.

THE COPINGERS AT LAVENHAM

The de Veres did not keep The Priory for long, and it was bought at the end of the 16th century by Henry Copinger, the newly appointed Rector of Lavenham. Copinger was granted the rich living at Lavenham by Edward de Vere after he had resigned as Master of Magdalen College, Cambridge. Copinger had links with Lavenham through his grandfather, a rich clothier who had been a church benefactor.

Almost as soon as Copinger had taken up his post, he came into conflict with de Vere, who was refusing to pay the church tithes on his park at Lavenham. Copinger threatened to resign unless de Vere paid up, and even though de Vere grudgingly agreed to settle his account, Copinger spent the rest of his life, and around £1,600 in legal fees, in trying to maintain the rights of his church.

Copinger and his wife jointly made a will that set up a charity to benefit four needy parishioners, which were to be selected by his five sons. By the time Copinger's widow had died, there was only one son left, who chose himself as the needy parishioner on the grounds that he was 'very aged and low in estate'! Incredibly, he won his case.

The Priory remained the Copinger home for almost 100 years, and from the early 18th century it was bought and sold a number of times, and was owned by the local doctor, members of the clergy, and several farmers. The house became empty in the 1960s, and began a decline which left it in a terrible state of disrepair until it was rescued by the present owners, the Casey family.

THE RESTORATION OF LAVENHAM PRIORY

In 1979 a sprawling mess of broken timbers, sagging roofs, and crumbling plaster enclosed in a nettle-filled garden was put up for sale at auction. It was bought by Alan and Gwenneth Casey, who then faced the formidable task of trying to restore The Priory to how it would have been in 1600, and to make this damp, dilapidated ruin a comfortable home. 15 years later, Lavenham Priory is magnificent, proudly displaying carefully restored crown post roofs, original wattle-and-daub panelling, fine mullioned windows, and patterned brick floors.

The magnificent 500-year-old crown post roof of the Priory's Great Chamber is a remarkable survivor.

THE PRIORY THROUGH THE AGES

The Priory is a two-storey dwelling that has been adapted and enlarged since the 13th century. The first part to be built was the splendid Great Hall, although this was considerably altered during the 15th and 16th centuries, when it was elongated and a solar was created on the floor above. The upper floor is now reached by the Jacobean staircase (where a painting by Bossanyi is displayed), although the original staircase was where the Tudor fireplace now stands. In the 15th century, a long five-bay house was added at right angles to the Great Hall. The front part of this building is called the Merchant's Room and was probably used as business premises.

On the upper floor, the Painted Chamber, so named because remnants of some Elizabethan wall-paintings have been found, would have been one of the principal bedchambers in the time of Henry Copinger. The Solar, also on the upper floor, has some beautiful Elizabethan strapwork painting over the fireplace, and during restoration it was found that the 500 year-old crown-post roof timber was of such good quality that it needed very little repair.

■ For 15 years The Priory has influenced everything that we think and do. As time passes we are simply becoming a part of the house. ■
Alan and Gwenneth Casey

Somerleyton Hall

LOWESTOFT

AN IMPOSING EARLY VICTORIAN PALACE WITH ELEGANT FURNISHINGS, EXTENSIVE GARDENS AND A FAMOUS MAZE: FOUR AND A HALF MILES NORTH-WEST OF LOWESTOFT ON THE B1074.

Although there has been a house on the Somerleyton site since the mid-1300s, the imposing palace that can be seen today dates mainly from the last century. Only a few walls and foundations of the earlier house were left when the new extravagant Victorian mansion was erected between 1844 and 1851.

The Fitzosbert family built the first house around 1240. In 1604, the estate came to John Wentworth, who built himself a comfortable Tudor-Jacobean mansion that was to survive virtually intact until the 1840s. Sir Morton Peto, who bought Somerleyton in 1843, was a highly successful Victorian entrepreneur. Born in 1809, he was apprenticed to his uncle as a bricklayer, inheriting the business when his uncle died. He became one of the biggest railway contractors of the 19th century, building railways in Canada, Denmark, Russia and Britain. He also built Nelson's Column and won the contract for the Houses of Parliament. In 1847 he became Liberal MP for Norwich, and was made a baronet eight years later.

By the early 1860s, Sir Morton's fortune began to decline. He was forced to sell the house and its splendid contents only 12 years after it was completed. In 1863, Sir Francis Crossley, a Yorkshire-based carpet magnate, bought Somerleyton Hall and the house has been in possession of the family ever since.

Sir Morton employed the talented sculptor John Thomas as his architect. The house was rebuilt in red bricks dressed with Caen stone. Unfortunately, the soft Caen stone has weathered badly at Somerleyton and the beautiful carved stags on the courtyard gate pillars had to be completely recarved in 1975.

Sir Morton wanted his house to be mainly Jacobean, but the campanile tower is decidedly Italianate. It once held a small observatory from which the spire of Norwich Cathedral could be seen. On the opposite side of the courtyard is a stable block with a magnificent Vulliamy clock, a model of the clock intended for the Houses of Parliament but discarded because it was too expensive. The central wing has a pinnacled and columned three-storeyed stone porch in Elizabethan style, with a delicate oriel window on the first floor.

Somerleyton has some quite dazzling rooms. These include the Oak Room, with carvings by Grinling Gibbons; the library, now used as a family sitting room, with a collection of 5,000 19th-century books; and the white and gold ballroom that served as a hospital during World War II.

Wingfield College

WINGFIELD

A FINE GEORGIAN EXTERIOR HIDES BEAUTIFULLY RESTORED MEDIEVAL TIMBER-FRAMED BUILDINGS IN THIS PEACEFUL SUFFOLK VILLAGE: SIX MILES EAST OF DISS OFF THE A143 OR B1118.

The story of Wingfield College is a remarkable one. The College and its 'Collegiate Church' were founded in 1362 by Sir John Wingfield, a close friend of the Black Prince. The Wingfields later married into the powerful de la Pole family, Dukes of Suffolk, who gave large donations to the College and church in return for prayers being said for them.

Below: With its rich harmony of styles and luxurious fittings, Somerleyton Hall epitomises the early Victorian era of self-confident expansion.

Below left: The spectacular Great Hall at Wingfield College dates from c1300 and is an important example of its kind.

The College flourished throughout the 14th and 15th centuries, with buildings accommodating the boys and masters, offices and a splendid Great Hall arranged around a small quadrangle. Disaster struck for the College in 1542, when, along with many religious establishments, it was closed during the Reformation, surrendered to King Henry and fell into ruin.

In the 18th century, the College fell into the hands of Squire Buck, whose preference was for a new Georgian house, rather than an old medieval hall. But rather than pull the old hall down in order to rebuild, Buck decided simply to put a false front on the building. A number of false ceilings and floors were also added, and the Great Hall was divided into three smaller rooms. The front of the house was given an elegant neo-Classical façade with 19 Georgian windows – seven of which are completely false and close inspection shows that there are no rooms behind them.

The medieval buildings remained hidden until the present owner, Ian Chance, discovered them. The Great Hall now stands as it did in the 14th century, complete with fire-blackened beams from many past feasts and intricately carved wall panels. Since 1981, the College has been the venue of Wingfield Arts and Music, providing an atmospheric setting for recitals, talks, and exhibitions.

■ Standing in the Great Hall at Wingfield you can wonder at life continuing in this ancient building for over seven centuries. It is a unique combination of the Arts and Heritage. ■
Ian Chance

Euston Hall

THETFORD

A 17TH-CENTURY HALL WITH A FINE COLLECTION OF STUART PAINTINGS, DOLL COLLECTIONS AND A WILLIAM KENT TEMPLE: THREE MILES SOUTH-EAST OF THETFORD ON THE A1088.

This late 17th-century painting shows Euston Hall and Church.

In 1902 a great fire raged at Euston Hall. The south and west wings were gutted, destroying, among other priceless treasures, the 18th-century ceilings painted by Verrio. Only the north wing remained. The burned wings were quickly rebuilt, but were demolished in 1952 so that the Hall that can be seen today dates mainly from the 1740s.

The house was originally built between 1666 and 1670 for the Duke of Arlington, Charles II's Secretary of State and a loyal supporter of the Stuart cause. He made a splendid match for his daughter Isabella when she was only five years old, betrothing her to Henry FitzRoy, the illegitimate son of the King and Barbara Villiers. Henry FitzRoy was made the Duke of Grafton, and Euston Hall, which he inherited from Arlington, has been the family home of the Graftons ever since.

Euston Hall was probably one of the first English country houses to have the luxury of a mechanically pumped water supply. The diarist John Evelyn visited Euston in 1671, and commented on the 'pretty engine' which pumped an abundant supply of water from a nearby canal for all the house's needs with enough left over to run the fountains and a corn mill.

Henry FitzRoy enjoyed his inheritance for only five years before he died. His son, the 2nd Duke, commissioned Matthew Brettingham to remodel the house. Brettingham faced all three wings with red brick, as well as building the stable block in 1750–1755, and these buildings remained untouched until the disaster of the fire in 1902.

Euston Hall possesses a magnificent collection of 17th-century courtly paintings. Since Henry FitzRoy's origins were indisputably Stuart, Stuart portraits fill every corner of the house. Charles I's painting is by Van Dyck, and Charles II's and Barbara Villiers' are by Lely. The portrait of Nell Gwyn, who was Barbara's famous rival for Charles II's affections, hangs rather unceremoniously in a side corridor.

A portrait of the Duke of Orleans is virtually hidden in a corner of the room known as 'The Square' on the first floor. Orleans had a somewhat debauched reputation, and was married to Charles II's favourite sister, whom it is said he tried to poison. There are many fabulous treasures to be enjoyed at Euston Hall, including splendid Chinese plates, fine 18th-century furniture, and Stubbs' famous painting *Mares and Foals by the River at Euston.*

NANCY PARSONS AND THE 3RD DUKE

Anne, the wife of the 3rd Duke of Grafton, ran away with the Duke of Upper Ossary when her husband embarked upon a flagrant affair with Nancy Parsons, the daughter of a tailor from London with many a scandalous dalliance to her name. When the 3rd Duke became Prime Minister, he was lampooned unmercifully for flaunting Nancy at all sorts of public events, and even before the Queen. When he was forced to resign, Nancy disappeared from his life and he later remarried.

Holkham Hall

WELLS NEXT THE SEA

■ **I have no particular favourite amongst the rooms or works of art at Holkham – I love the whole house, because it is friendly and has no ghosts.** ■
Lord Coke

THIS MAGNIFICENT 18TH-CENTURY PALLADIAN MANSION IS OWNED BY THE COKE FAMILY. IT BOASTS A DAZZLING DISPLAY OF TREASURES, INCLUDING A FABULOUS COLLECTION OF PAINTINGS, SOME BY OLD MASTERS, ELEGANT WILLIAM KENT FURNITURE, BEAUTIFUL BRUSSELS AND MORTLAKE TAPESTRIES, AND CEILINGS BASED ON INIGO JONES DESIGNS: TWO MILES WEST OF WELLS-NEXT-THE-SEA.

Holkham Hall sprawls majestically in its 3,000-acre park a mile from the wild and windswept north Norfolk coast. At the turn of the 17th century, the land on which the Hall and its park now stand was little more than a desolate heathland, covered with scrubby bushes and sparse grass. When Thomas Coke told his friends where he planned to build his new home, many reacted with horror at the thought of a magnificent palace being placed in such a wilderness. That the designs for Coke's new house were inspired by buildings he had admired in the warm and gentle climate of Italy made his choice of location seem even more strange to his friends.

Today, as the visitor strolls across the rich lawns and enjoys the shade of abundant oaks and beeches, it is difficult to imagine that it was once an uncultivated heath. Some of the trees were planted as early as 1712 in anticipation of the splendid park that was to follow. Visitors may picnic next to the peaceful lake or wander through acres of landscaped gardens and parklands. Or they may prefer to admire Kent's great obelisk or the monument to the architectural achievements of 'Coke of Norfolk'. But at the centre of all this is the resplendent Hall itself, offering the visitor the chance to see 2,000 years of fine art, all housed in one of the largest and most grand 18th-century palaces in the world.

This painting by Gheeraerts portrays Edward Coke, Lord Chief Justice and founder of the family fortune. It hangs in the Drawing Room opposite a portrait of Thomas Coke, the builder of Holkham.

THE COKES IN HISTORY

The Coke (pronounced 'Cook') family is an ancient one, but their fortune can be traced back to one man – the brilliant lawyer Sir Edward Coke. Coke was appointed Attorney General in 1594 by Queen Elizabeth I after the previous incumbent was promoted to Master of the Rolls. His appointment was the result of a bitter power struggle, with the Earl of Essex, Robert Deveraux, supporting his protégé Francis Bacon, and the powerful Cecil family backing Sir Edward.

When James I became King of England and Scotland, Coke remained loyal to the Crown, and was appointed Chief Justice of the King's Bench in 1613. He was dismissed only three years later for taking the view that common law was more important than the 'king's perogative'. In 1628, Sir Edward was largely responsible for the 'Petition of Right', which meant that it became illegal to imprison anyone without a trial, to levy taxes without permission of Parliament, or to billet soldiers on individuals.

During his legal career, Sir Edward was involved in a number of famous cases, the most notable being those of Sir Walter Raleigh and Guy Fawkes. Guy Fawkes was executed for high treason in 1606 after he tried to blow up James I and his parliament. Sir Walter Raleigh stood trial for treason when James I succeeded Elizabeth I, and was executed in 1616 after the failure of his expedition to bring back gold from the Orinoco River. Sir Edward was involved in the prosecution of both men.

Five generations later, Thomas Coke was created Earl of Leicester, about ten years after he started to build Holkham Hall. The Earl was predeceased by his only son, and so the title became extinct, although the Hall was passed to the Earl's nephew Wenman Roberts. Wenman changed his name to Coke in 1750, and his son was Thomas William Coke, the famed 'Coke of Norfolk'. Despite his support of the American Colonies during the War of Independence from the British, Coke of Norfolk was popular for his agricultural achievements. In 1837, he was made 1st Earl of Leicester of the second creation by Queen Victoria.

Coke of Norfolk's son, the 2nd Earl, continued his

THE SCANDALOUS LIFE OF JANE DIGBY

When she was 17 Jane Digby, one of Coke of Norfolk's granddaughters, married Lord Ellenborough, who was in his mid-50s After four years of marriage Jane left Ellenborough to pursue an affair with an Austrian prince and her divorce caused a tremendous sensation in Victorian England. The Austrian prince did not keep Jane's affections for long, and she left him for one of King Ludwig of Bavaria's courtiers. The courtier was swopped for a Greek count, and then an Albanian of dubious repute. She was in her 50s when she married a Bedouin sheikh, and seems to have lived happily ever after.

'COKE OF NORFOLK' AND HIS FARM

Thomas William Coke was 21 when he inherited Holkham in 1776. He was deeply interested in agriculture at a time when farming was generally regarded as rather menial. Each summer, he organised 'sheep shearings' where hundreds of people would gather to exchange views on horticulture and livestock. The agricultural shows of today were based on Coke's annual events. Coke also pioneered the concept of 'four crop rotation', where wheat, grass, barley and root crops were rotated every four years, a system that was used into the 1940s. Coke is known to have planted over one million trees by the time he died, aged 88.

father's agricultural improvements. He planted belts of trees to protect his farmland from the sea wind, and helped to finance the railway to Holkham in the 1860s. The 2nd Earl married twice and had 19 children. The 4th Earl re-established Holkham Hall's connection with the arts, and many concerts were given in the Gallery. Holkham Hall is now run by the son of the 6th Earl, Viscount Coke.

THE FIRST EARL OF LEICESTER

Thomas Coke was born in 1697. Ten years later he was an orphan, inheriting a vast fortune from his Norfolk estates. Coke was born in an age when it was considered fashionable, and even necessary, for the sons of the wealthy and high-born to spend some of their youth travelling. These 'dilettanti' of the 18th century prided themselves on their love of the arts and each year flocks of rich young men left England to travel and to provide themselves with handsome collections of paintings, sculptures and other treasures.

The young men gathered together in art galleries and at archaeological excavations, and everywhere they were seen to be buying art. Inevitably, not all purchases were good ones, and a large number of fakes and worthless pieces were proudly shipped home. However, this mass acquisition of artefacts had a major impact on the architecture of private houses. It was important that all these priceless possessions be appropriately displayed. Many houses had their libraries enlarged, and had fine galleries installed to display their treasures. Holkham's state rooms were intended to show Coke's collections to their best advantage.

When he was 15, Thomas Coke set off for Europe on the Grand Tour that was to last for almost six years. He was drawn to Italy in particular, mainly because of his interest in classical art and literature. He began to collect books, paintings, sculptures and other works of art, choosing with remarkable skill and taste for one so young. His purchases included a set of Leonardo da Vinci's notebooks and some rare Greek manuscripts.

Holkham's stunning Marble Hall is modelled on a Roman Temple of Justice, in true Palladian style. The fluted columns of alabaster were brought by river and sea from Derbyshire.

In Italy, Coke met Robert Boyle, 3rd Earl of Burlington, and they quickly discovered a common passion for architecture. Burlington introduced Coke to William Kent, who was to become one of the greatest architects of the 18th century. The friendship between Coke and Burlington flourished, and in May 1712 Coke was invited to Chiswick where he met Kent again. The three of them began to discuss plans for Coke's palace at Holkham and for Burlington's 'villa' at Chiswick.

Coke was the first Postmaster-General, and the present Viscount holds the hereditary position of sub-postmaster at Holkham. Coke was created Earl of Leicester in 1744, and died 15 years later. Holkham Hall was not finished at the time of his death, and it was left to his wife, Lady Margaret Tufton, Baroness de Clifford, to carry out Coke's plans for its completion. It is sad that Burlington, Kent and Coke did not live to see Holkham completed in all its splendour.

THE BUILDING OF HOLKHAM

Holkham is one of the finest examples of Palladian revival architecture in England and its grandeur has inspired many other mansions to adopt the Palladian style. Although plans had been drawn up by 1720, work did not begin in earnest until 1734, perhaps because Coke's fortunes suffered from speculation in the South Sea Bubble. Bricks were made on the estate from clay found just outside the park, and are a fine yellow-brown colour well suited to the bleak Norfolk landscape.

Although Kent was responsible for the design of the house, both Coke and Burlington contributed ideas at every stage. Matthew Brettingham, an architect from Norwich, was engaged as Clerk of the Works to oversee the building process. The

The richly coloured South Dining Room was known during the 18th century as the State Bed Chamber Apartment. Here guests would await an audience with the important occupant of the Green State Bedroom.

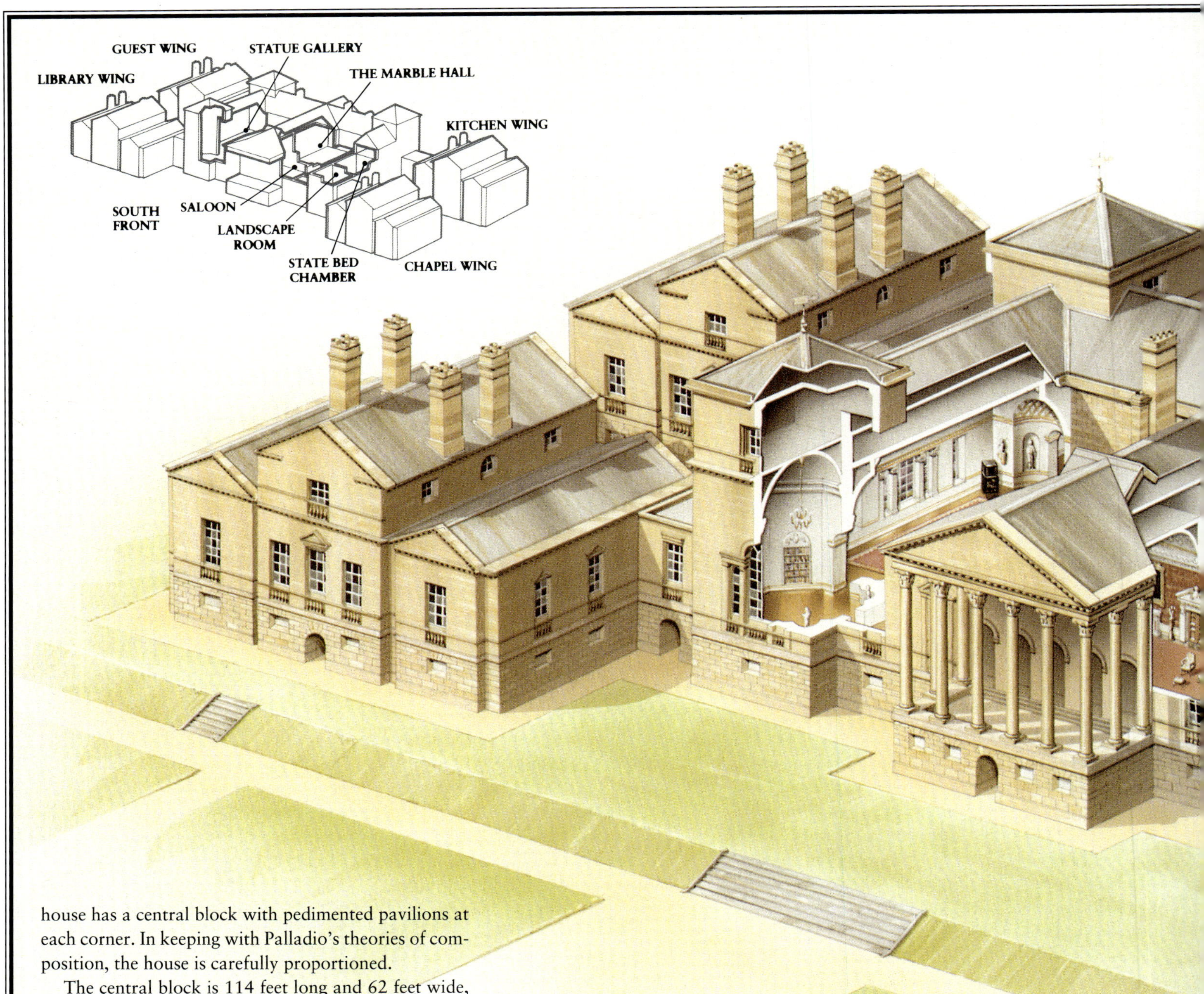

house has a central block with pedimented pavilions at each corner. In keeping with Palladio's theories of composition, the house is carefully proportioned.

The central block is 114 feet long and 62 feet wide, and the wings are all 60 feet by 70 feet, joined to the central block by corridors. The Hall was completed in 1762, and very little has been changed since then. The 2nd Earl added the north porch, and built the orangery and the fountain with statues of Perseus rescuing Andromeda from the sea-monster.

HOLKHAM'S TREASURES

Holkham has room after room of glittering splendour. Everywhere, there is evidence of Kent's outstanding talent, especially in the exquisitely carved scrolls, shells, cherubs and flowers on the ceilings, the walls and the furnishings. Coke's state rooms were never intended to be every day living quarters – they were meant to show off his incredible collection of art, and to dazzle the visitor with a display of Palladian magnificence.

The house is entered by the 2nd Earl's modest porch which leaves the visitor totally unprepared for the exuberant glory of the famous Marble Hall modelled on Vitruvius' design for a Temple of Justice. Fluted columns of Derbyshire alabaster soar 50 feet up to the lofty carved ceiling, the entire height of the house. Niches behind each of the columns hold full-length classical statues and a grand flight of Portland stone stairs sweeps up to the doorway surmounted by a bust of Coke.

The beautiful North Dining Room is a cube of 27 feet, excluding the niche in which stands a fine custom-made serving table of red porphyry topped with green Egyptian marble. The dome in the ceiling is based on a delicate gold and white design by Inigo Jones and is complemented perfectly by the fine Axminster carpet. One of the busts over the fireplace is of Aphrodite and is said to have come from the Parthenon. In the last century dinners at Holkham were lavish affairs, with a weekly average of 14 sheep, a bullock and a wide range of poultry and fish being eaten by the family and their large retinue of servants.

The 105-feet Statue Gallery and Tribunes hold one of the best private collections of classical sculpture in the world, collected by Coke over a 40-year period, and the design of the room is deliberately plain so as not to detract from them. Perhaps the most important is the bust of Thucydides, thought to be one of the earliest individual portraits in Greek art. The statue of Diana was reputedly owned by Cicero and was bought by Coke in 1717. Both statue and bust date from around 4BC.

The next room is the drawing room, hung with rich red velvet and fine paintings. The marble chimneypiece is from an Inigo Jones design, while above it is Pietro de Pietri's *Madonna in Gloria*. Some of the pictures have not been moved since they were originally hung here in 1773. The gorgeous saloon is hung with the original crimson Genoa velvet, and remains the principal reception room of the state apartments. Ruben's masterpiece *Return of the Holy Family* adorns one wall, and was

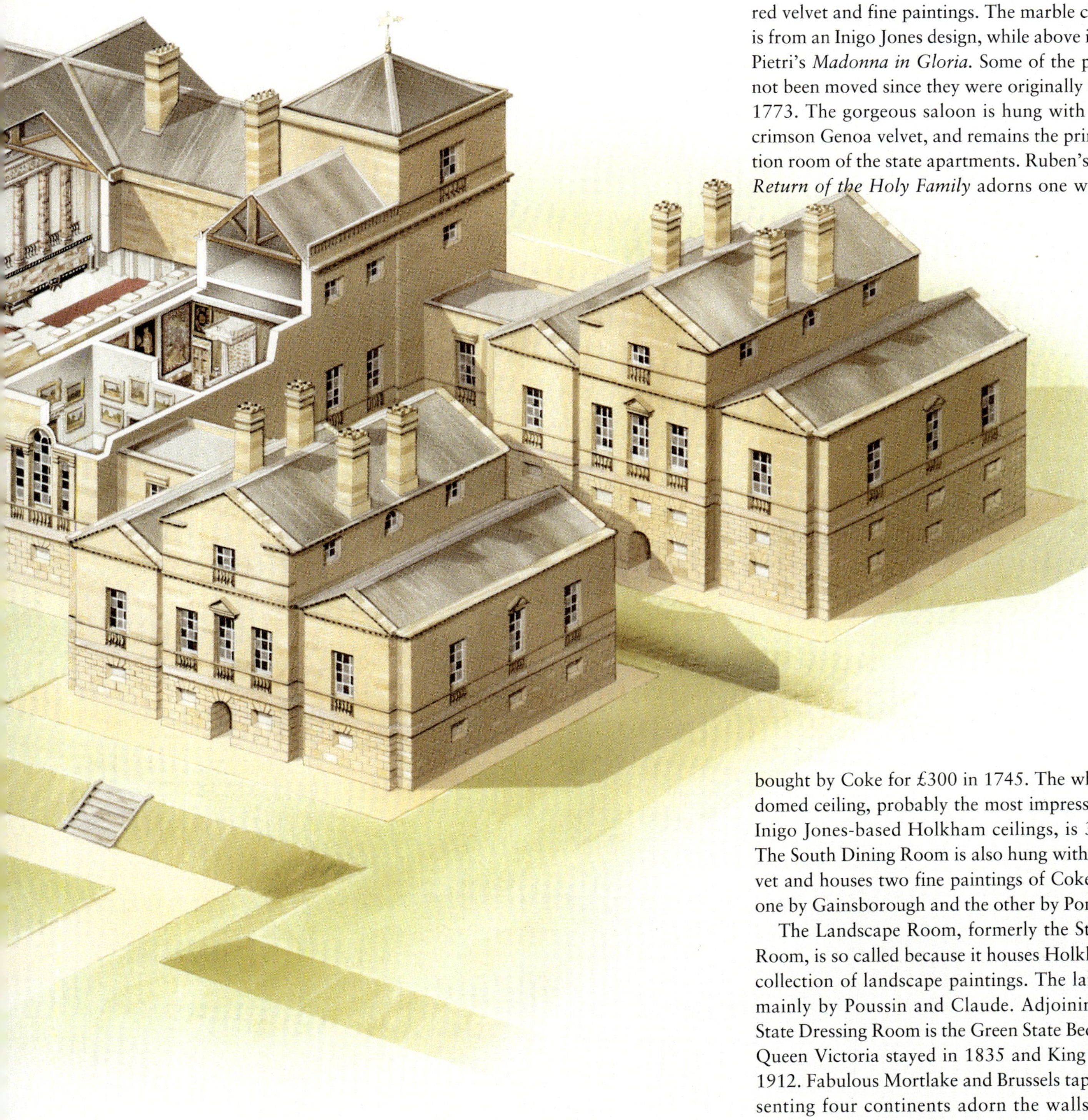

bought by Coke for £300 in 1745. The white and gold domed ceiling, probably the most impressive of all the Inigo Jones-based Holkham ceilings, is 32 feet high. The South Dining Room is also hung with crimson velvet and houses two fine paintings of Coke of Norfolk, one by Gainsborough and the other by Pompeo Batoni.

The Landscape Room, formerly the State Dressing Room, is so called because it houses Holkham's superb collection of landscape paintings. The landscapes are mainly by Poussin and Claude. Adjoining the Green State Dressing Room is the Green State Bedroom where Queen Victoria stayed in 1835 and King George V in 1912. Fabulous Mortlake and Brussels tapestries representing four continents adorn the walls. The North State Dressing Room and Bedroom and the State Sitting Room contain more fine art, most notably Bastiano di Sangallo's copy of the Michelangelo mural for the Palazzo Vecchio in Venice.

Houghton Hall

KINGS LYNN

WALPOLE'S SPLENDID PALLADIAN MANSION WITH EXQUISITE TAPESTRIES AND SUMPTUOUS STATE ROOMS WITH WILLIAM KENT MURALS: TEN MILES NORTH-EAST OF KING'S LYNN OFF THE A148.

Sir Robert Walpole, 1st Earl of Orford, and Prime Minister of England from 1730 to 1741, was born in 1676. While he was First Lord of the Treasury and Chancellor, his brother-in-law and ally, Charles, 2nd Viscount Townshend, was Secretary of State, and between them they wielded a formidable amount of power. When the relationship between these powerful men began to break down, Walpole's decision to build himself a glittering new palace at Houghton, a mere ten miles from Townshend's ancestral seat of Raynham Hall, infuriated Townshend.

By the time Walpole became Prime Minister, he had managed to engineer Townshend's resignation from the government, and Townshend retired to Raynham in bitter defeat. While Walpole lavishly entertained his influential friends from government and politics at Houghton, Townshend left the area altogether, and refused all invitations to visit.

But Walpole did not spend all his time at Houghton eating, drinking and hunting. He built up a fine collection of paintings by 120 Old Masters, as well as vast collections of furniture and sculpture. After his death in 1745, his feckless grandson sold most of the pictures to Catherine the Great, and they now grace the walls of the Hermitage Museum in St Petersburg. In 1797, Houghton passed to the Cholmondeley family, but it was not until 1913 that this magnificent palace became their permanent home.

Building at Houghton Hall was started in 1721 on the site of two earlier houses. The village of Houghton was demolished, and its inhabitants relocated outside the park gates; it then became known as New Houghton. It was not unusual in the 18th century for villages to be moved to suit their landlords. Walpole's house was originally designed by Colen Campbell, but James Gibbs added the cupola-like domes at each corner, and suggested that the main building material should be hard-wearing yellow sandstone brought by sea from Whitby.

Walpole left the entire interior design to William Kent, who added marble fireplaces, carved woodwork, many of the murals and much of the furniture. Kent's masterpiece is the cube-shaped 'stone hall' which has a plaster ceiling frieze by Atari and Bugutti, and reliefs over the fireplace and door by Michael Rysbrack. The other state rooms are also splendid. One of the dressing rooms is hung with rare Mortlake tapestries, while the Regency White Drawing Room has Louis XV tables laden with Sèvres porcelain.

The richly decorated rooms at Houghton Hall were suitably grand for Walpole's powerful political guests.

Chatsworth

BAKEWELL

ONE OF BRITAIN'S GREATEST HOUSES, WITH LAVISH ROOMS, PRICELESS COLLECTIONS AND MAGICAL GARDENS,: THREE MILES EAST OF BAKEWELL OFF THE B6012 BASLOW TO ROWSLEY ROAD.

Visitors have come to Chatsworth since the first house was built here in 1552 by the redoubtable Bess of Hardwick and her second husband, Sir William Cavendish. Two husbands on, Bess had Mary, Queen of Scots in the house several times as a prisoner, but little was done to update what must have already been a magnificent Elizabethan house until her Cavendish successors – created Dukes of Devonshire in 1694 for helping William of Orange to the throne – added a new South Front in 1687. Once rebuilding was in the blood, the other four sides were rapidly converted in rich classical style between 1700 and 1705. A century later the 6th Duke added a huge new North Wing, with rooms even grander than those of the earlier building, which became 'a museum of old furniture and a walk in wet weather'. Impressive though Chatsworth is from the outside – some of the window frames were even gilded on the outside – the treasures inside are overwhelming. Everything is on the most lavish scale. Painted gods swirl dizzily overhead in the monumental Painted Hall. The Great Stairs (one of 17 staircases in the house) lead to the 1st Duke's State Rooms on the second floor. The

THE EMPEROR FOUNTAIN

The 6th Duke's gardener, Joseph Paxton, designed and constructed the Emperor Fountain – a jet of water which shoots up some 280 feet from the Canal Pond – to honour a projected visit by Czar Nicholas in mid 1840s. Its construction involved draining the moor into an eight-acre man-made reservoir on high ground above the house, and the ambitious scheme was completed in just six months, after which the Czar failed to arrive.

The sight of Chatsworth from any angle is quite breathtaking, but this view, with the Emperor fountain and canal pond in the foreground, is one of the most famous.

6th Duke thought them all 'useless display' and wanted to make bedrooms out of the whole lot, but these were never rooms for relaxed living. Instead, they display the awesome wealth and power of the Cavendishes, with superb carved panelling, lavishly-painted ceilings and priceless objects at every turn. The overall impression is of polished wood, gold leaf and rich fabrics. Don't miss the *trompe-l'oeil* violin apparently hanging on a door in the Music Room. The chapel looks just as it did three centuries ago, and you can almost see the curly-wigged courtiers of Charles on the stiff-backed chairs, while the library, once the Long Gallery, took its present shape in the 1830s, and prepares us for the enormous dining room, like an outpost of Buckingham Palace, and the 6th Duke's Sculpture Gallery, a rather chilly assembly of neo-classical marbles typical of the first half of the last century.

Chatsworth's gardens, too, merit superlatives. There is formality, with the rectangular Canal Pond and with its huge Emperor Fountain. The Cascade has tumbled down the hillside since 1696, when the copper Willow Tree fountain, designed to spray unwary visitors, was already in place. More informal are the rockeries, including the waterfall which tumbles 45 feet over the Wellington Rock, the grotto and the tree-lined slopes of the arboretum, all conjured up by Paxton's magic.

■ In spite of the scale and grandeur of Chatsworth, it is still what it was designed to be – the home of the Cavendish family. This is due to my wife's skills as a decorator. She has turned large rooms which could have been unwelcoming into friendly and hospitable places for our family and all our visitors. ■

His Grace,
The Duke of Devonshire

Chillington Hall

Codsall Wood

A country house revealing the architectural style of Sir John Soane: between Albrighton and Codsall, off the A41; close to M54 junction 3.

The urban sprawl from the direction of Wolverhampton has not yet spread as far as Chillington Hall, which stands in the Park 'enlarged and improved' by 'Capability' Brown. The prestigious architect Sir John Soane was the abiding inspiration behind this striking red-brick house, having been offered the commission in about 1786 by Thomas Giffard. The Giffard family had held the Chillington estate since the 12th century.

Soane, whose masterpiece was to be the Bank of England, built on the foundations of an earlier Tudor mansion, and incorporated into his design a south wing built 60 years earlier. There have been few changes to the fabric of the hall since then, so, despite not being all of one build, Chillington represents one of Soane's most inventive forays into the design of country houses.

Through the entrance hall, with its screen of slender Ionic columns, is the saloon, occupying what had been the Great Hall of the Tudor house. This large, rectangular room is crowned by an oval dome; the only available light comes in from a lantern at the top. It illustrates Soane's love of contrasting curves later to be seen in many of his interiors in the old Bank of England. The fireplace is perhaps later – but looks earlier – and features armorial fragments from the old house.

Three other rooms – the drawing room, dining room and library – also reveal Soane's idiosyncratic styling. The Morning Room, in the older south wing, offers a more relaxed ambience. The splendid early 18th-century Staircase Hall, opening onto a fine wooden staircase with delicately carved tread-ends, features frivolous plasterwork of figures and busts.

Within the park is the Pool, a great lake created by Brown and embellished with temples and bridges, which was described by the architect, James Paine, who himself designed one of the bridges, as 'one of the finest pieces of water, within an inclosure, that this Kingdom produces.' It is worth a visit to Chillington simply to walk around the Pool.

Whitmore Hall

NEWCASTLE-UNDER-LYME

A CAROLINE MANOR HOUSE IN RICHLY COLOURED BRICKWORK: FOUR AND A HALF MILES SOUTH-WEST OF NEWCASTLE-UNDER-LYME OFF THE A53.

Whitmore Hall has been the home of the Mainwaring family and their ancestors since 1086, though the fabric of the building has undergone a number of changes in the intervening years. One thing is unchanged, however; the house has changed hands only through inheritance, and has never been sold.

Whitmore Hall is revealed at the end of a delightful tree-lined avenue. Typical of its age, the hall has nine bays, two storeys, sash windows and elaborate chimney stacks sprouting from a hipped roof. The south front of the house – all richly coloured brick, dressed stone and balustrades along the top – was added in 1676, to conceal the original, half-timbered Elizabethan façade. Most of the back part of the hall was destroyed by a fire of 1880.

The interior is 18th century in style. The downstairs rooms lead off from a classical central hall, which boasts some 18th-century portraits of the Mainwaring family. In the long drawing room, decorated in understated greens and creams, are various 18th-century paintings and fine Georgian furniture – including a William and Mary walnut cabinet. On the other side of a hallway is the part-panelled dining room, containing a funeral hatchment.

The Admiral Room takes its name from Admiral Rowland Mainwaring, a larger-than-life figure whose preliminary sketches were used by Luny for his painting *The Battle of the Nile*. The painting hangs here, alongside a portrait of the admiral himself.

The stable block is as handsome as the house itself. Dating from about 1600, the rustic wooden stalls are still in place. They are divided by Tuscan pillars and topped with elaborate arches, whose shapes are repeated on the back wall. Behind the Hall is delightfully landscaped parkland whose principal features are an extensive lake and woodland garden.

A double avenue of lime trees draws the eye to the impressive entrance of Whitmore Hall.

Eyam Hall

EYAM

A COMFORTABLE LATE 17TH-CENTURY HOME EVOKING MEMORIES OF REMARKABLE SELF-SACRIFICE: IN THE CENTRE OF EYAM, THREE MILES NORTH-WEST OF BASLOW OFF THE A623.

Plague put the village of Eyam on the map in 1665. Part of Eyam Hall was already in existence then, but for the most part this typical Derbyshire manor dates from 1671, when Thomas Wright, a forebear of the present owners, built it for his son John. Their portraits are still in the house. The building has changed little since their day. It is modest in size, part of the village rather than standing aloof, and gives the impression that the Wrights must always have been in the thick of local affairs. Behind its elegant gateway on the village street its entrance front, with two solid wings and central doorway, has leaded windows that add glittering life to a restrained façade. Once inside, the comfortable prosperity of the building is all-embracing. The large entrance hall sets the tone, with its beamed ceiling and

THE PLAGUE AT EYAM

Near Eyam Hall stands Plague Cottage, where in 1665 Mary Cooper took as lodger George Viccars, a tailor. An order of cloth arrived damp and, unknown to him, infected with bacillus from the plague which was at that time raging in London. He spread it out to dry in front of the fire, allowing the plague-carrying fleas to escape. Soon Viccars died, followed by Mary's son and several neighbours. The Rector, William Mompesson, persuaded the villagers to quarantine themselves so that the plague wouldn't spread beyond the village. For a year they stayed put, eating food left for them on the village boundary and burying their own dead. The plague was contained, but of 350 people in Eyam, 259 died.

Far left: The Tapestry Room at Eyam Hall has some beautiful examples of the art, which have recently been cleaned and restored.

Left: This bedroom is furnished with many 17th-century pieces, including the splendid tester bed.

wide 18th-century fireplace. Two huge settles at each side of the fire have been in the house since at least 1694, and in the rare 17th-century cedar coffer the present owners discovered early bedhangings – some can be seen elsewhere in the house. Major John Wright, whose swaggering portrait hangs here, served in America in 1777. The staircase, probably Jacobean, may have come from another house – no one is quite sure – and romantic tradition says that the heart it incorporates was for John Wright and his bride Elizabeth when they moved into their new home.

The Tapestry Room is hung with examples of several different periods, including a 15th-century Flemish tapestry. Several have been unceremoniously cut up to fill the walls, like draught-proof wallpaper. Engraved on the library window is an 18th-century poem in praise of Fanny Holme, 'ye pride of natures beauteous Powers', but as she never married into the family, she presumably never occupied the magnificent 17th-century bed, with its solid wooden roof, in the next room. In the dining room, once part of the original kitchen, the table is set for a Victorian dinner party, while in the kitchen proper the present owners have uncovered the fireplace of around 1700 and furnished the room with old kitchen implements, much enjoyed by children in weekly 'hands-on' recreations of the past.

■ The particular attraction of Eyam Hall is that it is essentially a family home, not a museum. My family greatly enjoy living in such a beautiful place, full of memories of the many generations of Wrights who have gone before. ■

Nicola Wright

Melbourne Hall

MELBOURNE

LITERARY, ROYAL AND POLITICAL CONNECTIONS, AND A GARDEN INSPIRED BY VERSAILLES: ON THE EDGE OF MELBOURNE ON THE B587.

In the 13th and 14th centuries, the Bishops of Carlisle used to come to Melbourne to escape from the troublesome Scots, and used the superb Norman church next door as their cathedral. From the 15th century their house was let to a succession of absentee landlords, who included Thomas Cromwell, Lord Chancellor of England. Then, at the end of the 16th century, the current lessee, Sir Francis Needham, decided to make Melbourne Hall his home and set about the substantial amount of work needed to make it habitable. A large part of the house was demolished and rebuilt, and the oldest part of the building we see today dates from that period.

The Hall was again altered considerably by Sir John Coke, Secretary of State to Charles I and ancestor of the hall's present owners. Further classical additions, designed by Smith of Warwick, followed in the 18th century, with the result that the interior of the house is a pleasantly confusing muddle. It has certainly known the great and the good – and bad – including two of Queen Victoria's Prime Ministers, Lords Melbourne and Palmerston, and Lady Caroline Lamb, mistress of Lord Byron, who was banished here before her formal separation from her husband. They would still recognise much of the furniture and many of the pictures, which include Stuart courtiers by Lely and royal portraits by Kneller.

A conservatory-style Edwardian Billiard Room, added to the Hall in 1911 by roofing the space between the two wings, serves as the visitors' entrance, but most of the house is mid 18th century in character. The formal drawing room has four symmetrical doorcases, while there is good 17th-century panelling in the dining room, once the Great Hall. This is probably the only room which Sir John Coke might still recognise from his original house.

It is Thomas Coke, Queen Anne's Vice-Chamberlain, whom we must thank for Melbourne's greatest glory, the Versailles-inspired garden laid out with advice from the royal gardeners, London and Wise. This rare survival was begun in 1704 with 'terraces, sloops, verges and fleets of steps' running down to the lake, or Great Basin. To the south there are radiating avenues of lime trees, with statues, including the massive 'Four Seasons Vause' supplied by the leading London maker, Van Nost. A grotto, near the chain of pools, has an inscription from Lady Caroline Lamb. Most spectacular of all are the yew tunnel, nearly 300 feet long, and a delicate wrought-iron arbour, the Birdcage, designed and made by Robert Bakewell. It cost Coke £120, and nearly bankrupted Bakewell. With gilded leaves rambling over its filigree dome, and suns, moons and flowers decorating its walls, it has no equal in Britain.

■ At Melbourne great care has always been taken, with limited resources, to bring together the work of great artists. Hopefully this can be seen in the architecture, pictures, furniture and the gardens here. The owners of the house have always taken an interest in all these things, which contributes to the atmosphere of the place as a family house of history. ■

Lord Ralph Kerr

Haddon Hall

Bakewell

■ **The charm of this great old house lies in its defiance of the onslaught of the centuries. Completely unspoilt, Haddon Hall is now as it has always been.** ■
His Grace,
The Duke of Rutland CBE

Haddon, one of England's most welcoming and magical houses, with its idyllic garden on a wooded hillside and romantic legend of elopement, lay untouched from the late 17th century until its sympathetic 20th-century restoration by the 9th Duke of Rutland: one and a half miles south of Bakewell on the A6.

'All Derbyshire is but a world of peaked hills which from some of the highest you discover the rest like steeples … as thick as can be,' wrote that indefatigable traveller Celia Fiennes when she visited the county in 1697. Yet this inhospitable landscape has long cradled two of the most remarkable houses in England – the princely Chatsworth and, just over the hill, Haddon. 'It's a good old house, all built of stone on a hill, but nothing very curious as the mode now is,' Celia commented in her sharp way. Hers is not a judgement that history has agreed with, for less than ten years after her visit the Manners family, who had owned Haddon since 1567, left the house for Belvoir Castle when they were raised to the Dukedom of Rutland. For 200 years Haddon slumbered like the Sleeping Beauty's castle. It was kept ticking over, repaired where necessary, but as changes of taste swirled around it – as the fashions for Baroque, Palladian, neo-Classical or High Victorian laid their sometimes heavy hand on other houses – Haddon remained unchanged, its grey towers with their blanket of ivy floating magically over the dense trees, as if waiting for their Prince Charming to breathe the breath of life into them once again.

THE MARQUIS OF GRANBY

And like all the best fairy stories, that of Haddon has a happy ending, for Prince Charming did come, though he was a Duke rather than a prince. The 9th Duke of Rutland, while still the Marquis of Granby, came back to Haddon at the beginning of this century and began its restoration. The care with which it had been kept since the 1700s meant that his task, which he carried out with enormous sympathy, not just for the structure of the house but also for its unique atmosphere, was less daunting than it might have been. The Duke (he succeeded his father in 1925) insisted on two things – that as much as possible should be preserved in the house, and that, where it was necessary to replace, the highest standards of craftsmanship were to be used. Work began in 1920, and by his death in 1940 he had seen beauty awaken at Haddon once again.

DOROTHY VERNON'S ELOPEMENT

Is the elopement of Dorothy Vernon with Sir John Manners a romantic fiction? No-one knows, but their marriage brought Haddon to the Manners family. Dorothy's father, Sir George, supposedly disapproved of Manners – even though his father was Earl of Rutland – so in 1563, during a wedding party, Dorothy slipped away from the Hall, down the garden steps and over the packhorse bridge to where Sir John was waiting. They rode through the night, and were married next day. If there was a quarrel, it was patched up, for Sir George left Haddon to them on his death in 1567.

EARLY HISTORY

The beauty of Haddon is not simply the result of the 9th Duke's restorations, of course. Like many fine houses, it owes its particular character to its past – a past that begins with the gift by William the Conqueror of the manor and village of Nether Haddon to his illegitimate son Peverel, who is recorded as being in possession of them by the Domesday Book. It seems likely that Peverel, or his successor at Haddon, William Avenel, built some sort of defences on the top of the limestone outcrop above the River Wye, covering much the same area as the Hall does today, although there is no evidence of a keep. Norman stonework remains at the bases of several of the towers, especially the one still known as Peverel's Tower at the highest point of the rock, and provides a solid foundation for subsequent building. In 1195 the king granted a licence to the Vernons, who were descended from Avenel, to build around Haddon *'muro exalto XII pedibus sine kernello'* – a wall 12 feet high without battlements. Much of that wall, with later battlements, still exists. It formed a large open courtyard, with the chapel, once the parish church of the now vanished Nether Haddon, at one corner.

The most significant event in Haddon's development came around 1370, when Sir Richard de Vernon built a new and up-to-date wing right across the centre of the courtyard. It held – and still holds – the typical medieval layout of hall, parlour, kitchen and other domestic apartments. The buildings, with their varied roof-lines and mixture of stone, still look much as they did when they were built, except for the later two-storied porch, added in around 1450. The mid 16th-century north-west gate tower, approached by a steep climb from the river valley, is the highest accent in the collection of elements that make up Haddon, and there are steps leading from its archway into the courtyard.

ELIZABETHAN TIMES

Bay windows and tall chimneys were added in Tudor times, but the most magnificent – and the last – of the additions to Haddon came around 1600, when Sir John Manners, who had reputedly eloped with the heiress Dorothy Vernon, built the Long Gallery. He was no doubt spurred on by the example of the Countess of Shrewsbury, Bess of Hardwick, whose gallery at Hardwick Hall was completed three years earlier, as well, no doubt, as his pride in the ownership of an already considerable house. From the terraced garden it is a pattern book for late Elizabethan building, with huge windows whose leading and diamond panes are deliberately set at different angles so as to glitter in the sun. And with the Long Gallery, development at Haddon virtually ceases. It is like an insect fixed in time by its capture in a bead of amber, perfect and unchanged.

The 9th Duke of Rutland helped to polish it, and it is fitting that the first rooms we see are the bedroom and inner chamber he used as he directed operations. Occupying the medieval place of honour, above the main entrance, they were built at the beginning of the 16th century by Sir Henry Vernon, and were given new plaster ceilings and honey-coloured panelling more than a hundred years later. Some of the detritus of domestic life that the Duke's operations uncovered are on display in the museum in the lower courtyard. It is in these everyday objects that we come closer to life at Haddon over the centuries. A child's shoe, a pot of dice, even wood and brass washing tallies, with intricate revolving dials that helped to keep track of 'Ruffes, Bandes and Cappes, Boothose, Pillowberes and Towells', speak directly to us of our ancestors.

PROVIDING FOR BODY AND SOUL

In the Chapel of St Nicholas, too, we can feel the nearness of the past, for all the owners of Haddon have worshipped here, from the Norman era to the time the Manners family moved away to Belvoir. The south aisle and the font are Norman (though the font cover is Jacobean), and the north aisle was added when Sir Richard Vernon built his great hall in the 1370s. Later still is the 15th-century chancel, and the roof was renewed as late as 1624. Even more remarkable than this wide span of dates is the reappearance, after centuries of being hidden under layers of Puritan whitewash, of the riot of 14th- and 15th-century wall paintings. The most conspicuous is of St Christopher carrying the Christ Child. It is a scene painted as vividly as if it were taking place in the River Wye below the Hall, with the saint surrounded by leaves and flowers, his feet sending swirling eddies rushing through the water. There are less complete paintings showing scenes from the life of St Nicholas, and three grinning skeletons as a reminder of our mortality. Among the chapel's other treasures are nine alabaster panels carved with scenes from the life of Jesus. They still retain the colour that was applied more than 500 years ago when they were made.

After spiritual nourishment in the chapel, where better to go than the kitchen? Once open to full height of the building, it was divided by a wooden ceiling in the 16th century, but it still gives the impression of past

Haddon Hall reflects a sense of history and continuity which can only come from remaining in the same family for over 800 years. The gardens step down in terraces to the River Wye below.

feasts. Huge solid tables, their tops in places worn thin by centuries of chopping and cutting, stand by the vast fireplaces. Bread was baked in the domed ovens off the kitchen and given to the village poor from the dole cupboards that still survive in the larder.

Across the Screens Passage, with its Roman stone altar to Mercury which was dug up in a nearby field, is one of the glories of Haddon – the Banqueting Hall. Perhaps here, more than in any other room in the Hall, we can understand how a great house was the centre of the community. It takes little effort to imagine the rush-strewn floor, the long tables seating 50 or so of the family and retainers, the tallow candles and flaring torches, the highly-spiced food, the dogs – and the rats – fighting for scraps, the noise, even the smell. The only part of this room less than 350 years old is the splendid roof, put up by the 9th Duke in 1924 using timbers from the Rutland estates. The screen, one of the best in the country, dates from about 1450 and supports a musicians' gallery. The tapestry behind the table on the dais was woven in France, but displays the English royal coat of arms. Thought to be a gift to the Vernons from Henry VIII, it commemorates the link between Henry's elder brother, Prince Arthur, and his treasurer, Sir Henry Vernon. Arthur, who often visited Haddon, died before his father, leaving a huge question about how English history would have been altered if he, and not Henry, had become king.

THE FAMILY ROOMS

Communal living in the hall may have been conducive to the feudal spirit, but the Vernons required privacy too. So beyond the Hall was a chamber for family use, originally the same height, but divided by a ceiling in about 1500. When Sir Henry Vernon had the ceiling installed, he had it painted, too, and, wonderfully, the work survives, like a slightly faded patchwork quilt suspended above the room. Against a background of chess-board squares are panels with the Tudor Rose (Sir Henry keeping on the right side of his royal employer?) and the badge of the Earls of Shrewsbury, the Talbot Dog – also perhaps a shrewd move, for Sir Henry had married the Earl's daughter Anne. It is a room of great warmth, despite the feeling that Sir Henry may have protested his loyalty too much, where Tudor elegance and manners had their full expression.

Upstairs, above the dining room, is the Great Chamber, its character largely of the 17th century, when the plaster frieze and the ceiling over the bay window were added, and when the panelling, once painted green and gold, were introduced. It holds part of Haddon's fine collection of tapestries, which for two hundred years hung from the Tudor iron hooks on walls throughout the empty building. Taken down for restoration in 1898, they were stored in a room that suffered badly in a fire in 1925. Sixty pieces were totally destroyed, so what we see today is only a fraction of that rich collection. Pride of place goes to a set depicting the Five Senses, woven at the Mortlake factory in the early 17th century for Charles I, and sold after his execution.

The Earl's Bedroom next to the Great Chamber was created in about 1500, and was used by the then Earls of Rutland between 1641 and their departure, as Dukes, to Belvoir in 1703. With an adjoining dressing room, they are comfortable but by no means grand.

THE LONG GALLERY

For grandeur, we need to look to the Long Gallery, reached by massive semicircular oak steps. Many Long Galleries are of greater dimensions

and contain more rare paintings and fine furniture, but the Long Gallery at Haddon is exceptionally beautiful, due in some part to the quality of the light streaming in through the leaded windows. The oak panelling has been lightened by graining to resemble walnut, and is divided into arches by Corinthian columns. The family crests of the Vernons and the Manners – the boar's head and the peacock – are carved in the oak. The coved plaster ceiling, with its typical geometrical patterns, is not too heavy or distracting, yet adds texture to the view along the Gallery. It is this room that leaves the greatest impression on its visitors, and a special feeling of gratitude to its Prince Charming, the 9th Duke, who can be seen with his heir in the 1933 painting of Haddon by Rex Whistler over the Gallery fireplace.

THE GARDENS AND GROUNDS

While the Long Gallery was being built, Sir John Manners also turned his attention to the garden. He built the terraces with their strong walls and fine balustrades, and the long flight of steps that leads down towards the river. Altered and replanted in the 1640s, the gardens needed wholesale clearance when the 9th Duke and his Duchess began their restorations. The replanting was, like the whole reawakening of the house, done with excellent taste and discretion, so that no other English garden is so well integrated with the house it surrounds, or so memorable in its variety of effects. This is no attempt to recreate a period garden, but a creation which succeeds on its own, superb terms to perfectly complete the magic of Haddon.

NORTH OF ENGLAND

PELE TOWERS, needed for security in the wild lands of the north, became part of comfortable houses in more settled times: as at Levens Hall, that gorgeous Elizabethan mansion full of ghosts which understandably refuse to leave it and its topiary. The same is true of Muncaster Castle, with its superlative views over Eskdale, while Raby Castle bares its savage teeth in County Durham. Further south, civilised grandeur peaks in the baroque magnificence of Castle Howard and the Georgian stylishness of Harewood House, while Carlton Towers represents Victorian Gothic at it most weird and exciting. Newby Hall is a Wren-style dream in red brick. Gillow furniture and birds of prey distinguish Leighton Hall. Charlotte Brontë knew Norton Conyers and Wordsworth lived at Rydal Mount. Browsholme Hall belongs to the hereditary Bowbearers of the Forest of Bowland, Sledmere House takes its charm from generations of Sykeses, while Leghs have resided at Adlington Hall through seven centuries.

Adlington Hall

ADLINGTON

A HANDSOME MANOR HOUSE, IN CONTRASTING ARCHITECTURAL STYLES, THE HOME OF THE LEGH FAMILY SINCE 1315: FOUR MILES NORTH OF MACCLESFIELD OFF THE A523 STOCKPORT ROAD.

Right: Fine craftsmanship is displayed in Adlington Hall's Angel Roof, dating from 1505.

Cheshire is a county renowned for its 'black and white' architecture, but even in the midst of so many architectural gems, Adlington Hall will certainly not disappoint its visitors. On the site of a hunting lodge, the hall is built around a quadrangle and was at one time surrounded by a moat. Since the beginning of the 14th century Adlington has been owned by the Legh family, whose ancestors include King Stephen and one Gilbert de Venables, who was knighted by William the Conqueror on the battlefield at Hastings. A later Legh fought at Poitiers and was listed as one of the Black Prince's Esquires

The Great Hall was built by Thomas Legh at the end of the 15th century, first in timber, then refaced in brick and stone. The rest of the house was added in 1581, by another Thomas Legh, mostly in the half-timbered style so typical of this area. The north front was rebuilt by yet another Thomas Legh in about 1670.

Successive owners have made further additions, reflecting the changing tastes of successive generations, and the result is an intriguing amalgam of architectural styles. The black and white, half-timbered façade of the east front is the one that first greets the visitor, though entry to the house is through a tall and handsome portico that rests on four Ionic columns.

Adlington's glory is the Great Hall, the first impression one of space. The hall is 45 feet long, 26 feet wide, and the roof-ridge is fully 38 feet high – a splendid example of the hammer-beam style, which is richly embellished with mouldings and carvings. Two oak trees support the east end of the hall, all that now remain of the original hunting lodge, and above the panelling of this noble apartment are large murals. Some of these murals had at some stage been plastered over and were only rediscovered when a member of the family damaged the plasterwork while playing shuttlecock.

The dining room, by contrast, is altogether simpler

THE ADLINGTON ORGAN

Adlington Hall boasts a particularly fine organ, its pipes topped by trumpet-playing cherubs, which can be found in the Great Hall, between a pair of carved oak trees. It was made in about 1670 by 'Father' Bernard Smith. By 1805 the organ had been damaged, and remained silent until 1959, when it was restored to full working order. It is now the largest 17th-century organ in the country, and none is in better repair.

Below: The quadrangle at Adlington Hall is a fine setting for the splendid black-and-white architecture.

Below right: The magnificent organ by Bernard Smith.

in style, with plainer panelling, and here the decoration is mostly provided by family portraits. The walls of the beautifully proportioned drawing room are divided into panels by fluted Corinthian columns. Above the doors and the marble fireplace are carved festoons of fruit and leaves. A minstrels' gallery provides an alternative view down into the Great Hall.

The gardens were landscaped in the style which 'Capability' Brown had popularised. At one time they featured such exotica as a hermitage, a Chinese bridge and even a mock castle. Today's visitors can still see a Temple to Diana and take a leisurely stroll along the Yew Walk and Lime Avenue.

Arley Hall

NORTHWICH

A VICTORIAN RED-BRICK RESIDENCE IN A NEO-JACOBEAN STYLE: FOUR AND A HALF MILES NORTH OF NORTHWICH OFF THE A559.

The Arley estate has been in the Egerton-Warburton family since the 15th century, though the Hall itself is a Victorian edifice. It replaced an 18th-century house which was itself built onto an earlier timber-framed house. It was Rowland Egerton-Warburton who, in 1832, approved the plans for the building we see today, which is a symmetrical, many-windowed design every bit as conservative as its owner. The architect was a local man, George Latham of Nantwich. Today it is the Hon. Michael and Mrs Flower who care for the Hall, and extend a welcome to visitors.

The entrance is through a red-brick gatehouse topped with a wooden clock tower, part of a group of outbuildings which includes a handsome cruck-framed barn dating back to the family's first occupancy of the estate. The barn now offers refreshments and light meals in authentically antique surroundings.

The sturdy façade of the Hall itself is enlivened by diamond-shaped patterns in the brickwork, heraldic beasts and ornamental chimneys which have been given an anachronistic 'barley-sugar' twist. The few genuine Jacobean details, salvaged from older houses, cannot disguise the fact that Arley Hall represents both a style and a self-confidence that typify the Victorian era.

While Arley Hall boasts few paintings of note, the spacious rooms, with their high ceilings, are full of fine craftsmanship – particularly voluminous fireplaces, wood panelling and plaster work. The wooden bookcases in the library reveal something of a taste for Gothic eccentricity. The drawing room provides an intimate space for some of the family's treasured possessions, while the dining room contains virginals dating back to 1675. Throughout the house are a number of long-case clocks and some fine porcelain.

Having invested in the solid virtues of bricks and mortar, the Hall's founder next sought to cater for his family's spiritual welfare. Architect Anthony Salvin was called in to create a private chapel, largely in the Decorated Gothic style that became so popular during Victoria's reign. But Rowland Egerton-Warburton's energies extended far beyond the Arley estate, and he took it upon himself to both build and repair buildings in some of the nearby villages.

The 12 acres of gardens are a special delight. Originally laid out by Rowland Egerton-Warburton while the Hall itself was under construction, they have been brought to their present condition through the attentions of Lady Ashbrook, the mother of the present owner. There are many garden styles to enjoy, including a splendid double herbaceous border, yew hedges, topiary, a walled garden, a herb garden and a colourful collection of more than 200 varieties of rhododendrons. An avenue of clipped *Quercus Ilex* contrasts with the grove and its informal woodland walks.

Top: The present Arley Hall is the latest in a succession of houses on the site.

Above: The delightful gardens at Arley received the 'Garden of the Year' award in 1987.

■ **Although the beauty of my family's home is disputed, its power is great. It can repel violently or attract irrevocably. To many its exotic towers, domes and pinnacles are preposterous, but to others its inimitable British quality offers a special fascination. We are held in its spell particularly at dusk when its commanding profile reminds us of eastern minarets, tales of Arabian Nights and the romances of the Round Table. Then, to those who love this home, it fleetingly becomes a palace to be cherished all the more.** ■

William Bromley-Davenport

Capesthorne Hall

MACCLESFIELD

BLACKENED TOWERS RISE UP FROM VICTORIAN BRICKWORK, SURROUNDED BY BEAUTIFUL PARKLAND: FOUR AND A HALF MILES WEST OF MACCLESFIELD OFF THE A537 AND THE A34.

The Bromley-Davenport family has owned land in Cheshire for almost a thousand years. From the time of Domesday the heads of the family had undertaken the role of Chief Forester, a post which carried the responsibility for maintaining law and order in the forests of Leek and Macclesfield. Since then many family members have served in parliament, providing Westminster with both a Chancellor and a Speaker. The present owner, Walter Henry Bromley-Davenport, is Lord Lieutenant for Cheshire.

The original 15th-century Hall is long gone; nothing remains now except some grassy mounds and a commemorative monument. The present Hall is more recent, dating from 1719, with major rebuilding in 1837 by architect Edward Blore, who largely created Capesthorne Hall in the form familiar to visitors today.

Visitors may well think twice before describing the exterior of the Hall as 'beautiful'. Some have admired its unique English character, others have called it frankly grotesque. Few, however, would cavil at its situation, amidst 60 sweeping acres of parkland, gardens, woods and lakes.

The house is announced from a distance by smoke-blackened towers, domes and pinnacles rising up from the Cheshire countryside. The entrance hall leads immediately into the Sculpture Gallery, where visitors can admire Capesthorne's important collection of classical marbles and later busts. In the Saloon it is not difficult to imagine the scene during one of the dances and festivities that were frequently held here. The unusual chairs and sofas were made in Ceylon, especially to be displayed at Capesthorne.

The drawing room, one of many reconstructed by Anthony Salvin after a disastrous fire in 1861, which destroyed the central part of the house. The twin fireplaces, brought here from the family's town house in Belgravia, bear the date 1789 and are splendid examples of Coade stone. Through the drawing room is the Bromley Staircase, lined with portraits of the Bromley family. Upstairs, outside the Dorothy Davenport Room, is a fascinating collection of watercolours painted before the fire in *c*1837 by James Johnson and Edward Blore. Further on is a family tree that traces their unbroken descent from the Norman Conquest.

In the Queen Anne Room is a monumental fireplace displaying the family arms, portrait busts, reliefs of Roman emperors and classical priests. The Coalport china displayed in the two alcoves was the inspiration behind the apple green walls and contemporary fabric.

In an area well represented by historic parkland, Capesthorne's 60 acres lose nothing by comparison. There is a trio of lakes, formed by damming a nearby stream, around which are shady walks and scenic views back towards the house. A mirror trout of over 33lbs, taken in 1983 by a lucky angler, proved to be a record catch for Cheshire. In summer the water surface is brightened by the floating blooms of the yellow waterlily. There are lovely walks at any season of the year, though in springtime they are enhanced by profusions of bluebells and rhododendrons.

This portrait of Speaker Bromley was painted by Michael Dahl.

Dorfold Hall

NANTWICH

A GABLED JACOBEAN HOUSE, AT THE END OF AVENUE OF LIME TREES: A LITTLE WAY WEST OF NANTWICH ON THE WREXHAM ROAD.

Ralph Wilbraham's portrait hangs in the dining room of Dorfold Hall, to the right of the mantlepiece. It was he who built this handsome Jacobean house, to celebrate in brick and stone the success he and his family

DISHARMONY OF LANDSCAPING!

In 1862 Wilbraham Spencer Tollemache had the path and gardens of Dorfold Hall re-designed by William Nesfield. These changes were wrought, so the story goes, while his wife was away on holiday. On returning she was apparently so displeased with the results that she refused to speak to her husband for three months!

were enjoying in the legal profession. The main block and the two forecourt lodges are of the same period, dated 1616. Dorfold Hall may have been the site of the manor of Edwin, the last Saxon Earl of Chester, and a grandson of Lady Godiva, whose place in folklore was secured by one short, but memorable, horse ride.

By the end of the 18th century Dorfold was one of Cheshire's most important hunting centres. The name 'Dorfold' is derived from the Saxon word 'Deofold', indicating a cattle enclosure or deer park. Even today this remains a quiet and well-wooded corner of the county.

It is remarkable that Dorfold survived the Civil War. Its second owner, Roger Wilbraham, took the Parliamentarian side, an allegiance which led to the house being plundered by Royalist forces in 1643. After five generations of Wilbrahams, Dorfold was bought by another legal man, James Tomkinson, who planted many of the fine trees in the garden, and added the stables for his two dozen hunters. The house has since been handed down to the Roundell family. Dorfold was the last hall in the district to relinquish the 'open house' hospitality of Georgian times, boasting its own butchery, bakery and brew-house.

The Great Chamber's barrel-vaulted plaster ceiling, executed in 1621, is very special; there are few better Jacobean examples in England. The original chimneypiece, with its Doric columns and family coat of arms, is still in place, as is the ornate panelling. The chamber offers a suitable setting for a selection of fine 16th- and 17th-century furniture and modern family portraits.

■ Dorfold Hall remains a beautiful family house, all fully lived in, which to many visitors gives it a special appeal. ■
R C Roundell

Peover Hall

KNUTSFORD

CENTURIES OF HISTORY IN MELLOW BRICKWORK, HIDDEN DOWN A COUNTRY LANE: THREE MILES SOUTH OF KNUTSFORD, OFF THE A50.

The original Peover Hall was replaced in 1585, as an engraved stone over the original entrance reveals, and the house provides a potted story of architectural styles down the years. Peover (pronounced 'Peever' hereabouts) was the brainchild of Sir Randle Mainwaring, whose family had already held land here for centuries.

The irregular exterior of the three-storey house reveals a curious mixture of Tudor and Elizabethan styles; numerous alterations down the years have failed to produce the symmetrical façade no doubt envisaged by Sir Henry Mainwaring, who added a wing about 1760. We can only surmise that his plans extended to demolishing the rest of the old house, and completing the building, but if that was the case, the plan was never carried through. Today some frontages are square, while others are gabled.

Peover Hall is now owned by Randle Brooks, whose good stewardship has extended to a sympathetic remodelling of the house and creating some delightful gardens and wooded parkland. The old Georgian wing, found to be in poor condition, was demolished and replaced by a new block in an Elizabethan style. While Peover cannot boast of any royal personage having 'slept here', it was requisitioned during the World War II by General George Patton of the US Army, and served as his headquarters. Tank tracks can still be recognised in the park.

Inside, the décor, too, reflects personal taste rather than a single unified style. What was once the kitchen is now the Great Hall, dignified by two monumental fireplaces, displays of armour and an unusual ceiling plan in which the beams are laid diagonally. The Long Gallery at the top of the house is open to the pleasing curves of the original Tudor roof timbers; here are displayed many of the family's treasures. The bedrooms are noted for a collection of four-poster beds, pride of place going to an enormous bed, dated 1559, which came from Tamworth Castle.

Peover also has unique Caroline stables, built in 1664 for Thomas Mainwaring, with 13 wooden stalls and an ornamental plaster ceiling.

Peover Hall and its lovely gardens are in a peaceful corner of Cheshire.

Rode Hall

Scholar Green

An attractive red-brick house, set in deep woodland above a reed-fringed lake: about three miles south of Congleton off the A34 Newcastle-under-Lyme road.

Rode Hall is still owned by the family that built it. The Wilbrahams have been a notable Cheshire family since the 13th century, and before the present Hall was built, a timber-framed house occupied this site. Then, in about 1700, Randle Wilbraham built a house of such modest proportions that within a few years it had been downgraded to become the servants' quarters. It wasn't until the present Hall was built, in the middle of the 18th century, that the Wilbrahams finally occupied a family seat which properly reflected their position in society. The architect is thought to have been John Hope, who is probably best known for designing the Piece Hall in Halifax.

It was Randle Wilbraham III who had the house refaced in stucco during yet another extensive programme of renovation in the early part of the 19th century. This redundant stucco was, however, removed in 1927, and it is once again a handsome red-brick house that greets visitors at the end of the driveway – albeit a house that reflects a distinctly convoluted architectural history.

The house contains a number of excellent family portraits, with the last four generations of Baker Wilbrahams represented in the Entrance Hall, once a billiard room. Following the death of Joshua Reynolds, his niece settled his medical bills with a self-portrait of the artist. His doctor was George Baker, and this painting too is on display.

Many of the rooms retain their Regency elegance, including the delightful library with its original fitted bookcases designed by Gillow. Other examples of Gillow furniture were made especially for the other rooms of Rode Hall. The main staircase, still blessed with carved balusters and rococo plasterwork, is now the only room in the house to have kept its Georgian features.

The oval Ante-Room has been redecorated in Regency style, with walls of the deepest blue to set off a collection of gouache paintings. The dining room betrays the handiwork of Lewis Wyatt: cool, elegant and almost entirely unadorned. Above the black marble fireplace is a portrait of Randle Wilbraham, the owner responsible for the building of the house in the 1750s.

The house is set in a Repton landscape, with formal gardens which were laid out in 1860 by William Nesfield. The kitchen garden has been restored and is now on view to visitors.

Rode Hall enjoys a charming vista over its gardens towards the surrounding wooded countryside.

Meols Hall

Southport

An object lesson in the restoration of a fine old house: one mile north of Southport off the A565 Preston road.

Even when judged by the fluctuating fortunes of many of our country houses, Meols Hall has had a chequered history. The Fleetwood and Hesketh families have a long and distinguished pedigree in this part of Lancashire, acquiring both land and upward mobility into the local gentry. Meols Hall came by marriage into the possession of Sir Thomas Hesketh, though unlike the other houses owned by the family, it served merely as a rectory.

Ironically, it took a family disaster to give the Hall a new lease of life. During the 1830s Sir Peter Hesketh-Fleetwood had founded a new town on the Lancashire coast to the north of Blackpool which, without a hint of false modesty, he named Fleetwood. Despite every good intention on his part, this ambitious enterprise foundered, bringing the family almost to its knees in the process. The family estates were sold in order to settle mounting debts, leaving just Meols Hall to be the family home.

The core of this comfortable house is actually a farmhouse dating back to the 16th and 17th centuries (an engraved stone on a back gable announces a date of

1695). However, in spite of the stylistic clues, the main reconstruction did not take place in the 1720s, as might be supposed, but in the 1960s. The present owner, Roger Fleetwood Hesketh, and his brother Peter share an avid interest in Georgian architecture, and through their joint endeavours they have incorporated the Hall's two fairly unprepossessing 17th-century wings into their modifications, reviving the Georgian style in a most handsome manner.

The inspiration came from them, while many of the materials – stonework, slates and bricks – were salvaged from other old houses that were suffering the unkinder fate of being demolished. These recent additions have blended remarkably successfully with the older sections.

As well as creating a family home, one of the principal reasons for restoring the Hall was to provide a suitable place for displaying a collection of family portraits and other paintings. These include landscapes by Poussin, a biblical scene by the Dutch artist, Jan Brueghel and works by other artists including Reynolds and Salvator Rosa. The commodious library was built to accommodate a life-size painting, by James Ward, of Sir Peter Hesketh Fleetwood's Arab stallion.

Though it has a 16th- and 17th-century house at its heart, Meols Hall is essentially a creation of the 1960s.

Browsholme Hall

CLITHEROE

A SPECTACULAR HOUSE OF PINK SANDSTONE, AT THE EDGE OF THE FOREST OF BOWLAND: FIVE MILES NORTH-WEST OF CLITHEROE OFF THE B6243.

Browsholme Hall has been the seat of the Parkers since the 14th century, making them one of the longest established families in Lancashire. What visitors see today at Browsholme is an unpretentious yet dignified house, largely as built by Edmund Parker in 1507. The major additions in the 18th and 19th centuries have not, happily, compromised the building's architectural unity. Gabled wings stand proud from the sandstone façade, while fluted columns either side of the front door create a classical focal point. Browsholme used to be taller; in the 18th century the attic floor was removed, leaving the house three stories high.

There is more to see inside than the modest exterior might suggest. Each successive generation of Parkers has added to the 16th-century furniture – which includes period chests and four-poster beds – to assemble a veritable storehouse of antiques. Thomas Lister Parker, a particularly assiduous collector, became a patron to a number of artistic luminaries; J W M Turner was one of the painters who benefited from his largesse. A Turner watercolour of Browsholme, painted in 1799 and showing the house before its major alterations, hangs outside the dining room.

To show his paintings in, literally, the best possible light, Parker hired Jeffrey Wyatt to create a spacious drawing room with red walls in which to display them. The eye is first caught by Luny's dramatic *Battle of Trafalgar*. Wyatt designed the dining room too, and the Regency style of these apartments contrasts with the studiedly antiquarian appearance of the older rooms, with their panelling, suits of armour, elephant tusks and displays of archaeological finds.

Until it was blocked off at one end to create space for the library, the stone-flagged, heavily-beamed hall extended the full length of the west wing. The main staircase is dominated by a huge window of medieval stained glass which may possibly have come from the ruins of nearby Whalley Abbey. Parker's catholic tastes are revealed in the vast array of textiles, ceramics, Jacobean relics and costumes on display.

The urbane Parker divided his time between provincial Lancashire and sophisticated London society. His lavish lifestyle and taste for buying fine paintings eventually outstripped his means, unfortunately, forcing him to sell Browsholme to his cousin. The Hall's present owner is descended from another branch of the same family.

THE BOW-BEARERS OF BOWLAND

The seemingly endless trees which once covered area of the Forest of Bowland are now long gone, but it was once a vast hunting forest where the monarchs of the day, and their well-heeled subjects, could enjoy the chase. The Parkers of Browsholme Hall traditionally held the title of Bow-bearers of The Forest of Bowland.

Hoghton Tower

PRESTON

A FORTIFIED HOUSE, HIGH ON A LANCASHIRE HILL, WHERE KING JAMES I FAMOUSLY KNIGHTED A LOIN OF BEEF: FOUR AND A HALF MILES SOUTH-WEST OF PRESTON OFF THE A675.

Castellated Hoghton Tower is a prominent landmark for miles around, and at first sight it could almost be a fortified town. The de Hoghton family have owned land here since the Norman Conquest, though the family name is actually Saxon and means 'high wooded hill'. It was Thomas Hoghton who, in 1568, built Hoghton Tower on a hilltop between Preston and Blackburn. He eschewed the prevailing taste for Italian architecture to create a battlemented house which even at that time was something of an anachronism. The house has been in the family's unbroken possession ever since. It was one of the first houses to be opened to the public – in 1946 – and today it is Sir Bernard Hoghton, the 14th Baronet, who welcomes visitors and who continues to restore the house.

Restoration has certainly been needed, for by the early years of the last century the buildings had fallen into romantic decay, tenanted only by weavers and gamekeepers. The founder would surely approve of Hoghton Tower as it is today. Behind the imposing façade the buildings are grouped around two courtyards: one part was for the servants, the other consisting of the banqueting hall and residential rooms.

THE ROYAL VISIT

There are many reminders of a famous visit by King James I, including the King's Bedchamber. Downstairs, in the King's Hall, he laid his hands on two men suffering from scrofula, an ailment held to be curable by a royal touch. In the imposing banqueting hall, with its minstrel's gallery, the king famously 'knighted' a haunch of beef (known as sirloin ever since) during one of the many gargantuan feasts this room has witnessed. Another notable visitor was William Shakespeare who performed in this room with Thomas Hoghton's own troupe of players. Leading off from the banqueting hall is the Ladies Withdrawing Room, to which the ladies would retire after dinner, leaving the men to pass the port bottle at ever-decreasing intervals.

The Buckingham Room, magnificently panelled in oak, takes its name from the Duke of Buckingham, the favourite courtier of King James. Adjacent is the state bedroom, with its elaborately carved four-poster bed. The exhibition room contains a unique collection of Chinese teaware, while a splendid display of dolls' houses can be found in the North Bedroom.

In 1800 Hoghton Tower was described as 'the only true baronial residence in Lancashire', and it still retains both the character and atmosphere that earned it that description.

A NOBLE ROAST

The story has passed into folklore about how King James I was so impressed with a joint of roast beef that he touched it with his sword. 'Arise, Sir Loin', he was heard to say, adding a new word to the language in the process. Fewer people will be aware that this intriguing incident actually took place in the splendid banqueting room at Hoghton Tower, on August 17th 1617. The king's host on this occasion was Sir Richard Hoghton, the first baronet. And quite an occasion it must have been, with more than 100 local members of the local 'squirearchy' assembled to greet their monarch.

Leighton Hall

CARNFORTH

A GOTHIC FACADE SEEN AGAINST A FRIEZE OF LAKELAND HILLS: THREE MILES NORTH OF CARNFORTH OFF THE A6.

Many of Britain's great houses are situated within acres of beautiful parkland, but few can boast a lovelier setting than Leighton Hall. Behind the house, and beyond the estuary of the River Kent, the mountains of Lakeland create a distinctive backdrop. The theatrical effect is heightened by the Hall's Gothic façade in white limestone.

Leighton Hall's story can actually be traced as far back as 1246, when Adam d'Avranches built a fortified manor on this site. Since then there have been 26 owners of the property, though it has been sold only twice. Every owner but one has been Roman Catholic, and during Penal Times a priest was always kept hidden in the house. That one exception, George Middleton, was a distinguished Civil War cavalier who was both knighted and made baronet on the same day in 1642. Albert Hodgson was the unfortunate incumbent when, during the 1715 Rising, the hall was sacked and burned by Government troops.

Far left: Long delicate pillars in the hall support a landing above the lovely curved staircase.

Left: Few houses could boast as beautiful a setting as that which Leighton Hall enjoys.

A NEW HOUSE ARISES

It was George Towneley who rebuilt the house, in 1763. He conformed to the tastes of the time by choosing the Adam style. He also laid out the park and gardens. A few years later, in 1800, the Hall underwent a major face-lift, with a castellated façade in the prevailing neo-Gothic style being added to the building. George Towneley died childless, however, and the Hall came into the possession of the Gillow family whose furniture business, based in Lancaster, became famous as a byword for quality.

When Richard Thomas Gillow (known throughout the county as the 'Old Squire') reached the age of 70, he assumed his days were numbered, and so neglected to carry out more than minor repairs to the fabric of the Hall. In fact he was to live for a further 29 years, and as a consequence it was a rather dilapidated Hall that was handed down to his grandson. Today, it is Mr and Mrs Gillow Reynolds who welcome visitors to Leighton, and the Hall has been restored to its full splendour.

FINE GILLOW FURNITURE

The hallway is a fine example of the Gothic revival, and through the charming little library is the panelled dining room. The family's own furniture is, not surprisingly, well represented here and throughout the house. The large expanding dining table is thought to be the prototype of all leafed tables. One of the pictures in this room features Richard Gillow, the son of the firm's founder.

The large window in the drawing room offers a panoramic view of the Lakeland mountains – a beautiful outlook from a room full of beautiful examples of Gillow furniture, including a games tables and an ornate lady's work-box. The Victorian style of the principal bedroom is exemplified by the magnificent four-poster bed, which was the bridal suite of Mr Reynolds' grandparents.

Once the billiards room had been converted into a music room, the house rang to many a musical evening, including a particularly memorable concert by the singer Kathleen Ferrier. On the landing at the top of the staircase are a couple of pictures that illustrate how the Hall would have looked between 1763 and 1800, before the front was re-faced.

LAWNS AND LONGBOWS

The grounds really should not be missed. Here is a shrubbery walk, an essential ingredient of a Victorian garden. The lawn, extending the full length of the kitchen garden, is where rival archers would bend their longbows during their archery competitions. The sundial on the rose lawn is the sole relic of pre-Jacobite Leighton. Children can try to unravel the mystery of the Caterpillar maze. The brew-house at the back of the house has now been converted into a tea-room; there is also a gift shop. Leighton Hall plays host to a number of special events throughout the year, from antiques fairs to performances of Shakespeare plays. A permanent and very popular feature is the largest collection of birds of prey in the north of England.

At one time, much of the food consumed at Leighton was hunted using falcons. Leighton Hall again has a fine collection of these aristocratic birds, though this one, Busby, a local buzzard, was brought in with a broken wing.

■ When I was a child I loved playing in all the odd corners and staircases in the house. I hope that everyone who visits Dalemain will be infected by the warm welcoming atmosphere which I feel is so much part of this family house. ■
Robert McCosh

Dalemain

PENRITH

CENTURIES OF HISTORY ARE REVEALED AT THIS SURPRISING HOME: THREE MILES SOUTH-WEST OF PENRITH AND M6 JUNCTION 40; BETWEEN THE A66 AND THE A592.

Like many of the best houses, Dalemain, situated where the Lake District mountains change to softer rolling countryside, has its secrets. The elegant 18th-century front, built of beautiful pale-rose sandstone, hides a building that stretches back through the centuries to the Saxons, who established one of a chain of small forts here. A Norman pele tower, the oldest surviving part of the house, was standing when Hugh de Morville fled to his brother John, its owner, after being involved in the murder of Thomas à Becket. The Layton family, who held Dalemain from the 13th to the 17th centuries, added the buildings round the courtyard. These include the medieval Great Hall, with its Tudor ceiling, and the Priest's Hiding Chamber, originally reached by climbing the kitchen chimney, but accessed now from the housekeeper's room. The haunted Solar holds 'The Luck of Dalemain', a superb wine glass of about 1730 engraved with the Hasell coat of arms.

Lady Anne Clifford, a rich heiress, whose portrait hangs here, left a legacy to her 'secretarie' Sir Edward Hasell, and he used it to buy Dalemain in 1679. His descendants still live here. Another Edward added the classical Georgian front that transformed the jumble of old buildings, with their unexpected changes of level and winding passages, with a series of fine rooms. The star of the show is the Chinese Drawing Room, with its hand-painted Chinese wallpaper featuring a riot of pheasants, peonies and butterflies. It is complemented by Chinese Chippendale chairs and an English fireplace carved with spirited dragons.

The fine workmanship of the splendid cantilevered oak staircase at Dalemain is set off by the warm colour of the walls and a fine array of paintings, including works by Van Dyck.

All around the house are fine family portraits, china and silver, and saucy Cumbrian double-seated courting chairs rub shoulders with more elegant furniture. A fascinating nursery comes complete with rocking horse, Noah's Ark, dolls house and Dinky cars. The Tower has a museum of the local Yeomanry, including swaggering 19th-century uniforms, and a countryside museum occupies a fine range of early farm buildings surrounding a courtyard.

■ Walking through the house is a remarkable journey through 400 years of architectural history, as reflected in the taste of one family. ■
Lord Inglewood

Hutton-in-the-Forest

PENRITH

EARLY ROMANCE MINGLES WITH VICTORIAN COMFORT IN THIS FAMILY HOME: FOUR AND A HALF MILES NORTH-WEST OF PENRITH, THREE MILES FROM M6 JUNCTION 41 ON THE B5305.

Sir Gawain is said to have stayed with the Green Knight at Hutton, which was then surrounded by dense woodland. In 1292 Edward I was a visitor during the heyday of the royal hunting forest of Inglewood. However, by the 1350's the de Hoton family found it necessary to build the fortified pele tower as protection against the Scots and the border reivers. The Fletchers bought it in 1605 and began its development into the fascinating and comfortable home we see today. The Long Gallery,

The inspiration for The Long Gallery at Hutton came from the great Jacobean and Elizabethan houses of southern England. Such rooms are a rarity in the north.

rare in the north, was built in 1630, and the classical east front, an unexpected and dramatic addition to this solid house, in the 1680s.

One of the Fletchers was killed fighting for Charles I in 1645. His granddaughter married into the Vane family – her husband's uncle, Sir Henry Vane, had been in Cromwell's government and was executed as a traitor in 1662. The 18th-century Fletcher Vanes improved the garden and grounds rather than the house, and spent much time following country pursuits – one of them employed John Peel, whose portrait hangs in the house, as his huntsman.

Hutton gained its present form in the 1820s, when Salvin designed the dominant south-east tower, and added battlements to the 'pele'. The impressive Stone Hall at its base contrasts with the later rooms, warm with panelling, good furniture and family pictures. The charming Cupid Staircase, with its carved cherubs, and the Cupid Room, with its delicate plaster ceiling of 1744, testify to the romantic associations of the house. There is a more formal air about Salvin's dining room, and the Long Gallery retains its Jacobean flavour.

Levens Hall

KENDAL

A REMARKABLE ELIZABETHAN HOUSE AND WORLD-FAMOUS TOPIARY GARDEN: FIVE MILES SOUTH OF KENDAL ON THE A6 AND A591; NORTH-WEST OF M6 JUNCTION 36 ON THE A590.

Levens is pre-eminently an Elizabethan house. Even without the Queen's arms in painted and gilded plasterwork, displayed so prominently above the fireplace in the Great Hall, the building's origins are apparent from the comfortable gables and mullioned windows in the grey rough-cast of the exterior. Yet, like many northern houses, it has at its core a defensive pele tower, built by the de Redman family, who held the manor from the 12th century, as protection against Scots invaders. There is also a later 17th-century servants' wing, but it is the grand ground-floor rooms, adapted or added by James Bellingham from around 1580, that are the real pride of Levens.

A century later Bellingham's great-grandson had gambled away the whole estate – it is said that Levens came to Colonel James Grahme, a relative, on the turn of the ace of hearts. It passed, often through the female line, to Grahme's descendants, the Bagots, who still live at Levens. This long, unbroken tradition, has created an atmosphere of care and comfort and has ensured that Levens is still full of family furniture and possessions. There are notable plaster ceilings in the main rooms, and, in the two drawing rooms, huge carved overmantels dated 1595. The one in the larger room is heraldic, while the other depicts Hercules and Samson, the elements, the four seasons and the five senses – a typical Elizabethan mixture.

The house has some fine furniture, much of it brought to the house by Colonel Grahme at the end of the 17th century. Grahme, who was Privy Purse and Keeper of the Buckhounds to James II, and his wife Dorothy appear in superb Lely portraits, while other paintings include a portrait of Anne of Hungary by Rubens. One of the Bagot ancestors married the Duke of Wellington's niece, bringing into the family a number of Napoleonic relics, including his cloak clasp of two bees, taken after Waterloo, and a superb Sèvres chocolate service made for the Emperor's mother. The earliest English patchwork quilt, made by Colonel Grahme's daughters from rare Indian cottons in about 1708 can be found in a dressing room upstairs. The family even owns one of the bowls Sir Francis Drake was using on Plymouth Hoe as the Armada was sighted. The dining room contains the finest set of Charles II walnut chairs in existence. At Levens, there is a superbly achieved balance between relaxed living and show, which makes this house one of the most covetable in the country.

■ We are delighted to welcome visitors to Levens because we like to share its warmth, historical associations and beautiful setting. We are all fortunate that Levens is so complete, with its early furniture, magnificent interiors and glorious gardens. ■
Mr Bagot

LEVENS TOPIARY

The formal gardens at Levens were laid out for Colonel Grahme by Monsieur Beaumont between 1694 and 1712, and the Countess of Suffolk, Grahme's daughter, insisted the design was maintained even after it became unfashionable. Thanks to her, Monsieur Beaumont's original plantings can still be seen on the parterre – huge beech hedges and yews clipped into all manner of fantastic shapes, most of them much bigger than intended and now more romantic than formal in spirit. Walking among them is like being part of an oversized chess game. With its tercentenary in 1994, the Levens garden is a miraculous survival.

The 300-year-old hedges and topiary at Levens are lovingly cared for, and the annual clipping takes the four gardeners about four months to complete.

Holker Hall

Holker

A Victorian country house and a haunt of the Dukes of Devonshire: three and a half miles west of Grange-over-Sands on the B5278.

Holker is the sort of house where at every turn you expect to see the hearty clergymen and eager young noblemen, discreet, elderly housemaids and animated younger daughters of the aristocracy straight from the pages of Anthony Trollope. For the Holker that the visitor sees is largely a creation of the third quarter of the 19th century. This former home of the Dukes of Devonshire, preferred by some of them to the splendours of Chatsworth, and still lived in by a branch of the Cavendish family, has its origins in a house built in the 19th century by George Preston, whose family bought land once owned by Cartmel Priory. The estate descended by marriage to the Lowthers, who added the north wing and reconstructed the rest before it came into Cavendish ownership.

The whole house was extensively altered in 1840 by Lord George Cavendish, created Lord Burlington at William IV's coronation. He had it rendered with Roman cement and made romantically Gothic. A disastrous fire in 1871, destroyed the whole of the west wing, including valuable paintings and furniture. The 7th Duke of Devonshire commissioned local architects Paley and Austin – then among the best country-house designers in Britain – to rebuild the wing in pale red sandstone in a grand yet relaxed Elizabethan style, complete with large bay windows and copper dome.

Holker Hall has an enormous amount of character and its appeal is enhanced by the lack of restriction on its visitors, who may wander at will through the rooms.

What is notable about a visit to Holker is the lack of restriction – visitors may wander at will through a series of fine, panelled rooms without roping and regimentation. The library sets the tone, with deep armchairs, French furniture and family portraits. Henry Cavendish, scientist – he discovered nitric acid – and recluse, is remembered by his microscope and copies of his learned works, and there is a portrait by Richmond of Lord Frederick, assassinated in Phoenix Park, Dublin in 1882.

The drawing room retains its original red silk walls, while the spectacular chimney-piece in the dining room, of local marble and finely carved wood, one of several throughout the house, incorporates a Van Dyck self-portrait. Fine craftsmanship is everywhere – every one of the hundred or so balusters of the main staircase is different, for example – and each room retains some of that joyous sense of jewelled clutter loved by the Victorians. One of the bedrooms has Wedgwood plaques and blue Jasper Ware on the fire surround, another has furnishings from 1937 when Queen Mary stayed at Holker. The family used to play carpet bowls down the gallery, a spacious and sunny contrast to the hall, which speaks of winter evenings round a roaring fire. In the extensive gardens, formal and informal by turns, is the only surviving monkey puzzle tree planted from seeds which were brought to England in 1837, and superb magnolias and rhododendrons.

Mirehouse

Keswick

Victorian literary giants were frequent visitors to this northern Lake District house: three and a half miles north of Keswick on A591.

Apparently isolated between the severe heights of Skiddaw and the glittering waters of Bassenthwaite Lake, Mirehouse, was first built for the 8th Earl of Derby in 1666, sold by him to the Greggs 22 years later, and was the meeting place of some of the greatest literary figures of the 19th century. Left in 1802 by the last of the Greggs to John Spedding of nearby Armathwaite Hall, who had sat at the same school desk with Wordsworth, Mirehouse was extended to its present size between 1792 and 1883. What we see today is a traditional family home, full of decent furniture and family pictures, but this comfortable house was not just appreciated by the Speddings. John's son, James, devoted his life to the study of Sir Francis Bacon – some of his collection of Bacon's papers, as well the many volumes Spedding produced about him, are in the Smoking Room – and was an intimate friend of Tennyson, Thackeray and Edward Fitzgerald. It was while staying at Mirehouse that Tennyson, whom Spedding met at Cambridge, walked the shores of Bassenthwaite, composing *Morte d'Arthur*, and the local scenery got into the poem.

Fitzgerald, who was a schoolfriend of Spedding, met Tennyson at Mirehouse, and his chess set can still be seen in the study. Here, too are manuscripts from Wordsworth, Southey and Hartley Coleridge, who were both neighbours and friends of the family. In the library, its bookshelves arranged by the present John Spedding according to Bacon's 'studies', it is his elder brother Tom whose portrait has pride of place. A leading Cumberland figure, he too had his literary friends, including Thomas Carlyle, who often called on 'the Genius of the hills' on his way to Scotland. Another Spedding, Anthony, was a friend of John Constable, whose painting of Anthony's Hampstead home hangs in the red-walled Music Room. Today's visitors to Mirehouse can trace the steps of the Speddings' friends through the pleasant grounds and woodlands to St Bega's Church on the shores of the lake, where Tennyson's Sir Bedivere carried King Arthur – 'a chapel nigh the field ...
That stood on a dark straight of barren land.'

■ We hope that, while this is an unusually literary house, our visitors will feel welcome in what is our home rather than a museum, and will bring their children to enjoy the secrets and surprises of an old house, as well as the live piano music which we have when the house is open. ■
Clare and John Spedding

One specially delightful part of Mirehouse is the schoolroom/nursery, where this child's sewing machine can be seen.

Muncaster Castle

Ravenglass

VICTORIAN COUNTRY HOUSE LIFE IN A HAUNT OF THE DUKES OF DEVONSHIRE: A MILE EAST OF RAVENGLASS ON THE A595.

The Romans built a fort on the edge of the Lake District to protect Ravenglass harbour and the entry to Eskdale. In the Middle Ages, a castle was built on the original Roman foundations. The pele tower still survives beneath later stonework, but virtually everything we see today dates from the 1860s. Lord Muncaster, a member of the Pennington family, who came to Muncaster in 1208 and still keep it as their family home, commissioned Salvin to extend and remodel both the medieval remains and a modest 18th-century house, built to his own design by a predecessor. Its situation is wonderful, with a spectacular view over the Lake District mountains from the famous half-mile long terrace, and its gardens full of rhododendrons.

The Victorian building is solid and workmanlike, rather than spectacular. Two massive towers on the garden front add weight and grandeur to the outside, while inside there are individual touches, like the hall with its enclosed staircase, and the octagonal library, with a brass-railed gallery and fine, vaulted ceiling. The rooms have splendid woodwork and panelling, from Britain and the Continent, and carved chimney-pieces, including one by Adam, brought from other houses. The furniture includes both an Elizabethan four-poster and a superb set of Charles II walnut settees and chairs. The house also contains a collection of glittering silverware by Storr and a wonderful series of family portraits from the 17th century to the present.

THE 'LUCK OF MUNCASTER'

King Henry VI fled to Muncaster after the Lancastrian defeat at the bloody Battle of Towton in 1461, when 30,000 men died one snowy Sunday. He was found wandering on the fells by a shepherd – the place is now marked by an 18th-century folly tower – and was taken to the castle for shelter. To show his gratitude for the help he was given, the King gave Sir John Pennington a enamelled glass drinking bowl, the 'Luck of Muncaster'. Legend says – and events seem to support it – that while this precious heirloom remains unbroken, the Penningtons will hold Muncaster.

The drawing room at Muncaster, in lovely Wedgwood shades, displays a fine collection of paintings.

Rydal Mount

AMBLESIDE

WORDSWORTH'S HOME AND GARDEN IN THE HEART OF THE LAKE DISTRICT: ONE AND A HALF MILES NORTH OF AMBLESIDE OFF THE A591.

Rydal Mount owes its fame to its most famous tenant, William Wordsworth. He came to this lime-washed yeoman's house on May Day 1813. 'The weather is delightful and the place a Paradise' wrote his sister Dorothy, and it was to remain his home until his death in 1850. His was a large household – it included not only the poet and his wife Mary, but his three surviving children and Mary's sister Sarah Hutchinson, as well as Dorothy. The move was partly financed by Wordsworth's appointment as Distributor of Stamps for Westmorland, which brought him his first (and only) steady income, and earned Browning's scorn: 'Just for a handful of silver he left us,' he wrote in *The Lost Leader*, 'Just for a riband to stick in his coat.'

Detail from Margaret Gillies portrait of William and Mary Wordsworth, dated 1839.

More than half of Wordsworth's published poetry was written at Rydal Mount, a house with origins in a farm built in 1550 – the dining room still has its early timbers and slate floor and was enlarged about the middle of the 18th century. Wordsworth was particularly attracted to the traditional style of the house, as well as by its spectacular views over Rydal Water and Windermere. He never owned the house – leased from the le Flemings of nearby Rydal Hall – and so did little to alter the house, concentrating his efforts on creating the garden.

It was 120 years after his death that a descendant, Mary Henderson, bought the property and gathered most of the furniture and mementos of the poet that visitors now see. Even in his lifetime, however, and especially after he became Poet Laureate in 1843, sightseers – sometimes as many as 100 a day – climbed the steep lane and loitered in the hope of glimpsing the great man. To avoid them, he worked in his attic study, his only addition to the house. Here are kept many of his first editions, including his poetic autobiography, *The Prelude*, published after his death, and his *Guide to the Lakes*, as well as the sword of his drowned brother John. Elsewhere in the house are other touching reminders, including William's reading glasses and his leather picnic case, used in his protracted walks over the fells. There are mementoes of Dorothy too, including her portrait in the library. She was William's mainstay for many years, and her gradual decline into mental breakdown after Sarah's death in 1835 was yet another tragedy he had to bear.

Rydal Mount was the Wordsworths' much-loved home and a source of inspiration to the poet.

Wordsworth believed that a house and its garden should harmonise with each other and with the locality, and at Rydal Mount he put this into practice. The garden, one of the most important of its date, is still much as he left it, with terraces stretching across the hillside. The highest was already there when he took over the house, but he added two others, one so that Dorothy could be pushed in her invalid chair to enjoy the view. Wordsworth would pace along them, booming new poems to himself.

WORDSWORTH'S OPEN HOUSE

Despite Wordsworth's praise of 'the bliss of solitude', the literary and fashionable world, as well as tourists, visited him at Rydal Mount. William Wilberforce and 19 of his family were somehow accommodated in 1817. In 1825 Sir Walter Scott came, more modestly, only for breakfast. Dr Arnold and his son Matthew were close friends, and American pilgrims included Emerson and Hawthorne. Swinburne, then just 11, received kind encouragement from the old man. Even Dowager Queen Adelaide came, in 1840. Wordsworth proudly showed her the garden, including the still-surviving stone summer house he had built, and the view over his beloved lakes.

Bramham Park

WETHERBY

ITALIANATE MANSION WITH FRENCH-STYLE FORMAL GARDENS IN THE HEART OF YORKSHIRE: FOUR AND A HALF MILES SOUTH OF WETHERBY OFF THE A1.

Robert Benson inherited a fortune and a parcel of land at Bramham Moor from his lawyer father when he was just a baby. Twenty-one years later, in 1697, inspired by his travels on the Grand Tour of Europe, he decided to build Bramham Park as his summer house, masterminding the whole project himself. He designed the house in the style of a 16th-century Florentine villa and set it in 70 acres of formal gardens. A successful political career as Lord Treasurer to Queen Anne, as British

Ambassador to Spain and as Treasurer to the Household of George II, led to him being created Lord Bingley in 1713 and enabled him to build up a superb collection of furniture, pictures, books and artefacts.

His grandiose schemes were nearly ruined by his descendent, George Lane Fox, 'the Gambler', whose riotous life in the company of the Prince Regent left him with debts of £175,000. In 1828 fire gutted the north wing and destroyed part of Benson's priceless collections. 'The Gambler' simply could not afford the restorations, so the house was abandoned. It was not until the beginning of this century that his grandson began to rebuild, following Benson's original plans. The Lane Fox family still live at Bramham Park.

The elegance of the east front, with its colonnaded wings and a sweeping carriage ramp, is more than matched by the interiors. The glowing colours of the library and the East Room provide a splendid backdrop for what remains of Benson's fine collection of 17th- and 18th-century books and gilt tableware, including dinner plates presented to him by Queen Anne. The Long Gallery houses a collection of portraits, principally by Kneller, but including Sir Peter Lely's portrait of young Popham Conway, who unwisely picked a quarrel with one of the best duellists of the day and was killed in the resulting encounter. Here too are portraits of James Fox, a Member of Parliament, whose red hunting coat was repainted black in case his constituents' should think that he might prefer hunting to parliamentary activity, and of Marcia Lane Fox, who was temporally disinherited for marrying a Catholic neighbour against her father's wishes. A delightful portrait in the North Room is of Harriet Benson, Robert's only legitimate daughter.

Naworth Castle

BRAMPTON

STRANGE BEASTS STAND GUARD IN THE GREAT HALL OF THIS BORDER CASTLE: ONE AND A HALF MILES NORTH-EAST OF BRAMPTON OFF A69.

You can see the Scottish Border from the towers of Naworth Castle, which was built by the Dacres in 1335 on a commanding site overlooking the valley of the River Irthing. The approach is by a long drive that gives a wonderful view of both the castle and the rugged Cumbrian countryside. Within the strongly-walled courtyard other phases of Naworth's history become apparent – the large, mullioned windows of about 1520, and the huge walls of Lord William's Tower, built by the third son of the 4th Duke of Norfolk after he married a Dacre heiress and reconstructed the decaying castle at the turn of the 17th century.

Portraits of 'Bold Willie', a Howard, and his wife are on show in the Great Hall. They were ancestors of the Earls of Carlisle, whose family home Naworth remains, although for two centuries they mainly lived at Castle Howard. As a result, little was changed at Naworth, and much of what we see today is the result of a very faithful restoration by Salvin after a disastrous fire in 1844. Under the massive roof of the Great Hall, the largest in the north-west, are French tapestries bought by the 5th Earl from the Duc d'Orleans' collection after the French Revolution. There are also four remarkable statues of heraldic beasts – bull, gryphon, sheep and dolphin – from the time of the Dacres, holding Howard banners. At the entrance to the dungeon at the base of the Dacre Tower is a very rare 'yett' or iron door, while in the Old Library, once the Dacres' private chapel, is a gesso panel designed and painted by Burne-Jones who, like other Pre-Raphaelites, was a friend of the artistic 9th Earl. Viewing by appointment only.

Left: The Great Hall at Bramham Park is a perfect cube, ten metres in each direction. It is furnished with mainly 17th-century oak pieces and paintings include works by Reynolds and Kneller.

Below left: This 17th-century Imari vase is on show in the Long Gallery at Bramham Park.

Below: Strong walls still surround the buildings and formal garden at Naworth Castle.

■ I have lived at Harewood since I was six, which is some 65 years ago. This is the Yorkshire landscape I grew up with and have loved ever since I can remember; I can't imagine living anywhere else and hope I never have to. ■
Lord Harewood

Above: An 18th-century clock in Harewood's Old Library.
Below: The south façade of Harewood House.

Harewood House

HAREWOOD

A SHOWPIECE PALACE WITH ROBERT ADAM INTERIORS, CHIPPENDALE FURNITURE AND 'CAPABILITY' BROWN PARKS: MIDWAY BETWEEN LEEDS AND HARROGATE AT THE JUNCTION OF THE A61 AND A659.

From unpromising beginnings – according to the Domesday Book, Harewood belonged to three Saxon chieftains, Tor, Sprot and Grim – the Lascelles family has created a treasure house. Displaying an artistic instinct which has not erred in over 200 years, they have employed only the finest craftsmen to build and embellish the house which is still their home.

A Lascelles came over to England with William the Conqueror. Later Colonel Francis Lascelles fought for Parliament in the Civil War and went on to become MP for the North Riding, beginning a long family tradition of parliamentary service. A fortune derived from sugar plantations in the West Indies enabled his grandson to buy Gawthorpe and Harewood and his great-grandson, Edwin Lascelles, to realise his dream of building a grand new house on the hill.

THE PLANNING STAGES

Rejecting the first set of plans drawn up by William Chambers, Edwin then commissioned John Carr of York, after the latter had proved himself by building a satisfactory stable block. After entrusting Carr with building the house, a farm and model village, he then referred the plans to the then up and coming Scottish architect, Robert Adam. Though Adam changed little of the Palladian exterior of the house, the interior was entirely committed into his care, resulting in a glorious series of State Rooms. He determined the prevalence of the classical motif in the decorations, oversaw the delicate and elaborate plasterwork designs and even selected all the carpets. He commissioned Thomas Chippendale, born only a few miles away at Otley, to provide all the furniture and furnishings, a task which he performed with both flair and sympathy. The simple elegance and understated opulence of even his inlaid and gilded pieces are the perfect complement to Adam's room schemes.

THE BUILDING OF HAREWOOD

The foundation stone was laid in January 1759, but it was not until 12 years later that the house became habitable. The following year, 'Capability' Brown submitted his plans for landscaping the park, creating a 'natural' undulating vista from the house down to the artificial lake. Planting woodland and altering the lie of the land took nine years and cost £6,000 but created an idyllic and supremely English setting for this gem of a country house. The only major alterations since then were carried out in the mid 19th century when the architect of the Houses of Parliament, Sir Charles Barry, transformed the south façade by removing the classical portico and adding a massive terrace, resplendent with a 'folded ribbon' Italianate garden, a central fountain and fine statuary. A careful restoration programme in recent years has undone some of his less sensitive remodelling of the interiors and allowed Adam's designs to re-emerge as the dominant theme.

The first glimpse of Harewood House is intimidating, soaring above the level parkland, with neither buildings nor trees to soften the approach. Visitors cannot fail to be impressed by the sheer size and magnificence of the north façade. The entrance to the house is dominated by an uncompromising classical pediment and pillars. The entrance hall itself is equally stern and cold, its walls and ceilings covered with roundels depicting stories from classical myth: even the alabaster figure of Adam, by Jacob Epstein, which stands sentinel here, is of heroic masculine proportions. Do not be deterred by this imposing beginning, for the rooms that follow are a mix of the splendid and the domestic. Regency furniture, coronation chairs and Chippendale pieces give way to comfortable sofas; Lascelles and Canning portraits by Reynolds and Gainsborough mingle with photographs of current members

ROYAL CONNECTIONS

The present Earl of Harewood's mother was the Princess Royal, daughter of King George V. Evidence of this royal connection can be seen throughout the house. There are family photographs of six reigning monarchs, from Queen Victoria to the present Queen, and of the Westminster Abbey wedding of the late Earl and the Princess Royal, including one where the bride's signing of the register is watched by a king, two queens and two archbishops. Princess Mary's sitting room and dressing room, the latter incorporating decorative features from the demolished Harewood House in Hanover Square, are among the rooms open to the public.

Left: This architectural detail is from Adam's fine ceiling in the Long Gallery at Harewood House.

of the family. Overall, however, the impression is that these are State Rooms created simply for their visual effect. While it is easy to imagine a family gathering together in Barry's library or Adam's music room, with its glorious round ceiling design mirrored in the pattern of the carpet, it is difficult to envisage this in the more formal surroundings of the Rose or Cinnamon Drawing Rooms.

HAREWOOD'S COLLECTIONS

There are treasures to be seen everywhere: superb Sèvres pieces in the China Room, including a tea service given to Marie Antoinette in 1779, and delightful views of Harewood House by Turner, Girtin and Richmond.The gallery, which extends the length of the west end of the house, hosts a famous collection of Chinese porcelain and Italian pictures including a Tintoretto and a Titian.

Stockeld Park

WETHERBY

A SMALL PALLADIAN MANSION, ON THE EDGE OF THE VALE OF YORK: JUST OFF THE A661 HARROGATE ROAD.

The Middleton family originally lived in this delightful country house. Wealthy landed gentry, owning extensive estates in the rich agricultural lands between York, Harrogate and Ripon, they commissioned a Palladian-style mansion from James Paine, the celebrated architect, who, at the tender age of 19, was responsible for supervising the construction of Nostell Priory. Stockeld Park, built between 1758 and 1763, is one of the finest examples of his work.

The agricultural depression at the end of the 19th century forced the Middletons to put the estate up for auction. Like many other Yorkshire country houses, it was bought by a successful textile magnate, Robert Foster. He was the grandson of the founder of Black Dyke Mills at Queensbury, once world famous for its production of fine, mohair-based cloth for suiting, now better known for its excellent brass band.

Robert Foster might not have had the ancestry of the Middletons, but he certainly had the finances that they lacked. He built a substantial new wing onto the house for his domestic staff, turned the old chapel into a library and converted the orangery into a new chapel in the grounds. Even more dramatically, he decided to alter the approach to the house, closing the old drive from the south lodge and building a new one from the north. To do this, he had to carry out major engineering works, raising the level of the new drive and building a new portico to disguise the fact that visitors now entered the house through what had been a window at first floor level.

The house is approached through parkland and the main entrance leads straight into the charming Oval Hall. An elegant cantilevered circular staircase, with crinoline balustrading, defies gravity to soar several storeys; even the doors off the hall are curved to match its oval contours. Large windows make the house light and airy and give wonderful views of the surrounding parkland and woods. The rooms have clean and simple lines, the only touch of extravagance being the elaborate plasterwork of the cornices. The dining room boasts one of the first gas fires ever installed and in the library is a fireplace which belonged to the Queen Mother. Furniture and pictures collected by several generations of Fosters add a personal touch to this pleasant house, which is not a museum showpiece but a comfortable family home for the descendants who still live here.

Stockeld Park's spectacular cantilevered circular staircase has delicate crinoline balustrading.

A 16th-century Venetian andiron from Sledmere House.

Sledmere House

DRIFFIELD

A GEORGIAN HOUSE WITH OPULENT STATE ROOMS, ANCESTRAL HOME OF THE SYKES FAMILY: SEVEN MILES NORTH-WEST OF DRIFFIELD OFF THE B1253.

Descended from successful Yorkshire merchants, the family of Sir Tatton Sykes can trace their ownership of Sledmere House back in an unbroken line to the middle of the 17th century. It was Richard Sykes, a High Sheriff of Yorkshire, who demolished the old Tudor house and began construction of a new red-brick mansion in 1751. His brother, 'Parson Sykes', created a baronet for his pioneering agricultural work, inherited the estate and it was his son, Sir Christopher, who transformed the house. Acting as his own architect, though consulting John Carr and Samuel Wyatt, he encased the house in Nottinghamshire stone and added new ranges to the north and south. He then engaged 'Capability' Brown to landscape his 2,000 acres of parkland – a job that entailed demolishing the old village and rebuilding it out of sight to the east.

A disastrous fire in 1911 left only the four walls standing, though an efficient salvage operation saved virtually all the contents of the house. It was rebuilt, to the original designs, by the York architect, Walter Brierley, who reinstated plasterwork from the original moulds and redecorated the house following contemporary watercolours of the rooms.

The grim and forbidding aspect of the exterior is entirely belied by the opulence of the interior. Remarkably intricate plasterwork ceilings and friezes, picked out in paint and gold, are a feature of every room: each one is different, though classical themes prevail – note the lyre motif in the music room which houses the famous Sledmere organ created for the original house. Pillars of every order, classical statuary and plaster reliefs are an ever present reminder of the 18th-century obsession with the antique. The extraordinary collection of rare books and illuminated manuscripts built up by Sir Christopher and his son has sadly been dispersed but its setting, a combined library and gallery, is on a monumental scale. The Turkish Room, an eastern fantasy, with tiles made in Damascus, is a memorial to the 6th Baronet, an eminent orientalist, who restored the house. The Stable Block and pictures in the Horse Room celebrate the justly famous Sledmere Stud.

Complex patterns line the walls of the Turkish Room at Sledmere.

Burton Agnes Hall

DRIFFIELD

MATCHLESS ELIZABETHAN CARVINGS MAKE THIS MANSION, AS MAGNIFICENT INSIDE AS OUT: SIX MILES NORTH-EAST OF DRIFFIELD ON THE A166 BRIDLINGTON ROAD.

The same family has owned this property since Roger de Stuteville built a manor house here in 1173. The builder of the Elizabethan mansion was Sir Henry Griffith, who employed Robert Smithson, Master Mason to Queen Elizabeth, as his architect. Uniquely, his plans have been preserved, revealing not only the unity of the design but also how little has been changed. In the 17th century the property passed to Sir Matthew Boynton, a Royalist who changed sides and was appointed Governor of Scarborough Castle by Cromwell. His son rebelled in favour of the king and was killed in 1651 in the advance of the Royalist army from Scotland. An 18th-century stepfather nearly ruined the family. 'Handsome Jack' married the widow of the 6th Baronet, spent a fortune and brought hersons up 'in every sort of vice' – one of them married a circus rider, whose father kept the Black Swan Inn in York. Later generations proved more responsible and have extensively restored this delightful house.

THE GHOST OF ANNE GRIFFIN

Burton Agnes has a ghost – of Anne, youngest daughter of Sir Henry Griffin. When her father began to build the Hall, Anne was entranced with the plans and could not wait to live there. Unfortunately she never got the chance. Fatally wounded by robbers, she declared she could never rest unless part of her remained in 'our beautiful home as long as it shall last' and made her sisters promise that they would preserve her head within the Hall forever. When they buried her in the churchyard her ghost walked until they fulfilled their promise – and walks again if she is disturbed.

A turreted early 17th-century gatehouse is a foretaste of the glories to come. The perfect symmetry of the red brick mansion, three storeys high, with two square and two compass bays, is preserved by having the entrance door at the side of one of the bays. A profusion of Biblical, allegorical and mythological figures are carved into the remarkable Elizabethan screen and massive alabaster chimney-piece, almost the height of the wall in the Great Hall. The Red Drawing Room is an incredible example of brilliantly painted and gilded Elizabethan panelling with another outstanding carved chimney-piece depicting the Dance of Death. Extraordinary plasterwork ceilings, intricate carvings on the staircase and bedroom panelling and a superb collection of family portraits, make this a house to remember.

The fine craftsmanship of the alabaster chimney-piece in the entrance hall at Burton Agnes dates from Elizabethan times.

Burton Constable Hall

Hull

A MAGNIFICENT ELIZABETHAN MANSION, WITH 200 ACRES OF 'CAPABILITY' BROWN PARKLAND: SEVEN AND A HALF MILES NORTH-EAST OF HULL VIA THE A165 AND THE B1238.

The Constable family have lived in Burton Constable Hall ever since it was built in *c*1570. Wealthy Yorkshire landowners, related by marriage to many of the leading county families, the Constables have kept a low profile over the centuries. Their relative obscurity in the annals of history is completely at odds with the splendour of their ancestral home.

There has been a building on this site since at least the Middle Ages and a medieval manor house survives as part of the present building, comprising the north wing and its tower with projecting staircase turret. In the later 1560s Sir John Constable added the Great Hall and another tower and wing to harmonise with those existing. The west front with its gallery was added shortly afterwards. Much of the building described in a survey of 1578 as 'one goodly manor house of aintient building' still exists, concealed behind later work. Until the 18th century a turreted gatehouse and two courtyards protected the house from the public road to the east. As it stands today, however, the house owes most to a sensitive remodelling which took place under William Constable in the late 18th century. While retaining most of the original exterior, he employed some of the most illustrious architects and craftsmen of the day to transform the interior into a series of elegant Georgian rooms. Robert Adam, James Wyatt and John Carr all contributed designs for the interior alterations, Timothy Lightoler added the new stable block and Thomas Atkinson the orangery.

The exterior of the house is graceful and imposing: three storeys high, built of red brick, with stone mullioned and oriel windows and castellated towers, it has a pleasing symmetry. The focal point of the east façade is the pillared entrance, surmounted by a pediment displaying the family coat of arms. Inside, the 30 rooms open to the public are maintained as if the squire was still living there and are crammed with furniture and pictures collected by the family over many generations. One of the particular delights of the Hall is that pieces by master craftsmen stand side by side with the work of estate joiners. Thomas Chippendale supplied the chairs, sofas, firescreens and side tables in the ballroom, but John Lowry, a former estate apprentice, who went on to set up business in London, was responsible for the superb nine-piece pedestal table and chairs in the dining room.

William Constable's own influence on the house he remodelled is evident in many of the rooms. Like other 18th-century gentlemen, he shared the twin passions for antiquity and science. Classical themes dominate in the dining room, where the free standing and relief plaster sculptures are by William Collins of London; marble slabs, brought back by Constable himself from one of his Grand Tours of Italy, rest on Chippendale tables in the ballroom. In the Museum Room is a display of his remarkable collection of 18th-century scientific instruments and the six remaining examples of his thirty-four guns. Each room is different, from the extravagance of the Chinese Room, to the simple elegance of James Wyatt's ballroom.

Detail from a scagliolia table top made by Bartoli.

■ **Although this is still a family home, nothing gives us more pleasure than to share our treasures with those who visit us from all over the world every year.** ■

The Hon. Simon Howard

Castle Howard

YORK

PALATIAL SPLENDOUR ON A MONUMENTAL SCALE AT THE FAMILY SEAT OF THE HOWARDS: ABOUT 12 MILES NORTH OF YORK OFF THE A64 MALTON ROAD.

The Castle Howard branch of this famous family descends from Thomas, fourth Duke of Norfolk, who was executed by Elizabeth I for plotting to marry Mary, Queen of Scots. Fortunately, he had made more prudent marital arrangements for his three sons, marrying them off to the three daughters of Lord Dacre, one of the greatest landowners in the north of England. Lord William married Elizabeth, and through her, inherited vast estates in Cumberland, Northumberland and at Henderskelfe in Yorkshire. His great-grandson, Charles Howard, was imprisoned for Royalist sympathies in 1646 but, having bought his freedom at the cost of £4,000, changed sides and was rewarded for his military service to the Commonwealth with one of only two hereditary peerages created by Oliver Cromwell. Cannily foreseeing the Restoration, he switched loyalties again and was created Earl of Carlisle by the new king, Charles II.

The sundial at Castle Howard.

CONTINUING PUBLIC SERVICE

His descendants were all equally active in politics, serving in the House of Commons, as Lords Lieutenant of the Northern Counties and at Court. Nineteenth-century earls included an ordained clergyman and an accomplished artist, friend to Burne-Jones and William Morris. Of the three sons of Geoffrey Howard, Parliamentary Secretary to the Prime Minister, Herbert Asquith, only one survived World War II: Mark died in France and Christopher was killed while serving in the RAF. George Howard returned from the war to find that the Trustees had begun to sell the contents of the house, assuming that no-one would ever live there again. Defying these expectations, he not only took up residence at Castle Howard but also began a programme of restoration and opened the house and grounds to the public in 1952. His four sons continue to administer the estate today. Like their father, they pride themselves on maintaining Castle Howard as one of the premier stately houses of England and also a much loved family home.

The Atlas Fountain was installed in the 1850s and is fed by a half-million gallon reservoir in Ray Wood.

BUILDING CASTLE HOWARD

Charles, 3rd Earl of Carlisle was responsible for building Castle Howard. A powerful and ambitious courtier, who was soon to be made a Gentleman of the King's Bedchamber and acting Earl Marshal of England, he decided, like many of his contemporaries, to build himself a fitting country seat to replace the old castle at Henderskelfe which had been seriously damaged by fire in 1693. His choice of architect was as extraordinary as the scale of his plans. John Vanbrugh had no experience of architectural design, theoretical or practical, but what he lacked in training he more than made up for in flair and imagination. Taking his inspiration wherever he could find it, he had no compunction about mixing architectural styles or building the largest dome on a private house in England. Defying convention, he took advantage of the lie of the land to make the most of the views across the Howardian Hills, building the house to face north and south rather than the traditional east and west. Vanbrugh was fortunate in having Nicholas Hawksmoor to advise him on the technical aspects of his plans, and Hawksmoor was able to turn his fantasies into solid reality.

By the time Vanbrugh died in 1726, his grandiose schemes for Castle Howard were almost complete. All but the west wing of the house had been built and in the grounds he had introduced a curtain wall, complete with bastions, mock fortifications, 11 different towers and a gatehouse whose massive arch and pyramid were

THE 'BRIDESHEAD' LOCATION

Brideshead Revisited, Evelyn Waugh's classic story of love and loss, was filmed at Castle Howard in 1981 and a more perfect location for the house whose spirit permeates the book would be hard to imagine. Life then imitated art. Lord Howard decided to use the opportunity to begin restoring rooms in the shell of the south front. The Garden Hall was created by Julian Bicknell in the spirit of Vanbrugh and, echoing a film scene in which Charles Ryder painted murals at Brideshead, Felix Kelly painted a series of delightful panels around the walls depicting imaginary Vanbrugh follies. Fact and fiction thus merged to sublime effect.

intended as a foretaste of the splendours to come. His last work was the Temple of the Four Winds, a Palladian style building with a dome, four Ionic porticos and elaborate finials. Hawksmoor survived Vanbrugh by ten years but, crippled by gout and unable to leave London, he made little further contribution to the work. His most important addition was probably his finest work – the Mausoleum, which dominates a hilltop a mile away from the house. As examples of the differing styles of Vanbrugh and Hawksmoor, the Temple of the Four Winds and the Mausoleum could not be more eloquent: where the Temple is startling in its flamboyance and defiance of convention, the Mausoleum is restrained and modest. Circular, with a cupola and a colonnade, its elegance is only marginally diminished by the later addition of a staircase and an unusual walled platform.

THE END OF AN ERA

Not surprisingly, when the 3rd Earl died in 1738, having spent over £78,000 on his palatial new home, he chose to be buried in the crypt beneath the Mausoleum Chapel. His death brought to a conclusion an era which had seen unprecedented experimentation with architectural styles. The 4th Earl was persuaded to employ his brother-in-law, Sir Thomas Robinson, to complete the house – a decision he was later to regret when Robinson added a Palladian west wing which, though a triumph of traditionalism, was completely out of keeping with Vanbrugh's buildings. C H Tatham was commissioned to finish the interiors of this wing in about 1800 and substantial alterations were made later in the century. During World War II a girls' school was evacuated to Castle Howard and, during their time there, two-thirds of the south front and the entire dome were destroyed by fire. Restoration work is an ongoing process.

FIT FOR A QUEEN

The full magnificence of Castle Howard is best appreciated from the south, where it is viewed in dramatic outline against the horizon. Visitors enter the house by a tourist entrance which has been used for that purpose for over 100 years. The sheer scale of the Grand Staircase and the vast, echoing rooms are imposing, and there is no denying the splendour of the bedrooms and dressing rooms that follow. Four-poster beds of every conceivable design contrive to reduce the height of the ceilings. Queen Victoria slept in the 18th-century bed with its unusual circular top, which dominates the Castle Howard Dressing Room. On the occasion of her visit in 1850 gas was first installed, and her entrance was heralded with a display of flames spelling out 'God Save the Queen' on the hall balcony.

A corridor has been turned from a utilitarian necessity into a novel Antique Passage, where antiquities from the 4th Earl's collections are displayed. The Great Hall is a triumph of Vanbrugh's art on an altogether different scale. Fifty-two feet square, its vastness is accentuated by the heavy pillars which draw the eye up to the wrought iron balcony of the gallery and the dizzying height of the dome 70 feet above. The plunging horses and arresting figure of Phaeton, tumbling from Apollo's chariot, are an entirely appropriate subject for the ceiling of the dome. By comparison with such monumental grandeur, the rest of the house seems positively domestic, but a series of glittering State Rooms provide the setting for a collection of fabulous paintings, with works from Holbein and Rubens to Gainsborough and Reynolds.

This portrait of Lady Mary Howard by Jackson is one of many commissions from the artist by the Carlisles.

Below: The Music Room contains two Broadwood pianos and a small harp, as well as a fine collection of paintings.

Carlton Towers

GOOLE

VICTORIAN GOTHIC AT ITS MOST MAGNIFICENT IN THE YORKSHIRE HOME OF THE DUKE OF NORFOLK: SIX MILES SOUTH OF SELBY OFF THE A1041.

■ **I treasure most the amazing Venetian Drawing Room where I can remember, as a small child, having the Christmas tree with real candles, and the butler standing by with a wet sponge to put them out as they burnt down, in case there was a fire.** ■
His Grace,
The Duke of Norfolk

Carlton has passed down entirely by inheritance since the Norman Conquest. From the family of Robert de Brus, who is recorded as its owner in the Domesday Book, it descended to the Stapletons, who were among the most renowned knights of the middle ages. Sir Miles Stapleton saw active service against the Scots under Edward I and became Steward of the Household to Edward II. He was one of the hundreds of Englishmen slain at the battle of Bannockburn in 1314. His grandson, another Sir Miles, belonged to the intimate circle of that great patron of chivalry, Edward, the Black Prince, and was therefore one of the founder members of the Order of the Garter. His younger brother was also a Knight of the Garter and held the powerful and dangerous post of Warden of Calais at a time when that part of France belonged to England. A renowned jouster, he won the family its crest, a Saracen's head, reputedly by killing an Infidel during a tournament in the presence of Edward III and the captive kings of Scotland and France. In the 15th century, a Stapleton married the heiress of the Beaumonts, descended from the last Crusader kings of Jerusalem. With her came the barony of Beaumont, an honour which, unusually, could pass through the female line and be held by a woman in her own right.

This chair, one of a set in the Inner Hall, dates from the 17th century, when it would have had a walnut frame and split cane seat. The chairs were transformed to this gold and red style in the 1840s for the 8th Lord Beaumont.

THE PRICE OF FAITH

Despite the Reformation, the Stapletons remained loyal to their Roman Catholic faith. The village church, which was a manorial chapel associated with the family, inexplicably avoided suppression in 1547 and remained in Catholic hands throughout the 16th century. It was not until 1611 that its existence was finally discovered by the authorities, who compelled it to convert to Anglican rites. The Stapletons refused to conform, even at this late stage, and though they continued to be buried in the village church (but not by the Anglican rector), they held all their religious services in the house at Carlton for the next three centuries.

With the Restoration of the monarchy, Miles Stapleton was created a baronet, an honour for which he had to pay the financially straitened Charles II the princely sum of £340. Sir Miles' faith, as well as his title, were to cost him dear. He spent large sums of money not only in installing and equipping a private chapel in the Long Gallery of the house, but also in bribing the local Carlton constable not to reveal the names of practising Catholics to the Wakefield Assizes.

A NARROW ESCAPE

Unable to hold any of the official positions which would normally have been open to his class because he was a Recusant, Sir Miles kept a low profile, thereby managing to keep out of trouble most of the time. Inevitably there were some nasty moments, the worst of these in 1680 when Sir Miles was accused of complicity in the 'Popish Plot', a supposed conspiracy among Catholics to massacre Protestants, burn London and assassinate the king which was 'uncovered' by Titus Oates. The plot was, in fact, a total fabrication by Oates, but the story gained popular credence and about 35 people were judicially murdered as a result. Arrested and taken to York to be tried for High Treason, Sir Miles was lucky to escape with his life: a special jury of his Yorkshire peers acquitted him outright. The narrowness of his escape was emphasised by the fact that Father Thomas Thwing, his chaplain, was refused a special jury because he was a priest and was condemned to death on the perjured evidence of a couple of notorious informers, becoming the last Catholic priest to be martyred in England. Thwing was hanged, drawn and quartered at York in October 1680.

The unfortunate Sir Miles was again a victim of anti-Catholic hysteria at the 'Glorious Revolution' of 1688 when James II fled to the Continent and William and Mary became his Protestant successors. An armed mob broke in, seized him and several members of his household and carried them off. However, at a loss to know what to do, they released their captive unharmed a few miles away. Sir Miles died in 1705 and the baronetcy he had purchased so expensively became extinct. His estates were inherited by his nephew.

THE ECCENTRIC ARCHITECT

The 9th Lord Beaumont commissioned someone as eccentric as himself to fulfil his fantasy of living in a medieval castle. Edward Welby Pugin, son of the more famous architect, ruined his career and bankrupted himself trying to prove that it was his father, and not Sir Charles Barry, who had designed the Houses of Parliament. His plans for Carlton Towers were never completed, the present building being only half the size he envisaged. Work on a great hall, a chapel and a massive keep had to be abandoned when Lord Beaumont's money ran out.

RACEHORSES AT CARLTON

His grandson, Thomas, was a successful breeder of racehorses: in partnership with Sir Thomas Gascoigne, he produced Hollandaise, the winner of the first St Leger in 1778. The following year, he won the race again with his own horse, Tommy. Not only did Thomas add extensive new stables to the house at Carlton, he also had portraits of his favourite horses painted, some of which still survive.

His ambitions were not entirely confined to racing. He also put in a claim to revive the dormant barony of Beaumont. It was not until 1840 that it was eventually allowed – too late for Thomas, but his great nephew, Miles Thomas, became the 8th Baron Beaumont.

Miles Thomas decided that his ennoblement should be commemorated by the creation of an appropriate family seat. A man of many talents, who had dabbled as a dramatist and a poet, he fancied himself as an architect as well, undertaking the remodelling of the house at Carlton along Gothic lines.

TRANSFORMING THE HALL

Perhaps because he inherited at only six years old, his son, Henry, turned out to have megalomaniac ambitions for his family home. He was responsible for the transformation of the perfectly worthy Carlton Hall into the Gothic fantasy, Carlton Towers, a project which was to occupy him for the rest of his life and drive him into bankruptcy. Perhaps it was fortunate, from a family point of view, that he died comparatively young and his younger brother, Miles, a professional soldier, inherited a palatial new home and what little remained of the once great estates.

The following year he married Ethel, daughter and heiress of Sir Charles Tempest of Broughton Hall, near Skipton, whose fortune saved the day. When he was killed in a shooting accident in 1895, only three years after inheriting, everything, including the title, passed to his one-year-old daughter, Mona. As Baroness Beaumont, Mona owned Carlton for 76 years. In 1914 she married Lord Howard of Glossop, heir presumptive to the Dukedom of Norfolk, and had eight children, all of whom were given a name beginning with the letter 'M': Miles, Michael, Mariegold, Martin, Miriam, Miranda, Mirabel and Mark. Her eldest son, Miles, born in 1915, inherited the baronies of Beaumont and Howard of Glossop from his parents and, in 1975, succeeded his cousin as 17th Duke of Norfolk and Earl Marshal of England.

It is his younger son, Lord Gerald Fitzalan Howard, who, with his wife and children, has recently taken up residence in Carlton Towers, maintaining an unbroken family tradition which stretches back to the Norman Conquest.

This detail from the magnificent fireplace in the Venetian Drawing Room shows the family coat of arms.

CENTURIES OF HISTORY

Given the personal and family glory achieved by his ancestors in the middle ages, it is understandable that Henry, Lord Beaumont decided to create a medieval fantasy at Carlton Towers. Though the exterior is overwhelmingly Victorian Gothic, the core of the house is genuinely much older. Traces of the original medieval house have been found and the three-storey block to the left of the main entrance is the Carlton Hall of 1614. The long wing to the right was added around 1777 and later given another façade. Though the idea was good – giving the house a unity of design it had previously lacked – its execution was disappointing and the 9th Baron, had no compunction in starting again.

His architect, Edward Welby Pugin, was more accustomed to building churches and the ecclesiastical influence is very strong in his designs for Carlton. Pugin's grandiose schemes involved refacing the entire building with concrete to make it look like stone, and adding a superabundance of extravagant 'medieval' details, turrets and battlements, gargoyles and coats of

Far left: A French vase which can be seen in the drawing room.

Left: The walls of the Picture Gallery display works of art which mostly come from the Tempest Collection.

arms. A curved flight of stairs leading to the entrance appears almost like a bridge over a moat and is guarded by two talbots, each holding a heraldic banner. The façade of the long east wing has huge armorial panels, Gothic arches and tracery in the mullioned windows, so that it resembles some medieval baronial Great Hall and has become the new focus of the building.

By the time the external alterations had been completed, Lord Beaumont had quarrelled with Pugin and taken on a new architect, John Francis Bentley. Interestingly, he too was principally a designer of churches, most famous for his Byzantine-style Roman Catholic cathedral of Westminster. Carlton Towers was the only major country house commission he took. Nevertheless, the interiors he created here are a triumph, a dazzling interpretation of medieval themes on a scale which would have been impossible in the Middle Ages.

MAGNIFICENT INTERIORS

The Outer Hall is a foretaste of the splendours to come and, appropriately enough, the visitor is greeted by a bust of the 8th Lord Beaumont, who masterminded the transformation of the house. The ecclesiastical character of the beamed and stencilled ceiling, the tiled floor and the stained glass window is intentional, for it served as a temporary chapel when Cardinal Manning, visiting Carlton in 1876, celebrated Mass here. The Inner Hall is the first of a series of State Rooms which extends to the east. There is a church-like quality to this room too, with its heavily panelled walls and ceilings, its decorated archways and its elaborately carved minstrels' gallery. Bentley went to great lengths to procure the overall effect, designing the huge chandelier, some of the furniture and the fabulous stained glass window.

Through enormous and intricately carved double doors lies the most important room in the house, the Venetian Drawing Room. Occupying the site of the 18th-century chapel, this vast room is a showpiece for the art of Bentley and Knox. Venetian glassware gave

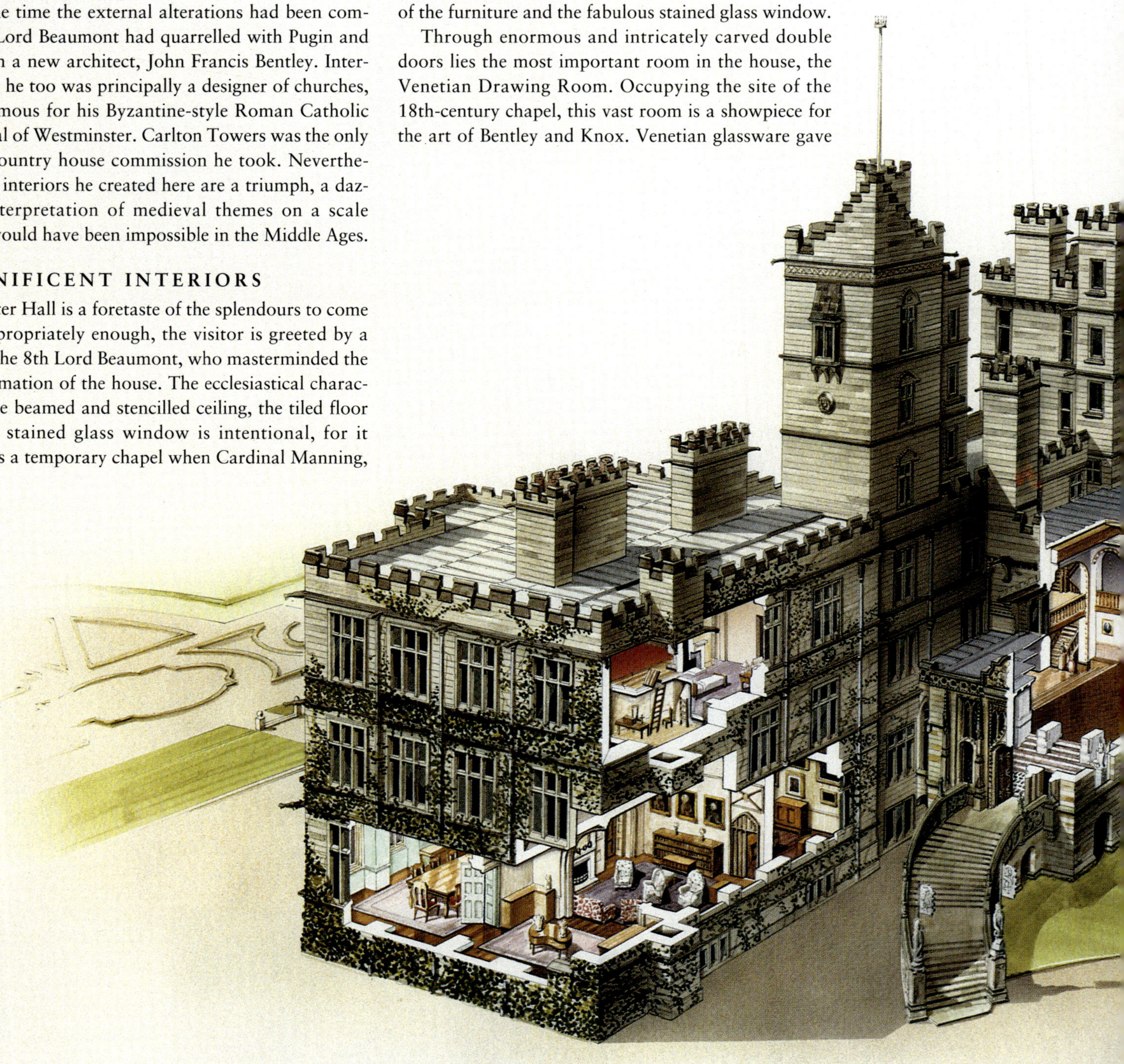

the room its name and the theme was picked up in the painted panels between the cabinets on which the artist, N J Westlake, portrayed characters from the *Merchant of Venice*, irreverently referring to them as 'Shylock, Boldlock and Padlock'. There is fine plaster-work and a magnificent cornice, but the glory of the room is the fireplace – a breathtaking extravaganza of heraldic design.

Beyond this room is the Picture Gallery, another vast room, but this time decorated in restrained style. The Tempest collection of pictures are displayed here, together with two banners painted to look like tapestry and bearing the arms of the last Stuart Pretender. Double doors at the far end suggest an endless suite of rooms, but in fact open onto a brick wall. It was at this point that Lord Beaumont's money ran out.

The Main Staircase is appropriately grandiose, the first flight of stairs framed by a stencilled Gothic arch whose shape is echoed in the splendid stained-glass window on the landing: de Havilland again devised the heraldic glass in the window and Bentley designed the Beaumont lions, borne as tournament helm crests, which Knox carved to form the newel posts.

At the top of the stairs lie the old nurseries in the Jacobean part of the house. Glass panels in the floor reveal the Priest Hole, constructed in 1614, between the chimney stacks in the old house and accessed by a trapdoor hidden in the base of a cupboard.

Carlton Towers is open only occasionally.

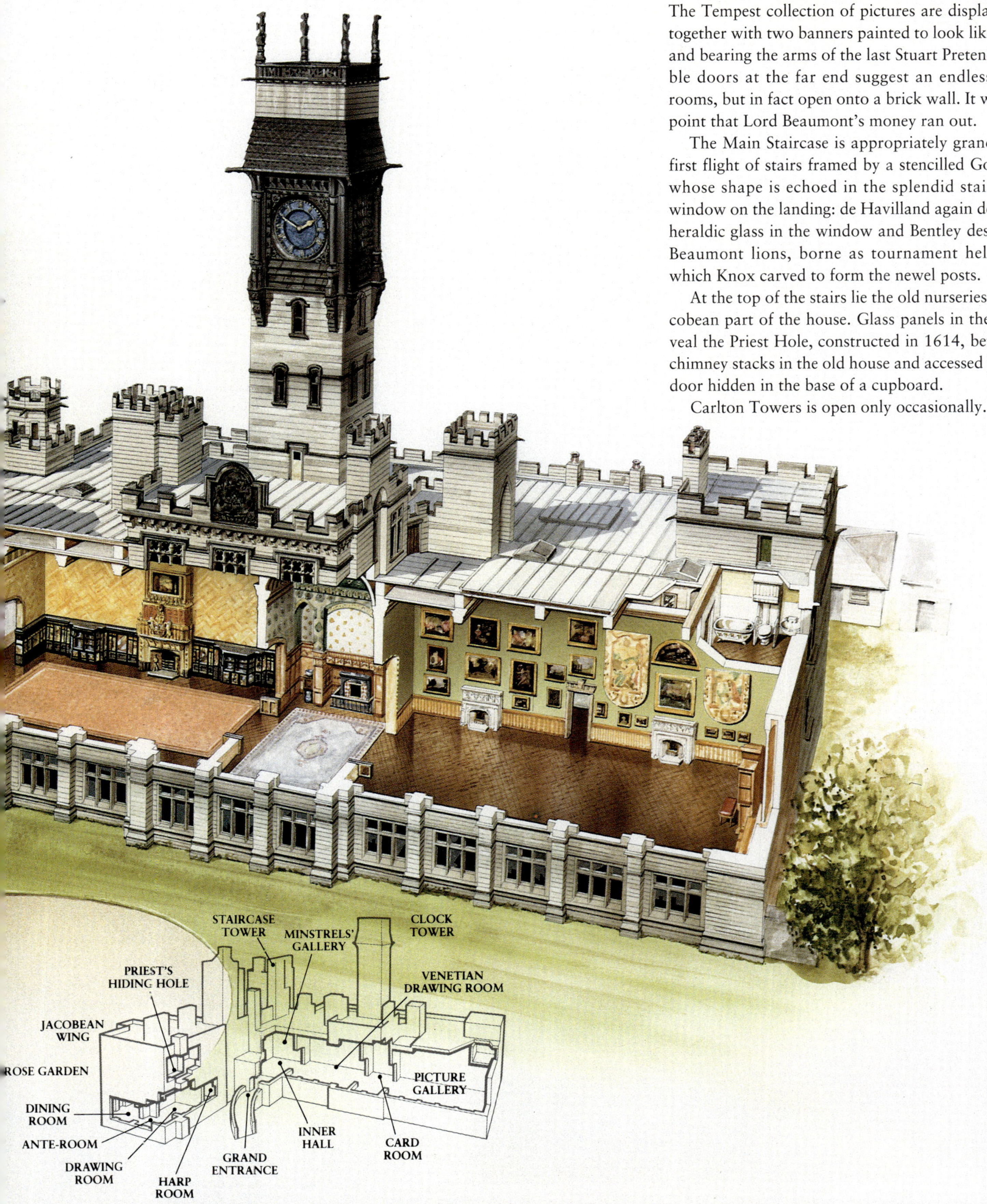

Allerton Park

Knaresborough

The most important Gothic Revival stately home in England: four miles east of Knaresborough at the A1/A59 intersection.

William Mauleverer, a Norman knight whose name meant 'poor hunter', gained a rich prize when he was rewarded for his services to William the Conqueror with lands at Allerton. The estates remained in his family, descending in the direct male line, for 600 years. The medieval Mauleverers collected a fine array of titles, including premier baron of England in 1448, and their splendid effigies can be seen in the Church of St Martin at Allerton. Continuing the family tradition of military service, but not of loyalty to the Crown. Sir Thomas Mauleverer raised regiments of horse and foot for Parliament in the Civil War and was one of the signatories of the death warrant of Charles I.

The Hon. Richard Arundell, Member of Parliament for Knaresborough, who inherited the estate in the 18th century, used his experience in Whitehall as Surveyor of the King's Works to completely remodel the house, park and church. The results were so elegant that they attracted royal attention and were bought for Frederick Augustus, second son of George III. Better known as the Duke of York, he made his mark by building a 'Temple of Victory' on top of an artificially created hill, 200 feet high, in the grounds. According to local legend, these efforts inspired the popular nursery rhyme, *The Grand Old Duke of York*.

The present splendid baronial mansion was built between 1848 and 1856 and is a perfect Victorian ideal of medieval romance, with everything on the grand scale. The public rooms are almost oppressive in their vastness and in the opulence of their heavy wooden panelling, but the details of the intricate and delicate carvings in the woodwork, elaborate fireplaces and wonderful plasterwork ceilings are quite seductive. The Great Hall, a full three storeys high, is magnificent, drawing the eye up past the wooden gallery to the soaring carved and gilded rafters and the vaulted ceiling. The drawing room, on the other hand, is ablaze with gold – mirror and picture frames, furniture, even the clock on the mantelpiece are ornately carved and gilded. Appropriately, the house now belongs to a charitable trust set up by its owner, Dr Rolph, to ensure the preservation of restoration skills and historic crafts.

Duncombe Park

Helmsley

Newly restored mansion, set in uniquely important baroque gardens, now a National Nature Reserve: minutes from the Market Square in Helmsley.

In 1689 London goldsmith Sir Charles Duncombe paid £90,000, the most ever paid by a commoner, to purchase the Helmsley estate from the Trustees of the Duke of Buckingham. His family prospered, becoming first barons and then, in 1868, Earls of Feversham. With the turn of the 20th century their fortunes changed. The second Earl was killed at the Somme in 1916; the house was leased out and became a girls' school and, in 1963, the earldom came to an end with the death of the third Earl. His distant cousin, Lord Feversham, inherited the estates and, in 1985, took advantage of a break in the school lease to take up residence in the family home. It was a brave decision: after so many years of institutional use the house was little more than a shell and, ten years later, the restoration programme is only half completed.

The terrace at Duncombe Park leads to a fine Doric temple. It stands amidst landscaped grounds which are not only beautiful, but also historically important, predating 'Capability' Brown by some 60 years.

Duncombe Park was originally built about 1713, to the designs of William Wakefield. Sir Charles Barry, architect of the Houses of Parliament, was responsible for the north and south pavilions and the addition of a charming forecourt which perfectly complements the attractive proportions of the classical façade. The house was seriously damaged by fire in 1879, but rebuilding was undertaken according to the original designs and the principal rooms remain a fine example of late 19th-century 'grand interiors'. Most of the 18th-century contents were destroyed in the fire – less than a fifth of the pictures survived – but Lord Feversham's personal collection of English and Continental furniture and family portraits find an appropriate setting in the palatial splendour of the public rooms.

Standing in a clearing, surrounded by some of the tallest and oldest hardwood trees in the country, Duncombe Park has an imposing frontage, though ornamental urns and a double-sided staircase soften the severity of its classical lines. Inside, the formality of the pillared hall is offset by the exuberance of the carved panelling, the furniture and fittings reflecting the range of styles available in the 18th and 19th centuries.

The grounds are uniquely important. Laid out some 60 years before the 'Capability' Brown era, they have been virtually untouched for 250 years, a rare survival of the naturalist style of landscape, which forms a classical English setting for an ancient house with a new lease of life.

Fairfax House

YORK

THE FINEST GEORGIAN HOUSE IN YORK, PAINSTAKINGLY RESTORED TO HOUSE NOEL TERRY'S COLLECTION OF PERIOD FURNITURE AND CLOCKS: IN CASTLEGATE

In 1759, Charles, Viscount Fairfax of Emley, purchased a house and land at Castlegate, overlooking the River Ouse, for his daughter, Anne, the sole survivor of his nine children. The gift was made to compensate Anne for her disappointment in marriage: at the 11th hour, when the bridal parties were already assembling in London, he had prohibited her marriage to William Constable of Burton Constable, on the grounds that the groom was not assiduous enough in his attendance at week-day Mass. Fairfax himself was a devout Catholic. His refusal to take the oath of allegiance during the Jacobite troubles in 1745 cast doubt on his loyalties, but, despite unfounded rumours that he was secretly harbouring troops at his country home, Gilling Castle, he weathered the storm. He poured a fortune into building a fine new town house for his daughter but his efforts to please her were in vain. She suffered acute nervous disorders, and tried (in vain) to find a cure in retreat at Cambrai and in Brussels. The two of them occupied the house in Castlegate for 11 winters, but when he died she sold it within a year and returned to spend the last 21 years of her life alone at Gilling Castle.

Between 1772 and 1865 the house changed hands six times, at one time belonging to the mother of Colonel Thornton, a notorious eccentric who was publicly horse-whipped for refusing to honour a lost wager of 1,000 guineas. After 1865 it was no longer a private house, first becoming offices for the York Friendly Societies and then, in 1919, its front first floor rooms were converted into a ballroom. The future of Fairfax House remained uncertain until it was purchased by the York Civic Trust in 1981 and restored to house the Noel Terry Collection.

The house probably dates from around the 1740s but the exterior was extensively remodelled and the interiors transformed by Fairfax in 1759. His architect, John Carr of York, was responsible for the overall scheme and, in choosing his favourite craftsmen, for the implementation of his detailed plans. The Palladian entrance hallway is a triumph of his art, where a carefully contrived vista of archways entice the visitor into his more flamboyantly decorated public rooms. His portrait hangs over the library fireplace, resplendent with a Greek key design. Attentive to every last detail, Fairfax purchased and demolished the house next door to increase the light to his superb Venetian window on the staircase.

Splendid though it is, Fairfax House proved no consolation for poor Anne Fairfax, thwarted in love by her father.

AN ENTHUSIASTIC COLLECTOR

Noel Terry, a member of the famous York chocolate-making family, spent 50 years amassing his superb collection of Georgian furniture and was determined that it should remain an entity on display to the public in York. The strength of the collection is in its mid 18th-century carved mahogany furniture, but there are also earlier and later pieces. Little concerned with the relationship between the pieces, he was only interested in building up a private collection of individual masterpieces which is one of the best in the country.

Kiplin Hall

CATTERICK

CHARMING JACOBEAN HOUSE, BUILT FOR THE FOUNDER OF THE AMERICAN STATE OF MARYLAND: SEVEN MILES EAST OF RICHMOND ON THE B6271.

The builder of Kiplin Hall was a local man, George Calvert, who rose from comparatively humble beginnings to the highest political eminence. After graduating from Trinity College, Oxford, he became a Member of Parliament in 1619. James I appointed him a member of the Privy Council and made him Secretary of State. In 1625, however, he announced his conversion to Roman Catholicism and, as a result, was obliged to resign his post. As compensation, he was given an Irish baronetcy, becoming the 1st Lord Baltimore.

The title was to be significant, for Calvert was to become deeply involved in American affairs. In 1622 James I had granted him Newfoundland, but the climate was not to his liking. Charles I proved more receptive to his complaints and in 1632 he was granted the territories which now comprise Maryland. Unfortunately, he died before the Charter could be issued, so it was his son, Cecilius, who officially founded the state. Both his younger son, Leonard, and his grandson, Charles, were governors of Maryland province, and the city of Baltimore took its name from the family title. Even today, the family maintains its connections with the United States and, though Kiplin Hall is now in the hands of a charitable trust, it has never been sold outside the family.

Kiplin Hall was built in the period 1622-25, before Calvert's conversion and exclusion from office. His choice of architect is not recorded, but the pretty, three-storey house, built of red brick, is quite delightful. Rectangular in shape, with a square tower in the middle of each side, its rooftops are a forest of chimneys, gables and domes. The widow of the 4th Lord Baltimore married Christopher Crowe, who had been British Ambassador to Leghorn in Italy. He was responsible for carrying out a series of improvements to the house in about 1720, including, most dramatically, replacing the staircases in the north and south towers with a central one. Restoration work is gradually progressing on this house, where the rather haphazard arrangement of the rooms only adds to its charm.

Newby Hall

RIPON

ONE OF YORKSHIRE'S FINEST ADAM HOUSES, WITH AWARD-WINNING GARDENS: THREE MILES SOUTH-EAST OF RIPON OFF THE B6265 BOROUGHBRIDGE ROAD.

The present owner of this delightful William and Mary House is descended from William Weddell, who bought it in 1748 with a legacy from his uncle. A man of cultivated tastes, Weddell was a prominent member of the Dilettanti Club and made the Grand Tour of Europe in 1765-6. Returning with a large collection of classical sculptures, he had to enlarge the house to accommodate them all. John Carr of York added the two east wings, remodelled the main block and planned the Statue Gallery which was completed by Robert Adam. Later owners added a Regency dining room, a Victorian wing and 25 acres of gardens.

The gardens at Newby Hall are a charming blend of formal and informal plantings, and stretch down to the banks of the River Ure.

The red brick exterior of the Hall, with its stone facings and balustrading, is gracious but the interiors are the true glory. The beautifully proportioned entrance hall, with its splendid plasterwork, is a suitable introduction to the house. Elegant family portraits by Sir Thomas Lawrence, Pompeo Batoni (the leading painter of English visitors to Rome) and Angelica Kauffman complement the Adam, Chippendale and Hepplewhite furniture. But this is no ordinary house, and there are surprises everywhere. The Circular Room is a delightful William Blackwood design, with ceiling roundels copied from murals at Herculaneum and *trompe-l'oeil* curved doors, painted with classical motifs to look like wall panels. The Motto Bedroom is a charming conceit by Lady Mary Vyner, with old French mottoes painted round the ceiling and on the furniture – even the hip bath has not escaped its worthy proverb.

Two of the rooms are particularly outstanding. The Tapestry Room, completed in 1776, was purpose built to house the glorious Gobelin tapestries ordered from the Paris factory by William Weddell nine years before. Woven by Neilson, on a unique dove-grey background, they incorporate medallions of the 'Loves of the Gods' and floral ornaments. Chairs and sofas, specially commissioned by Adam from Chippendale, incorporate matching tapestry upholstery, each depicting a different spray of flowers. This the only set of Chippendale furniture to retain its original upholstery, and the Gobelin tapestries are one of only five sets made for English patrons. The room has survived quite remarkably in its entirety.

Adam's Statue Gallery is extraordinary for different reasons. Designed in the style of a Roman interior, with two square rooms and a central rotunda, its remarkable plasterwork, alcoves, arches and pedestals provide the perfect setting for Weddell's famous collection of ancient statuary.

Norton Conyers Hall

Ripon

A CHARMING MANOR HOUSE, THE SEAT OF THE GRAHAMS SINCE 1624 AND PROBABLY THE INSPIRATION FOR THORNFIELD HALL IN CHARLOTTE BRONTE'S *JANE EYRE*: THREE MILES NORTH-WEST OF RIPON ON THE WATH ROAD.

Richard Graham was descended from a Scottish family who had made a dubious name for themselves in the Borders for cattle stealing and riotous behaviour, yet this considerably more respectable kinsman established the family fortunes in the service of the Duke of Buckingham. In 1623, he accompanied the Duke and the future Charles I to Spain to woo the Infanta, and returned to England with dispatches so swiftly that James I added the pair of wings to his coat of arms. These are still part of the family crest. When Buckingham was murdered, Richard became one of Charles I's Gentlemen of the Horse and was given a baronetcy. A Royalist during the Civil War, he was wounded at Edgehill and, according to family legend, again at Marston Moor near York in 1644. A scar in the wood of the main staircase is pointed out as the mark made by his horse's hoof, red hot after his frantic ride home from the battlefield.

Only marginally less dramatic were the poisoning of the 4th Baronet in 1755 – he died after drinking tea intended for his mistress – and the enforced sale of the house and all the other Graham property by the 7th Baronet in 1862 to pay off his gambling debts. His son, who served in the Crimea and was nursed by Florence Nightingale, married an heiress and repurchased the family home.

Though rebuilt in Stuart times, when its distinctive Dutch gables were added, the Hall betrays its medieval origins in the heavy panelling and staircase; the room and bed in which James II spent the night in 1679 are suitably atmospheric. Family portraits by Sir Peter Lely, Sir Godfrey Kneller and Romney are complemented by a delightful series of water-colours and lithographs of 19th-century notables.

Charlotte Brontë is said to have visited in 1839 and the legend of a mad woman imprisoned in the attics of Norton Conyers is believed to have inspired her later novel *Jane Eyre*.

Above: The Hall at Norton Conyers contains an array of fine paintings and some rare furniture.

Portraits of the servants of a household are a rare occurrence. This one is of Sarah Ellis, housekeeper to the 5th Baronet.

THE WRONG CUP OF TEA

The 4th Baronet died in 1755 after drinking tea which had been poisoned. It was not he who was unpopular, though, for the tea was intended for his housekeeper mistress, Eleanor Brady. The fact that she was Irish and, presumably, Roman Catholic would not have endeared her to her fellow servants in those days of religious bigotry. Her volatile temperament, coupled with the fact that she called herself 'Lady' Eleanor and arrogantly lorded it over the below-stairs household could well have provoked thoughts of murder.

■ From Jane Eyre: 'It (Thornfield Hall) was three stories high, of proportions not vast, though considerable; a gentleman's manor-house, not a nobleman seat.' I feel sure that these words were in part inspired by Charlotte Brontë's visit to Norton Conyers, and, both inside and out, the house must look very much as it did at that time. ■

Sir James Graham, Bt

Ripley Castle

HARROGATE

ONE OF THE PRETTIEST CASTLES IN ENGLAND, HOME TO THE INGILBY'S FOR OVER 670 YEARS: THREE MILES NORTH OF HARROGATE ON THE A61.

■ No historical drama could ever survive with a cast as diverse as the one which has occupied Ripley for 28 generations, yet the Castle has such a 'lived-in' quality that you get the feeling that half of them never left the stage. It is a house of wonderful charm, eccentricity and humour. ■
Sir Thomas
C W Ingilby, Bt

The colourful and eccentric Ingilbys have lived at Ripley Castle since the 1320s when Thomas married Edeline Thweng, heiress to the estate. Despite attaining high office in the judiciary, he is best remembered for saving the life of Edward III when he was attacked by a wounded boar while hunting. This act of valour won him a knighthood, but the Ingilby's Catholicism cost them dear. Sir William joined the conspirators in the 'Pilgrimage of Grace' and was only saved from execution by Henry VIII because he had advised against taking action. His son, Francis, trained as a Jesuit priest in the seminary at Rheims, returning to England in 1584; captured two years later, he was convicted of treason and hung, drawn and quartered at York. Beatified in 1987, he is the only Ingilby likely to become a Saint. His brother, William, narrowly avoided execution for treason when he was unjustly implicated in the Gunpowder Plot.

Loyalty to the Crown proved equally hazardous: Sir William was fined over £700 for 'delinquency' in supporting Charles I during the Civil War and his son briefly fled into exile with James II. More prosaically, in 1794, the then baronet and his wife abandoned their six small children by escaping to Europe to avoid their creditors. It was ten years before he could pay them off and return home.

The medieval fortifications of Ripley Castle were built to provide protection from marauding Scots but later baronets added a 16th-century tower and an 18th-century mansion house. Designed by John Carr of York, this is the most elegant part of the castle, with furniture by Chippendale, whose father was a joiner on the Ripley estate, and Hepplewhite. The Continental residence of various Ingilbys, both enforced and voluntary, is reflected in the Venetian chandeliers and Italian plasterwork ceilings and statuary. Most fascinating of all are the tower rooms: the library, with its huge 18th-century table, 5,000 books and the 1386 foundation charter of Mount Grace Priory; above it, the Tower Room, with a fabulous plasterwork ceiling, where James I slept in 1603 and, on the third storey, the gem of the castle, the perfectly preserved Knight's Chamber of 1555. A priest hole is hidden behind the panelling and the door leading to a spiral staircase has a prominent false handle to delay attackers.

TROOPER JANE

'Trooper Jane' helped her brother, Sir William, raise a troop of horsemen from Ripley and went to the assistance of the Royalist army which was besieging York. Disguised as a man and wearing a full suit of armour, this doughty lady not only fought at Marston Moor but also saved her brother's life in defeat by hiding him in the priest hole. Oliver Cromwell arrived at Ripley that night demanding admittance. Jane allowed him to sleep in an armchair in the library, sitting opposite him with a pair of pistols hidden in her lap, to ensure that her brother's hiding place was not discovered.

Sion Hill Hall

THIRSK

AN EDWARDIAN COUNTRY MANSION, HOUSING THE MAWER COLLECTION OF ANTIQUES: AT KIRBY WISKE, OFF THE A167 TOPCLIFFE TO NORTHALLERTON ROAD.

■ We take a great delight in showing visitors around. Brenda takes pride in her displays of period costume – many on mannequins in room settings – and I am particularly interested in the many different clocks which are on show, and all up, running and chiming. ■
John Bridges

One of the last great country houses to be built before World War I changed English social life for ever, Sion Hill Hall is a monument to the days when living was gracious and servants were plentiful. It was built for Mr Percy Stancliffe in 1912-3 by Walter H Brierley, the 'Lutyens of the North', on the site of an earlier house, of which a Georgian stable block and a Victorian walled garden are all that remain.

The influence of Lutyens is evident in the solid but pleasing red brick exterior, with soaring chimneys and rows of large neo-Georgian windows which create such a light and airy atmosphere inside. The epitome of Edwardian elegance and simplicity, the interiors form a perfect backdrop for the collection of Georgian, Regency and Victorian antiques which were assembled over 50 years by Herbert Mawer, the owner since 1961. Sion Hill Hall is no museum piece, however – strolling through the magnificent hall or pausing in the intimate Edwardian Boudoir, the feeling is very much that of a family home. Don't miss the Civil War hoard pot, unearthed locally in 1985, which contained one of the largest treasure troves then found in the north of England: gold and silver coins and a receipt for a quantity of cheese supplied to the Royalist Army. Buried in anticipation of the King winning the war, when the cheese account would be paid, its owner was doubly unfortunate in that the Royalists were defeated and he was never able to retrieve his pot of gold.

Right: This French-style bracket clock is among the delightful items to be seen around Sion Hill Hall.

Above left: Sion Hill's Inner Hall reflects an age of gracious living.

Above: The influence of Lutyens on Sion Hill's architect is clearly apparent.

Sutton Park

SUTTON-ON-THE-FOREST

A CHARMING EARLY GEORGIAN COUNTRY HOUSE, SET IN ELEGANT TERRACED GARDENS: EIGHT MILES NORTH OF YORK ON THE B1363 HELMSLEY ROAD.

Though the Sheffields have only lived in this house since 1963, they have undoubtedly made it their own. Descended from a Sir Robert Sheffield who was clubbed down by a butcher while suppressing the Norfolk uprising of 1549, the family won fortune and title by loyal service to the Crown. One descendent commanded the *White Bear* during the defeat of the Spanish Armada. Tragedy struck Edmund, Lord Sheffield, created Earl of Mulgrave in 1625, when his three sons were drowned while crossing the Humber at Whitgift. His great-grandson, who, like his father, inherited as a child, went on to become a friend of Queen Anne, serving as her Privy Councillor and Lord Chancellor. He was rewarded with the Order of the Garter and made Duke of Buckingham; his London house, sold to the king in 1762, is now better known as Buckingham Palace.

On the premature death of his legitimate heir, there was a contest over the inheritance between his widow and his natural son, ending in a division of the property. Charles Sheffield acquired the Normanby estates in Lincolnshire and it is his descendants who purchased Sutton Park, a mid 18th-century house, set in acres of well-timbered and ancient parkland.

The somewhat severe lines of the house, four storeys high and boasting two graceful wings, are complemented by formal gardens to the south, featuring three terraces, the lowest of which is a water garden, complete with fountain. A pillared entrance hall leads into a series of elegant and pretty rooms with delicate but exuberant plasterwork ceilings by Cortese, opulent chandeliers and large windows opening on to the gardens and park. Sheffield family portraits dating from the 17th and 18th centuries are quite at home here among the antiques collected over several generations.

Surprises do lie in store, not least in the unusual and striking wall decorations: the ornately carved pine panelling of the Morning Room was brought from Potternewton Hall in Leeds, while the Chinese Drawing Room has rare and beautiful Chinese wallpaper, patterned with birds and trees, which is as old as the house. It is a great tribute to the present owners, who have undertaken extensive and sympathetic restoration work in both house and gardens, that their innovations are undetectable to all but the most expert eye.

■ I love this house so much for its position facing south, which makes it full of sunlight; secondly, I never tire of looking at the wonderful plasterwork created by Cortese in the 18th century; thirdly, the proportions of the rooms are perfect – the doors and chimneypieces are all in their right positions, and one steps out into the garden, which my husband and I created, where there is always something of interest all year round. ■

Mrs Sheffield

Sutton Park is now the Yorkshire home of an illustrious family.

Raby Castle

DARLINGTON

LINKS WITH CANUTE AND RICHARD III AT A ROMANTICALLY-SITED CASTLE: 12 MILES NORTH-EAST OF DARLINGTON, OFF THE A688

Part of King Canute's castle may be built into Raby's walls, but it was in the 14th century that the intensely romantic building we see today was begun. Romance was not, of course, its purpose. When the Nevill family built Raby there were constant threats from Scotland, and the surrounding landscape, now tamed by centuries of cultivation, was harsh and unwelcoming. The 30 foot curtain wall has long since gone, but the huge feudal castle, which grew gradually through the generations, retains much of its medieval impressiveness.

It was here that Richard III's mother, Cicely Nevill, 'The Rose of Raby', was brought up by her father, the 1st Earl of Westmorland. The royal connection did not help the 6th Earl, who led the Rising of the North in 1569, intended to put Mary, Queen of Scots on the throne. Defeated, he fled abroad and Raby was taken by the Crown. After more than 50 years of neglect, it was sold to the Vane family. The second Sir Henry Vane to live at Raby was executed by Charles II, but the Vanes eventually became Barons Barnard, Earls of Darlington and Dukes of Cleveland. The last Duke died in 1891, and Raby is now owned by Lord Barnard.

Approached through the gatehouse, the only survivor of the outer walls, is the awesome bulk of Clifford's Tower, built in about 1378. Other reminders of the original castle are Bulmer's Tower and the perfect 14th-century kitchen, with its ox-sized fireplaces, and the servants' hall. The spectacular Nevill Gateway leads to the cobbled Inner Court. The long tunnel was created by John Carr when he restored and reshaped the castle in the 1760s. Indeed, many of the rooms seen today were built or decorated in the 18th and 19th centuries. Most impressive are Carr's Gothic entrance hall of 1783, with its vaulted ceiling and blood-red columns, and the Octagon Room, built in the 1840s by William Burn in the French style, with silk-covered walls, gilded furniture and fine china. Burn was also responsible for lengthening and redecorating the huge Baron's Hall, 130 feet long, where the Rising of the North was planned. It still retains its medieval minstrels' gallery.

This four-poster bed at Raby Castle has beautiful Chinese painted silk hangings.

The magnificent contents of the castle were all collected after the 1st Lord Barnard, furious at his son's marriage, sold everything in 1714 and tried to destroy the whole building. Favourite for many visitors is the marble statue of a chained and naked Greek slave girl by Powers. Delicately erotic, it caused a sensation at the Great Exhibition of 1851.

Rokeby Park

BARNARD CASTLE

AN EXTRAVAGANT AMATEUR ARCHITECT'S SUBLIME ITALIANATE VILLA, IN A BEAUTIFUL SETTING: FOUR MILES SOUTH-EAST OF BARNARD CASTLE, OFF THE A66 SCOTCH CORNER ROAD.

If buildings could fly like homing pigeons, Rokeby Park would surely wing its way from its northern perch to the Venetian mainland. For this ochre-painted house is a villa in the purest Palladian style, a poised composition of a tall central block and lower, retiring wings, all with pyramid roofs, following in its wake. It was designed for himself by Sir Thomas Robinson, on the site of the old Robinson mansion, some distance from the still-surviving medieval tower of the Rokeby family, from whom the Robinsons bought the estate during the Civil War. 'Long Sir Tom' was the son-in-law of the Earl of Carlisle, for whom Vanbrugh was building the baroque Castle Howard, but Robinson's taste was for the neo-classical style. Rokeby was to be both a home and a show place.

The lower ground floor rooms are not lofty, but each has its characteristic decoration, especially the breakfast room, which is enlivened with cut-out 18th-century prints. But it was on the *piano nobile* – the main floor – that Robinson expended most of his talent and money. The fine music room is a fitting introduction to the startling grandeur of Rokeby's principal room. The full height of the house, the Saloon is an apartment that should be filled with the music of Handel for full effect, for it is of the same stately richness, from its gilded ceiling to the marble fireplaces and the doorways, surrounded by columns and crowned with triangular pediments. Sir Tom wrote to the Earl of Carlisle, 'My chief expense has been in Palladian doors and windows', and one can see why.

A Member of Parliament, Sir Tom was nearly

always in debt because of his high living, and spent a period of time as Governor of Barbados to escape from his creditors. When in London he was a director of entertainments at Ranelagh Gardens, and he appears both in Hogarth's picture *The Beggar's Opera* and in Fielding's novel *Joseph Andrews*. His extravagance meant he had to sell Rokeby, just 30 years after it was built, to John Sawrey Morritt, whose family still lives here. It was Morritt's son who introduced one of the house's most celebrated inhabitants, the Velasquez painting known as *The Rokeby Venus*, which had pride of place in the Saloon for about a century until she finally went to the National Gallery. Yet even her beauty could not rival the magnificent setting of the house and nearby Greta Bridge, memorably painted by J S Cotman.

A CHARITABLE MAN

In the 18th century Dr John Sharp restored the ruins of Bamburgh Castle and ran a remarkable charity under the terms of Lord Crewe's will. There was a free school, an infirmary with its own dispensary, a free lending library for the use of the poor, and a mill where corn was ground and sold very cheaply. Dr Sharp also set up one of the first coastguard and lifeboat stations in the country (the chains he used for rescue are still in the castle), set up a safety beacon on the coast and provided homes for shipwrecked sailors.

Left: Detail of an 18th-century painting of the north aspect of Rokeby Park.

Bamburgh Castle

BAMBURGH

A DRAMATIC SITE AND A FASCINATING HISTORY FOR THIS RESTORED CASTLE: IN BAMBURGH, 14 MILES NORTH OF ALNWICK VIA THE A1 AND THE B1342.

If you want a castle that really looks like a castle, Bamburgh's the place. Its setting is superb, and it crouches ferociously on its fearsome crag like a whole medieval town. Beyond it, only the empty dunes and cold North Sea, with Holy Island, once under the castle's protection, on the horizon. This outcrop of basalt has been defended since the Iron Age. After the departure of the Romans, Bamburgh was a royal Saxon capital and was sacked by the Vikings. It fell easily to William the Conqueror, but with its new Norman keep and walls was absolutely impregnable until in 1464 Edward IV's new artillery earned it the dubious honour of being the first castle ever to be shelled into submission. Thereafter Bamburgh, with its walls broken and its roof shattered, succumbed to the elements.

The Forster family held it from the reign of James I until the early 18th century, when it passed to Lord Crewe, Bishop of Durham. He left the castle as part of a charitable trust and it was sold in 1894 to the 1st Lord Armstrong, whose family still owns it. It was repaired and restored in the 18th century, but in the 19th century was extensively reconstructed in turn-of-the century Gothic.

The State Rooms, which are on the landward side of the castle, include the panelled Great Hall, with an impressive hammer-beam roof and a musicians' gallery. The Hall houses an excellent display of armour from the Tower of London's Royal Armoury collection. Elsewhere in the castle there is fine furniture and porcelain, portraits of many of those associated with the castle's history, and, in the lower rooms of the Keep, fetters and man-traps. The upper rooms are let and are not open to the public.

Bamburgh Castle is perched on a basalt outcrop, looking out over the North Sea, the Farne Islands and Lindisfarne Castle on Holy Island.

The 11th Duke of Northumberland.

Alnwick Castle

ALNWICK

THE ANCESTRAL HOME OF ONE OF THE NORTH'S GREATEST FAMILIES, THE PERCYS, DUKES OF NORTHUMBERLAND. ALNWICK CASTLE COMBINES THE GRIM REALITIES OF MEDIEVAL WARFARE AND SOME OF THE MOST GLORIOUS OF 19TH-CENTURY STATE ROOMS WITH AN OVERWHELMING DISPLAY OF TREASURES: OFF NARROWGATE IN ALNWICK, A MILE WEST OF THE A1.

'When the Duke of Northumberland is willing to receive visits from the neighbouring gentry,' read an early 19th-century notice at Alnwick, 'a flag is hung upon the highest turret as a signal that he may be approached.' In these more democratic days visiting times are both more regular and more generous, but the castle still demonstrates the tremendous aristocratic pride, wealth, power and influence of the Percy family. They came over with William the Conqueror, but the line can be traced back further, to the Emperor Charlemagne's grandmother. Alnwick came to the Percys in 1309, and it has remained one of their principal homes – along with Syon House near London (see page 69). Yet it was not the Percy family who founded and built the first castle at Alnwick. Another of the Conqueror's companions, his standard-bearer Gilbert Tyson, was the first Norman to own the site, but forfeited it after rebellion against the king in 1095. It passed to Yvo de Vescy the following year, and it was he who founded the castle we see today. His son-in-law completed the main form of the castle before his death in 1147.

MEDIEVAL ALNWICK

It must have been an intimidating sight in the Middle Ages, with its circular shell keep, studded with fearsome towers, and the outer wall, enclosing the two baileys also bristling with bastions. Alnwick has kept its shape through more than 800 years, though inevitably there have been alterations, repairs, renewals and, certainly inside, wholesale transformations. It might not have been so, however, for, after the barons revolted against King John in 1212, among them Eustace de Vescy, the king ordered its total destruction. Fortunately it survived both that threat and burning by Alexander, King of Scotland, as well as a siege by Prince Edward after John de Vescy had backed the rebel side against Henry III in the Battle of Evesham.

A piece from one of two great Meissen dinner services in the dining room.

The last de Vescy died at Bannockburn in 1314, but by then Alnwick had already been sold to Henry, 1st Lord Percy of Alnwick. He immediately began strengthening the castle, a task carried on by his descendants. We enter the castle today through one of the earliest and best of the additions, the barbican and gatehouse, built around 1310. Stone figures crowding the battlements – 18th-century replacements of the originals – give the impression of an ever-watchful garrison. A moat used to lie between the defensive barbican, the best that survives anywhere in Britain, and the gatehouse, and was crossed by a drawbridge that pivoted vertically on a central arch.

CENTURIES OF CHANGE

Once through the gatehouse and on the well-trimmed lawns that have replaced the medieval clutter and confusion in the West Bailey, we can see just how well the Percys protected themselves from the Scottish incursions, political feuding and troublesome neighbours that constantly harried them. Not that everything in sight is genuine medieval work, for, like most castles, things have changed as a result of warfare and fluctuations of taste. On the outer wall, for example, the Auditor's Tower is genuine 14th-century work, while the Clock Tower dates from around 1760 and Falconer Tower from the mammoth restoration of the building undertaken by Salvin for the 4th Duke of Northumberland in the mid 19th century. In the East Bailey, reached through the Middle Gateway, is the least altered of Alnwick's outer defences, the Constable's Tower, which is almost as it was built more than six centuries ago. The Postern Tower, too, is little changed, and now houses a museum of finds from an earlier period of Northumbrian history, when the Romans defended their furthest outposts.

The massive central keep has changed considerably since the de Vescys' day. Entry to its inner courtyard is through the superb twin Octagon Towers, built by the 2nd Lord Percy in about 1350. Into the gateway is incorporated a Norman arch, a reminder of the first castle on this site, and great wooden doors from the 17th century. Much of the courtyard was rebuilt in what has been described as a 'Wagnerian' style by Salvin around 1854, but it retains its early 14th-century well, complete with its wooden pole and wheels. The work that Salvin altered was not original, but dated from the restoration of the castle in the 1760s to 1780s by James Paine and Robert Adam, whose work for the 1st Duke of Northumberland (they had been Earls since 1377) at Syon House still remains in all its splendour. Adam's work at Alnwick was described at the time as 'in the gayest and most elegant style of Gothick architecture', but it was not a style that the 1st Duke was happy with, and the 4th Duke, perhaps a more serious character than his ancestor, found it thin and unconvincing. We may regret what was lost in the 1850s – and indeed only a few chairs and fireplaces remain from Adam's extensive scheme – but Salvin certainly made up for it in medieval grandeur. His is the Prudhoe Tower, the castle's tallest, which adds the necessary accent to the views of the castle on its bluff of land above the River Aln that Sir Walter Scott complained was lacking. Most impressive of all is Salvin's approach to the main doorway of the keep, with its Brobdingnagian arches and massive stone vaulting, entirely fit for a descendant of the Holy Roman Emperor.

TRANSFORMATION AT ALNWICK

When the 4th Duke carried out his restorations in the mid 19th century, he had a definite idea of what he was aiming to achieve. He had seen Italian castles that married the feudal aggressiveness of strongly defensive medieval architecture to the most opulent of Renaissance interiors. He was determined to do the same – creating a home for his extensive collection of Italian pictures, while attempting also to raise the artistic standards of British interior decoration and craftsmanship. His rooms were also, of course, to show off the wealth and magnificence of one of England's greatest aristocratic families. So today's visitor to Alnwick gets two experiences for the price of one – a full-blown medieval castle and one of the richest of 19th-century houses in the country.

The Duke insisted that Alnwick's new interiors should be as authentically Italian as possible, so he entrusted the planning of the decorative scheme to the Director of Rome's Capitoline Museum, the Commendatore Canina. With Canina worked two experts on 16th-century art, Montiroli and Mantovani, the Florentine carver Bulletti and the sculptor Taccalozzi, who was responsible for the numerous impressive chimney-pieces in the castle.

Things begin modestly enough in the low Entrance Hall, with its geometrical display of arms and armour from the 2nd Duke's Percy Tenantry Volunteers, raised to fight Napoleon. From it rises the Grand Staircase, lined with marble and looking like an import from the most magnificent of Victorian town halls. But this municipal experience hardly prepares you for the impact of the range of State Rooms at the top. At once you are in the Guard Chamber – not a draughty, stone-lined chamber of the Middle Ages, but a hugely impressive room, almost square, with Venetian mosaics underfoot, one of the many heavily compartmented and gilded ceilings at Alnwick above you, and statues of Justice and Britannia looking down rather accusingly at visitors' presumption in entering the ducal halls. Here, too, are the first of the many wonderful paintings in the castle, including a harbour scene by Claude, Canalettos

Above: Alnwick Castle's forbidding walls belie the magnificence of the rooms within.
Below: Alnwick's library houses many thousands of volumes in two tiers of oak bookcases.

This portrait of Hugh, 1st Duke of Northumberland (1750-1786) is by James Barry. Full of energy and enterprise, the 1st Duke changed the face of the Alnwick Castle estate with landscaping and up-to-date methods of farming.

of Windsor Castle and the Duke's Syon House, and a portrait of the 10th Earl of Northumberland by Sir Anthony Van Dyck.

And so the overwhelming procession of rooms begins. In the Ante-Room next door are three paintings by Titian, at least one of which has been in the family for more than 300 years. *The Bishop of Armagnac and his Secretary* certainly hung in Northumberland House in central London in 1671, and probably came to Alnwick when that house was demolished in 1874. There are pictures by Licinio and Palma Vecchio and parts of a fresco by Sebastiano del Piombo here too, as well as furniture by Adam and a pinewood ceiling, carved and gilded by members of the Alnwick School, who were drawn together by the Duke under the leadership of the skilled local carver John Brown, whose work can be found throughout the state apartments.

The library, which holds 16,000 books, occupies a complete floor of the Prudhoe Tower. Here, the Italian exuberance seen elsewhere in the castle shows itself in the ceiling with its carved trophies representing History, Poetry, Painting and the Sciences among the gilding. The bookcases, more restrained, are of light oak inlaid with maple, and a brass-railed gallery gives access to the upper stacks. There are Regency chairs from Northumberland House, and marble busts of Shakespeare, Newton and Bacon.

The Saloon once stood where the 42 feet long music room now displays itself. Here the ceiling is even richer, the chandeliers glitter yet more brightly and the paintings include works by Van Dyck, William Dobson and Mignard, as well as chairs by Linnell and a pair of top-quality Boule cabinets. Here too, are Canaletto's paintings of Northumberland House and of Alnwick itself, showing how ruinous its walls and towers had become before the 1st Duke began his restoration.

THE HEIGHT OF SPLENDOUR

It is most of all in the Red Drawing Room, however, where we can understand what Marcel Proust was driving at when he muttered the mystical words 'Duchess of Northumberland', a mantra that conjured up the wealth and lineage of the aristocracy. Dominating this palatial apartment are two French cabinets, the most famous of all Alnwick's furniture. They were made for Louis XIV in 1683 by Cucci at the Gobelins factory, and sold at the Louvre in February of 1751. In 1822 the 3rd Duke purchased them from Robert Fogg Junior, a well-known London 'chinaman'. They are stunning works, with deeply-carved stands, brilliant *pictra dura* panels and gilding on mouldings surmounted by Louix XIV's cypher. Made for one of the wealthiest and most ostentatious of European courts, it is an indication of the quality of the workmanship and decoration at Alnwick that they seem entirely at home in this room. On the walls, hung with red and gold damask, are more priceless paintings – a portrait by Andrea del Sarto, a *Crucifixion* by Guido Reni and Lanfranco's *Nativity*.

The Basilica of San Lorenzo in Rome was the inspiration for the ceiling, carved in St John's pine, in the rather more restrained dining room, on the site of the medieval Great Hall. Pieces from two great Meissen dinner services are on show, one painted with exotic animals and the other with scenes from *La Fontaine* The white marble fireplace, the lightest note in this rather sombre room, is supported by large sculpted figures of a faun and a somewhat restrained bacchante, both carved by Italian workmen. Between them are the arms of the 4th Duke and his Duchess. Indeed, the whole room is dedicated to the family. Shields of arms appear on the ceiling, and there are family portraits, mainly from the 18th and 19th centuries, around the walls.

THE PERCY FAMILY

The generations of Percys they portray included some of the most remarkable of the family. The 1st Duke of Northumberland, raised to the title in 1766, not only restored the castle, with the help of James Paine as well as Adam, but also completely reorganised the running of the entire Percy estates. Modern farming methods were introduced and acres of woodland planted. With this experience under his belt, he was appointed Lord Lieutenant of Ireland, and undertook diplomatic missions for George III. The State Coach, now on display in the coach house, was used by the 3rd Duke at the coronation of the French King Charles X in 1825, when he represented George IV as Special Ambassador. On the death of the 4th Duke, in 1865, the *Newcastle Journal*, its entire issue black-bordered, called him 'Algernon the Benevolent, the greatest of all the Percys'. Seven thousand of the poorest people in Northumberland filed past his coffin at Alnwick, for he had worked tirelessly for their welfare, and the Minster bells tolled solemnly as the funeral train passed through York.

Such activities seem a world away from the war-filled times of the earlier Percys. The first Earl was instrumental in deposing Richard II and helping Henry IV to the throne, but later quarrelled with him, too, rebelled and was defeated at the Battle of Shrewsbury – all of which is chronicled by Shakespeare in his histories. The Wars of the Roses found the subsequent two Earls on the side of the Lancastrians. The 2nd Earl was killed in the first battle of the war, at St Albans, and the 3rd at the Battle of Towton in 1461. Alnwick then changed hands several times as the estates were confiscated, captured by the Scots, retaken by the English and eventually restored to the Earls of Northumberland. Even though the 4th Earl enjoyed the Yorkist Edward IV's favour, he too came to an unhappy end, murdered in a tax riot in 1489.

'The Magnificent' 5th Earl was a typical Renaissance man – cultured, given to display and a trusted servant of the monarch. But his successor, 'Henry the Unthrifty' led a less charmed life. He made the mistake of falling in love with Anne Boleyn, and was forced by Henry VIII to arrest Cardinal Wolsey. His brother – who was his heir – was executed for taking part in the 'Pilgrimage of Grace', and the 6th Earl died in poverty, leaving the estates to the Crown. They were restored by Queen Mary. Throughout the Tudor years the Percys were in the thick of religious and political intrigue. The 9th Earl's cousin Thomas Percy, then Constable of Alnwick Castle, was one of the Gunpowder Plot conspirators, and suspicion fell on the Earl, too, who was imprisoned in the Tower of London for 17 years. He was known as 'the Wizard Earl' because of his study of chemistry and astronomy.

ALNWICK'S PARKLAND

'Capability' Brown was called in by the 1st Duke to landscape the park at Alnwick. He transformed the rugged Northumberland scenery into the beautiful sweeps of grass and carefully planted groups of trees which provide a fine, though perhaps unauthentic, setting for the castle. The Duke's enthusiasm for making his grounds as picturesque as possible also led him to construct some of the minor pleasures of the estate, including Robert Adam's Brizlee Tower of 1781, two miles away on a hilltop. It is 78 feet tall, in the Gothic style and crowned with a large cast-iron basket in which to light a beacon for ducal festivals. Adam's brother John designed the Lion Bridge in 1773, a medieval vision of battlements and lookouts, with the Percy's crest, a statant lion, guarding its parapet, a proud symbol of this noblest of families.

GALLANT HOTSPUR

Most famous of the Percys was Hotspur, son of the 1st Earl. An energetic, fiery and inspiring man, he was 12 years old when won his nickname at the siege of Berwick in 1378. He led the English forces at Otterburn in 1388, but in 1399 he was proclaimed a traitor by Richard II. Richard was deposed and Henry IV took the throne, but the Percys were soon at loggerheads with him. At the Battle of Shrewsbury the rebellion was crushed and Hotspur was killed. Shakespeare's *Henry IV* is in part a celebration of 'gallant Hotspur', who 'kills me some six or seven dozen of Scots at breakfast ... and says "Fie upon this quiet life! I want work".'

One of a pair of ebony cabinets, made by Cucci at the Gobelins factory in 1683 and now on display in the Red Drawing Room.

Chillingham Castle

ALNWICK

A STRONG BORDER CASTLE, NOW BEING RESTORED, WITH A HERD OF PREHISTORIC CATTLE: 15 MILES NORTH OF ALNWICK OFF THE B6348.

This solid, square fortress encapsulates 800 years of history. It has been besieged, received royal visitors and it has enjoyed the refinement and extravagances of the 18th and 19th centuries, but it has never lost its medieval flavour.

Sir Walter Scott may have used Chillingham as his model for Osbaldistone Hall in *Rob Roy*, for this impressive open square of a castle, with its four great corner towers, has been famous in the borders for centuries. Held by the Grey family since they took it by force in 1245, it remains the home of their line to this day, though soldiers burned the castle's north wing in the 1940s, and rot ravaged the place until Sir Humphrey Wakefield, who married into the Grey family, began its rescue and restoration in the 1980s. Visitors today still see work in progress, but the medieval spirit of the castle is already strongly stirring again, helped by newly-introduced antique furniture, armour and tapestries and the careful restoration of plaster and metalwork, carving and masonry.

A FAMILY TO RIVAL THE PERCYS

The work has revealed more of the building's history – including a bundle of Tudor documents hidden in a walled-up fireplace. Such discoveries help to put the long history of the Grey family into perspective. Only ten years after the original tower was captured they entertained Henry III at Chillingham, and Edward I followed in 1298. By that time the castle had taken on much of the appearance we see today, for Sir Thomas Grey was allowed to 'crenellate' or fortify it in 1344. A moat gave added protection and made the dungeons, with their sinister oubliette, in which prisoners were thrown and forgotten, even more dank and alarming than they are today. As one of the most important families in the north – often in rivalry with the Percys at nearby Alnwick – they played an important role in helping to keep the Scots from causing trouble. The armoured effigy of one, Sir Ralph, who died in 1443, is found on a magnificent tomb in the church at the castle's gates. Seventy years later Chillingham was captured by James IV's Scottish soldiers. Within two days they were defeated a dozen miles away at Flodden Field, and Chillingham was back in the hands of the Greys. The Percys brought guns to bear on the castle in 1536 when the Greys refused to join the 'Pilgrimage of Grace' against Henry VIII, but repairs were quickly made, and by the beginning of the next century extensive reconstruction had been carried out, including the most memorable feature of the castle's interior courtyard, the cloister range with its stumpy columns and statues of the 'Worthies'. Inside, a recently-repaired Jacobean ceiling gives some idea of what has been lost.

THE LAST 300 YEARS

More changes followed, with Georgian additions in 1753 and, after a fire in 1803, new state apartments in the East Range, which suffered badly when the house was unoccupied. George IV's architect from Windsor Castle, Wyatville, was called in for further modifications by Charles Grey, 5th Earl of Tankerville – this title was originally acquired by one Sir Ralph Grey of Chillingham in 1409, when he stormed the castle of Tancaville in Normandy. The 5th Earl was responsible for importing the two great marble chimney-pieces in the Great Hall from the magnificent Wanstead House in Essex, built by architect Colen Campbell in 1720

Outside, grass had been brought right up to the castle walls in the 18th century – the moat is now a huge tunnel under the south lawn. Wyatville added long avenues of trees and designed a new formal garden on the site of the medieval tournament ground. Its elaborate hedges and plantings survived until the 1930s, when it rapidly became overgrown and unrecognisable. It has recently been rescued from its near-desolation and now forms a replica of an Elizabethan garden well-suited to the grandeur of one of the north's most important castles.

WILD CATTLE

Older even than the castle, the 1,000 acre park at Chillingham has been walled since 1220. Uncultivated for more than 650 years, it is still medieval in its atmosphere. Within it roam Chillingham's most famous inhabitants, its herd of white cattle, the last of a species once found roaming England's primeval forests. Descendants of prehistoric wild oxen, their rough creamy-white coats contrast with black muzzles and tips to their curved horns. Usually shy, they can turn angry, as the 18th-century engraver Thomas Bewick found when he was chased up a tree as he sketched the dominant bull.

Chipchase Castle

WARK ON TYNE

THE SPECTACULAR MARRIAGE OF A MEDIEVAL CASTLE AND JACOBEAN MANSION: TWO MILES SOUTH-EAST OF WARK-ON-TYNE OFF THE B6320.

If you look north from the line of Hadrian's Wall you can see Chipchase Castle, high on its plateau above the North Tyne. It is a magical mix of medieval, Jacobean and Georgian, reflecting both the turbulent history of the area and the vicissitudes of its ownership. Like many Northumbrian houses, it began life as a defensive pele tower against the frequent Scots' raids – and against the neighbours and authorities, too, for the Heron family, who owned Chipchase from 1348, were a quarrelsome lot.

Whether they or their predecessors, the de Insulas, built the tower is not known, but it is a typical mid 14th-century building with massive nine-foot thick walls and corbelled-out corner turrets, but no battlements. The grooves down the side of the entrance door still hold the rare wooden portcullis, and a narrow spiral stair climbs right to the modern roof. There are three floors above the vaulted storeroom basement, two of which have kept their original fireplaces and garderobes. A room on the second floor, with its pointed windows, seems to have been the chapel, while the larger third floor held the Heron's private quarters.

TROUBLED TIMES

How long the tower stood alone is unclear, but by 1541 there was a stone manor house joined to it. It was from here the Herons, as Keepers of Tyndale, set out on Scottish raids, sometimes in defiance of their overlords. The entire history of the family seems to have consisted of skirmish, capture and bloodshed. In 1537 John Heron was accused of murder – but was later pardoned. His son, Sir George, was himself killed by the Scots at Carter Bar. The Heron estates, which were considerable, were inherited by Cuthbert Heron in 1591 when he was only six – and he was responsible for the Jacobean house which replaced the Tudor mansion at Chipchase in 1621. Its E-shaped south-east front makes it one of the north's best buildings of its time, with its two great bow windows – Victorian restorations, but very much in keeping – and the fanciful cresting over the porch tower.

Yet within 60 years of Cuthbert's confident gesture in building a new home, there was almost nothing left of the Heron fortunes. Mortgages and dowries, as well as the difficult political climate of the 17th century, had taken their toll. The family struggled on at Chipchase until 1727, when they were forced to sell. Ownership changed several times until it came to John Reed.

A NEW LOOK FOR CHIPCHASE

Reed obviously found the Jacobean house dark and gloomy, for he added sash windows throughout. He even went to the trouble of putting false windows on the pele so that the south-west side of the house is symmetrical — if you can make the mental effort to ignore the turrets on the medieval tower. He transformed the interiors at Chipchase, too, with elegant plaster ceilings and fine doorcases, particularly in what is now the billiard room, where there is also a superbly-carved wooden overmantle — a survivor from the previous house. Father Time and other allegorical figures are drawn on an ornate cart with winged horses, while Muses stand in attendance, angels and cherubs flutter overhead and grotesques ride on exotic animals. Other rooms in the house are comfortable rather than spectacular, with good furniture and porcelain, and with wide views over the valley.

The view of Chipchase Castle from the south-west illustrates its development from defensive pele tower to splendid family home.

Meldon Park

Morpeth

A superbly sited William IV house with fine interiors reminiscent of a gentlemen's London club: west of Morpeth, south of the B6343.

■ The fine plasterwork in the Main Hall, which was added by Lutyens in the 1920s, helps to create a warm welcome. Meldon is a home of warmth and has our undivided affection. ■
Michael Cookson

The ghost of Meg of Meldon, a miserly local witch, used to appear as a little dog that haunted the bridge over the River Wansbeck below Meldon Park. She lived in the old house, Meldon Tower, about a mile away across the park and was married to Sir William Fenwick of Wallington. He bought the estate in the time of James I from the Heron family, owners since the 14th century. Meg's granddaughter married the 1st Earl of Derwentwater, and the Meldon estate stayed in the Earls' ownership until the 3rd Earl was beheaded on Tower Hill for joining the Old Pretender's rebellion in 1715. Meldon was then confiscated and went to swell the endowments of Greenwich Hospital, until they sold it in about 1830 to shipping magnate Isaac Cookson, in whose family it remains.

Cookson commissioned the Newcastle architect John Dobson, who had the largest practice in the north of England, to design for him a new house. It was to be built on a site overlooking the old deer park and would be surrounded by fine trees. From the south front of the new house the ground gradually slopes down to the Wansbeck. Dobson made full use of this sunny view, with floor-to-ceiling windows in the main rooms on this side – the two drawing rooms and the library – giving a feeling of space and light to the whole house. A large square house, beautifully built of yellowish sandstone, Meldon exudes a spirit of quiet and prosperous calm, without the heaviness that would have been imposed upon it by the Victorians of ten years later.

There is a pretty conservatory tucked away round the side, while the main entrance has a simple portico leading to the restrained delights of the interior. Most impressive is the huge staircase, the like of which adorns many a London club. It is imposing and grand, but, even with the wooden balustrade that replaced the original light metal between the wars, still has the lightness of touch that you can find throughout the house. The comfortable library continues the club-like theme. One section of the bookcase has false book-fronts disguising double doors into the Small Drawing Room, while the Large Drawing Room, with its full-length windows to two sides, demonstrates Dobson's style of linking the landscape outside to the understated elegance inside, making Meldon one of most attractive houses of its time.

The elegantly simple exterior of Meldon Park, looking south over its finely manicured lawns and gardens.

Preston Tower

Chathill

Border life five centuries ago is brought to life in this medieval tower: a mile south of Chathill, off the A1

Some of the north's greatest houses had their origins in defensive pele towers to which, over the centuries, more comfortable quarters have been added. Preston Tower, one of 78 peles listed in 1415, is different. For more than three centuries it barely developed from its original form – and the Preston Tower that we see today is only half of that.

It was built in the 1390s by Sir Robert Harbottle, a trusted friend of Henry IV, who appointed him Sheriff of Northumberland and Constable of Dunstanburgh Castle. Robert was a contemporary of the fiery Harry Hotspur and fought alongside him against the Scots in the Battle of Otterburn in 1388. A display in the Tower illustrates life during those turbulent times. One of Robert's descendants was the gloriously-named Sir Guiscard Harbottle, one of six knights killed at Flodden Field in 1513 – in hand-to-hand combat with King James IV himself. The Flodden Room in Preston Tower recounts the story of Guiscard's part in the battle, and of Flodden's impact on the history and literature of Scotland and the north.

When England and Scotland were united by James I and VI in 1603, Preston Tower was partially demolished. Stone from two of its towers was used to build adjoining cottages and farm buildings, and the Tower gradually decayed for the next 250 years. It was not until 1864 that Henry Baker Cresswell, whose family have owned the Tower since the 1820s, came to the rescue. He removed the agricultural additions and built up its rear wall to make it weatherproof. He also added the clock, which he made himself. His home was the Georgian house next door, and part of the Tower was made to hold tanks of water for it, pumped from a nearby spring.

The attractions for us today, besides the fascinating historical displays, is the impression of life under threat from the Border Reivers – bands of marauding Scots – at the beginning of the 15th century. Two rooms, on the floor above the spartan guardroom and grim prison, have been furnished in period style. Do not expect comfort. Rough stone walls, reed-strewn flag stones and simple wooden furniture with animal skin covers were the order of the day, and Preston Tower gives an authentic glimpse of an unromantic past.

Seaton Delaval Hall

WHITLEY BAY

VANBRUGH'S MONUMENTAL MASTERPIECE, DEALT A CRUEL HAND BY FATE, IS STILL IMPRESSIVE: THREE MILES NORTH OF WHITLEY BAY ON THE A190.

By the time Sir John Vanbrugh came to design his masterpiece at Seaton Delaval he had already produced both Castle Howard and Blenheim Palace. Never one for tame classical copying, he used the opportunity given by Admiral George Delaval to build a house on this windswept northern coast to indulge his taste for the dramatic – and dramatic Seaton Delaval certainly is. As a former playwright, Vanbrugh knew how to utilise scenery for impressive effect, and the north-facing entrance front of his main block – strangely, it largely ignores the sea – is hugely powerful, almost aggressive, with its towers and turrets and the enormous columns casting sinister shadows that dwarf the central doorway. Even the garden front is monumentally and magnificently intimidating.

The wings, low and spreading, now hold the main rooms of the house, for Seaton Delaval did not have a lucky history. Admiral Delaval died in 1723 after being thrown by his horse (an obelisk in the park shows where it happened), and Vanbrugh died in 1726 – both before the house was complete. One wing was burned in 1752, while an even more disastrous fire in 1822 destroyed most of the interior of the main block. It stood empty for almost 150 years until Lord Hastings, the present owner and a direct descendant of the Delavals, began its partial restoration.

From the outside the Hall appears to be once again whole and complete, but the Great Hall of the central block is semi-ruinous, open to the roof and still bearing the marks of the devastating flames. Blackened statues stand in their niches and a delicate iron gallery, now restored, gives access to vanished floors. In the Mahogany and Tapestry Rooms on the north side there is a display of family portraits and documents, and some rare mahogany panelling survives, while the vaulted basement could have held supplies for an army. In the West Wing, open only by special appointment, the former kitchen is now the entrance hall, and in this and the other habitable rooms are furniture and paintings that were rescued from the blaze, as well as items from Melton Constable in Norfolk. Over in the opposite wing, Vanbrugh's fine stables, like a pagan temple, still have the horses' names above the classical niches holding their mangers. The stalls have their original finely-moulded timberwork and paved floors.

AN ACTOR AND A JOKER

Most famous of the Delavals was Sir Francis, who entertained lavishly at the Hall in the 18th century, when Seaton Delaval was '... a fairyland of light, music and beauty'. A friend of Garrick, he played Othello at Drury Lane, with his family taking other parts – and the House of Commons adjourned specially to watch. Visitors to the Hall suffered from his practical jokes. While they slept their beds would be lowered into baths of cold water, and bedroom walls would suddenly disappeared to reveal their *deshabille* to others. A brave soldier as well as a playboy, his charred portrait is in the West Wing.

In the grounds at Seaton Delaval is this statue of Samson slaying a Philistine.

Below left: The fireplace in the entrance hall has a frieze on the mantel showing a Roman wedding march.

Below: Seaton Delaval's south elevation conceals the sad fact of the part-ruined interior of the Hall.

WALES AND THE MARCHES

HOUSES IN THIS REGION of the country rejoice in long histories and curious juxtapositions, like the Egyptian mummy in Bodrhyddan Hall. The building history of Burton Hall stretches from the Middle Ages all the way to work by Sir Clough Williams-Ellis, the playful architect of Portmeirion in this century. Little Malvern Court, similarly, is medieval with 19th-century building by Joseph Hansom, who gave his name to the cab. There is drama in the Malvern Hills, where you can imagine Sir Ivanhoe jousting at Eastnor Castle, a splendid fake Norman fortress of 1812. Penhow Castle is the real thing – the oldest lived-in castle in Wales – and Hellen's is still home to descendants of the Mortimers, great Marcher warlords. Times of peace brought elegance as the Morgans held sway from Tredegar House in its graceful 17th-century brick, while Weston Park, another grand brick edifice, bulges with Old Master paintings.

Burton Court

EARDISLAND

A LARGELY 19TH-CENTURY HOUSE WITH A FINE COLLECTION OF COSTUMES: FIVE MILES WEST OF LEOMINSTER ON THE B4457.

This portrait of Queen Elizabeth I at Burton Court is attributed to Zuccarco (1558-1603).

Although parts of the Great Hall at Burton Court date from the 14th century, most of it was constructed in the 19th and early 20th centuries. From the 17th century, it was owned by the Brewster family, but they sold the house in 1865 to John Clowes, an MP and Victorian country gentleman, who had the house 'Victorianised' by Frederick Kempson.

In 1895, when his son, Colonel Peter Legh Clowes, married the heiress of the Warren Steamship Line, John Clowes gave Burton Court to the couple as a wedding present. They did not take up residence until the Colonel had retired from the army after the Boer War in 1901. When the family, complete with three-year-old son, arrived by carriage to Eardisland, the villagers unhitched the horses and pulled the carriage up to the house, where a great feast celebrated the homecoming.

The years up to World War I were times of great prosperity for the Clowes family. In 1912 a rising young architect called Clough Williams-Ellis, later famous for the gloriously eccentric Portmeirion village in north Wales, was brought in, and he added the distinctive projecting porch on the east front. However, the story is sadder from this point, for the couple's only son was killed towards the end of World War I, and the 1,050-acre estate went into decline after the Colonel died in 1925. It was sold and broken up in 1950.

Inside the house, the most important room is the 14th-century Great Hall with its complicated, arch-braced, sweet-chestnut timber roof, and a richly-carved chimney-piece dated 1654. Around the house an array of period and oriental costumes is displayed, and Burton Court also has a working model fairground.

Below: Although it has medieval origins, Burton Court is a monument to Victorian prosperity.

Eastnor Castle

LEDBURY

A FAIRYTALE CASTLE SURROUNDED BY A VERDANT ARBORETUM AND LAKE: TWO AND A HALF MILES SOUTH-EAST OF LEDBURY OFF THE A438.

When lawyer John Cocks, the 2nd Baron Somers, sought a rapid passage into the aristocracy, the size and splendour of the family home were seen as key indicators of status and fortune. His investment in a castle had the desired effect, for soon after its completion he became the 1st Earl of Somers. However, neither status nor castle brought him happiness at home, for he was abandoned by two wives. Funds to build the castle were made available both from family wealth and from the sale of properties in Gloucestershire and Worcestershire, and the result was Eastnor Castle, completed in 1824 for £85,923. 13s. 11d. The symmetrical design was by Robert Smirke, later the architect of the British Museum, who chose to create a Norman Revival style fortress at Eastnor, with simple Gothic interiors. Only about half of these remain. Gothic enthusiast Augustus Pugin was commissioned to decorate the drawing room in the high Gothic style in the 1850s – the furniture, the lavish chimney-piece, and the great iron chandelier are all his work. More embellishment was commissioned by Charles, the 3rd Earl Somers, over the next two decades and recent restoration work has been most effective.

Below right: No expense was spared at Eastnor Castle to match Baron Somers' aspirations.

Many of the items on display at Eastnor were collected during the long travels of the 3rd Earl. Something of a connoisseur, he collected Italian furniture, Flemish tapestries, Renaissance art, arms and armour. He also acquired a stunningly beautiful half-French wife, Virginia Pattle, reputedly falling in love with her when he saw her portrait by Watts's, which is now in the Little Library. She and her seven sisters were known as 'Pattledom', and this vivacious group were welcomed with open arms by London's artistic elite. One of the sisters was the photographer Julia Margaret Cameron, and some of her work is also on display in the house. The excitement and glamour of partying with the likes of Tennyson, Browning and Ellen Terry was a far cry from Eastnor, and Virginia rarely visited the castle, though her two daughters were brought up there. Both had unhappy marriages to sons of dukes: one a depressive, the other homosexual. The elder daughter, Isabel, went through a scandalous divorce from Lord Henry Somerset, which left her ostracised. She divided the estate between her son and her cousin, Arthur, the 6th Lord Somers and grandfather of the current owner James Hervey-Bathurst.

A 19th-century creation, in the Norman Revival style, Eastnor Castle has all the appearance of a romantic medieval fortress.

Hellen's

Much Marcle

HELLEN'S HAS SEEN BETTER DAYS, BUT IS STRONG ON EXCITING TALES FROM ITS LONG HISTORY: FOUR MILES FROM LEDBURY, OFF THE A449.

Hellen's is a rather dilapidated house with a thrilling history, and there are reminders of its story throughout the house. For example, James Audley, grandson of Yseult Mortimer Audley, was a life-long friend of Edward III's son, the Black Prince, and a monumental fireplace (still visible) in the lobby was decorated with the Prince's crest in honour of his visit. The Prince and his youngbloods are said to have held a raucous banquet here just before they sailed for the Battle of Poitiers in 1356. James rented the house from his uncle for a yearly payment of 'a pair of gilt spurs to be given at Easter'. One of these pairs can be seen at the top of the stairway.

For centuries, the inheritance of Hellen's followed a wandering course, mainly down the female line. Then it came to Hilda Pennington-Mellor, who married Swedish doctor and philanthropist, Axel Munthe, and bore him two sons. Their descendants live in the house today, and displayed among the many portraits in the lobby is a Flemish tapestry used as a tarpaulin to cover the Protestant family's goods when they fled Catholic Belgium in the 16th century.

The Staircase Hall was last decorated in the 17th century as part of a major modernisation for the marriage in 1641 of the guardian's 15-year-old daughter, Margaret, to 16-year-old Fulke Walwyn. During the Civil War Fulke gathered all the bravest men in Much Marcle and led them away, through the big gates and through Hellen's parkland to Ledbury, where a terrible battle took place. Margaret watched him go with great foreboding in her heart, and vowed that no-one should ever pass through that gate until her beloved Fulke returned. Sadly, they remain locked to this day. The house was subsequently taken over by Roundheads, who chased Fulke's Catholic chaplain around the house, cornering and killing him in the Queen's Room. His ghost is said to haunt Hellen's.

The estate was later returned to the family. Fulke's cousin, Lady Mary Wharton, later owned Hellen's, and at the top of the staircase is a snuff box which once belonged to her nephew Philip, Duke of Wharton. He died outlawed and in disgrace after a life devoted to carousing, black magic and intrigue. Mehetabble Walwyn's Room is named after a woman who fled Hellen's with a lover, and returned humiliated to live out her days behind the barred windows of the room.

A ROYAL AFFAIR

In 1326 Yseult Mortimer Audley was embroiled in a struggle for the crown. Audley's brother, Roger Mortimer, had fallen in love with Queen Isabella, the beautiful French wife of Edward II, and it is popularly believed that it was Mortimer who had the king killed. The triumphant couple assumed royal power, but in 1330 Isabella's son became King Edward III and captured them in Nottingham. Mortimer was hung, drawn and quartered without delay.

■ Why do my family and I love Hellen's – this shabby old mansion full of ghosts and 'things that go bump in the night'? Because it is the most romantic house in England. My mother's ancestors have lived here for some 700 years; terrible things have happened, no doubt, but also many happy and good things. It is a dear old home, and we love it. ■
Malcolm Munthe

Little Malvern Court

Malvern

A medieval priory with later additions, surrounded by gardens and fishponds: five miles south of Great Malvern on the A4104.

Little Malvern Court is a manor house which includes the remains of its original medieval priory. After Henry VIII's Dissolution of the Monasteries, this priory was leased to John Russell, who's son Henry was granted the freehold in 1554 by Mary Tudor. The Russells maintained their Catholicism through centuries of opposition, worshipping in a secret chapel in the roof (now exposed). Early in the 18th century, the Russell family line came to an end and ownership of Little Malvern was transferred by marriage to a member of another local Recusant family, Thomas Berington. His daughter Elizabeth was well known for the careful eye she kept on her finances – to the extent of charging her guests for food and lodging. Even her future husband, Thomas Williams, had to pay up during his first visit in April 1748!

Still he married her in the following year, and after the official opposition to Catholicism was relaxed in 1791, their daughter, Mary, converted the medieval Prior's Hall into a chapel.

In 1860 Joseph Hansom, designer of the famous cab, associate of Augustus Pugin and popular architect in Catholic circles, extended the house. This involved a new west range, with dining room, drawing room and the west entrance hall. The funding came from Ellen Balfe, an heiress from County Roscommon in Ireland, who had met the owner, Charles Michael Berington, in Rome. She and her eight children all died within six years. The mournful Charles then considered becoming a monk before marrying Patricia Mary Coxon, said to be an illicit descendant of Bonnie Prince Charlie.

Buried in the graveyard of Saint Wulstan's is the quintessentially English composer, Sir Edward Elgar, who became a frequent visitor to Little Malvern Court after meeting William Berington (one of Patricia's 12 children) at the Malvern Festival in 1929. The current owners, Tim and Alexandra Berington, have re-landscaped the lovely garden, which is still dominated by a giant lime tree under which Queen Victoria played in 1831.

MONKS OF LAZY HABITS

The small monastery was founded at Little Malvern early in the 12th century. Its dozen monks do not seem to have made their lives too demanding over the years. Food was plentiful from the five fishponds which they dug (still there), and they did so little to maintain the priory that when the Bishop of Worcester visited in 1480, he was appalled at its poor state. The monks were sent away for two years of penance, and the bishop set about restoring the place – the walls of the Priors Hall, scene of many a previous fishy feast, still show the marks of the work.

Moccas Court

Hereford

A simple Georgian mansion on the banks of the River Wye: about 13 miles west of Hereford via the A465, B4349 and B4352.

The Circular Drawing Room at Moccas has Parisian paper panels which are unique in Britain.

When Sir George Amyard married Catherine Cornewalle in 1771, he took on far more than a wife. The wealthy Huguenot banker had to adopt his bride's family name and arms as a condition of her inheritance of the Moccas Court estate, which had been in her family since the mid 17th century. He also appears to have agreed to replace the existing family home there, and approached Robert Adam to design a house. However, he took against the plans (or the cost), and commissioned a simple red brick house from a local architect, Anthony Keck. Building was completed in 1781, originally a rather severe box shape, but in 1792 the unusual bow-fronted porch was added under the arched Venetian window.

Inside, the rooms are grouped around a dramatically top-lit central staircase, reached via the narrow entrance hall, in the porch of which hangs a portrait of Catherine Cornewalle. Her family was devoted to music: all the women sang and played the harpsichord, among other instruments, and every summer an opera singer was engaged to stay and teach at Moccas Court. Most of the house's music was made in the South Drawing Room, which had its own specially-built chamber organ. However, this is long gone, and only the gilded frieze of musical instruments reminds visitors of the room's melodious past.

Moccas Court was a truly cultured house, for it also had a library with more than 3,000 books, and the view from this room of the River Wye is marvellous. The river features in a number of Thomas Hearne watercolours displayed around the house. All the rooms are sparsely but charmingly decorated, but the best of them is the Circular Drawing Room, where Adam's designs for a plaster ceiling, chimney-piece and doorcases were used. The walls are decorated with unusual wallpaper panels from the celebrated Reveillon workshop in Paris.

The Cornewalles occupied Moccas Court until 1916, but it was uninhabited for the next 30 years, at which stage its contents were sold off. Since the 1960s, it has been the home of the Chester-Master family, who have carried out many repairs in addition to refurnishing the house.

Above: The dining room at Sufton Court.

Sufton Court

MORDIFORD

A LATE 18TH-CENTURY PALLADIAN HOUSE ON A SITE OWNED BY THE HEREFORD FAMILY SINCE THE 12TH CENTURY: FOUR MILES EAST OF HEREFORD OFF THE B4224.

This pair of duelling pistols on display at Sufton Court date from the early 1800s.

Sufton Court was designed by James Wyatt and completed around 1788 as a new abode for the Hereford family, who were living less than a mile away in a house now known as Old Sufton. Wyatt created a four-storey Palladian house with a one-bay pediment in Bath stone, and the original marble fireplaces are still in place. It would seem that he was instructed to keep the servants as far distant from their masters as possible – their quarters were in an attic so arranged that no-one could see or be seen from below.

The building was evidence of new prosperity for the family, who were also able to afford to commission Humphry Repton in 1795 to landscape the park. He presented his designs in the 'Red Book', a copy of which can be viewed in the house today. This makes particularly interesting reading at the moment, because the present Herefords are replanting trees and carrying out other work to restore the garden to Repton's original plan.

The most famous member of the family was Nicholas Hereford, born in about 1330, who joined the Lollards – followers of the religious reformer John Wycliffe. Nicholas was one of a group of Wycliffe's disciples who translated the Old Testament into English in about 1382. His work included a phrase forbidding 'strong drink or cider', which is believed in some quarters to have earned that particular translation the name 'The Cider Bible'; it is now held in Hereford Cathedral. The Lollards were always in danger of arrest and the possibility of a horrible death at the stake, and Nicholas went to Rome to explain his views to the Pope. He was jailed, but escaped during a riot outside the prison, and subsequently decided that his views were dangerous! He then became one of the Lollards' greatest enemies, and was given royal protection by Richard II, which included not only security from persecution, but also the gift of a quantity of royal wines, and the yearly delivery of timber from wrecked pirate ships. The documentation is on display at the house, as is an earlier pardon issued to Henry de Hereford by Edward III. Henry was implicated in the assassination of Edward II in 1327, and was at risk of being hung, drawn and quartered. However, he fought for the new king with notable vigour in Scotland, and his earlier misdemeanours were forgiven. He was knighted and served as Member of Parliament for Hereford.

■ It is a matter of great pride that my forebears were responsible for the creation of a small part of this magnificent landscape. It is also an enormous responsibility to see that under our stewardship it is maintained for all to see. ■

J N Hereford

Hatton Grange

SHIFNAL

A FINE HOUSE BY AN UNDERESTIMATED ARCHITECT, WHOSE BEST-KNOWN ASSIGNMENT WAS THE FIRST IRON BRIDGE: ABOUT THREE MILES FROM SHIFNAL ON THE A464 WOLVERHAMPTON ROAD.

■ On a sunny summer day the bay window in the drawing room, overlooking the rose garden, is my favourite spot. ■
Meriel Afia
(formerly Kenyon-Slaney)

Hatton gets its earliest mention in the Domesday Book, when the estate was given to Gerald de Tournai as a reward for services rendered during the Norman invasion. Two centuries later the estate was bequeathed to the monks of Buildwas Abbey, about nine miles to the west, and Hatton became an outlying grange of the Abbey, where monks farmed the land and took fish from the ponds. After the Dissolution of the Monasteries in 1539, the ownership of the Grange passed through several hands before it was bought during the 1650s by the Slaney family, in whose good stewardship the house remains today.

It was Plowden Slaney who, in about 1760, elected to build a new house at Hatton for himself and his bride. He engaged a local architect, Thomas Farnolls Pritchard, and Hatton Grange appears to be Pritchard's only complete surviving country house, built with locally made red bricks, some from Hatton itself – this area is known for producing bricks of good quality, and this house is certainly in a fine state of preservation today. We know little about Plowden Slaney, apart from what can be surmised from a rather wistful portrait of him that gazes down from above the drawing room door. His coat of arms can be seen on the south front of the house.

The turn of the 19th century saw a few additions to the exterior – bay windows on the west front, a porch on the north and a large block to house the servants at the back, which must have almost doubled the overall size of the house. This extension was demolished in 1966, but a picture by Moses Griffiths, now hanging in the hall, shows how Hatton Grange would have looked in 1791.

The main feature of the dining room is the elaborate plasterwork, drawing from both classical Rococo and Gothic motifs. Indeed it was for his interiors – rather than purely architectural work – that Pritchard became known. The drawing room retains many original features, including a chimney-piece, for which the design can be traced back to Inigo Jones.

During both world wars Hatton Grange served as an auxiliary hospital, where wounded soldiers could come to convalesce. The bedrooms were turned into dormitories and the downstairs rooms were used for recreation. The Grange is surrounded by beautiful grounds and gardens, with delightful footpaths around the chain of medieval fishponds and the judicious planting of rhododendrons and azaleas creating some delightful romantic vistas.

THE FORGOTTEN ARCHITECT

Thomas Farnolls Pritchard, architect of Hatton Grange, has been rescued from virtual anonymity. Contemporary accounts rated him 'the principal architect of the county'. But he was largely forgotten until the late 1960s, when an unascribed book of carving designs was discovered in the American Institute of Architects' library in Washington. It took a good deal of detective work to link these designs to Hatton Grange and other country houses. Pritchard's other claim to fame are his plans for the first iron bridge, across the River Severn at Ironbridge. We remember that the engineering work was by Abraham Darby, but Pritchard's pioneering role in the creation of what has since become a symbol of the birth of the Industrial Revolution has largely been forgotten.

Moat House

SHREWSBURY

THOUGH OF MODEST PROPORTIONS, THIS IS ONE OF THE FINEST MEDIEVAL HOUSES IN SHROPSHIRE, SURROUNDED BY ITS ORIGINAL MOAT: JUST OFF THE A49 TO THE SOUTH OF SHREWSBURY.

'A genuine medieval experience' is how visitors may well describe Moat House, a timber-framed manor house which was built in about 1467. Lawley Hill provides a backdrop on one side, while a moat – still filled with water – once offered protection from all sides. The moat was actually here before the house, being dug to surround the previous house that occupied this site as early as 1290.

It is likely that the house was built for Thomas Acton, one of the leading Shropshire justices of his day. Inside the house a pair of heads, which probably represent Acton and his wife, carved into the bases of two corbels, can still be seen. Once there was a third head, now no longer in place, which may possibly have been that of Edward IV, the Lancastrian king who was murdered in 1471.

The Actons lived through some turbulent times – notably the Wars of the Roses – and supported the Lancastrian cause. They were fortunate indeed to survive with both their property and livelihood intact when a Yorkist king subsequently ascended to the throne. The act of jettisoning the effigy of a Lancastrian monarch may indicate that diplomacy was a fortunate family trait. The moat, the house and the rectangular 'island' on which it stands, have been excavated by archaeologists. They found remains, including what may have been of a palisade and a bridge across the moat, and evidence that there was a barn and other earlier buildings on the site. The lovely fish-pond, its banks now colourful with flowers, is yet another survivor from medieval times.

Moat House is box-framed, with later stone gables and an extension added in recent years, and the current owners, Peter and Margaret Richards, have created a comfortable atmosphere. There are, however, sufficient original features to offer revealing glimpses into domestic life during the 15th century. For example, in the old hall (now the dining room) it is not difficult to imagine yourself back in time by a few hundred years. The room is open to the roof, and the monumental roof-beams – mostly original – are delicately carved, many still bearing the adze-marks of the medieval carpenters. Above the crackling fireplace is a chimney breast constructed from massive blocks of dressed stone and around the room the exposed timberwork alternates with plastered panels, in authentic 'black-and-white' style.

All the components of a fine medieval building are at Moat House – timbers, exposed stone and a huge old fireplace.

Moat House is still surrounded by its original moat.

■ Moat House is, to us, an island of tranquility and stability in this turbulent and changing world. The peaceful and welcoming atmosphere greets you as you enter, ensuring its continuation as a comfortable home after 500 years of occupation. ■

Peter Richards

Shipton Hall

MUCH WENLOCK

A LOVELY ELIZABETHAN HOUSE IN AN IDYLLIC SETTING IN THE SHROPSHIRE COUNTRYSIDE: FOUR AND A HALF MILES SOUTH-WEST OF MUCH WENLOCK, JUST OFF THE B4378 CRAVEN ARMS ROAD.

Shipton Hall was built around 1587 by Richard Lutwyche to replace a much older black-and-white timbered house which had been destroyed by fire earlier in the century. It is said to have been the dowry of his daughter, Elizabeth, when she married Thomas Mytton, and certainly the Hall was to remain in the Mytton family for the next three centuries. The mellow stonework of the Hall and its Georgian stable block blends perfectly with the lovely countryside of Shropshire's Corvedale, and has been accurately described as 'an exquisite specimen of Elizabethan architecture set in an old-fashioned garden'.

Inside is a profusion of Tudor panelling and brickwork, as a counterpoint to the elegant Georgian décor, revealing much about the architectural transition from the timbered construction to the later use of stone and brick. In fact, many of the medieval timbers from the earlier manor house survive in the Shipton Hall of today. The plasterwork of the ceilings and chimneypieces is especially noteworthy, some of which are the work of Thomas Pritchard. Many of the glazed windows retain the original 15th- and 16th-century diamond-leaded panes.

Few could argue with the statement once made that Shipton Hall 'satisfies the artistic sense of even the most fastidious'. It's colour and form blend harmoniously with the delightful gardens which surround it.

Upton Cresset Hall

BRIDGNORTH

A MEDIEVAL MANOR HOUSE IN RED BRICK, TUCKED AWAY AT THE END OF A LEAFY SHROPSHIRE LANE: ABOUT THREE MILES WEST OF BRIDGNORTH ON UNCLASSIFIED ROADS.

The site of Upton Cresset Hall is ancient – it was mentioned in the Domesday Book, and nearby are the remains of a Roman settlement. The Hall was built in the 14th century as a timber-framed manor house, but was extended during Elizabethan times, when it was encased in brick, almost certainly made from the clay in the grounds of the Hall; it was at this time that the turretted, red-brick gatehouse was built. From that time the Hall has been the seat of the de Upton and Cresset families in an unbroken line.

The house is deeply associated with British history. Cressets fought for the Yorkists in the Wars of the Roses and for the king in the Civil War. Another, James Cresset, was Ambassador to Hanover during the negotiations for the Hanoverian Succession, and his correspondence is on display. The present owner, Bill Cash, is the Member of Parliament for Stafford. The Hall was originally encircled by a moat – now dry – and a small village grew up close by, but today it sits alone, apart from the gatehouse and a redundant Norman church, in this romantic site.

The house itself has had a chequered history. The 14th-century Great Hall, now the family's dining room, was once open to the roof-beams, but an extra floor of bedrooms was added. It is now in these rooms, reached by a Tudor staircase, that the massive timber roof-arches can be admired.

Weston Park

SHIFNAL

A TREASURE TROVE OF ART IN A SPLENDID PARKLAND SETTING: ON THE A5 ABOUT NINE MILES WEST OF M6 JUNCTION 12, TOWARDS TELFORD.

Weston Park, completed in 1617, was built on the site of an earlier medieval manor house and since that time it has been the family seat of the Earls of Bradford. Additions and alterations in the intervening years have created an extensive collection of buildings, in a number of different styles. In recent years, however, the present owners, the Earl and Countess of Bradford, have undone many of the Victorian alterations, to restore both the house and grounds to a condition more in keeping with the original 17th-century plan.

It was the redoubtable Lady Wilbraham's love of architecture which led to the building of the present mansion, and the library contains the original inspiration for Weston Park – a copy of Palladio's *First Book*

A DEVOTED CORRESPONDENT

Displayed in the West Marble Hall are over 1,100 letters written by Benjamin Disraeli (over a period of eight years after the death of his own wife) to Selina, the wife of the 3rd Earl of Bradford, and to her sister, Lady Chesterfield. At the time of this massive correspondence, both sisters were grandmothers and Disraeli was in his seventies. Many of these letters were dashed off in spare moments between official engagements. As he was Prime Minister for six of these eight years, the letters offer a fascinating glimpse into not only the great affairs of the day, but also into Disraeli's more private preoccupations.

of Architecture, printed in 1663. Notes on the flysheet, in Lady Wilbraham's own hand, reveal her knowledge of architecture and provide a good deal of information about the rebuilding of Weston Park.

ART AND LITERATURE

The interior is cool, airy and sumptuously appointed, with period furniture and art treasures collected by the family over the centuries – important paintings include works by Stubbs, Constable and Van Dyck. Displayed in the entrance hall are paintings that reflect the 3rd Earl's passion for horses, while the dominant feature of the adjacent Marble Hall is its floor with contrasting squares of white marble and black slate. The Tapestry Room, by contrast, is a symphony of pinks, its walls draped with beautiful tapestries woven at the famous Gobelin factory in Paris. They feature mythological scenes after the styles of Reubens and Watteau. The cool ambience of the drawing room sets off a series of family portraits, including one of Lady Wilbraham by Sir Peter Lely.

The library has a splendid collection of books, though one or two titles flatter to deceive and are, in fact, camouflaging two secret doors – note here such titles as *The Library of Useless Knowledge* and nine bogus volumes of *The American Peerage*! The dining room was created a century ago by combining several small rooms. The high ceiling gives a sense of space, and a recent redecoration has duplicated the motifs on the elaborate fireplace to embellish the doorways, dado and frieze. The finishing touch is provided by three fine family portraits by Van Dyck.

A pair of salons were created from what was formerly a courtyard, and are now used as galleries for an impressive display of landscape, genre and portrait paintings. The breakfast room is another which has been redesigned to set off pictures – in this case a collection of the best smaller portraits, including a painting of Sir George Carew by Holbein. Of the bedrooms, one of particular interest is the elegant Tent Room, which has been sumptuously redecorated in the French style, with a tented ceiling and walls which are hung with silk drapes.

Above: Weston Park's south front looks out over formal lawns to the 'Capability' Brown parkland beyond.

The dining room contains the finest paintings in the house, including portraits by Van Dyck.

THE PARK

The estate comprises almost a thousand acres, and is surrounded by a wall fully eight miles in length. The parkland highlights the handiwork of 'Capability' Brown, who made good use of the site's natural contours to create an intimate landscape of lakes and woodland. Footpaths meander past flowering shrubs and into a fine arboretum and the parkland is well-served by picnic areas. Here too is Pendrill's Cave, once the draughty home of a hermit of that name.

The formal gardens of Weston's South Terrace have been restored to their former glory, and include the Italian broderie, the long border and the rose garden. At one time fires smouldered beneath the orangery, allowing tropical fruit to be grown for the family's table, no matter how inclement the weather.

The Bag of the Great Seal of England, on display in the library.

Margam Country Park

PORT TALBOT

A COUNTRY PARK HAS BEEN CREATED AROUND THE SHELL OF MARGAM PARK: FOUR MILES SOUTH OF PORT TALBOT ON THE A48.

Close to the sea between Porthcawl and Port Talbot is Margam Country Park. The heart of this estate is the shell of the 19th-century mansion house, but the history of the area lies with the Abbey of Margam, founded in 1147 by Robert Consul, Earl of Gloucester. Given to the Cistercian monks from Clairvaux, the Abbey depended for its existence on sheep rearing on the outlying granges worked by the lay brethren, much of the wool being exported to the Continent from nearby Taibach. Margam was one of the wealthiest abbeys in Wales during the 12th century, but, following the Black Death, which reached Margam in 1349, the numbers of lay brothers dwindled, and by 1536, when Henry VIII dissolved the monastery, only nine monks were left.

AN ILL-FATED MANSION

The parish church incorporates the severe Norman nave of the Abbey church and also the richer west doorway and the windows above, and visitors to the country park can still see the remains of the wonderful dodecagonal Chapter House and some beautiful doorways dating from that early period.

In 1536 Margam Abbey was bought by Sir Rice Mansel, of Penrice and Oxwich. Although a house was built incorporating part of the Abbey, this was demolished in the 18th century to make way for the famous orangery designed in 1787 by Anthony Keck for Thomas Mansel Talbot to house the family's great collection of orange trees. His son, Christopher Rice Mansel Talbot, Liberal Member of Parliament for Glamorgan for 60 years from 1830, commissioned a large house from Thomas Hopper in 1830-5.

Dating from the 1780s, the famous orangery at Margam Park was restored in the 1970s, to be re-opened by Her Majesty the Queen during her Silver Jubilee visit in 1977.

It was one of Hopper's masterpieces, in the Tudor style, and built in warm red stone with a great octagonal tower, surmounted with pinnacles, rising in the middle. The internal appointments were those of a great Victorian country house, and when its owner died, his heir inherited very considerable wealth. By 1941, however, the contents were auctioned, and the mansion subsequently became derelict. Sadly it is now an empty shell.

A UNIQUE LANDSCAPE

The landscape of Margam is unique in South Wales, as it incorporates the barren uplands of Craig-y-Lodge and Tonmawr, as well as the lowland copses and lakes of the southern part of the park. There is a rich variety of bird life including many birds of prey, while mute swans and pochard inhabit the lakes, and you can occasionally see kingfishers. Margam supports the largest number of fallow deer in South Wales, while there is also a growing herd of Glamorgan cattle, a breed thought to have become extinct before 1918. In the old kitchen garden area a maze has now been created which, covering an acre, is thought to be the largest in the world. Margam Country Park also now displays more than 60 pieces of contemporary sculpture by British artists, including works by Kenneth Armitage, Barbara Hepworth and Elizabeth Frink.

MARGAM'S ORANGERY

The orangery at Margam Park is one of the largest and most famous in the country. Built by Anthony Keck for Thomas Mansel Talbot between 1786 and 1790, it was intended to house the collection of orange, lemon and citrus trees inherited by the Talbots from their Mansel forebears. Legend says that these trees were originally the gift of royalty shipwrecked on the nearby coast, and claimed by the Mansels as tribute. By the mid 18th century, the collection numbered about 100 trees, and an orangery 327 feet long had to be built to accommodate them.

Penhow Castle

NEWPORT

A MEDIEVAL CASTLE WHICH IS STILL INHABITED AND OFFERS A STIMULATING TOUR: FIVE MILES EAST OF NEWPORT ON THE A48.

Half-way between Chepstow and Newport is the romantic Penhow Castle, set on a steep grassy hill, interspersed with rocks, and considered to be the oldest castle in Wales which is still inhabited. First home in Britain of the St Maur family, more familiar to us, perhaps, as the Seymours, the square tower house was built by Sir Roger de St Maur before 1129. The

additional buildings continue around the courtyard, incorporating a 14th-century gatehouse, a Great Hall block of the 15th century, and a three-storey 17th-century wing.

In the Norman tower, an early medieval bedchamber has been recreated, warmed and catered for by a large fireplace. Nearby there are two halls, one above the other, both of them beautifully lit by traceried windows. The authentic atmosphere of the Middle Ages is unmistakable in the 15th-century Great Hall, with its tall screen separating the main part of the hall from the kitchen. Over the screen is a minstrels' gallery, and the timber roof is open to the rafters, which terminate in a decorative frieze.

In contrast to this medieval severity, the later panelled rooms from the reign of Charles II are elegant and comfortable. Plasterwork decorates the ceilings, while the doorcase with its broken pediment and fielded panels hung with paintings give a real flavour of the spacious classical period. The kitchen has a fine display of early equipment, including an open fire, a bread oven and a supply of water pumped by hand.

For the last 20 years, Penhow has been owned by film director, Stephen Weeks, who has lovingly restored and furnished this fascinating building which he originally found in a ruinous state. He also pioneered the range of Walkman audio-tours which guide visitors at their own pace, from secret passages to battlements, vividly recreating the drama and atmosphere of the period rooms along the way.

Left: The restoration of Penhow Castle has earned it three awards for Heritage Education. This is the 12th-century Keep Room.

■ Penhow is so special because, on a domestic scale, one can see how the British house developed from fortified tower through to the beginnings of the modern home. It has been my pleasure to tease out its history so that visitors can now explore the eight and a half centuries of the Castle's varied story. ■

Stephen Weeks

Bryn Bras Castle

CAERNARFON

A ROMANESQUE CASTLE NESTLING IN THE FOOTHILLS OF SNOWDONIA: ABOUT THREE MILES EAST OF CAERNARFON, JUST OFF THE A4086 LLANBERIS ROAD NEAR LLANRUG.

First impressions can deceive: the truth is that the battlements of Bryn Bras Castle were built – in about 1830 – for the pleasures of gracious living rather than to withstand a siege. A building had existed on this site for centuries, and the old road passing the castle is an ancient drovers' road that winds through the Llanberis Pass eastwards through Wales and on into England.

Bryn Bras was planned in a neo-Romanesque style for Thomas Williams, a Welsh attorney at law, and his wife, Lauretta. The architect is thought to have been Thomas Hopper, whose skills were also in evidence at Penrhyn Castle. Various additions since then, including much of the panelling and stained glass to be seen today, have created a building that is as charming as it is rambling. The towers, turrets and battlements create a dramatic silhouette quite in keeping with the romance and elegance of the interior. Many distinguished guests have enjoyed hospitality at Bryn Bras, including Edward, Prince of Wales, and Lloyd George – particularly when the castle was the home of millionaire Duncan Elliot Alves.

The splendid setting extends over 32 acres. The castle opens onto green lawns and flowering trees that gracefully blend into mature woodland. The gardens were created as a sanctuary of tranquillity, for the private pleasure of a few; now they can be enjoyed by many. The walled knot garden brings the formality of the Elizabethan era into an essentially Victorian garden. There are enchanting walks amongst shady groves and tumbling streams. One path winds uphill to a viewpoint offering a panorama that extends to Snowdon, Anglesey and the sea.

The library at Bryn Bras Castle includes one of the beautiful stained glass windows that were fitted to the castle in the early part of the 20th century.

■ We think Bryn Bras is a gem amongst the many castles in Wales. ■

Marita and Neville Gray-Parry

Not only restored but also refurnished and equipped, Tredegar's collections include this fine plate.

Tredegar House

NEWPORT

A MAGNIFICENT MANSION OCCUPIED FOR 500 YEARS BY THE MORGAN FAMILY, A POWERFUL AND INFLUENTIAL DYNASTY WHO HAVE LINKS WITH OWAIN GLYNDWR AND TUDOR AND STUART MONARCHS: FIVE MILES WEST OF NEWPORT ON THE A48 OR M4 JUNCTION 28.

Home to one of the greatest of Welsh families for over 500 years, Tredegar provided in the 18th and 19th centuries much of the wealth that enabled commercial and industrial development to take place in Newport, and the family were generous benefactors to the community, giving land for the Royal Gwent Hospital, as well as helping to encourage recreation and educational facilities in the area.

The Morgans, although they claim descent from the great princely families of Wales, are likely to have attained gentry status only in the early Tudor period, when they constructed a grand house to reflect their new social position. The earliest recorded owner was Llewelyn ap Morgan in 1402, but, implicated in Owain Glyndwr's rebellion, he was forced to surrender his estates. In 1485, however, Sir John ap Morgan assisted Henry Tudor to the English throne, and was rewarded with lordship over the area. The oldest part of the house, the south-west wing, probably dates from this period.

Tredegar was clearly a substantial house, but was unlikely to satisfy the ambitions of the greatest family in the district indefinitely. In 1645, after the Battle of Naseby, Charles I, his retinue and two troops of horse spent the night at Tredegar, courtesy of Sir William Morgan, and it was his grandson, another William, who created the house that we see today, financed largely by his marriage to his cousin, Blanche Morgan, who possessed great estates in Breconshire. In 1664, William started work on a tremendously grand house which was to take ten years to complete, consisting of two wings at right-angles to each other, forming a hollow square with the old medieval hall and the later offices.

Tredegar House is one of the most significant late 17th-century houses in the whole of the British Isles.

SYMBOL OF PROSPERITY

Tredegar's main façade is elaborate in design, presenting an intriguing problem of attribution – no architect for Tredegar can be definitely identified. Although there is some evidence of the influence of Inigo Jones, or of his pupil, John Webb, the decorative motifs would seem to be Dutch, perhaps created by British craftsmen-designers from Dutch or Flemish pattern books.

Whatever the answer may be, Tredegar was a wonder of Wales in the late 17th century, and symbolised the Morgan's power and influence for the following 250 years. The family's wealth increased, enabling Sir William to live a short but rich life, to marry a daughter of the 2nd Duke of Devonshire, and to be created a

THE ECCENTRIC VISCOUNT MORGAN

Evan Morgan, 2nd Viscount Tredegar, was a great eccentric who entertained literary and society figures such as H G Wells, Prince Paul of Greece and Nancy Cunard to weekend house parties that gained a certain local notoriety. He used to box with a kangaroo he kept in the park, had a remarkable empathy with birds and animals, and had a parrot which sat on his shoulder. Although he was a devout Catholic and a chamberlain to the Pope, he dabbled in black magic with his friend, Aleister Crowley, the occultist, a frequent visitor to Tredegar.

Knight of the Bath in 1725. The estates passed to his niece, Jane, and she married Sir Charles Gould, an astute lawyer, who changed his name to Gould Morgan and invested the Tredegar fortunes in industrial and financial projects. Developments which he financed during the 18th and 19th centuries included coal mines, the Tredegar Ironworks, the Monmouthshire Canal, the Sirhowy Tramroad and the Newport Docks.

A DECLINE IN FORTUNE

It was for loyalty to Disraeli that Sir Charles Morgan was created 1st Baron Tredegar in 1859. He was succeeded by one of the most colourful Morgans, Godfrey, who had survived the Charge of the Light Brigade. A nephew, Courtenay, succeeded in 1913, and he and his son, Evan, the last Morgan to live at Tredegar, indulged an extravagant life-style which was to lead John Morgan to sell the estate in 1951 to meet death duties. After more than 20 years as a school, the house, stables, home farm, gardens and 90 acres of parkland were purchased by Newport Borough Council, whose extensive programme of restoration continues.

TREDEGAR RESTORED

Entering the house, you come into the Side Hall, Victorian in style, but described in the inventory of 1688 as 'the Drawing Room that is hang'd with Gilt Leather'. Two framed pieces of this gilt and embossed leather are on display above the entrance to the dining room. The Morning Room is furnished as for the use of the ladies of the house in the early 19th century, with a fine Brussels carpet, rosewood furniture and a chaise-longue. The dining room, known in the late 17th century as the New Parlour, has fine, but restrained panelling from floor to ceiling, while its plasterwork dates from the 19th century.

With the New Hall, the whole tempo of the rooms changes. This was the original entrance hall and the first in the sequence of spectacular State Rooms. The fine panelling was originally matched by a splendid plasterwork ceiling, but this unfortunately collapsed in the 1950s. The Brown Room was the State Dining Room, with furniture and decoration which were calculated to impress, and the oak panelling carries a feast of baroque carving. Described in the 1688 Inventory as 'the Gilted Roome', the last State Room was designed to be, and remains the decorative climax of the sequence. Its pine panelling, grained to imitate walnut, has gilded mouldings and the chimney-piece also glistens with gold, the twisted columns on either side echoing those on the doorcase of the house. The stuccoed ceiling is the only 17th-century plasterwork on the ground floor; the central painting is after *The Glorification of Pope Urban VIII* by Pietro da Cortona.

ABOVE AND BELOW STAIRS

The fine staircase has a carved balustrade typical of the late 17th century, but it is probable that alterations were made in the 19th century. Situated over the Gilt Room is the panelled Best Chamber, its original plaster ceiling the most attractive in Tredegar. The King's Room was probably named after King Gould, Sir Charles Gould's father, but it was also used by Evan Morgan, the 2nd Viscount. The Blue Room was used by Princess Olga Dolgorouki, his second wife, as a private sitting room. A fine portrait of Evan Morgan's mother by Augustus John hangs here. Beyond the Master's Dressing Room and Bedchamber is the Cedar Closet, small, elegant and lavishly decorated, where favoured guests would sometimes be received.

In 1911 there were 22 indoor servants at Tredegar, and the house is fortunate in having a series of well-appointed rooms that give a clear idea of how a great house worked. Visitors can see the butler's pantry, the plate scullery, where the gold and silver plate was kept secure, the lofty kitchen which still has a roasting range complete with its elaborate spit mechanism operated by a 'smoke jack' in the chimney. There are separate rooms for making pastry and for various larders, a

The cool, classical dining room is authentically furnished in Victorian 'antiquarian' style.

The Gilt Room, always intended to be the most splendid room in the house, was used as a reception room for formal occasions.

Servants' Hall, where the under-servants took their meals, and the Housekeeper's Room, where the steward, the butler, the housekeeper and the cook ate.

THE ESTATE

Like other great houses, Tredegar was supported by a large estate with its own Home Farm, Brewhouse and even a private fire-engine. The magnificent stables were clearly built at the same time as the house, and they share the same characteristics. The plan of the gardens is most probably Tudor in origin, and the lovely Cedar Garden, overlooked by the State Rooms, was almost certainly laid out as a parterre. In the 1930s, a sunken garden was added between the house and the lake, and its herbaceous borders and rose beds are wonderfully colourful during the summer. The orangery dates from the early 1700s.

The remarkable Cefn Mabli shovelboard, now housed in the stables, is one of the most amazing pieces of oak furniture in the country, its top a single plank 42

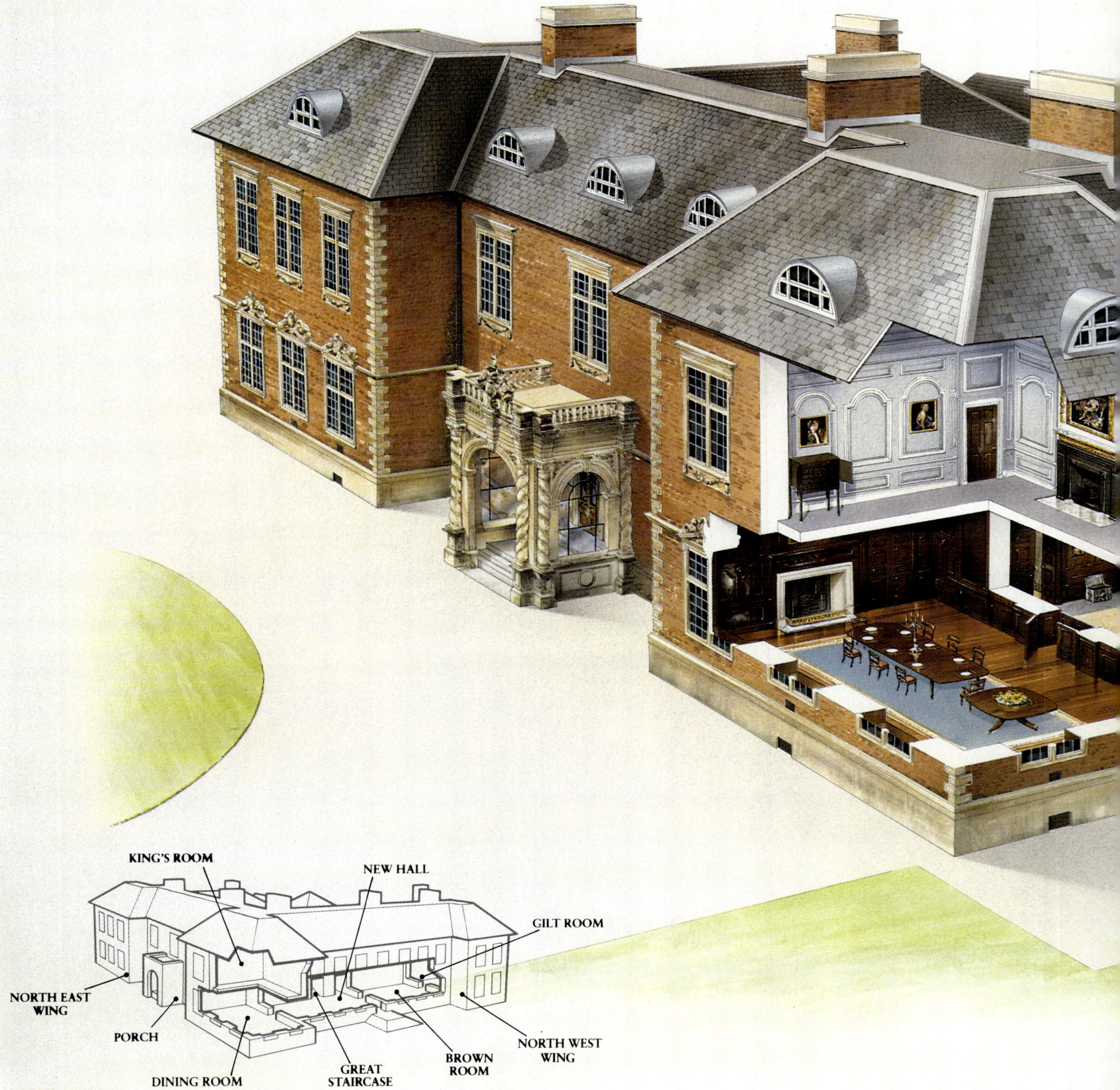

feet long. It was made in about 1640 for Cefn Mabli House, a property purchased by Courtenay, Lord Tredegar, in 1924. Although it has undergone some vicissitudes during the past 50 years, it is now restored, and could once again be a suitable surface on which to play the 17th-century equivalent of shove-ha'penny.

■ When you own a large old house you have two strokes against you – its size and its age. Such houses are a labour of love – a lot of love – even more labour and a great deal of money, but I personally do not grudge this. My family have been here for 700 years and it is not only my duty, but a great privilege and a hobby to maintain it to the best of my ability. ■
Colonel The Lord Langford

Above: *Bodrhyddan has a splendid collection of arms and armour, including this ceremonial sword.*

Bodrhyddan Hall

RHUDDLAN

A SPLENDID GRADE I LISTED BRICK MANSION WITH FINE PORTRAITS: THREE MILES SOUTH OF RHYL ON THE A547 RHUDDLAN ROAD.

Only a few miles from the North Wales coast, near Abergele, is Bodrhyddan Hall, standing in its own lovely parkland. It is probable that there has been a house on the site for 700 years, and certainly Bodrhyddan has been in the hands of the same family, the Rowley-Conwys for that long. The first dwelling was most probably of wattle and daub, and no trace of it now exists, but substantial parts of its 15th-century successor are incorporated in the present house, including the inner walls of the Great Hall, the cellar doorway, and Tudor stone flags in the Gun Room.

It was with Sir Henry Conwy, during the Commonwealth and Restoration periods, that the status of the family was enhanced. Though his loyalties have never been recorded, it would seem that he worked secretly for the king while engaged by Cromwell as High Sheriff of Flintshire. After the Restoration, Sir Henry was given a baronetcy by Charles II and it was this elevation which prompted his plans to rebuild the family home – plans which were actually carried out by his son, John.

Over the garden entrance is a date stone showing that Sir John Conwy built the house between 1696 and 1700. This was a mellow brick structure with stone quoins which comprises most of the present south front, and it was approached up the old drive which now forms a grassy avenue. Sir John's two-storeyed house was built in typical William and Mary style, with the Great Hall as its central feature. Towards the end of the 18th century, the Big Dining Room was constructed, most probably by Dean Shipley, who married the heiress of Bodrhyddan. In 1872, the house was brilliantly altered and enlarged for Conwy Grenville Hercules Rowley-Conwy by William Eden Nesfield, who added picturesque wings at each end, making the new main entrance face west, with a mile-long drive running down towards Rhuddlan.

The panelled Front Hall has a fine collection of armour, including two cap-a-pie suits made in Augsburg in the 15th century. Through the oak double doors is the Great Hall, with an inglenook around the fire, similar to those revived by Nesfield and Richard Norman Shaw only a few years earlier. Here, too, are the two most interesting pictures in the house, probably showing William Conwy and his wife, both by Marcus Gheeraerts the Younger, and dated 1606.

At the top of the staircase is the White Drawing Room, which used to be the library. The books have been replaced with some notable pieces of china, as well as items of special family interest. The small panels around the two fireplaces depict religious subjects, and came from the chapel of one of the Armada

A CHANCE ENCOUNTER

The Egyptian Room at Bodrhyddan Hall contains two mummy cases (one still occupied) and many small items which Richard and Charlotte Rowley brought back from their Egyptian honeymoon in 1836. They left behind an inscription of their names and the date, carved on a column of the Mortuary Temple of Rameses III at Thebes – an inscription which was noticed quite by chance by their great grandson during his visit to Thebes in 1978.

Bodrhyddan Hall, the home of Lord Langford and his family, incorporates features which span the five centuries of its existence.

galleons wrecked off the coast of Anglesey. At the foot of the stairs is the Big Dining Room, which, while only rarely used today for its original purpose, displays a distinguished group of family portraits, from Hogarth, Michael Dahl and John Vanderbank, to Ramsey, Hudson, Reynolds and Beechey.

Leaving the house by the garden entrance, you pass through what was the main doorway of the William and Mary house. Appropriately, the older central part of Bodrhyddan still boasts a formal parterre garden with a circular waterlily fountain. On the bottom lawn, between oak trees, is the only surviving pillar from Rhuddlan Castle, while, on the other side of the main drive in the Pleasaunce is Ffynnon Fair, St Mary's Well, housed in a charming octagonal wellhouse, inscribed with the name of Inigo Jones, 1612.

Tower

Mold

The only fortified Welsh border house in existence: one mile south-east of Mold town centre, off Nercwys Road.

Just to the south of the charming market town of Mold, in Clwyd, lies the remarkable fortified manor house of Tower. With its flank secure against the outlying slopes of the Clwydian Range, the house is set in deep parkland, the low, medieval tower reflected in the still waters of a picturesque lake.

Tower dates from the 15th century, and the poet, Hywel Cilcan, speaks of 'the fair Tower, a fortress 20 fathoms high', and praises 'the well-stocked table kept by Rheinallt'. This was the builder of Tower, Rheinallt Gruffydd ap Bleddyn, who featured prominently in the almost continuous border warfare that marked the 15th century in this part of the Principality. Rheinallt was one of the 'gallant captains' who defended Harlech Castle, and who carved out a special, if rather macabre, niche for himself in the annals of Welsh history. The story is told by the poet, Lewys Glyn Cothi, that in 1465 Rheinallt captured the Mayor of Chester in Mold Market Place, and taking him to Tower gave him a pie to eat – in the pie was a rope, with which the unfortunate Mayor was promptly hanged in the Great Hall.

The present owners, the Wynne-Eyton family, have owned Tower for 500 years, and although their house now has a tranquil air, this was not always so. Inside, the defensive purposes of the house are soon apparent. The basement has a shallow vaulted ceiling, while the ground-floor room has a fascinating segmental tunnel vault, built primarily for strength, and there is a late-medieval fireplace on the west side. The Great Hall is on the first floor, but this has been divided into two, and the original timber roof has gone. During the medieval period, Tower must have had crenellations with a wall walk for defensive purposes, but this was replaced by a harmonious parapet, presumably at the end of the 18th or the beginning of the 19th century. The panelled dining room on the first floor, which can seat 35 guests, is a most attractive room, its fabric clearly medieval, though the earlier panelling was replaced in 1870. More ordinary domestic rooms stand to one side of the tower, and this has always been the case – a Welsh awdle, or poem, refers to Rheinallt's tower with kitchens to one side. Indeed, you can still see two corbels inside the structure which must have supported an earlier floor.

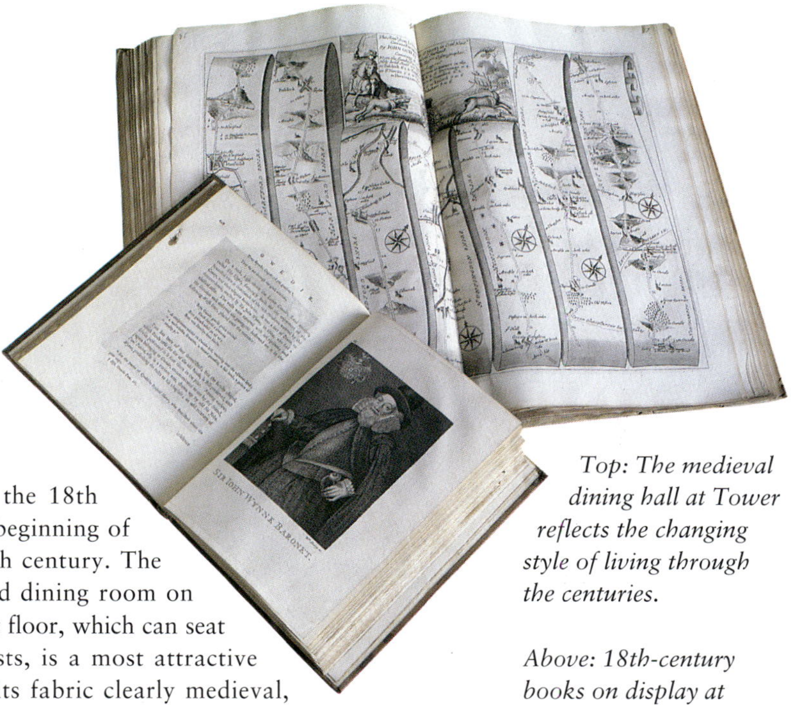

Top: The medieval dining hall at Tower reflects the changing style of living through the centuries.

Above: 18th-century books on display at Tower.

The south front was altered early in the 18th century, and the rooms that we see and enjoy today are very different in character from the original atmosphere of medieval severity. Here all is elegance, with large windows making the drawing room a pleasant place to be. The bedrooms also offer all the comforts expected of the classic country house. Tower has the special qualities that a long and distinguished history bring to a house which enjoys all the comforts and sophistication that we associate with modern living.

■ We love showing off our home to all our guests, whether they are coach parties partaking of afternoon tea or overnight bed and breakfast guests. ■
Charles Wynne-Eyton

SCOTLAND

SIR WALTER SCOTT played a major role in creating today's image of romantic Scotland and his house, Abbotsford, on the Tweed below the enchanting Eildon Hills, is testimony to his enthusiasms. His family, the Scotts of Buccleuch, own two of the grandest houses in all Scotland, Bowhill and Drumlanrig, packed with fabulous treasures. Meanwhile, the simple old Border laird's home of Traquair, which has played host to innumerable kings, is perhaps the most romantic house in all Britain. Further north, the grim MacLeod fastness of Dunvegan can claim Britain's nastiest dungeon and Glamis a particularly chilling monster, while the country's only remaining private army is based at Blair Castle. But Scottish history is not all violence – far from it – and all the graces of civilisation will be found in the 18th-century magnificence of Hopetoun House, the Scots Baronial ducal splendours of Dunrobin and Inveraray, the 19th-century Gothic of Scone Palace and the Edwardian opulence of Manderston.

Abbotsford

MELROSE

IN A SUPERB SETTING ON THE RIVER TWEED, ABBOTSFORD STANDS AS A MEMORIAL TO ITS REMARKABLE CREATOR, THE GREAT SIR WALTER SCOTT: TWO MILES SOUTH-EAST OF GALASHIELS.

By 1811, at the age of 40, Walter Scott could at last see financial security on the horizon. In 1804 he had moved to Ashiestiel, on the Tweed, to be nearer his job, for he was sheriff-depute for Selkirkshire. In 1805 he had established his popularity as a poet with the historical ballad *The Lay of the Last Minstrel* and had followed this to great acclaim with the heroic *Marmion* and the romantic ballad *The Lady of the Lake*. With the prospect of considerable earnings from his future writings, Scott borrowed half the £4,000 needed to purchase the farm of Cartley Hole, some six miles up the river from Ashiestiel.

SCOTT'S NEW HOME

The site was indifferent for farming, but Scott, attracted, no doubt, by its general location overlooking the river and its historic associations (it was the site in 1526 of the last clan battle in the Borders), could see its potential, and threw his prodigious energies and not a little money into creating a modest country cottage. Adding an armoury, a dining room, a study, a conservatory and three bedrooms to the existing farmhouse, he called it Abbotsford, after the river crossing below the house and its situation on land once owned by the abbey at Melrose.

By 1812 the family was ready to move in, and in that first summer, Scott spent every spare moment supervising the planting of the estate with oak and Spanish chestnut, while furiously composing *Rokeby* to pay for it all. In fact, the building of Abbotsford signalled the period of Scott's greatest creativity, for in 1814 he started the series of *Waverley* novels that would establish his lasting fame. He gradually bought more land and even planned to turn one farmstead into a model hamlet, to be called Abbotstown.

In 1822 the remains of the farmhouse at Abbotsford were finally demolished, making way for the main block which can be seen today, complete with courtyard walls and a gateway. The chief architect was William Atkinson, a noted castle-builder of the time, but Scott and his many influential friends all added their own ideas.

THE FLITTING

When Scott and his family moved into Abbotsford, he wrote a light-hearted account of their 'flitting' to a friend – 'The neighbours have been much delighted with the procession of my furniture, in which old swords, bows, targets and lances made a very conspicuous show. A family of turkeys was accommodated within the helmet of some *preux chevalier* of ancient Border fame; and the very cows, for ought I know, were bearing banners and muskets.' Clearly, Scott was already collecting some of the remarkable historical mementoes or 'gabions' as he called them, which lend the house such charm today.

Abbotsford is much more than a fine mansion. It is also the repository of the varied and fascinating collections amassed by Sir Walter Scott.

SCOTT'S COLLECTIONS

The house has great character, mixing Tudor and traditional Scottish styles, and its contents reflect their creator in an extraordinary way, for it is the treasure-house of a magpie with a gift for romantic history. The dark entrance hall is lined with oak panelling from the Auld Kirk at Dunfermline; other architectural details are copied from Melrose Abbey, and the whole is filled with an eccentric collection of armour, heraldic badges and historic knick-knacks, including two canon balls from the siege of Roxburgh Castle, 1460. These themes continue throughout the house, with a library ceiling copied from Rosslyn Chapel, desks presented by royalty or made from timber salvaged from the Spanish Armada, and every imaginable weapon, from Rob Roy's broadsword to a pistol belonging to 'Bonnie Dundee'. As well as family portraits, other evocative artefacts include Napoleon's cloak clasp of golden bees, discovered in his carriage after Waterloo, a drinking quaich which belonged to Bonnie Prince Charlie, and a pocket book worked by Flora Macdonald.

In the year after Scott's death, 1833, the house was officially opened to an avid public. The house passed eventually to his daughter Sophia, married to John Lockhart, who became the first biographer of the great man. Their daughter, Charlotte Hope-Scott added the west wing, including the chapel, giving much-needed employment to local labourers. Her daughter, Mary Monica, inherited in 1858, and today her granddaughter, Patricia Maxwell-Scott, is keeper of Abbotsford.

Ayton Castle

EYEMOUTH

A DRAMATIC EXAMPLE OF THE ROMANTIC SCOTTISH BARONIAL STYLE OF ARCHITECTURE, IN RED SANDSTONE: ONE AND A HALF MILES SOUTH-EAST OF EYEMOUTH ON THE B6355.

Though Ayton Castle is a true creation of the Victorian age, there has been a castle on the site since Norman times. In the 15th century it was owned by the Homes, but was confiscated by the crown because of their support for the Stuart cause. In the mid 18th century the estate was acquired by James Fordyce, who was the Scottish Commissioner for Lands and Forests, at which time the estate was important and rich enough to instigate the removal of Ayton village to a more distant location. That castle was completely devastated by fire in the early years of the 19th century.

The basis of the Ayton Castle we see today was commissioned by the 19th-century owner, William Mitchell-Innes, who chose Gillespie Graham to create for him a suitably grand, though not excessively large, residence – he was a practical man, who saw no need for rooms he could not utilise. His son, however, had a much larger family and found it necessary to extend Ayton soon after he inherited it in 1860.

In addition to adding new rooms, including an attic suite of nurseries, the castle was splendidly redecorated and the rich plasterwork of the ceilings remains a particularly fine feature. In 1886 the castle was sold to Henry Liddell, a Northumberland land-owner and it is his grandson, David Liddell-Grainger, who is the present owner.

■ **When I came to live at Ayton in 1955 it had been closed and managed by Trustees, and was unused and unappreciated. Since then I have restored it to its former glory and preserved it as a family home; it was a challenge in which I am proud to have succeeded, so that future generations may appreciate this truly great Scottish Castle which has been faithfully cared for.** ■
David Liddell-Grainger

Bowhill

SELKIRK

THE SPLENDID 19TH-CENTURY HOME OF THE SCOTT FAMILY, DUKES OF BUCCLEUCH AND QUEENSBERRY: THREE MILES WEST OF SELKIRK OFF THE A708.

'Sweet Bowhill' was Sir Walter Scott's fond name for this fine house in his *Lay of the Last Minstrel*, and he spoke with authority – as a kinsman of the owners, he was a frequent visitor. The Scott family had been prominent in Scottish history since the 13th century, amassing vast tracts of land in the Borders which included the Bowhill estate. One Sir Walter Scott fought with James IV at Flodden; another, knighted by James VI, was known as 'Bold Buccleuch' for his daring deeds in Border raids during the 16th century and was created first Lord Scott of Buccleuch. In 1663 Anna, the heiress to the Scotts, married James, Duke of Monmouth, natural son of Charles II, who was then created Duke of Buccleuch and Earl of Dalkeith (another Scott property). She had been granted the title Duchess of Buccleuch in her own right and so avoided the forfeiture of her position and estates when her husband was executed after his unsuccessful uprising.

A succession of marriages brought further titles and possessions to the Scotts, who are among the oldest families in Scotland, and Bowhill remains their main residence. Amidst beautiful forest and farmland between two tributaries of the Tweed, this imposing mansion contains some magnificent paintings, including works by Van Dyck, Canaletto, Reynolds, Gainsborough and Claude Lorraine, an outstanding collection of portrait miniatures and a fine display of porcelain and furniture. There are two rooms in the house devoted to memorabilia associated with the Duke of Monmouth and Sir Walter Scott.

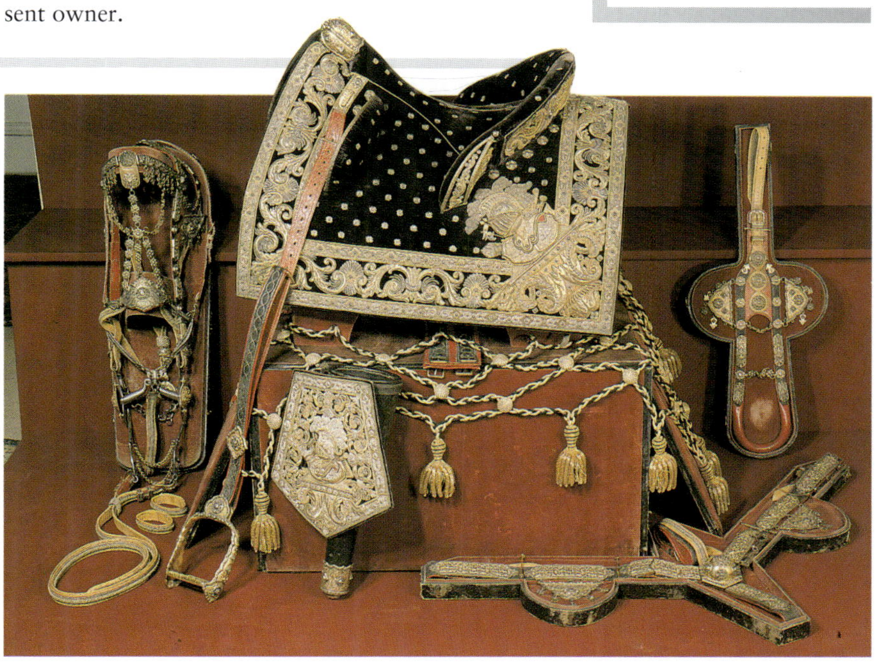

Above: The Duke of Monmouth's saddle.
Left: Winter *by Sir Joshua Reynolds.*

■ **The most special thing about Bowhill is that it is a family home, not an institution. It grows out of a superb landscape, where many generations have shared the delights of 'Sweet Bowhill' and its surroundings.** ■
The Duke of Buccleuch and Queensberry

Floors Castle

Kelso

A magnificent 18th-century mansion, remodelled in the 19th century, standing in a beautiful setting on the River Tweed: a mile north-west of Kelso.

The family home of the Innes Kers, Floors has been described as the largest inhabited mansion in Britain. It started its existence as a large house, built between 1718 and 1740 for the 1st Duke of Roxburghe, John Ker, and until recently it was believed that Sir John Vanbrugh had drawn up the plans, but it is now known to be the work of William Adam. Ker had been Secretary of State for Scotland, and the house was conceived as a mansion for a man of status.

THE ROXBURGHE PEERAGE CASE

On the 1st Duke's death in 1740, the house quickly passed through his son Robert to John, the 3rd Duke, in 1755. The death of his heir, an elderly cousin, in the following year, sparked off a celebrated crisis, the Roxburghe Peerage Case, with a number of distant relatives eagerly claiming the title. The matter was finally decided in 1812 by the Committee of Privileges of the House of Lords, who came down in favour of Sir James Innes. Taking the title 5th Duke and the name Innes Ker, Sir James was forced to sell his predecessor's famous library to cover the costs of his claim. The distinguished collection of antiquarian volumes attained huge prices – a first edition of Bocaccio's *Decameron* alone raised £2,260. Aged 76 and childless, it looked as though Sir James might be but a temporary solution to the problem of succession, but in his 80s, the old Duke confounded his eager relatives by fathering a son, who succeeded in 1823, aged just seven.

Right: Embellishments by William Playfair to the already splendid Adam mansion have given Floors Castle its unique appearance.

FORBIDDEN LOVE

The story of the 3rd Duke is a sad one. He was devoted to Queen Charlotte's elder sister, but Court etiquette forbade her marriage to anyone whose status was less than royalty. The frustrated lovers pledged themselves to celibacy, and the Duke turned his energies to book-collecting, dying unmarried in 1804.

THE CHANGING FACE OF FLOORS

The 6th Duke, James, was to further the family fortunes through his connections at Court, earning himself a peerage, and a state visit from Queen Victoria in 1867 – a summerhouse in the garden was built especially for her. The 6th Duke was also responsible for changing the face of Floors, engaging the great William Playfair, noted for his work in Edinburgh New Town, to remodel and extend the house. Playfair added a delightful roofscape of lead cupolas more reminiscent of French than Scottish architectural traditions, as well as features ranging from the Grand Ballroom to a Gothic-style chamber to hold the Duke's collection of stuffed birds.

While the outside of Floors has barely changed since that time, extensive remodelling of the interior was undertaken during the time of the 8th Duke, Sir Henry Innes Ker, who inherited it in 1892. A notable soldier, he served in the Boer War and World War I – a fighting tradition that was continued by his son, and by his grandson, the current (10th) Duke, who served in the Blues and Royals.

In 1903 the 8th Duke married American heiress, Mary Goelet, and over the next 33 years she devoted herself to the house. Her greatest contribution is probably the collection of antique tapestries, many brought from her Long Island home. A rich collection of French furniture was also acquired, but Duchess May, as she was known, did not neglect contemporary art, and there are paintings by Matisse and ornaments by Fabergé. Together they form one of the chief attractions of Floors today.

The drawing room at Floors Castle is among those remodelled at the turn of the century to house the superb set of Brussels tapestries brought by Duchess May. It also contains outstanding collections of furniture, porcelain and other works of art.

Left: Portrait of a Lady, *by Alexis Grimoux is among the works of art on display at Floors Castle.*

Manderston

DUNS

THE 19TH-CENTURY HOME OF LORD PALMER WAS ONE OF THE LAST GREAT CLASSICAL HOUSES TO BE BUILT: A MILE AND A QUARTER EAST OF DUNS, OFF THE A6105.

Before the architect John Kinross was called upon to improve Manderston, the old house, built in the late 18th century for Mr Dalhousie Weatherstone, was solid, square and unremarkable. In 1855, the estate was bought by William Miller who made his fortune in the trade of hemp and herrings! He went on to become Honorary British Consul at St Petersburg, then a Member of Parliament, which earned him a baronetcy in 1874. Sir William was the great-great-grandfather of the present owner, Lord Palmer, whose father was the last chairman of Huntley & Palmers, the biscuit company, before it was sold to an American company.

THE SPORTING BARONET

Sir William intended, as is usual, to leave Manderston to his eldest son, also William, but he unfortunately choked to death on a cherry stone at Eton in 1874, and the house passed to the second son, James. Sir James Miller was one of late Victorian England's most eligible bachelors and was accomplished as a sportsman, soldier and horse racing enthusiast. His sporting passion is reflected in the décor of the Ante-room where Diana, the goddess of hunting, is portrayed, and in the decoration of the ballroom and drawing room in primrose and white – Sir James's racing colours. James married Eveline Curzon, daughter of Lord Scarsdale, who was head of one of the most revered families in England. Sir James re-employed Kinross when he returned from the Boer War in 1901, instructing him to transform Manderston into a house which would surpass Kedleston Hall, his bride's ancestral home in Derbyshire, in style and grandeur.

With the warmth and richness of Kedleston reproduced, Lady Eveline must truly have felt at home on entering the vestibule, with its gorgeous panels of apricot alabaster from Derbyshire – and the dining room has the largest private collection of Blue John in Scotland. This very rare, semi-precious stone is found nowhere else in the world but in Derbyshire. In the hall, the fireplace with its elaborate plasterwork is almost an exact copy of one at Kedleston.

Sir James and Lady Miller held their one and only ball at Manderston in 1905 to celebrate the completion of the house. All too soon, their era was sadly over, for in January 1906, just three months after completion, Sir James died. A sportsman to the last, he died from pneumonia, exacerbated by hunting on a cold day.

FEMININE INFLUENCE

Lady Miller's feminine influence presides over many of the rooms. She also had a passion for fancy-dress soirees and loved to dress up as a Russian Tzarina, perhaps influenced by the miscellaneous collection that her father-in-law brought back from St Petersburg. At the Silver Staircase, picture her in full costume for dramatic effect!

The present Lord Palmer's great-grandmother embroidered the three Louis XVI chairs in front of the fireplace in the drawing room, and his grandmother worked on the corded silk of the four chairs opposite.

■ **We live in the whole of the house and it is very much our home – and judging by the comments in the visitors' book, this is very much appreciated, which is perhaps why we get so many return visits.** ■
Lord Palmer

BELOW STAIRS

One of the fascinations of Manderston is that the life of the servants is also depicted. There are still bell-pulls in the bedrooms; 'up' called a maid whereas 'down' indicated the requirement of a manservant. Pity the poor servants before 1960, when the lift was installed – everything had to be carried upstairs, including coal!

The servants' hall in the basement is now the Racing Room – Sir James' horse, *Sainfoin*, won the Derby in 1890 at 25-1, and he won £118,000 over a 16-year period! Off the Servants' Hall is the Biscuit Tin Museum, the largest private collection of Huntley & Palmer's tins.

The kitchen at Manderston has four ovens for varying temperatures. On the table beside the scullery door, a permanent jug of beer would be available to departing tradesmen. The dairyman's house has two carved heads below the Corbel, said to represent the tenant who paid his rent ... and the one who didn't.

THE STABLES

Sir James' stables are spectacular, and are widely accepted to be the finest in the world. Surrounded by Doric columns and marble panels, the horse population of Manderston must have considered themselves very privileged indeed!

Mellerstain House

Gordon

The great house of Mellerstain is one of the outstanding Georgian residences of Scotland: seven miles north-west of Kelso.

The estate at Mellerstain had changed hands several times before, in 1642, they were made over to one George Baillie of Jarviswood by Charles II. Of the house already on the site, called Whiteside (or Whytesyde), little is known and nothing remains today.

THE BAILLIES OF MELLERSTAIN

George's son Robert, a staunch supporter of the rebellious Duke of Monmouth, was condemned to death for high treason in 1684, and the estate was forfeited until after 1688 when Robert's son George returned from exile in Holland, in the retinue of the Prince of Orange, who was soon to be King William II.

This George Baillie, whose portrait by Sir John Medina may be seen in the Small Sitting Room, was married to the remarkable Lady Grisell Baillie, daughter of another loyal Covenanter. George rose to be a Lord of the Treasury (many books in the library bear his special bookplate, dated 1724), and in 1725 he laid the foundations of the new mansion at Mellerstain. Designed by the architect William Adam, who completed the two symmetrical wings, the building was completed by his son Robert. The gardens were laid out with a distant lake in the form of a Dutch canal – a reminder, perhaps, of the Baillies' exile.

Their younger daughter Rachel married Charles, Lord Binning, heir to the earldom of Haddington; their elder son Thomas inherited the title to become the 7th Earl, while their younger son George Hamilton inherited Mellerstain and changed his name to Baillie. A charming portrait of him by Ramsay hangs in the Music Room, near one of his wife, by Gainsborough. George had travelled widely, and, approving of the classical style then in vogue, employed Robert Adam to complete the house, including building a central block to link the existing wings.

Mellerstain is one of the great houses of Scotland to be built by the famous father and son architects, William and Robert Adam.

EXQUISITE INTERIORS

The interior of the house represents some of Adam's finest work. It is beautifully proportioned, and ceilings, fireplaces, mirrors and door furnishings have remained intact. The library is outstanding, its ceiling (*c*1773) painted in the original soft colours reminiscent of Wedgwood china. Four long panels in plaster relief run above the bookshelves, representing different tales from ancient Greece, and marble busts in high alcoves above the mahogany doors include one of Lady Grisell Baillie.

The music room ceiling is also exquisite, its decoration including eagles and sphinxes. Deep and ornate friezes run below the ceilings and around the doors, completing the harmony. The plasterwork of the Small Sitting Room is in a light Gothic style, unusual for Adam. The main staircase, sweeping up from the West Corridor, is pleasantly unpretentious, and the overall effect, offset by delicate 18th-century furnishings and a particularly fine collection of portraits, is delightful and airy. Adam did not finish his work – the barrel-vaulted ceiling for the long gallery was not carried out, but his plans may be seen on display there.

In 1841 Mellerstain passed to George's grandson, also called George, who in 1858 inherited the title 10th Earl of Haddington from his second cousin, assuming the name Baillie-Hamilton – his life-size portrait can be seen on the stairs, with that of his wife, Georgina. It was his grandson, Lord Binning, who commissioned Sir Reginald Blomfield to re-landscape the gardens leading down from the terrace in 1909, resulting in the attractive vista we see today.

LADY GRISELL BAILLIE 1665-1746

The beautiful daughter of a Scottish Covenanter, as a 12-year-old Grisell bravely visited Robert Baillie on her father's behalf. She went on to shelter her father when he was forced into hiding, and shared his exile in the Netherlands, along with Robert's son George. After the restoration of the Mellerstain estates, she and George were married in 1691 and went on to have two daughters. Lady Grisell Baillie is remembered not just for her heroism, but as an accomplished poet, and for her household book, which is considered a classic of social history. There are a number of portraits of her at Mellerstain, including a particularly striking one of her in maturer years by Marie Varelst, which dominates the Front Hall.

Neidpath Castle

Peebles

A romantic castle in a commanding position above the River Tweed: a mile west of Peebles on the A72.

Neidpath Castle started out as a defensive tower in the second half of the 14th century, and it was constructed in an L shape with a main block and a projecting wing to the west. Its history goes back to the powerful Frasers, who ruled over the entire shire – the last of the male line, Sir Symon, defeated the English armies three times in one day at nearby Roslin. The Lordship then passed through his daughter to the Hay family, who were subsequently ennobled, becoming Lords Hay of Yester, in 1488.

In 1645 Lord Hay was created 1st Earl of Tweeddale, and soon afterwards, in 1650, the castle was held for Charles I until Cromwell's artillery battered its massive walls and forced its defenders into submission. Later in the century the 2nd Earl made substantial alterations to the building, adding 17th-century comforts to the medieval tower. It was sold in 1686 to William Douglas, 1st Duke of Queensberry, but one of his descendants, the 3rd Earl of March, unfortunately allowed part of the west wing to fall into ruin. He also, in order to raise money, cut down the old trees around the castle, prompting Wordsworth to put pen to paper in a sonnet which began, 'Degenerate Douglas! Oh, the unworthy lord!'.

Still in a somewhat dilapidated state, Neidpath was inherited in 1810 by the Earl of Wemyss, ancestor of the present owner. The original entrance to the castle was on the ground floor, where visitors can also see a well, laboriously dug out of the hard rock, and the intimidating Pit Prison. The last person to be incarcerated here was one 'Brown of Frosthill' in 1594, but no records exist to tell us why he was imprisoned or the duration of his miserable sojourn.

In the 17th century a grand new entrance was created, leading directly to the Entresol Floor. Above the entrance is a goat's head, which features in the crest of the Hay family. The west wing is now in ruins, but it is still possible to appreciate its scale from the remains of walls and fireplaces.

Neidpath Castle, dating from the 14th century, sits above the River Tweed as a reminder of more turbulent times in the Borders.

Paxton House

Berwick-upon-Tweed

The largest private art gallery in Scotland, in a lovely Palladian mansion: five miles west of Berwick-upon-Tweed on the B6461.

Overlooking the River Tweed to the south, Paxton House numbers among its many attractions the largest private art gallery in Scotland, which is now an outstation of the National Galleries of Scotland. Furnished with fine rosewood pieces by William Trotter, the celebrated cabinet maker, the gallery was designed in 1811 by the architect, Robert Reid, who played an inspired part in designing Edinburgh's New Town – a grand scheme of Georgian terraces, crescents and squares.

The house itself was built in 1758 for Patrick Home of Billie, later the 13th Laird of Wedderburn. His intention was to create a fine home for himself and his prospective bride, one 'Miss de Brandt', who was a natural daughter of Frederick the Great. Home had met her at Charlottenburg Palace near Berlin and had fallen instantly in love, but the marriage was not to be, and his only reminder of his loved one was a pair of kid gloves she had given him – still on display in the house.

Paxton House is one of the best examples of Palladian architecture in Britain, of which there are many. It was the work of the celebrated Adam brothers, and Robert Adam later added decorative plasterwork to the main public rooms. The impressive mahogany furniture in the entrance hall, dining room, breakfast parlour and main bedrooms came from Thomas Chippendale, and all the pieces have stood the test of time with quiet pride.

Seventy acres of gardens and grounds surround the house and include lovely riverside walks and an adventure playground.

Paxton House offers a fine setting for the works of art which form this outpost of the National Galleries of Scotland.

Catherine Maxwell Stuart, the 21st Lady of Traquair.

Traquair House

INNERLEITHEN

SNUG IN THE UPPER VALLEY OF THE RIVER TWEED, SET DEEP AMID THE TREES, THE OLD GREY HOUSE OF TRAQUAIR LOOKS AS IF SOMEHOW IT HAS ALWAYS BEEN THERE, AND INDEED IT IS ONE OF THE OLDEST PERMANENTLY INHABITED CASTLES IN BRITAIN, WITH A HISTORY THAT GOES BACK OVER 800 YEARS: SIX MILES SOUTH-EAST OF PEEBLES.

The ancient house of Traquair was once called a castle, but it has never withstood a siege or been fought over in bloody battle. Its exterior is remarkably plain, its high. harled walls regularly punctuated with un-ornamented windows which break into the line of the high, steeply pitched roof. A hint of a turret in the centre marks one corner of the oldest section, but otherwise Traquair is refreshingly free of crenellations, castellations, machicolations, Gothic windows and all the other architectural paraphernalia without which no 18th-century stately home was considered complete. Yet, by its bulk and its bearing, and its romantic setting in the forest, it is every inch a castle. Visitors who flock to this Borders beauty spot will find that the fundamental honesty of Traquair is continued inside. With the exception, perhaps, of the library, there is little sign of lavish Georgian refurbishment or opulent Victorian High Gothic pastiche, and little to show in the way of unnecessary trinkets, for the family's fortune was spent in other, arguably more noble causes. To some Traquair is a monument to lost causes, the visible sign of a family that simply fought too often on the wrong side; to others, it is a quiet, living, breathing home, minding its own business and continuing much as it has done for hundreds of years.

MEDIEVAL TRAQUAIR

According to tradition – and tradition plays an important part at Traquair – the first building on this prime site, in a bend of the Tweed and the Quair burn, was probably a simple hut, used as a base for hunting in the surroundings of Ettrick Forest. This early reference dates the spot to about the year 950, but Traquair was first recognised as a royal hunting lodge in 1107 by King Alexander I of Scotland, who stayed here and granted its charter. Traquair remained a royal property until the 13th century and, though it was essentially little more than a fortified house, it was known at this time as Traquair Castle.

In 1491 the Earl of Buchan, an uncle of King James III of Scotland, purchased the house and estates of Traquair for the nominal sum of 70 Scots Merks (which translates as something under £4 – a tiny sum even for those times). The three-storey tower house which he bought, its outline still clearly visible, is today incorporated into one end of the main block of Traquair. The Earl of Buchan presented the estate to his son James Stuart, who became the 1st Laird of Traquair; he died on the battlefield of Flodden in 1513, fighting alongside King James IV. James Stuart was succeeded by his son, William, and by his grandson, Robert in 1540. Robert out-lived his father by only another eight years, and the property passed in turn to his brothers John, William and James.

MARY, QUEEN OF SCOTS

John Stuart, the 4th Laird, took on a prominent role in public life, becoming not only a close and loyal friend of Mary, Queen of Scots, but also captain of her bodyguard. Following the infamous murder of Mary's favourite, Rizzio, John Stuart planned her escape during the night from the scene of the crime at Holyrood Palace, and engineered her flight to Dunbar. (It is said that he also acted as a mediator when the traitors were finally exposed.) He received a knighthood at the time of the Queen's marriage to Lord Darnley.

In 1566 he welcomed the Queen, her husband and her baby son (the future James VI and I) to Traquair on a hunting expedition, and mementoes of this time may be found in the King's Room on the first floor of the old part of the house, including a magnificent quilt said to have been stitched by Mary and her ladies in waiting (the 'Four Maries' of the old song), and a splendidly carved crib. The four-poster bed in this room, with its golden canopy and drapes, was used by Mary, but on another occasion, when she visited Terregles House, the home of the Maxwells. Other relics relating to Mary, Queen of Scots, may be seen elsewhere in the house, including a simple rosary and crucifix, displayed in the Museum Room, and a carved panel of oak, showing the Royal Arms of Scotland, which was presented by the Queen to the 4th Laird and hangs in the entrance hallway. A copy of the warrant for her execution in 1587 is also shown nearby.

DANGEROUS TIMES

Despite his marriage to Janet Cox, Sir John left no children, and Traquair passed to the next brother, William Stuart, in 1591. William, the 5th Laird, also kept a high public profile, not only as Member of Parliament for Peeblesshire from 1593 to 1604, but as a Privy Councillor and Gentleman of the King's Bedchamber, and Commendator of Dryburgh. Like his brother, he was also to receive a knighthood, and from his initials on a window lintel, dated 1599, it is known that he was in a position to add to the home at that time. On his death, unmarried, in 1605, Traquair passed briefly to the youngest brother, James, a lieutenant in the King's Guard. Predeceased by his eldest son (he had nine children all told), the inheritance went in 1607 to his grandson John Stuart, who became the 7th Laird of Traquair and a key player in the complicated politics, both civil and religious, of his time.

History has been unable to make up its mind as to whether the 7th Laird was 'uniformly treacherous' in his conduct, or simply a man trying to hold his estates together in a dangerous and violent age, when supporting the wrong faction could mean the loss of every shred of livelihood. Born in 1600, John Stuart's rise to fortune was rapid; in 1633 he received the title 1st Earl of Traquair from Charles I, on a state visit to Scotland, and by 1636 had reached the peak of his political career when he was made Lord High Treasurer of Scotland – one of the most influential positions. His portrait, which hangs above the mantelpiece in the dining room, was probably painted around this time.

In 1639, however, John Stuart found himself forced into an awkward role as Royal Commissioner to the General Assembly which met in Edinburgh to support the Covenant, against the king. As the king's position weakened throughout the country, the 1st Earl refused to join the king's champion, Montrose, who was trying to raise an army, and while still claiming to be the king's man, he swore allegiance instead to Argyll, who was leading the Covenanters. In 1645 he wavered, sending his son, Lord Linton, to join Montrose, and reputedly using this as a chance to spy on the enemy. When Montrose sought refuge at Traquair after the disastrous battle of Philiphaugh, John Stuart pretended not to be home and refused to let him in – fortunately for Traquair, as it turned out, for the bloodthirsty Covenanter, General Leslie, was hot on his tail and would certainly have sacked the house.

Despite all this, on the direct influence of the king, the 1st Earl was readmitted to Parliament in 1646. In 1648, however, he and his son were captured at the Battle of Preston, where they had been defending Charles against the Parliamentarian army, and the next four years were spent as a prisoner in Warwick Castle. He died in poverty in 1659, but his legacy may be seen in more concrete terms at Traquair, where he added another floor to the house, and undertook improvements to the window casements.

A FAMILY TRUE TO THEIR FAITH

The 1st Earl's son, John Stuart, inherited a bitter legacy, and it was through his influence that the house became a great centre of Catholicism, in an age when anti-Catholic feeling ran high across the land. His first marriage to the Catholic daughter of the Marquis of Huntly resulted in temporary imprisonment and a staggering fine of £5,000. On her death a year later, apparently undeterred, he chose the devout Catholic Lady Anne Seton as his second wife. Her determination may be seen in the rather stern portrait which hangs in the King's Room, and it was probably around this time that the secret passageways, little back stairways and hidden cupboards were built in the house so that a priest could evade the frequent searches that took

A rosary and crucifix that belonged to Mary, Queen of Scots can be seen in the Museum Room.

Traquair is said to be the oldest inhabited house in Scotland. Its 'modern' wings date from 1680!

place. Despite the early death of her husband, Lady Anne successfully raised her children in the Catholic faith, against all the efforts of the Church authorities.

In due course, their second son, Charles, became the 4th Earl and 10th Laird of Traquair, but the times were hardly more peaceful. Shortly after his marriage in 1694 to Lady Mary Maxwell, daughter of the 4th Earl of Nithsdale, he was imprisoned in Edinburgh Castle under suspicion of Jacobite sympathies. The couple went on to have 17 children, including two sets of twins, and all of them survived. A touching list of their names and birthdays, hand-written by their mother, is among the family treasures displayed in the Museum Room. The Countess lived on to the great age of 87, dying in 1759.

CHANGES AT TRAQUAIR

Between 1695 and 1699, Charles turned his attentions to the house, remodelling and extending the two wings, under the supervision of the Edinburgh architect James Smith. The 10th Laird also drew up proposals to alter the outside of the house and bring it more into line with fashionable taste, but these were never carried out. He did succeed in laying out the formal gardens, including the pavilions at each end of the terrace which runs along the back of the house. These were to be the last major external changes at Traquair, as the family became more closely entwined in the doomed Jacobite cause. Charles was involved in the Jacobite rising of 1715, as part of a conspiratorial group known as The Braemar Hunting Party. On his death in 1741, his son Charles became 5th Earl and 11th Laird, and the house continued its role in the Jacobite conspiracies. This Charles Stuart left tangible signs of his influence on Traquair in the drawing room, where the old painted beams were covered over and the walls panelled in the simple, classical style he had admired so much in Italy. Embellishments were painted over the doorways in this room to symbolise the arts – drama, music, art and architecture. He also completed the distinctive decoration of the First Library in 1740 and his portrait by the Italian artist Annigoni may be seen in this room. Charles is the owner of Traquair who is supposed to have closed the famous Bear Gates for the last time, after a visit by Prince Charles Edward Stuart. After the final rebellion of 1745, the 5th Earl was imprisoned in the Tower of London for his Jacobite sympathies, and remained there for two years with his faithful wife, Theresa. The cost of living in relative comfort in the Tower was considerable, and ate further into the family's fortunes. When he died in 1764, childless, his brother inherited the title. Married to Christian Anstruther, whose lovely portrait by Jervis hangs in the dining room, he chose to spend much of his time in voluntary exile abroad, dying in Paris in 1779. His son became the 7th Earl and 13th Laird, but with very little money at his disposal he lived a quiet life, again mostly abroad.

The drawing room stretches across the full width of Traquair House, demonstrating how the original tower was gradually extended.

THE STEEKIT YETTS

Most old houses have their family stories and legends, and that of Traquair is one of the most famous. Visitors approaching the house from the Peebles direction pass by a pair of venerable old gates, somewhat overgrown and clearly unopened for many years. The old gates were erected around 1737-8 on the instruction of Charles, the 4th Earl and 10th Laird of Traquair, and old records reveal that they took several labourers and four gallons of ale to put up. The bear statues on each pillar, carrying the family motto 'Judge Nought', may have been added then or a few years later. The gateway would have served as the main entrance to Traquair, with a quarter-mile long avenue lined by tall trees, but the 'avenue', as it is still known, has been grassed over for centuries. The story goes that the gates were closed for the last time by the 5th Earl, as a gesture in support of Prince Charles Edward, or 'Bonnie Prince Charlie', after that would-be monarch had paid a visit to the house in 1745. In a fit of Jacobite fervour, the Earl ordered that they should not be re-opened until a Stuart king returned to the throne of Britain. A slightly less romantic, but hardly less poignant tale claims that they were closed much later, in 1796. According to this version, it was the 7th Earl who ordered the deed, devastated at the death of his wife Mary Ravenscroft (in Madrid), and he vowed they should not re-open until a new Countess came to Traquair. Whatever the case, the main drive down to the house today runs parallel with the old avenue.

The library has been restored to its 18th-century appearance and its collection of 3,000 books has remained almost intact since the library was first formed between 1700 and 1740.

THE ECCENTRIC 8TH EARL

Thus, in 1827, another Charles Stuart inherited the title as 8th Earl of Traquair. Charles was a shy man who developed some eccentric ways, but he took a keen interest in the house and its estates, encouraging the most modern farming practices. Some of the land had been sold off to pay his father's debts, and Charles was meticulous in the keeping of records, so that a clear picture of his careful stewardship may be drawn. Oddities to be found among his accounts include sums paid to the children of the village on the occasion of organised wasp-hunts.

Fascinated by many things, Charles had a particular interest in the sharpening of razors, and undertook this service free for his tenants; some of his own razors are displayed in the dressing room. His curiosity took him to the Great Exhibition in 1851, where he selected the rather heavy hand-blocked French wallpaper which adorns the dining room. A confirmed bachelor (it is said he placed stinging nettles in the beds of unwanted female suitors), he was succeeded by his sister.

SUBSEQUENT LAIRDS AND LADIES

Lady Louisa Stuart became 15th Lady of Traquair in 1861. She was also unmarried, and lived on alone in the house into her 100th year – her photograph may be seen in the Still Room. On her death in 1875 she left money for the building of Catholic churches in Peebles and Innerleithen, and Traquair passed to her cousin, Henry Constable Maxwell of Terregles, who took the additional surname of Stuart.

He was intrigued by gemstones from around the world and amassed a fine collection in a small room at the top of the house. Unfortunately the collection was sold off on his death by his sons, who had no idea of their real value. The 17th and 18th Lairds, Herbert and Arthur, were conservative bachelors, determined to change nothing in the house. Through their nephew it passed eventually to the care of Peter Constable Maxwell Stuart, who became the 20th Laird. He and his wife, Flora, were responsible for much of the careful restoration work at Traquair, as well as the study of the family's history, and this work is continued by their daughter Catherine, who was brought up in this lovely old house and became 21st Lady of Traquair in 1990.

Traquair's dining room, situated in the newest (late 17th century) part of the house, contains family portraits.

Thirlestane Castle

LAUDER

THE DRAMATIC, TURRETED SEAT OF THE MAITLAND FAMILY, BUILT AROUND A CENTRAL KEEP: OFF THE A68 IN LAUDER.

Below: Of all the wonderful plasterwork in the castle, the Large Drawing Room has the finest.

Bottom: With its towers and turrets, Thirlestane Castle was given an exceptionally romantic appearance by eminent architect, Sir William Bruce.

This fairy-tale castle has been the home of the Maitland family, Earls of Lauderdale, since the 13th century and the present owner, Captain the Hon. Gerald Maitland-Carew, and his family still live in one of the wings. The Maitlands came to Britain with William the Conqueror and headed north, settling in Northumberland until Sir Richard Maitland married a Thirlestane heiress in about 1250. Over the centuries the family became

powerful through their military and public service – One William Maitland was Secretary to Mary, Queen of Scots; his brother John was Lord Chancellor of Scotland in the mid 16th century and his grandson, also John, became one of the most important and controversial figures of 17th-century Scotland. Chief Scottish adviser and confidant of Charles II, he was made Secretary of State for Scotland at the Restoration and wielded unrivalled power and influence. On the occasion of his marriage to the Countess of Dysart, John Maitland was created Duke of Lauderdale and this prompted his remodelling of Thirlestane Castle into a suitably grand residence.

Sir William Bruce was the architect who created a splendid palace without destroying the character of the original castle. He also supervised the interior work, which included some magnificent plasterwork in the State Rooms. The Duke died in 1682, having been forced out of office by his opponents, and, having no male heir, his title died with him. His brother, Charles, became the 3rd Earl of Lauderdale.

When the present owner inherited the castle from his grandmother in 1972 a colossal amount of restoration work was required – the central tower was in danger of collapsing and dry rot had taken a hold in over 40 locations around the castle. With the help of grants and a preservation trust, an immense amount of work has been done to restore and preserve this splendid building. Visitors may well complete a tour of the castle with a crick in their neck from gazing up at all the wonderful ceilings – the richest of all is in the Large Drawing Room, but in every room it is worth looking upwards. Fine 19th-century French Empire-style furniture, vast gilded mirrors and one of the most comprehensive collections of family portraits in Scotland adorn the State Rooms. The charming nurseries house a delightful collection of historic toys, with some modern replicas, too, for visiting children to try, as well as a dressing-up chest. The kitchen, sculleries and laundries show another side of life at Thirlestane, and there is a Country Life Exhibition in the basement.

Drumlanrig Castle

THORNHILL

A CASTLE OF OUTSTANDING ARCHITECTURAL ELEGANCE, A PINK SANDSTONE MASTERPIECE SURROUNDED BY THE ROLLING HILLS AND WOODLAND OF THE QUEENSBERRY ESTATE: EIGHT MILES NORTH OF DUMFRIES ON THE A76.

Drumlanrig was a Douglas stronghold as far back as the 14th century and Sir James Douglas was Robert Bruce, King of Scotland's right-hand man. Indeed, the family crest of a winged heart surmounted by Bruce's crown, which appears in various forms throughout the house, stems from that alliance.

The present palatial structure was built around the

original castle by William Douglas, 1st Duke of Queensberry. It was finally completed in 1691, more than ten years after it was begun. An impressive horseshoe staircase and colonnaded archway lead up to the castle entrance and promise greater delights to come. The visitor is not disappointed, for this truly is a treasure trove of massive proportions. Masterpieces such as Leonardo da Vinci's *Madonna with the Yarnwinder*, Hans Holbein the Younger's *Sir Nicholas Carew* and Rembrandt's *Old Woman Reading*, which adorn the Staircase Hall, seem to have found a home of complementary stature.

The Front Hall used to open onto the inner courtyard but its archways were glazed in with the family crest, and portraits include those of James, Duke of Monmouth, eldest natural son of Charles II, and Ahmed ben Ahmed, Qadr an Nasir, Moroccan Ambassador 1706-7. There is also a rare Italian statuette, a French longcase clock and a section of tapestry needlework attributed to Mary, Queen of Scots (who is, incidentally, distantly related to the Douglases). A fine quality carpet embellished with the family crest was made in Ayrshire in 1985, proving that a high standard of craftsmanship can still be found.

A portrait of particular note hangs in the Morning Room. It is a modern painting of Jane, the present Duchess of Buccleuch, done in 1957 when she was the Countess of Dalkeith. The artist was John Merton and it is the only painting this century to have received a Royal Academy 'A' award.

A tour of the castle reveals room after room of priceless works of art, from the exquisite Grinling Gibbons carvings and Meissen Monkey Band in the drawing room to the Dutch and Flemish paintings to be seen in the Boudoir. From the early Douglases to the present-day guardians of the estate, the family motto of 'Forward' has true meaning. Rural land management and woodland conservation combined with a shrewd business sense will ensure that the stately Drumlanrig Castle and all its treasures can be enjoyed for many generations to come.

THE REFUGE OF THE BONNIE PRINCE

Drumlanrig Castle has played host to many celebrity guests throughout its history, from Mary, Queen of Scots to the first moon-walking astronaut, Neil Armstrong. No-one's visit has been more commemorated, however, than that of Prince Charles Edward Stuart, Bonnie Prince Charlie. The bedroom that he occupied on his retreat northwards on December 22nd, 1745, has been dedicated to his memory. A pastel of the Prince and an oil painting of his father hang either side of one window and several personal items, including his money box, rings, some miniatures and a camp kettle, are on display.

Standing four square on top of its hill, Drumlanrig Castle is one of the first and most important Renaissance buildings in Scottish domestic architecture.

Rammerscales

LOCKERBIE

A FINE PINK-STONED 18TH-CENTURY MANSION: FIVE MILES WEST OF LOCKERBIE ON THE A74.

This fine Georgian manor house was built in 1760 for one Dr James Mounsey. He was a local physician and a Privy Councillor at the Court of Empress Elizabeth of Russia. It was designed in the classical Palladian style, variations of which were appearing all around Britain during the Georgian era, from the city villa in Chiswick to the great country mansion. Largely unaltered during its 200-year existence, Rammerscales is an excellent example of the period. It is located high on the side of the Tinwald Hills overlooking Annandale. Since the end of the 18th-century the house has been under the ownership of the Bell Macdonald Family.

A focal point of the elegant interior is a long pillared hallway, leading to a stunning circular staircase. The kitchen quarters have been adapted to accord with modern conditions, but otherwise the interior remains as it was in Dr Mounsey's day. Elegant public rooms can be seen on the first floor and, on the top floor, the entire south side is taken up with the library. This comprises mostly of works collected by William Bell Macdonald of Rammerscales, surgeon, scholar, linguist and man of letters, who lived here during the middle years of the 19th century. Historical interest is provided by some relics of the Jacobite movement, including evidence of links with Flora Macdonald, who helped Bonnie Prince Charlie escape the Highlands in 1745. On a more modern theme, the house also boasts a fine collection of paintings, tapestries and sculpture by 20th-century artists.

■ I am particularly proud of the collection of family portraits at Arniston, representing members of each generation from the time of the acquisition in 1551 to the present day. The Arniston Memoirs tell much of their personalities. ■

Mr and Mrs Dundas-Bekker

Arniston House

GOREBRIDGE

A FINE PALLADIAN MANSION: ABOUT SEVEN MILES SOUTH-EAST OF EDINBURGH (VIA THE A7) ON THE B6372 NEAR GOREBRIDGE.

Arniston House is the family seat of the Dundas family, who first became established in the area in the 12th century, though the first house on this site was built in the early part of the 17th century. It was in the latter part of that century that the family came to prominence, when successive members of the family were appointed to the Scottish Bench. In the 18th century Robert Dundas went on to preside over the Court of Session, Scotland's supreme civil law court, and it was he who commissioned Adam to design a Palladian family seat which would be worthy of their status. Robert's son, Henry, ascended to the peerage as 1st Viscount Melville and there is a statue of him in St Andrew Square in Edinburgh.

The house contains a wealth of family portraits, from the 16th century onwards, including works by Ramsay and Raeburn, and the faces which look down from the walls contrive to be striking without any trace of aggression – a quality which is by no means universal in Scottish family portraits. John and William Adam's splendid mansion incorporates some of the original house, notably the panelled Oak Room, but fireplaces and decorative features were added. Other rooms, including the drawing room, dining room and library, have notable plasterwork and intricate friezes characteristic of the Adams' work, while the kitchen still has its Victorian food lift.

This is a house which has been continuously inhabited and cherished by members of the same family. The current owners, the Dundas-Bekkers, have devoted a great deal of time and energy into attacking an outbreak of dry rot and are engaged in an ongoing programme of restoration work. This does mean that some parts of the house are closed off from time to time, while the work is carried out, but there remains plenty to see.

Outside, the grounds have developed over the centuries too, from formal layouts to the more natural landscapes in the style of 'Capability' Brown. There is also an orangery.

Biel

DUNBAR

A 12TH-CENTURY TOWER HOUSE WITH 18TH-CENTURY ADDITIONS: FOUR MILES WEST OF DUNBAR, OFF THE B6370 NEAR STENTON.

This sturdy mansion, on high ground on the edge of the Lammermuir Hills, is, like many a Scottish mansion, based on a medieval tower house. Its battlements, however, date from towards the end of the 18th century. A further transformation of the building took place in the early part of the 19th century, when it was hugely extended in Gothic style by William Atkinson.

Much of Atkinson's work was later demolished, restoring Biel to something more akin to its original size, but some features remain, including the entrance porch, which was moved to its present site in 1952.

Owners of this interesting house have included the 1st Lord Belhaven, in 1647 and Admiral Brook in 1951, but since 1959 it has been under the proud ownership of the Mr Charles G Spence. The house stands in a fine terraced garden with many lovely shrubs and trees, and a stream running through. Nearby is 'The Cardinal's Hat', an ancient well which gets its name from the conical roof. By tradition the owner of Biel is responsible for keeping the roof in a good state of repair.

Biel, which has an early tower house embedded in its eastern end, stands on three south-facing terraces leading down to a lawn which is flanked by the Biel Burn.

Dalmeny House

SOUTH QUEENSFERRY

A TUDOR GOTHIC HOUSE WITH A RARE SET OF TAPESTRIES AND EXQUISITE 18TH-CENTURY FURNITURE: THREE MILES EAST OF SOUTH QUEENSFERRY, AND ABOUT FOUR MILES WEST OF EDINBURGH, OFF THE A90.

Any family who can trace their origins back into the depths of history will usually have a black sheep somewhere along the line, and the Rosebery's are no exception. James the 2nd Earl was imprisoned for riot and debt; he left his wife for a laundry maid and when she left him, he advertised for her to be returned as she had taken some of his linen – a two guinea reward was offered, 'and no questions asked'! The 3rd Earl did much to restore both the family name and its fortunes, and he freed the estate of debt, organised the farming and planted many trees.

Archibald John, Lord Dalmeny, was son of the 4th Earl, but predeceased his father and so never inherited the title. He married Catherine, daughter of the Earl of Stanhope and he and his wife were very much involved in the political and social life of the day. She had been a bridesmaid to Queen Victoria, and the queen visited Dalmeny and praised the view and the comfort she enjoyed here.

The 5th Earl came into his title at the early age of twenty. A brilliant scholar and distinguished historian, he collected paintings and objects relating to people he considered to be of historic interest, and wrote biographies of Peel, Pitt and Napoleon. He also amassed an extensive collection of books, part of which can be seen in the library.

THE BUILDING OF DALMENY

The original building, Barnbougle, was a 13th-century castle, built on the sea shore by the Mowbray Family. In 1662 Sir Archibald Primrose, father of the 1st Earl of Rosebery, bought the Dalmeny Estate and lived in Barnbougle Castle, but by the end of the 18th century the castle was in a bad state of repair. The Earl refused to make improvements, for he considered that it was good enough for them to live in. His son, the 4th Earl, did not agree, and decided to build another dwelling which he named Dalmeny House.

In 1814 two architects – William Wilkins and Jeffrey Wyatt – were commissioned to submit plans for the house. He preferred Wyatt's Tudor Gothic design to Wilkin's neo-classicial Greek style, but he obviously felt some loyalty to Wilkins because they had been at Cambridge together. He asked him to submit another design in the Tudor Gothic style, accepted it and Dalmeny House was born.

Not only did Wilkins design the house, he also designed some of the furniture, including sofas, stools and chairs. Twenty-nine sets of chimneys, numerous battlements, embrasures and turret shafts, at the then quite substantial cost of almost £5,000, were shipped from London. It is thought that Dalmeny was the inspiration for many 19th-century Scottish houses, by architects such as William Burn and David Bruce.

DALMENY'S TREASURES

The entrance hall has a stunning hammer-beam ceiling and a rare set of tapestries designed by Goya for Spanish royal palaces – only two sets exist outside Spain, and the Queen has the other. Several family portraits adorn the walls and there are two marble busts by Ernst Boehm, one of Lord Rosebery and the other of Gladstone, who stayed at Dalmeny House during the Midlothian Campaign.

Part of a famous collection of French furniture collected by Baron Mayer Rothschild is in the drawing room, brought into the family by Rothschild's only child, Hannah, who married the 5th Earl. Beauvais tapestries, designed in 1740 by Francois Boucher in Chinoiserie style, depict European fantasies of what life in China was like. A number of Sèvres pieces can also be seen, as well as busts of Louis XVI and Marie Antoinette.

Lord Rosebery's Sitting Room has been kept as it would have looked in the 6th Earl's lifetime. Around the room are paintings of racehorses and a display of the Rosebery rose and primrose racing colours. The link with racing goes back over 100 years when Baron Mayer founded a stud at Mentmore.

MEMORIES OF NAPOLEON

The 5th Earl wrote a biography of Napolean, and he built up an impressive and fascinating collection of furniture, paintings, and other items relating to the emperor. These are now displayed in the Napoleon Room. Also in this room, perhaps to balance the collection, is the red leather chair in which the Duke of Wellington planned the campaigns that were to lead eventually to Napoleon's defeat

Top: The drawing room

Above: Dalmeny was the inspiration for many later Scottish houses.

A porcelain dog which once belonged to Marie Antoinette.

Gosford House

Longniddry

A Neo-classical house by Robert Adam, set in lovely wooded parkland with a lake: north-east of Longniddry on the A198 Aberlady road.

This fine 3rd-century Roman statue is among the collections at Gosford House.

Damaged, repaired, rebuilt and surviving against all the odds as a delightful family home, the history of Gosford House has been a chequered one. In its early days the house could by no means have been described as a resounding success. It was built for the 7th Earl of Wemyss in the 1790s to a design by Robert Adam, and it is said that the site was chosen mainly for its proximity to good golf courses, rather than for its attractiveness. The Duke of Rutland described its situation as 'objectionable in the highest degree: a barren rabbit warren on a sandy shore stretching on all sides, and the country around being totally destitute of wood or fertilisation.' If the Duke noticed at all that planting had already begun, he certainly did not possess the vision to foresee the pleasing effect that its maturity would bring.

It was not only the situation that met with no favour. Lady Louisa Stuart considered that from a distance the house had the appearance of three great ovens and that the plan was 'absurd', though she did concede that the front was very pretty. It was not the criticism which prevented the 7th Earl from ever taking up residence at Gosford House, but the fact that he found it damp. The 8th Earl did not like the house either, pulling down the wings at each end and using the central block simply to house the family pictures, while he continued to live elsewhere. His successor was all set to demolish the whole building, but was dissuaded by his son, who became the 10th Earl in 1883.

Imposing Gosford House has a fine situation above Gosford Bay on the Firth of Forth.

Below: The exquisite Marble Hall demonstrates the 10th Earl's fascination with all things Italian.

A Shrewd Collector

The 10th Earl had a particular interest in the Italian Renaissance and built up a splendid collection of paintings, frequently at bargain prices – his first purchase was a Carlo Dolci from a London pawnbroker, and he later bought two beautiful paintings from a café proprietor in Italy. He made all his own purchases, disapproving of any collector who 'bought through other men's eyes and paid through his own nose'.

The 10th Earl restored the missing wings of the house and in 1890, 90 years after its completion, Gosford House at last became a family home. After the death of the 10th Earl in 1914, the house was used only infrequently and was requisitioned by the army during World War II. Part of the central block was gutted by fire in 1940 and extensive dry rot was discovered in the north wing in 1948.

Gosford House became a family home again in 1951, when the 12th Earl and his family took up residence in the south wing and began the transformation which has made this unfortunate edifice such a delightful home today. The Italianate influence of the 10th Earl is still very apparent, particularly in the remarkable three-storey Marble Hall, with its magnificent double staircase, central dome and splendid plasterwork.

Hopetoun House

South Queensferry

An elegant 18th-century mansion set amid landscaped parkland overlooking the Firth of Forth: one and a half miles west of South Queensferry.

Hopetoun House is an amalgamation in style of two eminent Scottish architects. It was originally designed by Sir William Bruce for Charles Hope, 1st Earl of Hopetoun, and completed in 1707. Then, in 1721, the architect William Adam was commissioned to enlarge the house. Work was continued after his death in 1748 by his sons, and the interior decoration was completed around 1767. Much of that original decoration in the main apartments still survives to this day. The two individual styles of architecture, both clearly discernible, are linked by the imposing entrance hall which was redesigned in order to harmonise with Adam's alterations.

Pride of place, above the white marble fireplace in the entrance hall, is given to a massive portrait of the 7th Earl of Hopetoun, who became the first Governor-General of Australia and was created Marquess of Linlithgow. On the opposite wall is a portrait of his son, the 2nd Marquess, who was Britain's longest serving Viceroy of India (1936-43). Both are wearing the robes of Knight of the Thistle. They are great-grandfather and grandfather of the present Lord Linlithgow, the 4th Marquess. The Hope family is descended from one John Hope, a Burgess of Edinburgh, who died in 1561.

The Yellow Drawing Room at Hopetoun House, lined with silk damask, displays craftsmanship of exceptional quality. Doors, window frames and chair rails are by the estate joiner; the stucco ceiling by the plasterer.

THE STATE ROOMS

Entered from the hall, the State Rooms were designed by William Adam and were decorated under the supervision of his son John. The yellow silk damask on the walls in the Yellow Drawing Room is repeated on the sumptuous sofas, and the walls are lined with fine paintings and glittering gilt mirrors. There are a large number of interesting paintings adorning the walls of the Red Drawing Room, while an array of fine family portraits by such artists as Sir Henry Raeburn, Allan Ramsay and Gainsborough grace the walls of The State Dining Room.

The chief decorative feature of the William Bruce part of the house is the front stairs. Here wood panelling with elaborate carving is enhanced by some decorative murals painted more recently in 1967 by Scottish artist William McLaren. These paintings were commissioned by the 3rd Marquess to commemorate his wife, who had died four years earlier, and a delightful cameo of that Lady Linlithgow is included in the first panel.

Elsewhere in the house there is a Family Museum which illustrates the fascinating history of the Hope family. A roof-top viewing gallery offers vistors a stunning view of the Firth of Forth and its famous road and rail bridges, indicator boards list other places and objects of interest. Various permanent exhibitions can be seen at Hopetoun: The Building of Hopetoun; Wildlife (in the stable's courtyard) and Horse and Man in Lowland Scotland (in the tack room).

Stevenson House

HADDINGTON

A DELIGHTFUL 16TH-CENTURY HOUSE, WHICH WAS RESCUED FROM NEAR TERMINAL NEGLECT IN THE NICK OF TIME: ONE AND A HALF MILES FROM HADDINGTON OFF THE A1.

The story of Stevenson House really begins in 1624 when it was bought by one John Sinclair, a laird's son who had made his fortune in commerce. In 1636 he became a baronet and from that time onwards he and his descendants continued to make alterations and improvements to their beautiful home – that is, until the early part of the present century when the 9th Baronet died without leaving an heir. When his widow also died, in 1931, Stevenson House was bought by William Brown Dunlop, but he never took up residence here. The property remained empty until it was commandeered during World War II to house Allied troops who, it has to be said, were not the most house-proud of guests.

When William died in 1946 his son inherited a house in a disastrous state. More than 300 windows were broken, including a skylight through which the rain, hail and snow could enter unhindered. Dry rot was as rife as the damp, and the garden was a jungle.

The Brown Dunlop Country Houses Trust was formed to save the house from ruin, but decay and the lack of electricity were not their only problems. The arrangement of some of the rooms was a real puzzle: the dining room was on the first floor of the south wing, while the kitchen was on the ground floor of the laundry wing. And it was quite clear that 1858 (the year the house had last been decorated) had not been a particularly good year for wallpaper!

Now, with all these problems solved, the structure is sound, the architecture is more practical and the décor is pleasing to the eye. The gardens, which took longer to tame than the house, are also delightful. In spite of fanciful stories of a spirit presence, the instant impression of Stevenson House is one of peace and goodwill; the lasting image is of a beautiful home which was nearly lost for all time.

Blairquhan

MAYBOLE

A HANDSOME TURRETED MANSION IN MAGNIFICENT LANDSCAPED PARKLAND, WITH A THREE-MILE RIVERSIDE APPROACH AND AN ELEGANT AVENUE OF LIMES: HALF A MILE SOUTH OF KIRKMICHAEL OFF THE B7045.

■ I think I and, I hope, our visitors appreciate and enjoy Blairquhan most because the building, its contents and its surroundings remain virtually as they were when the project was completed 170 years ago. ■
James Hunter Blair

The original tower house at Blairquhan was built for the McWhirters in 1346, and the present owners, the Hunter Blair family, are the fourth family to reside here. That house was sold to the Trustees of Sir David Hunter Blair, 3rd Baronet, in 1798, by which time it was becoming uninhabitable, so Sir David commissioned the Scottish architect William Burn to design a new house, which was completed in 1824. The walled gardens, laid out around 1800 by John Tweedie, have an unusual feature – in the main wall is a series of flues which allowed the wall to be heated in the winter to protect the fruit trees against frost.

The elegant entrance hall of this family home has a collection of landscape paintings by Scottish artists. Busts of Apollo, Napoleon, Wellington and Sir Walter Scott are displayed in the Saloon – a spacious room with a ceiling 60 feet high and 22 doors. A brass ventilator in the centre of the Saloon was originally used for heating, a fact much appreciated by Victorian ladies emerging from the chill of the dining room. The Small Drawing Room, once the Billiards Room, has walls which are lavishly lined with Thai silk, and a feature of the main drawing room is one common to all the great houses designed by William Burns – it overlooks a private garden. Books displayed in a black bookcase in this room are all school prizes.

In the dining room family portraits take pride of place, with a major work by David Allan of the 1st Baronet and his family displayed above the fireplace. The late Sir James Hunter Blair, the 7th Baronet, amassed an enviable collection of paintings by a group of artists known as the Scottish Colourists, now on view in the Picture Galleries on the ground floor.

A gruesome reminder of a bygone age is the Dool Tree near the kitchen courtyard, where wrongdoers, after a speedy trial by the laird, were hanged. Thankfully, this practice died out before the present house was built.

The picture gallery at Blairquhan contains an important collection of works by the Scottish Colourists.

Duart Castle

ISLE OF MULL

THE SEAT OF THE CLAN MACLEAN, SET HIGH ON A ROCKY PROMONTORY OVERLOOKING THE SOUND OF MULL: ABOUT THREE MILES SOUTH-EAST OF THE CRAIGNURE FERRY PORT FROM OBAN, OFF THE A849.

Duart would not be the fine castle it is today had it not been for the determination and foresight of Sir Fitzroy Maclean, 14th Baronet and great-grandfather of the present clan chief. Sir Fitzroy was only a boy when he saw the ruined Duart Castle for the first time and uttered the words, 'It is going to be my life's ambition to restore the castle as a family home and headquarters of the clan.' This he achieved, with the aid of Scottish architect Sir John Burnet, at the age of 76. Today, members of the Maclean Clan travel from all over the world to visit the ancestral home. Sir Fitzroy, a veteran of the Crimea, died a centenarian in 1936.

Earliest records suggest that the castle dates from the mid 13th century, since when the Clan Maclean have endured a colourful and sometimes bloody existence on Mull. The family history is peppered with fascinating tales and characters, such as 'Iain the Toothless Maclain of Lochbuie', who killed his own son and rival 'Eachuin of the Little Head'. Family feuds gave way to clan battles against the MacDonalds and the Campbells during the 17th and 18th centuries, when the Macleans lost Duart to enemy forces and the dilapidated castle was left to rot.

The castle today contains much memorabilia,

THE GENTLEMAN HIGHWAYMAN

One of Maclean's more infamous clansmen is one James Maclean (b.1724), 'The Gentleman Highwayman', whose story is told in a book on show at Duart. After squandering his fortune in 1748, James made a less than honourable attempt to amass another by means of highway robbery. This he did with great success. Maclean's nickname was acquired when, in 1749, he and an accomplice held up Horace Walpole in Hyde Park. His pistol went off accidentally, grazing the statesman's face, and the next day Walpole received a letter of apology from Maclean. His exploits were cut short, however, for in October 1750, he was hanged.

including some unusual horn snuffboxes and a horn container for wig powder dating from the early 18th century. The kitchen today is as it was in Sir Fitzroy Maclean's day and his new addition to the castle structure, The Sea Room, affords magnificent views of both the sea and the mountains. The Banqueting Hall, where the walls are nine feet thick in places, contains some family portraits and three regimental flags. The State Room is furnished as it was for the honeymoon of Lord Maclean and his bride (parents of the present clan chief) during World War II.

Finlaystone

Langbank

A delightful family mansion on the south bank of the River Clyde: about two and a half miles west of the end of the M8 (junction 31), on the A8 Greenock road.

The chief of the clan MacMillan is the current owner of this charming house and its popular Countryside Estate, but the story of Finlaystone begins far back in 1373. This was the date of the first recorded ownership – that of Sir John de Danyelstoun, whose niece was married to Robert II. Her son, Robert III was ancestor to a number of British sovereigns, justifying the family's boast that 'Kings come of us, not we of kings'.

Soon after the turn of the 14th century, the property passed by marriage to the Cunninghams, an old Ayrshire family, and in 1488 Alexander Cunningham was created 1st Earl of Glencairn, the first of 15 to hold that title. The 5th Earl, another Alexander, was known as the 'Good Earl', an outspoken supporter of the Reformation who was host to John Knox at Finlaystone. The most influential member of the family was William, the 9th Earl, a staunch supporter of the Stuart kings and a veritable thorn in the side of Cromwell's General Monk. After an inevitable period incarcerated in Edinburgh Castle during the Commonwealth, the Restoration came and Charles II made William Lord High Chancellor of Scotland.

James, the 14th Earl, was a friend of Robert Burns, who often visited Finlaystone – his name can be seen scratched into a window-pane as evidence of one particular visit – and the poet always maintained that it was the earl who had rescued him 'from wretchedness and from exile'. Burns named his son James Glencairn after the earl and wrote a lengthy lament for the earl when he died.

It was in this era that the house, already a noble building, was given its 18th-century façade. The square tower and kitchen wing date from the mid 19th century, when Finlaystone was sold to Sir David Carrick-Buchanan, Master of the Lanark and Renfrew Hunt. Just four years later he rented the house to George Jardine Kidston, who bought it after 15 years as a tenant and enlarged it further to house his nine children. Much of the interior was redesigned at this time and it is largely because of this work that the house has been listed. Finlaystone passed to Kidston's daughter Lilian, then to her daughter Marian, Lady MacMillan, who lives there today.

In addition to its fine furniture and paintings, Finlaystone houses a number of fascinating exhibitions – a collection of international dolls, Victorian flower books, other Victoriana and displays of Celtic art. A substantial part of the attraction to visitors here is the Country Estate, which includes formal gardens, walled gardens, woodland walks and adventure playgrounds, all set amidst the considerable natural beauty of this south Clyde area.

Left: Duart Castle was restored, not just as a family home, but also as the headquarters of the Clan Maclean.

Above: This charming oriental doll is among the international collection at Finlaystone.

Left: The drawing room at Finlaystone.

Below: Finlaystone House is at the heart of a splendid country estate, with formal gardens, walled gardens and areas of woodland, all in a beautiful natural setting overlooking the Clyde.

Inveraray Castle

INVERARAY

THE SLATEY BLUE-GREY CENTRAL TOWER AND CORNER TURRETS OF THE CASTLE, HOME OF THE CAMPBELL DUKES OF ARGYLL, MAY BE GLIMPSED THROUGH THE TREES FROM THE SHORE ROAD BELOW: A QUARTER OF A MILE NORTH OF INVERARAY.

The history of Clan Campbell dates back to 1266 and beyond, and could fill volumes, but the senior branch of the family, Earls of Argyll, moved into a fortified tower with a small settlement nearby, at the mouth of the River Aray, in the 15th century.

The dukedom was conferred on the 10th Earl by a grateful William of Orange in 1701; by 1720 the 2nd Duke, a great Hanoverian soldier, was thinking of remodelling the castle to designs by Sir John Vanbrugh, but it was his brother Archibald, succeeding him in 1743, who threw himself wholeheartedly into the task.

THE BUILDING OF THE CASTLE

Most of what can be seen at Inveraray today was planned by the 3rd Duke, including the township, the castle and the beautiful surrounding parkland. The years of unrest around 1745 were not the ideal time to be planning on such a scale in the Highlands, and a further problem was posed by the remoteness of this spot on Loch Fyne, some 40 miles by land or sea from the nearest road. Nevertheless, the foundation stone of the castle was laid in 1746, just yards away from the old tower (which was not demolished until 1773). The basic square structure, including the central tower, was completed by 1758, to a design by Roger Morris. One of the most appealing features of the estate was also built at this time: the watchtower high on Duniquaich was constructed in 1748, for the grand sum of £46.

Unfortunately the 3rd Duke did not live long enough to inhabit his new castle, although he visited it regularly, and his cousin, the 4th Duke, John Campbell of Mamore, was more interested in soldiery than building work. However, in 1770 his son John, who had fought as a colonel with the Argyllshire Militia at Culloden, became the 5th Duke, and took up the challenge. The inside of the castle, largely designed by Robert Mylne and in fine contrast to the rather severe exterior, was finally completed around 1788. Hardly changed today despite two serious fires, it is one of the chief delights of this enchanting castle.

With all the look of a sturdy fortress, Inveraray Castle is, in fact, a splendid 18th-century mansion which has seen neither siege nor skirmish.

THE INTERIOR

There is a great sense of space and light in the State Dining Room, which was created from one end of the Long Gallery when a modest entrance hall was built in the middle in 1772. The elaborate wall paintings of flower garlands and fruit, with little animals, faces, peacock feathers and anything else that took the artist's fancy, are encased in finely gilded panels. With the central friezes, it is very much in the French style made popular by the young Prince of Wales at Carlton House, yet it is the only work to survive of the two French artists Girard and Guinard. The quality of the painting here and in the drawing room is unique and exquisite, enhanced by the pretty French tapestry work on the gilded furniture.

The Tapestry Drawing Room, at the opposite side of the entrance hall, is hung with beautiful Beauvais tapestries, commissioned by the 5th Duke, with further painting on a delicate ceiling by Robert Adam. Appropriately to the floral theme of this décor, the room is dominated by a lovely portrait by Hoppner of the 5th Duke's daughter, Lady Charlotte, as 'Flora'.

THE VICTORIAN ERA

Modification of the exterior of the castle was undertaken by the 8th Duke, a prominent Liberal statesman. He considered elaborate plans by Anthony Salvin to turn the castle into a Victorian Gothic extravaganza, but settled in the end for simply adding conical roofs to the corner turrets, and a higher roof with gabled dormers, added in 1877–8. If the 8th Duke added style, his son and heir, the Marquis of Lorne, later Governor-General of Canada, added a royal touch through his marriage in 1871 to Queen Victoria's fourth daughter, Princess Louise. Sadly, there were no children, but the line passed through a nephew to the current (12th) Duke, who is, among his other titles, 26th MacCailen Mór, or Chief of the Clan of Campbell.

Kelburn Castle

Fairlie

An appealing mixture of styles distinguishes this castle, seat of the Earls of Glasgow: between Fairlie and Largs on the A78.

Kelburn is thought to be the oldest castle in Scotland to have been continually inhabited by the same family – and it is easy to understand their reluctance to leave. The situation overlooking the Clyde towards Cumbrae and Arran, and the beautiful glen with its waterfalls, would have been equally attractive when the first of the Boyle family settled here in 1140, though in those days it is more likely to have been selected as a strategic site for defending the western approaches.

Successive generations of the family combined their devotion to Kelburn with distinguished public service, and in 1699 David Boyle was elevated to the peerage as Lord Boyle. Becoming Earl of Glasgow just four years later, he was largely instrumental in pushing the Act of Union through the reluctant Scottish Parliament. The 7th Earl was Governor of New Zealand in the late 19th century and a museum in the grounds displays his antipodean collections.

Naturally, the castle has developed over the centuries, but the Norman keep remains at its heart. A William-and-Mary style mansion was built on in 1700 and a Victorian wing was added in 1879, but neither of these additions detract in the slightest from the original. Instead they comprise a delightful grouping which illustrates at one glance the long history which Kelburn has enjoyed.

Within the grounds a group of 18th-century farm buildings, neatly converted to resemble a village square, house craft workshops and exhibitions.

Kelburn Castle is at the heart of an historic estate that is still very much alive and working.

GENEROUS TO A FAULT

The Kelburn estate was almost lost in the 19th century, owing to the generosity of the 6th Earl. He built and endowed churches all over Scotland until he not only ran out of money, but ran up debts of £1million. His cousin and successor fortunately came to the rescue by selling his own lands to buy back Kelburn, but the rest of the family's considerable holdings were lost.

Sorn Castle

Mauchline

A 15th-century stronghold, extended in the late 18th and early 19th centuries, which once played host to James VI: three miles east of Mauchline on the B743.

The date 1409, carved into a stone in the castle wall, announces the ancient origins of Sorn Castle, set on a sandstone cliff right above the River Ayr. Its battlements, corbelling and crow-stepped gables distinguish the exterior, while inside can be found fine old oak ceilings which also bear witness to its great age. And yet, it is mostly the later additions of the 1790s and early years of the 1800s which characterise the castle today.

The earliest recorded owners of the Sorn estate were the Keiths, and from them the castle and land subsequently passed by marriage to the Hamiltons. During the reign of James VI, Sorn came into the ownership, again by the marriage of a Sorn heiress, of the Setons, Earls of Winton. The 1st Earl was a friend of James VI and the monarch honoured him by visiting Sorn for the wedding of his daughter, Isobel.

The 2nd Earl sold Sorn to the Loudoun family and they remained in residence from 1630 to 1728. The most illustrious member of that family was the formidable Countess of Loudoun, a tremendously energetic lady who involved herself most rigorously in the affairs of the estate and the village. Under her direction new roads were built, moorland was drained and many trees were planted, and much of the landscape we see today owes its beauty to her effective land management. Present-day visitors can enjoy lovely woodland walks in the grounds. The other great achievement of the redoubtable Countess was to attain the grand age of 100.

The Loudoun's sold Sorn in 1728 and there were a number of owners between that time and 1908, when the father of the present laird, T W McIntyre, bought it.

Torosay Castle

Isle of Mull

A 19th-century Scottish Baronial mansion in a magnificent setting on Duart Bay: one and a half miles south-east of the Craignure landing of the ferry from Oban.

■ I think what I most appreciate is how the house sits in the landscape – with formal terrace, a formal garden, parkland and in the distance the wild West Highland scenery. ■
Christopher James

Torosay Castle is no ancient seat of a clan chief, but a charming Victorian creation of modest proportions. It was designed by David Bryce in 1858, a grey stone mansion with the characteristic turrets of the Scottish Baronial style.

Inside, the house is Edwardian and the heavy oak staircase is overlooked by a remarkable collection of stags' heads and antlers. Around the house family portraits and other items reflect the 120 years of occupation by the Guthrie-James family, particularly in the library and archive rooms, which really capture the flavour of the era. And visitors are not only welcome, but actually encouraged to sift through the family history at their leisure. There is a fascinating collection of family scrapbooks from the turn of the century to browse through, as well as displays on travel in the Antarctic, sailing by windjammer and the story of a successful wartime escape by David Guthrie-James, the father of the present owner.

In April 1987, on his 30th birthday, Christopher James inherited the estate. As energetic and intrepid as his forebears most certainly were, he had spent the intervening years, between graduating from Edinburgh University (with a degree in agricultural economics) and taking up his inheritance, engaged in various projects overseas. Two years with the Voluntary Service Overseas in Indonesia were followed by three years on a rural development project in Uganda, before he returned to Indonesia to take up a post as consultant in a provincial development board. Now with his own 10,000-acre estate to manage, he shares the running of the house and gardens with his mother.

The house sits amidst 11 acres of delightful gardens which include a water garden, an avenue of Australian gum trees, a Japanese garden and many rare shrubs. An interesting feature is the Statue Walk, with 19 life-size figures by Antonio Bonazza.

The 19 life-size limestone figures along the Statue Walk were sculpted by Antonio Bonazza (1698-1763) and were brought to Torosay from a deserted villa in Padua in about 1900. The figures represent gamekeepers, gardeners, fishermen and women, all set off by a fuchsia hedge.

There are various ways of getting to Torosay Castle, including a special launch service from Oban which docks just a short walk from the castle. Foot passengers on the scheduled ferry from Oban to Craignure can complete the one and a half mile journey to the castle on a narrow-gauge railway which offers wonderful views along the way.

Balcaskie House

Pittenweem

An extended 16th-century tower house set in beautiful terraced gardens: a mile north-west of Pittenweem.

Before ever catching a first glimpse of the house, visitors to Balcaskie have a captivating view of the lovely gardens – showy formal terraces which were a real innovation for Scotland when they were first created in the mid 17th century. The property was bought in 1665 by the architect, Sir William Bruce, Surveyor-General of the Royal Works in Scotland, who is considered by many to have been the greatest of Scottish architects. It was he who brought Renaissance influences to bear on the Scottish Baronial style of architecture, and his commissions included the remodelling of Holyrood House, which is still the official royal residence in Edinburgh.

At Balcaskie he designed and laid out the gardens and extended the original tower house into the fine mansion we see today. The building of the house took six years, though the completion of the interior continued for several years more – William Bruce had a passion for perfection, and there is no denying that the result was impressive. In 1698 Balcaskie was bought by Sir Robert Anstruther and it is his descendant, Sir Ralph H Anstruther, who lives here today.

During the 19th century the Anstruthers employed W S Gilpin to add the impressive drive to the house from the west and to 'humanise' the edges of the plantations. The house was, by this time, also in need of some attention – Sir Walter Scott, who had a lifelong passion for great historic houses, once remarked that Balcaskie was 'much dilapidated', though he had nothing but praise for the restoration work which was then in progress.

Inside, the house is both spacious and elegant and is perhaps at its most spectacular in the dining room, with its beautiful frescoes and a splendid display of family portraits. The Gallery is a work of art in itself, while the library exudes an air of elegant relaxation which is conducive to quiet reading. Look out, too, for the family coat of arms, its three piles sable, representing the three nails on the Cross, symbolising the family's part in the Crusades.

Earlshall Castle

LEUCHARS

AN ELEGANT SCOTTISH MANSION BUILT IN TRADITIONAL STYLE AND SURROUNDED BY FINE FORMAL GARDENS AND PARKLAND: SIX MILES NORTH-WEST OF ST ANDREWS ON THE A919.

The private family home of the Baron and Baroness of Earlshall, Earslhall Castle has a long and fascinating history. It was built in 1546 by Sir William Bruce, ancestor of the present occupants, to a sturdy design with five-foot thick walls, musket loops and battlements. It was restored in the 19th century by renowned Scottish architect, Sir Robert Lorimer. His talents also extended beyond the castle walls to the gardens and the surrounding parkland, where his creation can be seen today. Fine lawns are bordered by sumptuous herbaceous borders and there are many delightful small gardens within the whole. There is a yew walk and a famous selection of topiary yews trimmed in the shape of chess pieces. Espalier fruit trees enclose the vegetable and soft fruits gardens; sweetly-smelling herbs abound in the herb garden and, for lovers of mystery, there is even a 'Secret Garden'. Beyond these formal gardens is a natural woodland walk. Two stone gateways in the garden bear prophetic inscriptions; the first says 'Here shall ye see no enemy but winter and rough weather', and the second 'Who loves a garden still keeps his Eden'.

Although Earlshall exudes the air of a warm and welcoming family home, that feeling of history, and the house and family's links with the past, has not been lost. The visitor to Earlshall may look at the actual bedchamber, complete with period furnishings, where Mary, Queen of Scots stayed during her visit in 1561. Indeed, it is said that the land surrounding Earlshall Castle was her favourite hunting ground. Jacobite relics, arms and armour, and some fine antique furniture, porcelain and paintings are on show throughout the castle.

One of the main attractions is the Long Gallery. Its unusual coved, painted ceiling depicts the coats of arms of the principal families of Scotland interspersed with paintings of fabulous and mythological creatures. On the walls, as a tribute to the feuds of a bygone age, there are more than one hundred Scottish broadswords. Also in this room, on a more gentle note, is the family crest: a romantic 'lynkit hearts' symbol incorporating the initials of Sir William Bruce (the great grandson of Earlshall's founder) and his wife. This motif can be seen on all the estate signs.

The weaponry theme of the Long Gallery is continued in the Rod and Gun Room which contains antique firearms, sporting guns and fishing tackle from yesteryear. Special exhibitions are also staged in this room. A set of bagpipes which were played at the Battle of Waterloo in 1815 is among the military trophies on show in the Museum Room, where there are also original letters written from Earlshall over 200 years ago.

THE RED SHOES

A long time ago there was a ball at the castle, to which a young girl was allowed to go, though she had to retire to bed before the ball was over. Drawn by her screams, other guests ran to find her sitting on a dark staircase, crying that her candle had been snuffed out and someone had stolen her red shoe. Despite an intensive search the shoe was not found. Many years later, when Robert Lorimer was restoring the castle for Mr McKenzie, his workmen removed some loose bricks at the foot of that staircase and found the little red shoe hidden behind the wall. A strange story, but even stranger is the fact that the daughter of the current owners, while occupying the same room as that little girl long ago, also lost a pair of red shoes which have still not been recovered.

Below: The intricately inlaid Augsburg casket on show at Earlshall Castle dates from 1710.

Bottom: Earlshall Castle looks down over a huge set of topiary chess pieces.

Blair Castle

Blair Atholl

■ I like to think that the castle recalls the traditions and the spirit of the Scottish Highlands and I am intent on ensuring that my ancestral home continues to survive as a major Scottish landmark. To see it visited and alive with people is as important to my hard-working staff as it is to me personally. ■
The 10th Duke of Atholl

Blair is everything a grand Scottish castle should be, with fairytale gables and turrets adorning a much older heart, and a history interwoven with stories of Jacobite heroes and Victorian eccentricity; 14 miles north-west of Pitlochry, off the A9 to Inverness.

The Murrays have lived at Blair Atholl since the earldom was conferred in 1629 on John Murray, Master of Tullibardine, but the history of the castle and the family dates back to David Strathbogie, the Crusader Earl of Atholl. In 1457 the earldom was conferred on the half-brother of James II of Scotland, Sir John Stewart of Balvenie, and since that time the names of Stewart and Murray have remained intertwined. It was Sir John who adopted the family motto – Furth Fortune and Fill the Fetters – taken from the instructions of King James III on the quelling of the rebellious Lord of the Isles, John Macdonald.

ROYAL CONNECTIONS

The 5th Earl of Atholl left a daughter, Lady Dorothea Stewart, and the title was held by her male cousins until her son, John Murray, Master of Tullibardine – with whom the story started – came of age. Through Lady Dorothea and the marriage of her sister-in-law to Patrick Lyon, later Lord Glamis, the Murrays of Atholl can claim a distant kinship with our present Queen.

The first John Murray was an ardent Royalist during the Civil War, and his death in 1642 left the Atholl estates vulnerable at a time of great turbulence in British history. Royalist support continued with his young son John, 1st Marquis of Atholl, and in 1644 Blair Castle witnessed a famous scene of crisis – and near disaster. Irish troops, freshly arrived under command of Alasdair Macdonald for a rendezvous with Royalist leaders, so alarmed the local Athollmen that a fight seemed inevitable. The situation was saved at the eleventh hour as the heroic Marquis of Montrose, the King's own lieutenant, stepped between the hostile armies, having walked 20 miles over the hills to keep his appointment. All quarrels forgotten, Athollmen and Ulstermen united behind a common leader.

Blair Castle soon became the target of Cromwell's army, who captured and held it from 1652. Despite hard-fought attempts by the 1st Marquis to regain his home, it was not returned to the Murrays until the Restoration in 1660.

Royalist skirmishes continued around Blair Atholl until the Battle of Killiekrankie in 1689, when the great soldier, John Graham of Claverhouse, 'Bonny Dundee', fought his last battle for the exiled James II. Fatally wounded, he was buried in the church at Old Blair and his helmet and breast-plate may be seen at the castle. Athollmen had been conspicuous at this local fight by their absence, for the 1st Marquis had shifted his alliance, thanks to his new wife, Lady Amelia Stanley, cousin to William of Orange. William's successor, Queen Anne, created John Murray, the 2nd Marquis, the first Duke of Atholl, in 1703.

Blair Castle sits splendidly amidst breathtaking scenery.

BLAIR AND THE JACOBITE CAUSE

When the Stuart cause revived in 1715, the Murrays found themselves a house divided. John, along with his second surviving son James, remained loyal to the monarchy, but John's first son William, Marquis of Tullibardine, sided with the Jacobites (thus forfeiting his claims to the Dukedom), and with his brothers Charles and George went into temporary exile.

Thus James Murray inherited the Atholl title on his father's death in 1724, and started on an ambitious scheme to create a new park and drastically 'improve' the castle. It is largely his work which we see inside the castle today, as he turned a simple fortified castle into one of the finest Georgian residences in the country.

James was hardly left in peace, however, for it was during this time that the family and the castle became caught up once more in the Jacobite revolt. In 1745 Prince Charles Edward Stuart landed at Glenfinnan,

A PRIVATE ARMY

In 1777 the 4th Duke responded to the call to arms in the American War of Independence, and raised a private regiment of soldiers from his estates. However, by the time the Atholl Highlanders were equipped and ready to fight, the war was over, and the regiment disbanded in 1783. When Victoria came to stay at Blair Castle in 1844, some 200 Athollmen formed a royal bodyguard. The young Queen was so enchanted by this gesture that she presented them with their colours in the following year, as the only private army in Britain. The Atholl Highlanders, still recruited largely from the estate, exist today as a ceremonial private bodyguard.

accompanied by the Marquis of Tullibardine, to reclaim the crown. He appointed James' brother, George, to be a lieutenant general of his army, and stayed for several days at Blair Castle on his triumphant journey south. As the Prince's fortunes changed, Hannoverian troops occupied the castle and Lord George brought his Atholl Brigade to lay siege to the family home (making it the last castle in the British Isles to be besieged).

RESHAPING THE LANDSCAPE

The 3rd Duke died in 1774, and his son John, the 4th Duke, retained the title for 56 peaceful years. His influence at Blair was considerable, and he earned the nickname 'the planting Duke' for his extensive afforestation of the estate.

The 4th Duke's youngest son, Lord Charles, had died of fever in Greece during the Greek War of Independence. His oldest son, John Murray, died unmarried, and ultimately the succession followed through a third son, James, whose son George Murray

Blair's entrance hall leaves visitors in no doubt that they are entering a very special place.

The 4th Duke of Atholl and his family, as portrayed in G David Allan's Conversation Piece.

Exceptionally fine carving lines the walls and ceiling of the Picture Staircase.

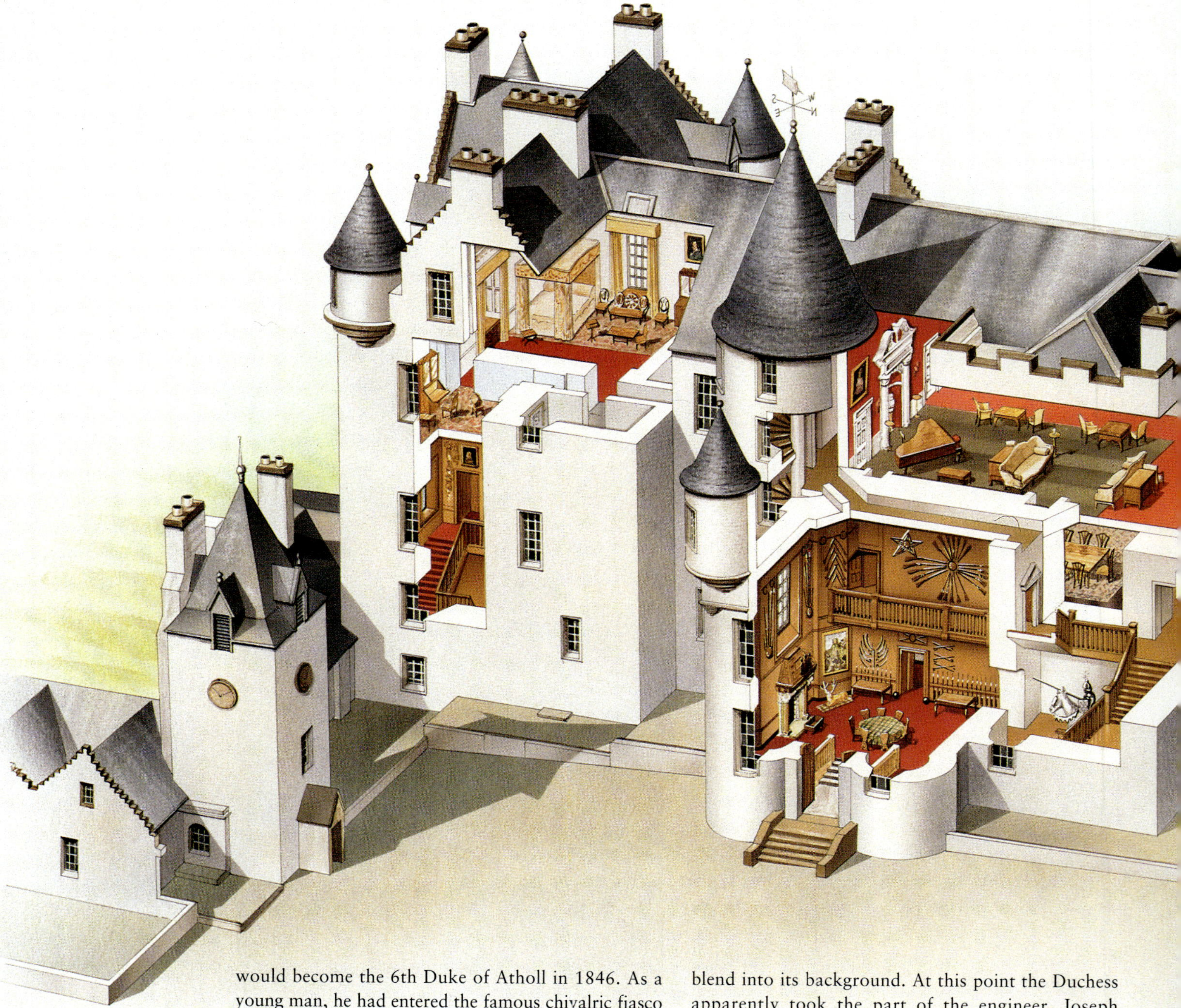

would become the 6th Duke of Atholl in 1846. As a young man, he had entered the famous chivalric fiasco of the Eglinton Tournament in 1839, as The Knight of the Gael – his specially made suit of full armour and his magnificent fancy-dress costume for the ball are both on display at the castle. The Costume Room also displays the Order of the Thistle awarded to the 6th Duke and his robes as a member of the Order of the Knights Templar.

It was during the 6th Duke's time that the railway reached Blair Atholl, and he took exception to it crossing the River Tilt just below his home. He reluctantly gave way, but demanded that the bridge should blend into its background. At this point the Duchess apparently took the part of the engineer, Joseph Mitchell, against her husband, and the elaborate lattice-work structure was built, as Mitchell himself agreed, 'somewhat more ornate than necessary'.

The 7th Duke inherited in 1864, taking the name Stewart-Murray, and he was largely responsible for turning what had become a Georgian mansion back into a romantic castle in the best Scottish tradition. He engaged the architects David and John Bryce, noted for their specialist skills in the 'Scottish baronial' style. Crow-stepped gables and blue-slate-roofed pepperpot towers were fully restored and Cumming's Tower was

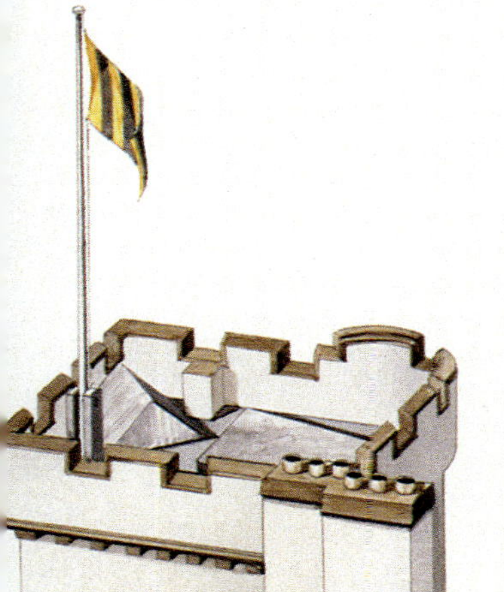

rebuilt to its original height. The entrance hall was added and the magnificent ballroom, popular still for Highland balls and grand dinners.

THE RED DUCHESS

The 8th Duchess was the formidable Katherine Marjorie Ramsay, an accomplished musician, who organised concerts for soldiers serving in both the Boer War and World War I. Despite her opposition to women's suffrage, she was elected Tory Member of Parliament for Kinross and Perthshire in 1923. Among her other achievements, notably in education, she promoted the first full English translation of *Mein Kampf*, in order to warn Britain of Hitler's real intentions. Becoming involved in the politics of the Spanish Civil War, she opposed the Munich Agreement and resigned her parliamentary seat. Defeated in the subsequent by-election and ridiculed as 'the Red Duchess', she spent much of the rest of her life assisting political refugees, until her death in 1960.

The 8th Duchess, fully supported by the Duke, was also largely responsible for opening the castle to the public in 1936, and in the first year a remarkable 32,500 visitors came to admire and enjoy the Atholl home and lands. It remains the most popular private castle visited in Scotland, for the 10th Duke, George Iain Murray, retains a keen involvement in all aspects of the castle and the estate.

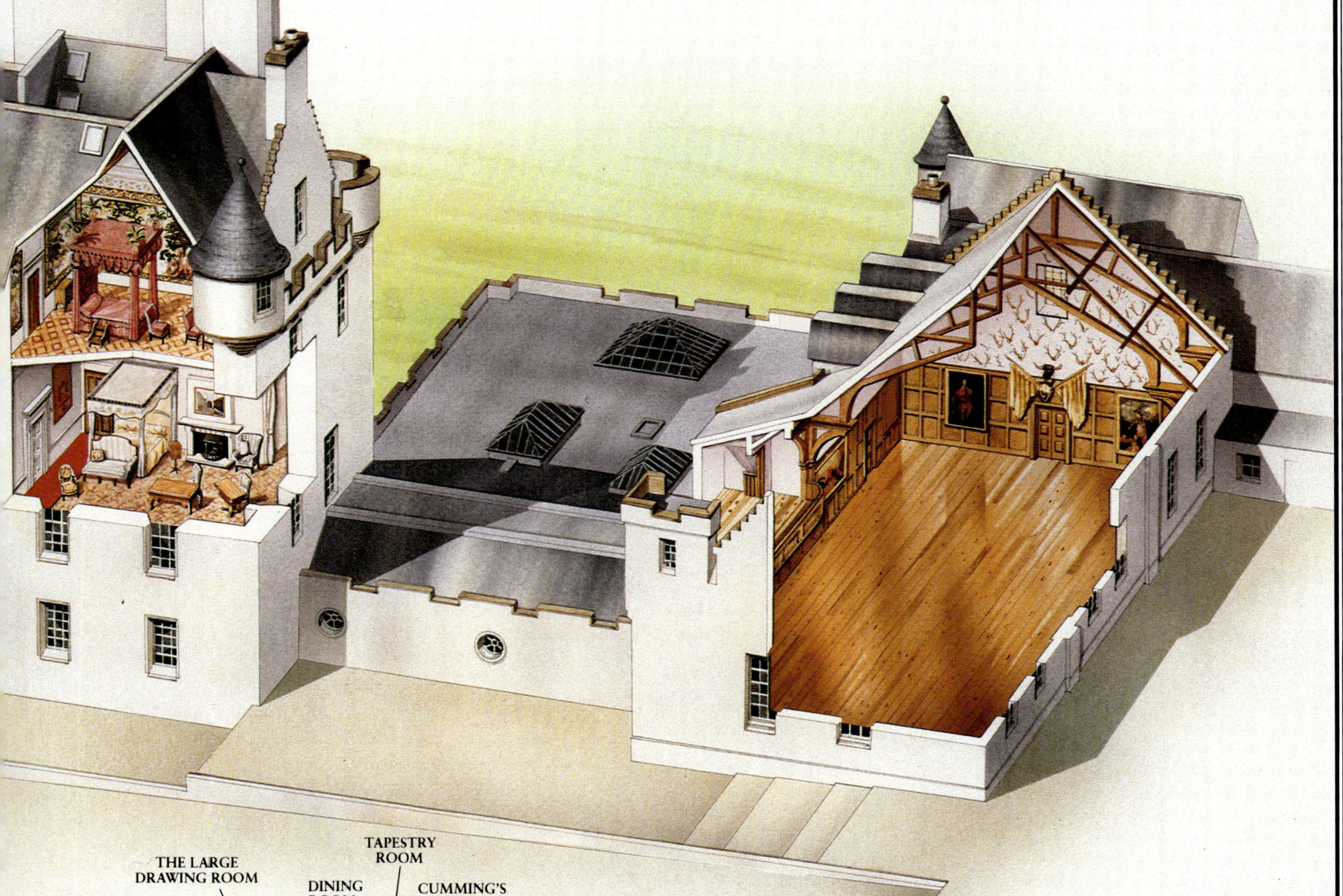

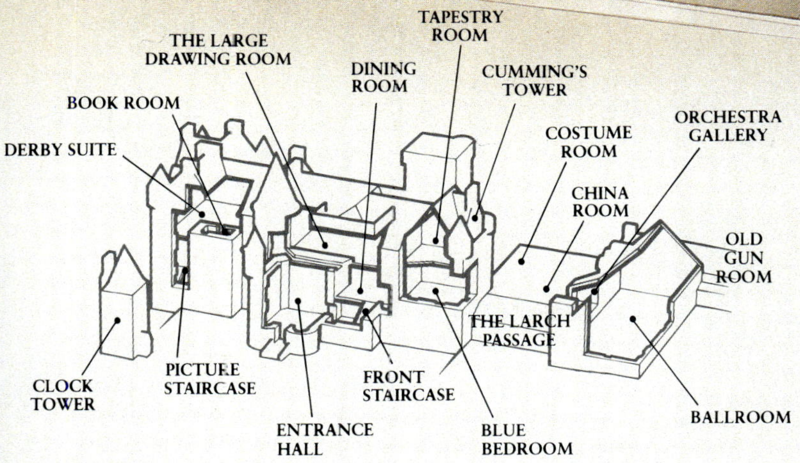

Glamis Castle

GLAMIS

A MAGNIFICENT AND MYSTERIOUS RED SANDSTONE CASTLE, IMMORTALISED IN LITERATURE BY WILLIAM SHAKESPEARE AND SIR WALTER SCOTT: 12 MILES WEST OF DUNDEE ON THE A94.

Early records of Glamis show that it was a holy place where, in the 8th century, St Fergus came from Ireland to preach and to live out his life. Today visitors can see St Fergus' Well near the kirk, and several Celtic stones found in the area date from this time. Later, Scottish royalty came to appreciate the lush Angus landscape and built a hunting lodge at Glamis for the King of Scots. Shakespeare's witches were rather previous in naming Macbeth 'Thane of Cawdor and of Glamis', as the actual thaneage (or lordship) was not granted to Glamis until 1264, a century after his death. The thaneage then became a feudal barony in 1376 when Sir John Lyon of Forteviot (Thane of Glamis) married King Robert II's daughter, Princess Joanna. And so began a line of feudal barons and later, earls which continues to flourish at Glamis to this day.

The silver nef in the dining room at Glamis bears the arms of the Strathmore family on its sails.

Below: Statues of Charles I and James VI and I, by Arnold Quellin, watch over the rugged and romantic outline of Glamis Castle.

THE LORDS OF GLAMIS

It was Sir John's son, the second Sir John Lyon, who began building the castle at the beginning of the 15th century. After his marriage, he built the east wing which now houses the Royal apartments. His son, Patrick Lyon, became Lord Glamis when he was granted a peerage in 1445. He was responsible for the addition of the Great Tower in 1484. There was also a fortified court surrounding the castle at this time.

Events at Glamis were tinged with tragedy during the life of John, the 6th Lord of Glamis. Unluckily for him, he married a Douglas, and from that time onwards he was subjected to a vendetta against him by King James V. He was eventually murdered and his beautiful wife was condemned to be burnt at the stake as a witch. The king also claimed Glamis Castle as his own and occupied it from 1537 to 1542.

Relations with the crown were improved in 1606 when the 9th Lord Glamis was created Earl of Kinghorn by James VI. Of his successor, the 2nd Earl, it is said that '... coming to his inheritance the wealthiest peer in Scotland, he left it the poorest'.

Unlike his father, however, Patrick, the 3rd Earl, was a great credit to the family. He repaid all debts and went on to restore and rebuild the castle to the fine specimen that stands today. Patrick obtained a new charter to his peerage in 1677 and henceforth the title became The Earl of Strathmore and Kinghorne. An interesting relic of this period is a motley (costume) belonging to the 3rd Earl's jester. It is on show in the Family Exhibition Room along with other relics such as a watch belonging to James VIII and a sword that the king gave to the 5th Earl on the occasion of the king's visit to Glamis.

The walls and ceiling of the 17th-century chapel are covered with paintings by Dutch artist Jacob de Wet. Other notable paintings include *The Fruit Market* by Frans Snyders in the Billiard Room and one of the 3rd Earl and his sons by Jacob de Wet in the Drawing Room.

A ROYAL WEDDING

The family became Bowes Lyon when the 9th Earl married a Durham heiress, Miss Mary Eleanor Bowes. The most famous Bowes Lyon is, of course, Her Majesty Queen Elizabeth, The Queen Mother. When Lady Elizabeth Bowes Lyon married Prince Albert, the Duke of York, in 1923, her mother, Lady Strathmore, created a suite of rooms for exclusive use of the royal couple when they visited Glamis. Although The Queen Mother was not born here, she spent most of her childhood at Glamis, and this is where she gave birth to her second daughter, Princess Margaret. The Royal Apartments are furnished with fine antiques and porcelain and family portraits, the most notable being one of The Queen Mother when she was Duchess of York.

THE GARDENS AT GLAMIS

The gardens at Glamis include a five-acre walled garden for vegetables, fruit and flowers and a delightful Dutch garden. On the east side of the castle is the Italian garden – about two acres enclosed within a high yew hedge and featuring two 17th-century-style gazebos. This garden is entered through decorative wrought-iron gates which were made to commemorate the 80th birthday of The Queen Mother. One of the most notable objects in the extensive grounds is a huge baroque sundial.

Scone Palace

PERTH

AN ELEGANT CASTELLATED PALACE DATING FROM THE 19TH CENTURY, WITH EARLIER FOUNDATIONS: THREE MILES NORTH OF PERTH ON THE A93.

Since the 9th century the site of Scone Palace has occupied a place in history for the coronations of Scottish kings. Early records tell of a monastery here and then an Abbey of Augustinian Canons, but the Abbey and the Bishop's House were burned down in 1559 by a mob incited by the sermons of John Knox. Fortunately, the Palace of Scone, residence of the Abbot and coronation place of kings, survived. It was around this early structure that the present palace grew, enlarged in 1802, in a Gothic style in keeping with its monastic past, by the architect William Atkinson. The palace was then under the ownership of David William Murray, 3rd Earl of Mansfield. He was the first Earl of Mansfield to have lived at Scone – the previous two considered life at Scone to be too austere, preferring to live in their comfortable southern estates. So the Murray family have the 3rd Earl to thank for the magnificent structure that exists today.

The interior is equally impressive. Visitors begin their tour of the State Rooms in the dining room, a grand room containing a unique collection of European ivories the majority of which were collected by the 4th Earl. They were carved in the 17th, 18th and 19th centuries in Bavaria, Flanders, Italy and France, and perhaps the most beautiful specimen is the French 17th-century sculpture of the Holy Family. A damask cloth covering the dining table was specially woven to incorporate the Mansfield coat of arms with Murray stars and crescents. A more recent acquisition, seen from the dining room window, is a beautiful Japanese tree, *Acer Worleei*, which was planted here by the Crown Prince of Japan.

The Gothic influence in design is nowhere more enchanting than in the pretty Ante-room, painted in white with architectural details highlighted in gold and silver. There is a Chinese theme to this room with its niches filled with vases from the Chien Lung period (1736-95) and some Chinese Chippendale chairs. The Gothic style continues in the majestic Long Gallery, some 142feet long, with an unusual floor of Scottish oak inset with bog oak. Family portraits line the walls, and the gallery also contains Lord Mansfield's unique collection of Vernis Martin ware: *papier maché* made by the Martin family in 18th-century France. The library is home to a fabulous collection of 18th- and 19th-century porcelain, including Meissen, Sèvres and Worcester – and a huge portrait of the 1st Earl. Outside, a tiny chapel stands on Moot Hill, where all the early Kings of Scotland were crowned. The Palace is surrounded by fine lawns, lush woodland and a famous pinetum.

At the geographical centre of Scotland, Scone Palace has also taken centre stage in Scottish history over the centuries.

THE STONE OF SCONE

Royal rulers have been crowned on the Stone of Scone for centuries, including our present monarch. It is thought that the stone was brought to Scone in AD838 and was kept here for some 500 years, but this fabled stone has an obscure history. Variously described as 'St Jacob's Pillow', a survivor from Biblical times; a Royal Stone of the Belgic kings or of the Picts; or even an altar stone to some awesome and long forgotten god – its origins are impossible to prove. Removed from Scone by King Edward I to Westminster Abbey in 1296, the stone now resides beneath the Coronation Chair.

Cawdor Castle

Nairn

An unusual and fascinating building, the 14th-century Cawdor Castle is surrounded by woodland and some of the finest Highland scenery: on the B9090 between Nairn and Inverness.

The early Thanes of Calder (early spelling) were appointed Sherriffs and Constables of Nairn. A thane was a kind of feudal baron holding land from the Crown, and was often a clan chief and a powerful individual answerable only to the King and to God. Not much is known of Donald, the 1st Thane of Cawdor but his successor, William, 2nd Thane, received a Charter of Thanage from King Robert the Bruce in 1310. This confirmed his hereditary thanedom and thus began a family line that survives to this day at Cawdor.

This statue of Agura, by Churyo Sato, can be seen in the Yellow Room.

BUILDING ON SUPERSTITION

Although there had most certainly been a fortified home of some description in the vicinity of the present Cawdor Castle, it is not until the time of the 3rd Thane of Cawdor (another William) that records began. A personal friend of King James II, William was granted a Special Licence by the king to build a castle. And so, around 1370 the foundations of the present structure were laid. The choice of site was decided through a mixture of tradition and superstition. A donkey led the way to a high, rocky position with water nearby and so, unchallenged, building went ahead on the site of the animal's auspicious choice. The fortified tower was built around a living tree, thought for centuries to have been a hawthorn; the marvels of modern science have revealed it to be a holly tree. Superstitious reasons for having a tree at its heart might be that the tree was a symbol of life and of luck and, as some people believed, as protection against lightning, fiends and fairies. Whatever the reasons for its planting, the unfortunate tree died in 1372, as soon as building work deprived it of daylight.

A superstitious ritual chose the site for Cawdor Castle, but that method has not failed the generations of thanes who have called it their home.

A sturdy and simple design typical of the period, the tower house does however have several unusual features; the dining hall, kitchens and sculleries were not adjoining the main structure but were grouped around a courtyard alongside other domestic buildings. Other oddities included an oubliette – a tiny dungeon with no windows, accessed (one way only) by means of a vertical chute, reputed to be used for relations or neighbours who fell out of favour with the owners.

A LEGACY OF SORROW

The Cawdor line proceeded without much incident until the death of John, the 8th Thane. His only heir was a daughter, born shortly after his death, who was to endure much suffering in maintaining her thanedom. Firstly she was kidnapped by the most influential man in Scotland, the Earl of Argyll. Then, for future recognition, the infant was branded on her hip with a key by her nurse and had the top joint of her little finger bitten off. Finally, in 1510, at the age of twelve, Muriel of Cawdor was married off to the son of Argyll, Sir John Campbell. However, it was a surprisingly long and happy union and the present owner is a direct descendant of those Campbells of Cawdor.

THE FORTRESS RESTYLED

The tower fortress of Cawdor Castle remained virtually unchanged until the 17th century when Sir Hugh Campbell, 15th Thane of Cawdor, transformed the simple tower fortress into an elegant and spacious mansion. A large family of nine children and a generous household of twenty-seven servants dictated the size somewhat, but the changes, both to the building and the interior, are a tribute to Sir Hugh's good taste and sense of style. The massive project was started in 1684 and did not see completion until 1702. Sir Hugh supervised the whole proceedings ensuring the craftsmen completed everything in 'the handsomest order, so themselves may have credit and Sir Hugh satisfaction.' The workers were paid partly in silver coin and partly in ground cereals.

After Sir Hugh's death in 1716 the estate was passed to his grandson John, 17th Thane of Cawdor, but it was a period of civil unrest, notably the Jacobite Risings, and John decided that it was prudent to remove his family to a safer environment. The family divided their time between London and their estates in Wales, leaving Cawdor in the capable stewardship of John's uncle, Sir Archibald Campbell. A peace loving man, Sir Archibald kept well away from the political wranglings of the time and contented himself with creating a new garden at Cawdor and undertaking a programme of improvements, both interior and exterior, of the castle.

A collection of the possessions of the great statesman, William Gladstone is on display at Fasque.

LORD CAWDOR'S RETURN

The estate was run by factors for the next hundred years, until the 1st Lord Cawdor returned in the early 19th century. At this time the castle was damaged by fire and it fell to his successor, John, the 1st Earl to carry out alterations and redecoration. Both the 1st and 2nd Earls inherited the sense of style and good taste of their ancestor, Sir Hugh, for the elegant building that stands today is in large part a tribute to their work.

The rooms are well-proportioned, many with stunning stone fireplaces, and striking décor – a perfect blend of historic and modern. Family portraits abound particularly in the drawing room, and of the modern works of art, one by Stanley Spencer of St Ives is of note. The tapestries in the Tapestry Room and the Tower Sitting Room are a legacy from Sir Hugh and his wife who acquired a fine collection. Antique furniture, including four-poster beds and Sheraton card tables, blend perfectly with the present family's modern pieces, which include ceramics by the current Lord Cawdor's brother.

THE SCOTTISH PLAY

Descendants of the Cawdor line may tire of the myths and half-truths that have grown around Shakespeare's Macbeth and its connection to Cawdor Castle. However, in the minds of the theatre-going public, Macbeth, King Duncan and Cawdor are inextricably linked. In fact, Shakespeare's play was an adaptation of a much earlier tale by a Scottish monk, Andrew of Winton. Andrew embellished the true story of the real Macbeth who was, in fact, killed in 1057, some 400 years before Cawdor Castle and the Thanedom of Cawdor came into existence.

Below: A particularly fascinating aspect of a visit to Fasque is the insight into the working life of the house. This fine array of brass utensils can be seen in the kitchen.

Fasque

LAURENCEKIRK

GLADSTONE'S SPLENDID VICTORIAN STATELY HOME, IN A BEAUTIFUL PARKLAND SETTING: ABOUT FOUR MILES NORTH-WEST OF LAURENCEKIRK VIA THE B9120 AND THE B974.

This fine golden stone mansion, complete with its battlements and a clock tower, was bought by Sir John Gladstone in 1829, and has been the home of the Gladstone family ever since. The successive generations have treasured Fasque for its quiet comfort and have created a home which is both gentle and unassuming. The name of Gladstone, of course, is familiar and that great Victorian statesman, W E Gladstone, four times Prime Minister, lived here from 1830 to 1851.

Inside the house very little has changed since Sir John's day. The impressive state rooms include a vast drawing room, a fine library and sumptuous bedrooms, all reached by a handsome sweeping double cantilever staircase, possibly the finest of its kind in the world.

For many visitors to Fasque, the most interesting aspect is, in many ways, the extensive servants' quarters. Here it is possible to obtain a vivid impression of the 'upstairs-downstairs' life and work of a large Victorian household. The kitchen, sculleries, washroom, knives hall, bakery and buttery are full of the domestic trappings of a bygone era, when the owners and staff of such estates formed a community which was largely self-sufficient. There are also collections of farming machinery and other local items.

Fasque is surrounded by spacious parkland, populated by a herd of red deer and a flock of Soay sheep, and behind the mansion the hills rise dramatically towards the Highlands.

The Gladstone Bag, as popular a design as ever, gets its name from Prime Minister W E Gladstone.

Braemar Castle

Braemar

A DELIGHTFUL LITTLE BROWN-HARLED CASTLE AMID THE TREES ALONG THE VALLEY OF THE RIVER DEE: HALF A MILE EAST OF BRAEMAR.

Its strategic location on the main route through the mountains has meant a turbulent history for Braemar Castle – not only has it changed hands several times, but has also been burnt out and deserted, and used as a garrison fort for Hanoverian troops determined to crush any further Highland rebellion. Later fitted out in the best 19th-century traditions of elegance, style and comfort, it is today the delightful family home of the Farquharsons of Invercauld.

NEIGHBOURHOOD FEUDS

The castle was started in 1628 by John Erskine, Earl of Mar, to fend off his belligerent neighbours along the valley – the Farquharsons, the Gordons and the Forbes – and its original structure as an L-shaped tower-house can still be clearly seen. The Earl of Mar was an important figure in Scottish politics, holding the position of High Treasurer of Scotland, and guardian to the young King James VI (later James I of England). The castle was to serve not simply as a symbol of the Earl's power in Deeside, but also as a hunting lodge.

The first serious conflict arose in 1689. While the current Earl of Mar supported the Hanoverian government, his neighbours the Farquharsons favoured the doomed Jacobite cause, and rallied to support the stand made by John Graham of Claverhouse ('Bonnie Dundee'). The Hanoverian troops on the trail of Claverhouse, under General Mackay, stopped off at Braemar Castle, but were routed by the Farquharsons in a surprise night-attack. The Farquharson leader, John, 'The Black Colonel', ordered the castle to be burned, to prevent its further use by government troops, and for 60 years it remained a forlorn, burnt-out shell.

This black Wedgwood teapot can be seen in the Morning Room at Braemar Castle.

Braemar Castle now sits peacefully amidst a landscape that was once torn apart by family feuds and bitter neighbourhood skirmishes.

JACOBITE SYMPATHIES

During this time the political situation changed, as the current John Erskine, Earl of Mar, fell out of favour with the new king, George I. Disillusioned, he swapped sides, whole-heartedly supporting the Jacobite uprising of 1715, and indeed raising the standard of the Young Pretender, 'King James VIII', in Braemar village, on the site where the Invercauld Arms may be seen today.

The Jacobites were soundly defeated at Sheriffmuir and the Earl of Mar forfeited his estates to the government. They were eventually bought up in 1732 by John Farquharson, 9th laird of the neighbouring estate of Invercauld. He too had fought with the Jacobites, and suffered capture and imprisonment as a result; however, his refusal to take part in the uprising of 1745 led to the plunder of his estates by the Prince's followers, and in 1748, keen to see peace restored once more, he agreed to lease the castle to the War Office for 99 years, in exchange for a small annual payment.

REBUILDING BRAEMAR CASTLE

Braemar Castle was rebuilt, and remains one of the best examples of a Hanoverian fort. Turrets were extended, a rectangular rampart was constructed with projecting salients to make the classic 8-point star shape, and the interior was worked on by the two young sons of the great architect William Adam, one of whom, Robert, would later outstrip his father's fame. When the garrison withdrew in 1797 they left behind some graffiti carved in the woodwork – the sign of a bored soldiery.

The castle was restored to the family, and it was the 12th Laird of Invercauld who made it the comfortable family home that can be enjoyed today. Inside, the low-ceilinged public rooms are decorated in rich, warm colours that, with the thick castle walls, give an air of cosiness. The furnishings, including pieces by Chippendale and Hepplewhite, are elegant and decorative, giving a real sense of space and harmony, and revealing the influence of the grandmother of the present laird, Mrs Zoë Farquharson of Invercauld, a great beauty of her day whose portrait may be seen just inside the drawing room. Among the family treasures on display is a huge uncut cairngorm, weighing 53 pounds and believed to be the biggest in the world.

Dunrobin Castle

Golspie

THE FAMILY HOME OF THE EARLS AND DUKES OF SUTHERLAND SINCE THE 14TH CENTURY: HALF A MILE NORTH OF GOLSPIE ON THE A9.

Like most ancient Scottish castles, Dunrobin started out as a keep, or tower and is named after its originator, Earl Robin. It was built in the early 1300s and subsequent enlargements in the 17th, 18th and 19th centuries created the splendid, gleaming, turreted castle that today's visitors see. The original keep is still at its heart, and a tour of the castle as a whole gives an illuminating impression of the development of architectural style over the centuries.

The overall impression of the state rooms, bedrooms and nurseries recalls the lifestyle of the Dukes of Sutherland in Victorian times. The furniture, pictures – including some Canalettos – family heirlooms and *objets d'art* have been carefully displayed in their original settings wherever possible, creating a true reflection of Dunrobin Castle as a family home and not simply as an historical exhibit.

There are a few surprises, though, notably when visitors step into the Sub Hall. Here, instead of the fine décor and furnishings one might expect to find is, as large as life, a 19th-century fire engine! Still in working order, it is hung with fire helmets and buckets – and watched over by the baleful stare of the collection of stags' heads on the wall.

Beyond the castle walls, in a converted summer house, a museum has been set out to display various collections which reflect the wide-ranging interests of the family over the centuries, ranging from ornithology to Egyptology.

Equally as grand as the castle, the magnificent formal 19th-century gardens were modelled on those at Versailles. They were designed by Barry, who was the architect not only of Dunrobin's Victorian extension but also of the Houses of Parliament.

The splendid, gleaming, turreted Dunrobin Castle owes its appearance largely to 19th-century rebuilding.

Dunvegan Castle

Isle of Skye

THE LAST GREAT CASTLE HOME OF AN ISLAND CLAN CHIEF TO HAVE RETAINED ITS TRUE IDENTITY: AT THE END OF THE A850 IN NORTH-WEST SKYE, ABOUT 20 MILES FROM PORTREE.

This stronghold of the Clan MacLeod is still occupied by the clan chief – the 29th to be precise – who can trace a history back to the last Norse Kings of Man and the North Isles. The castle has been their home for nearly 800 years, and it is almost certain that it occupies the site of an earlier fort, which may predate it by 1,000 years.

Naturally enough, various additions have been made over the centuries, but the most substantial alterations were made by the 25th Chief, between 1840 and 1850. He commissioned Robert Brown of Edinburgh, at a cost of £8,000, to add dummy pepperpot towers and defensive battlements, and to undertake the rebuilding of the north wing.

Every room has its own story to tell. The drawing room is where you can see the famous Fairy Flag of Dunvegan, its fabric now protected by glass to prevent visitors from cutting off pieces to take home for good luck! The dining room forms the largest suite of rooms in the castle, with ancestral portraits covering over 300 years of family history. The library has a collection of books of historical and family interest, including the *Dunvegan Armorial*, compiled in 1582-4. Only six feet away from the gracious surroundings of the drawing room is the dungeon, where prisoners were thrown, through a trap in the guardhouse floor, and left to die.

THE FAIRY FLAG

Many castles claim connection with legends, but how many can actually produce tangible evidence? Dunvegan's Fairy Flag is said to possess magical powers, for it was given to the family by a fairy who married one of the MacLeods. When she had to return to her people, she left it to protect his family from harm and bring them luck. Less romantic is a claim that it was the war banner of Harold Hardrada, King of Norway, who was killed in 1066.

Dunvegan is linked with one of the most romantic stories of Scottish history. One of the illegitimate sons of the 22nd Chief married the daughter of Flora MacDonald, who helped Bonnie Prince Charlie escape from government troops, and Flora herself lived at Dunvegan for a time.

Dunvegan Castle has a dramatic setting on the sea loch, a fitting situation for a family that goes back to the Norse kings.

The Historic Houses Association

As President of the Historic Houses Association, I am delighted to welcome this excellent publication. All the houses featured in the book are members of the Association which represents nearly all the most important privately owned houses in the country, from great palaces to smaller manor houses.

The Historic Houses Association exists to promote the interests of privately owned historic houses. We believe that in almost all cases the best possible solution for the heritage and the nation is that the families who occupy these houses (many of whom built them in the first place) should continue to live in them. This is certainly the cheapest solution, since the cost to the nation of maintaining them in public ownership is very substantial. Equally important is that the occupation of the private owner gives a special dimension to the house which is missing once it is taken into institutional ownership. The public who visit them have shown on numerous occasions that they like the 'atmosphere' that comes with individual ownership. Every house is cherished by its owner and this special feeling is made abundantly clear to visitors.

Apart from the houses featured in the book, the Historic Houses Association has over 1200 other members. Although these other houses are not necessarily open to the public on a regular basis, they all play an important part in their local community and virtually all of them will be involved in some way with social and charitable events. Thus they play a vital role in the fabric of this country, particularly in the rural community where so many of them are situated.

Over eight million people visited the houses featured in this book in 1993, many of them from abroad. They provide a vital tourist as well as a heritage resource and are one of the main reasons why overseas visitors choose to come to this country. However, they do impose a very considerable burden on their owners. This is partly financial since the costs of upkeep are often enormous. Sharing your house with the public can also require considerable dedication and patience and the willingness to sacrifice your privacy.

Given the importance of these houses to the nation it seems reasonable that the owners, many of whom face substantial repair liabilities, should get more help from the government to shoulder their responsibilities. The Historic Houses Association has an active campaign to improve the position of the private owner through tax and other incentives. The Association also assists its members with a wide range of practical problems facing the private owner, such as insurance, conservation, security etc. The Heritage Conservation Trust was set up recently as a charity to help owners with the cost of conservation of works of art and has now helped a number of owners with the restoration of their pictures.

I am sure that this book will add considerably to the enjoyment of all those readers who visit the houses included. Not only is it a valuable companion guide, but it also gives a fascinating insight into features of houses and family that are not normally covered in a guide book.

If you would like more information about the Historic Houses Association you should apply to the Association's headquarters at 2 Chester Street, London SW1X 7BB, telephone 0207–2595688

William Proby
President

Index

Acknowledgements

The Automobile Association wishes to thank the following photographers, libraries and organisations for their assistance in the preparation of this book.

The Althorp Estate 94a, 94b, 95a; **Athelhampton House** 21b; **Blairquhan** 204; **Boughton House** 95b; **Boughton Monchelsea Place** 79b; **Bowhill** 189b; **Bowood House** 38a, 38b; **The Bridgeman Art Library** 28c *A View of Longleat by Jan Siberechts (1627-1703) (Ackermann & Johnson Ltd London),* 39 *Corsham Court, Wiltshire, The Picture Gallery, plasterwork by Thomas Stocking and fireplace by Scheemakers,* 52a, 52b *The Duke of Marlborough in Garter Robes by Sir Godfrey Kneller (1646-1723) Blenheim Palace, Oxfordshire,* 53 *Fall of Lille, Marlborough tapestries 1708 Blenheim Palace, Oxfordshire,* Cover, 56 *Broughton Castle (John Bethell),* 65 *Empress Alexandra Feodorovna (Werner Collection, Luton Hoo),* 67a *Philip II & Mary I, 1558 by Hans Eworth (Trustees of the Bedford Estate),* 71a *Loseley House,* 75b *3rd Duke of Richmond & family watching horses in training on the Downs by George Stubbs (1724-1806) (Goodwood House),* 76a *Earl of Arundel in his Gallery by Daniel Mytens (1590-1648) (Arundel Castle),* 96a *Charge of the Light Brigade, Balaclava (Private Collection),* 96b *Field Marshall the Earl of Cardigan by Carlo Marochetti (1805-67) (Crown Estate/ Institute of Directors, London),* 113 *Euston Hall & Church by English School (Private Collection),* 133 *Meols Hall (John Martin Robinson),* 134 *Hoghton Tower,* 140a *Portrait of William & Mary Wordsworth 1839 by Margaret Gillies (1803-87) (Dove Cottage Trust),* 162 *Portrait of 1st Duke of Northumberland by James Barry (1741-1806) (Syon House);* **Burghley House** 102a; **A Casey** 111; **Castle Howard** 147a, 147b; **Chenies Manor House** 62; **Chipchase Castle** 165; **Country Life Picture Library** 3, 28a, 29, 35a, 35b, 118, 145b, 158, 159b; **Duart Castle** 205a; **Duncombe Park** 152; **Dunvegan Castle** 219b; **Earlshall Castle** 209a, 209b; **Eastnor Castle** Cover, 170c; **Elton Hall** 97a; **English Life Publications Ltd** 33a, 33b, 69, 71a, 90, 91, 100, 101, 102b, 114a, 114b, 115a, 115b, 128a, 128c, 135a, 135c, 136a, 160a, 160c, 161b, 163, 177a, 177b, 177c, 189a, 214a; **Mary Evans Picture Library** 82b; **Eyam Hall** 121a, 121b; **Fairfax House** 153; **Fursdon House** 16, 17a; **Grimsthorpe Castle** 104; **Haddon Hall** 122, 123; **Hagley Hall** 93; **Robert Harding Picture Library** 159b, 168/9, 171, 176; **Harris (Belmont) Charity** 78, 79a; **Hartland Abbey** 17b; **J Henderson** 218b; **Hever Castle Ltd** 82a, 83, 84, 85a, 85b; **M Holford** 107b, 186/7, 193a; **Hutton in the Forest** 136b; **Ilsington House** 22b; **Hector Innes** 2/3, 190a, 191, 192; **Jarrold Publishing** 52c; **Kelburn Castle** 207; **Lamport Hall** 97b; **A Lawson** 129a, 129b; **Longleat** 31b; **Margam Country Park** 178; **Muncaster Castle** 139b; **The National Motor Museum Beaulieu** 49a; **Naworth Castle** 141c; **Newby Hall** 154; **Nunwell House** 49b, 49c; **Hugh Palmer** 10/11, 14, 208; **Parham Park** 77; **Penhow Castle** 179a; **Pencarrow House** 13a; **Photos Horticultural Picture Library** 109; **Powell Cotton Museum** 86; **Prideaux Place** 13b; **Rex Features Ltd** 28b, 160b, 194b; **Lord Romsey** 51b; **Sherborne Castle** 24; **Southwick Hall** 98; **Spencer House** 70; **Squerryes Court** 87; **Stanford Hall** 99a, 99b, 99c; **Stansted Park** 51a; **Stratfield Saye** 60; **The Sussex Archaeological Society** 75a; **Sutton Park** 157c; **Syndication International** 73b; **Tapeley Park** 19; **Thirlestane Castle** 198a; **J Tims** 20; **Tredegar** 180a (Rex Moreton), 180b, 181a, 181b; **Wakefield & Partners** 164a, 164b; **Warwick Castle** 92b; **Andy Williams Photo-Library** 80; **Wilton House** 40a, 40b, 40c, 41a, 42, 43; **Woburn Abbey** 46/7, 66, 67b; **Zefa Picture Library (UK) Ltd** 8/9, 76b.

All remaining pictures are held in the AA Photo Library with contributions from:
S Abraham 44a, 44b, 44c, 45; **M Adelman** 61b; **M Alexander** 193b, 194a, 195a, 195b, 196, 197a, 197b, 200, 201a, 201b, 201c, 202a, 202b, 202c, 205b, 205c, 205d; **A Baker** 27a; **P Baker** 119; **J Beazley** 135b, 146a, 188, 215; **M Birkitt** 1, 41b, 68a, 68b, 92a, 103a, 103b; **E Bowness** 137, 140b; **D Corrance** 198b, 203; **D Croucher** 74; **S L Day** 22a, 23a, 23b, 25a, 25b, 25c, 37a, 37b; **R Fletcher** 48, 50b; **D Forss** 73a, 82c; **J Henderson** 216a, 217a, 217b, 217c, 218a; **A Lawson** 32; **C Lees** 167a, 167b, 167c; **J Loan** 139a; **S & O Mathews** 166, 199; **J Miller** 72; **R Moss** 12,15, 21a, 26, 27b; **J Mottershaw** 126/7, 131a, 131b, 132a, 132b, 148a, 148b, 149a, 149b, 149c, 155a, 155b, 156, 157a, 157b; **R Newton** 30, 31a, 128b, 179b; **R Shape** 138, 190b; **A Souter** 33c; **F Stephenson** Cover, 36, 57a, 57b, 58a, 58b, 59a, 59b, 59c, 63a, 63b, 64a, 64b; **M Trelawney** 71b, 105a, 105b, 106, 107a, 108a, 108b, 108c, 108d, 110a, 110b, 112a, 112b; **W Voysey** 50a; **R Weir** 214b, 216b, 219a; **J Welsh** 88/9, 120, 170a, 170b, 172, 173a, 173b, 184a, 184b, 185a, 185b; **L Whitwam** 141a, 141b, 142a, 142b, 143a, 143b, 144a, 144b, 145a; **T Woodcock** 161a.

Maltings Partnership for supplying colour perspective cut-away illustrations with contributions from Stephen Capsby, Eric Brown, Michael Foster and Jonathan Preston.